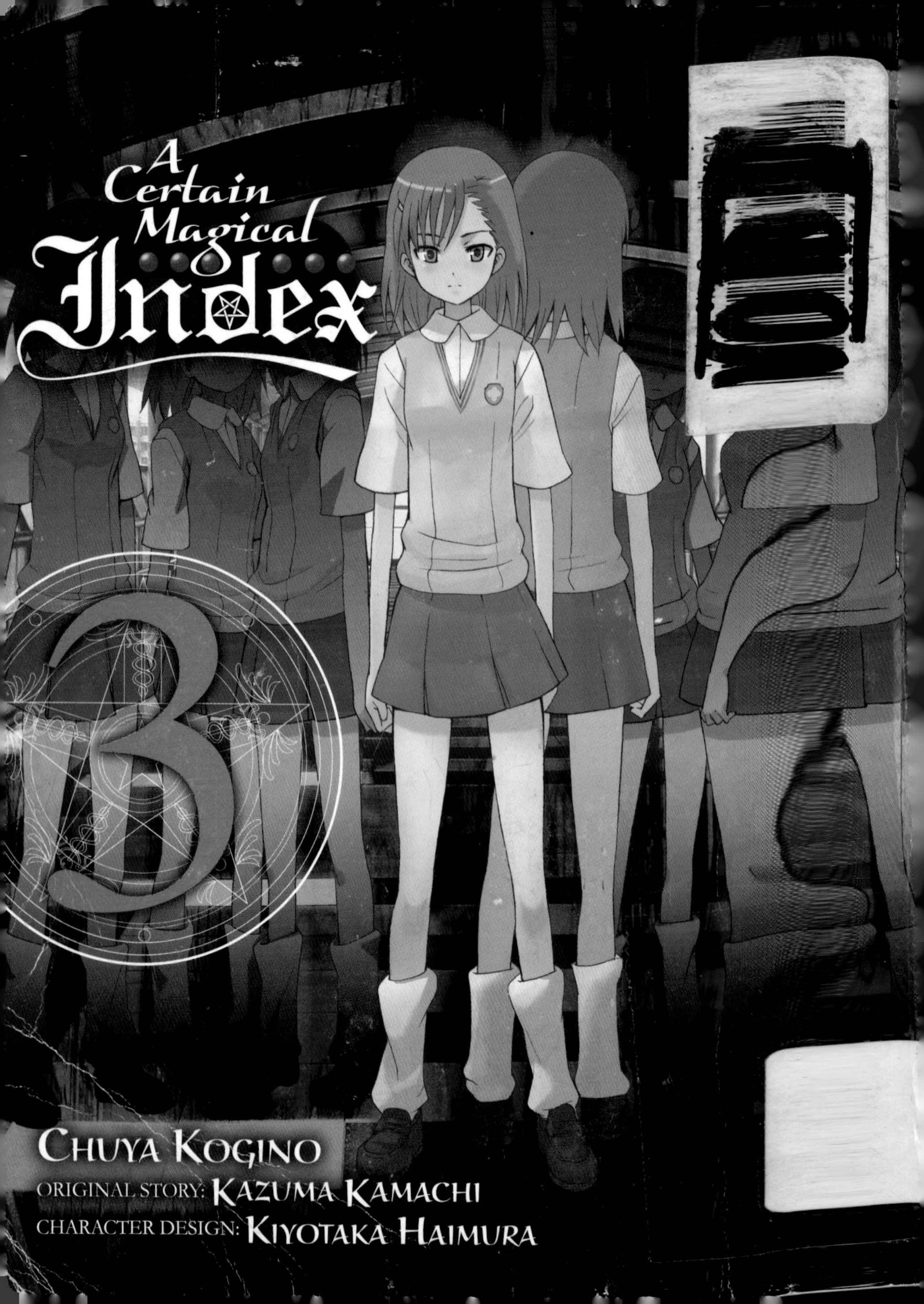

A Certain Magical Index
3
Chuya Kogino
Original Story: Kazuma Kamachi
Character Design: Kiyotaka Haimura

A Certain Magical Index 3

ORIGINAL STORY:
CHUYA KOGINO   KAZUMA KAMACHI

CHARACTER DESIGN:
KIYOTAKA HAIMURA

A CERTAIN MAGICAL INDEX ❸ TABLE OF CONTENTS

Index Librorum Prohibitorum

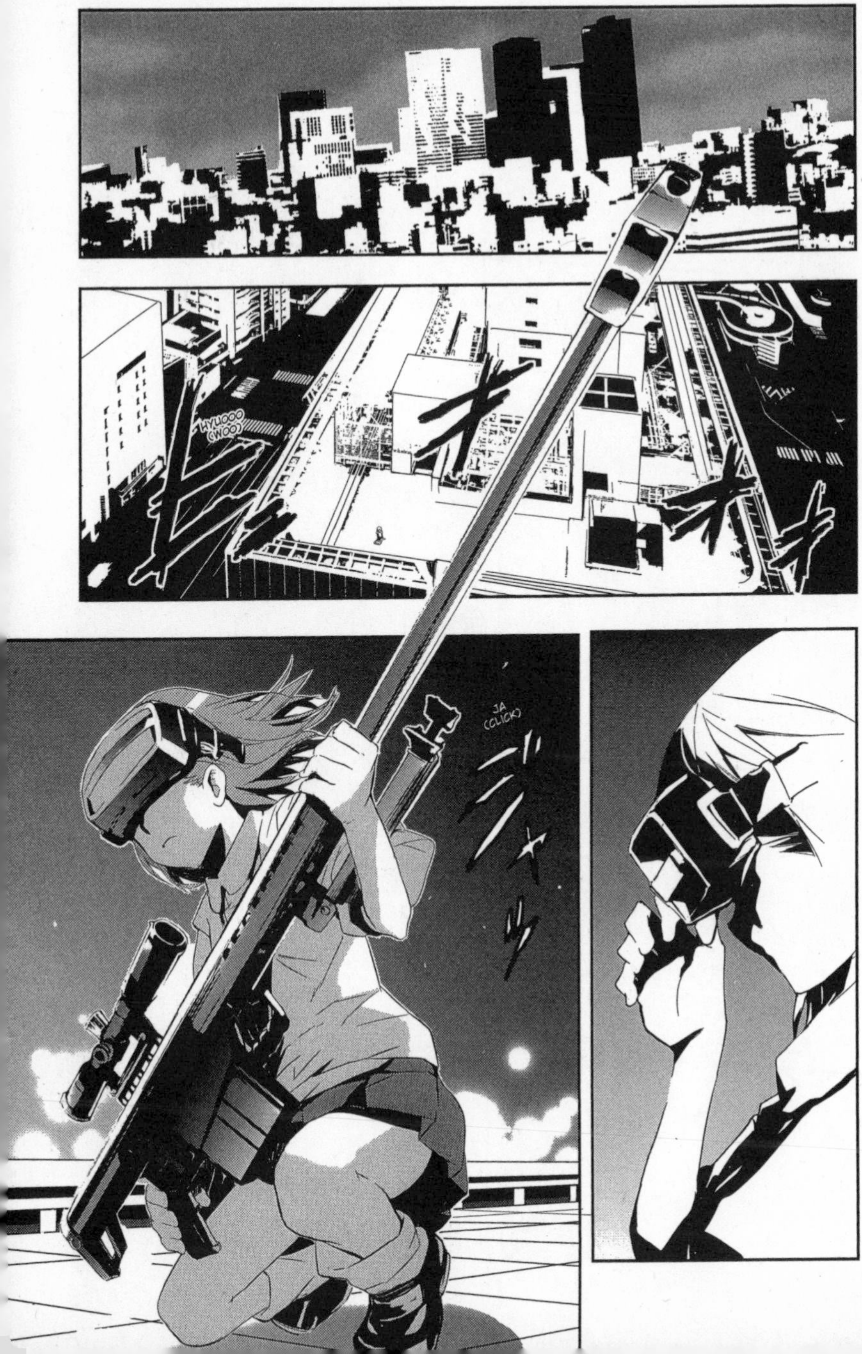
HYUOOO (WOO)
JA (CLICK)

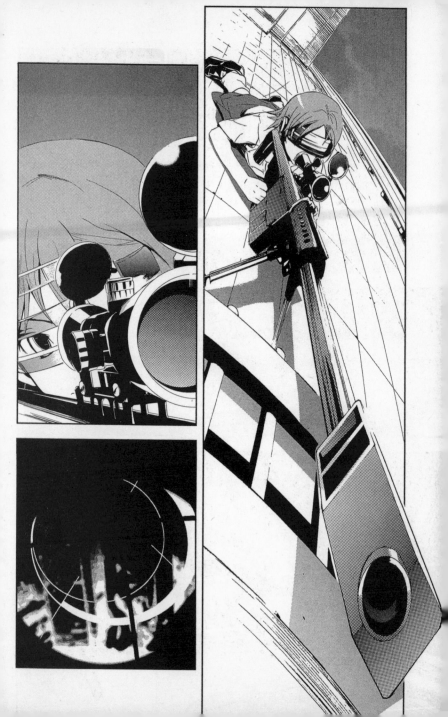

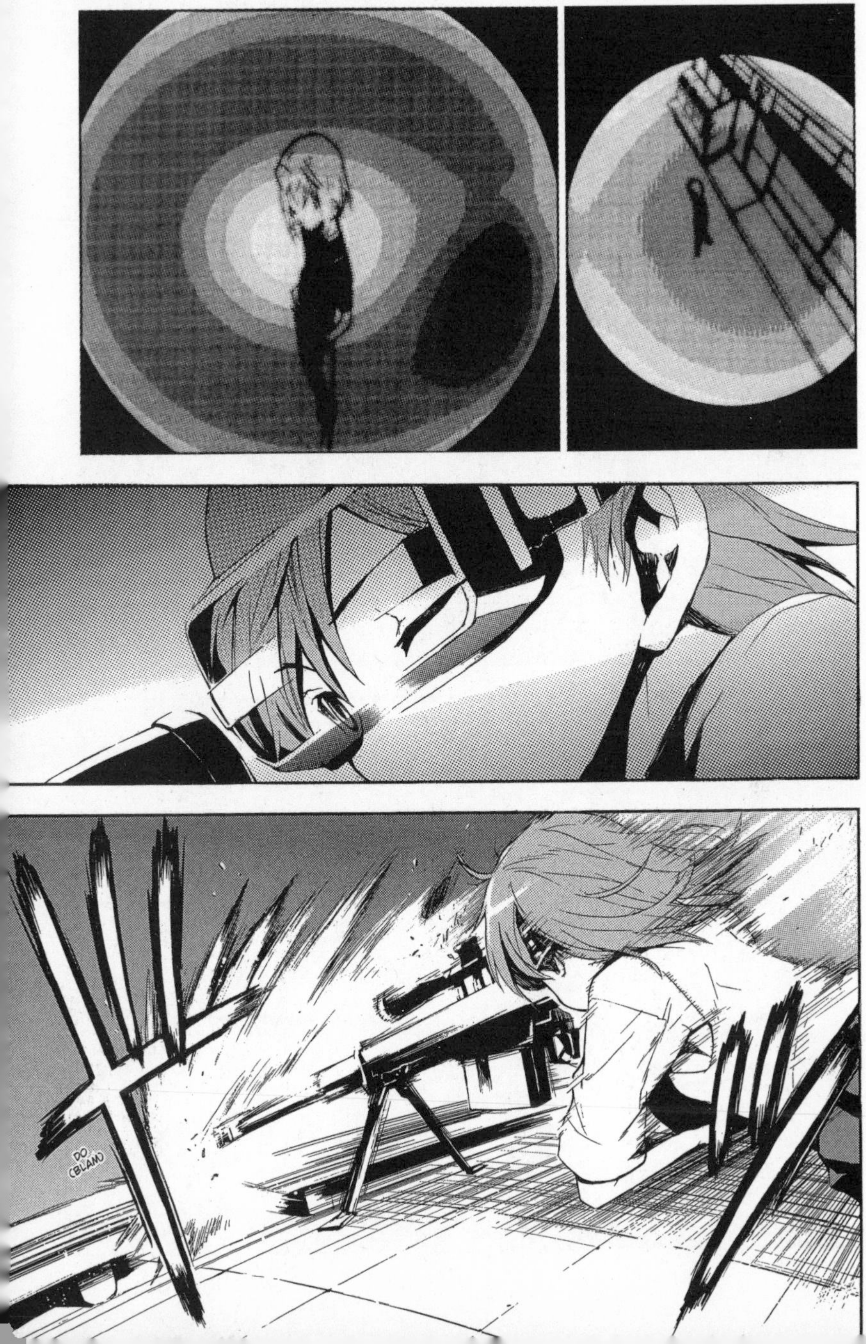
DO
(BLAM)

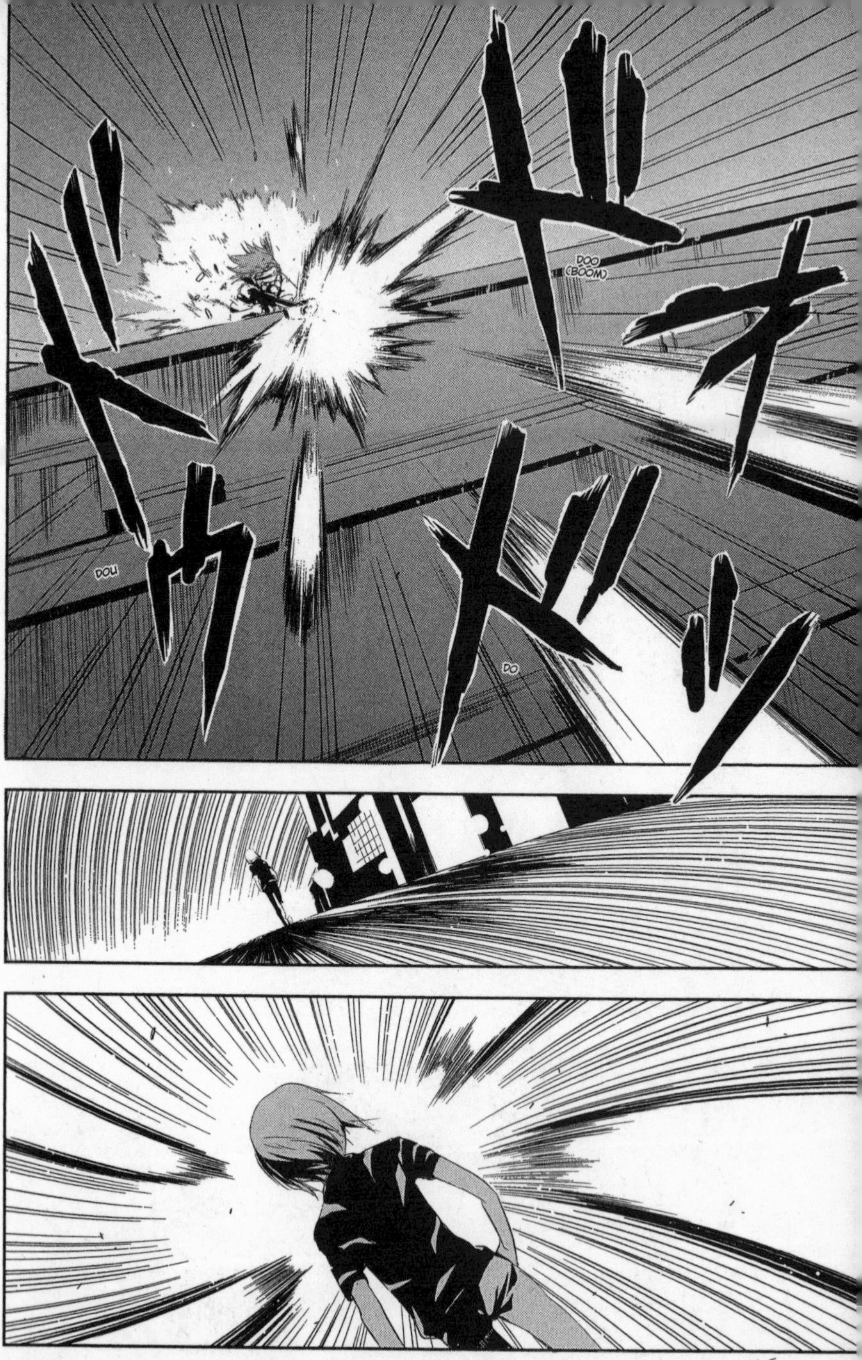
DOO (BOOM)
DOU
DO

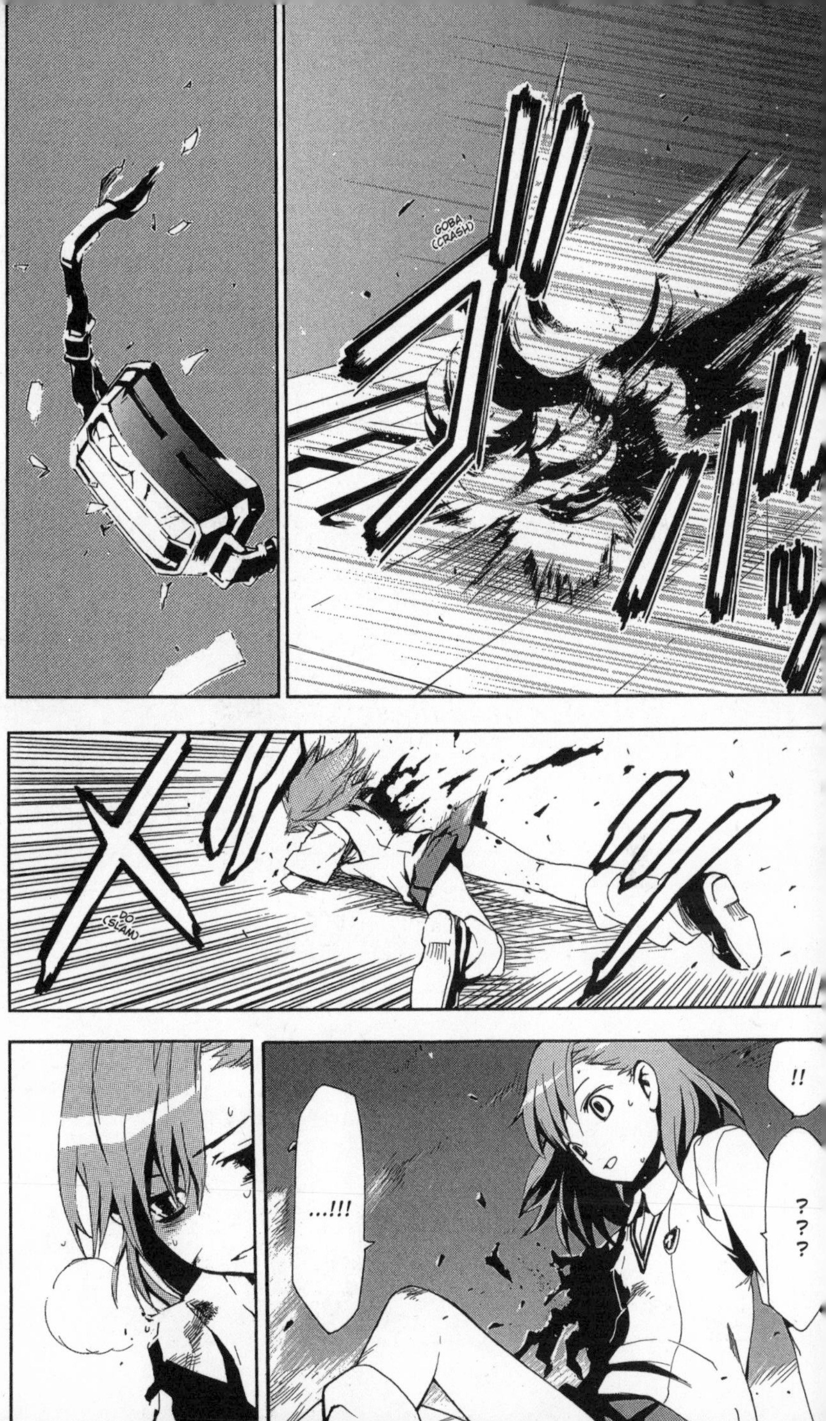
GOBA
(CRASH)
DO
(SLAM)
!!
???
...!!!

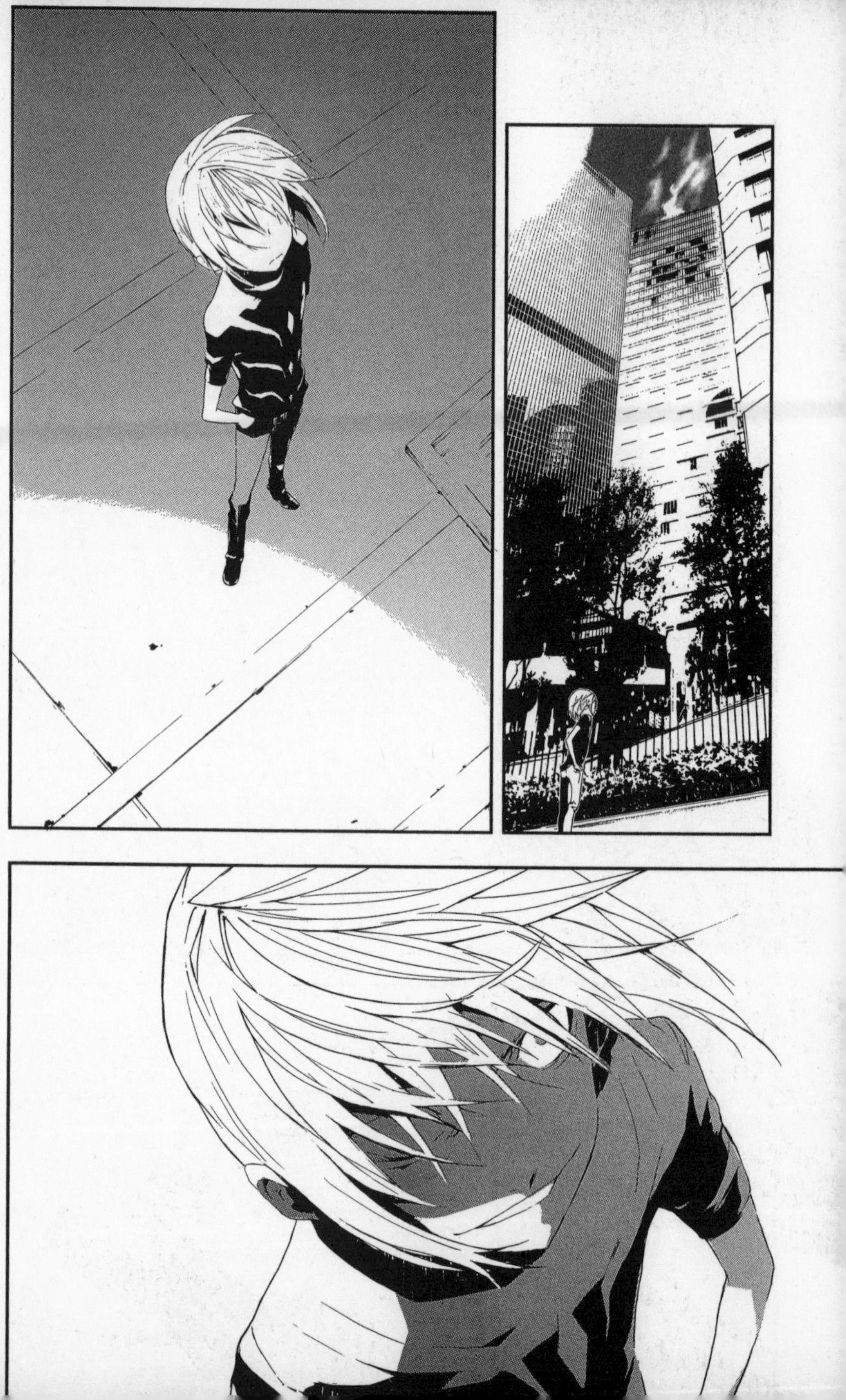

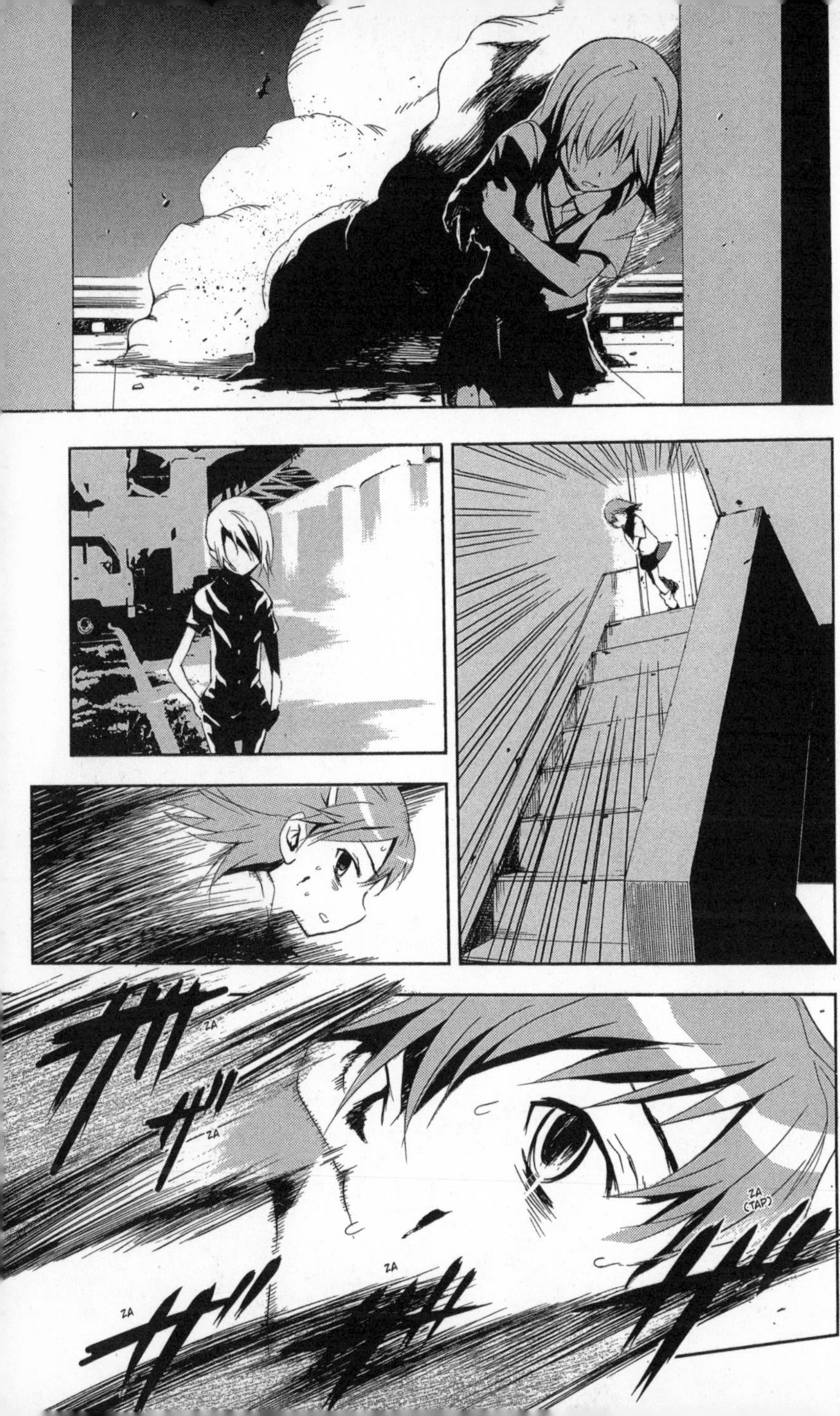
ZA
(TAP)
ZA
ZA
ZA
ZA

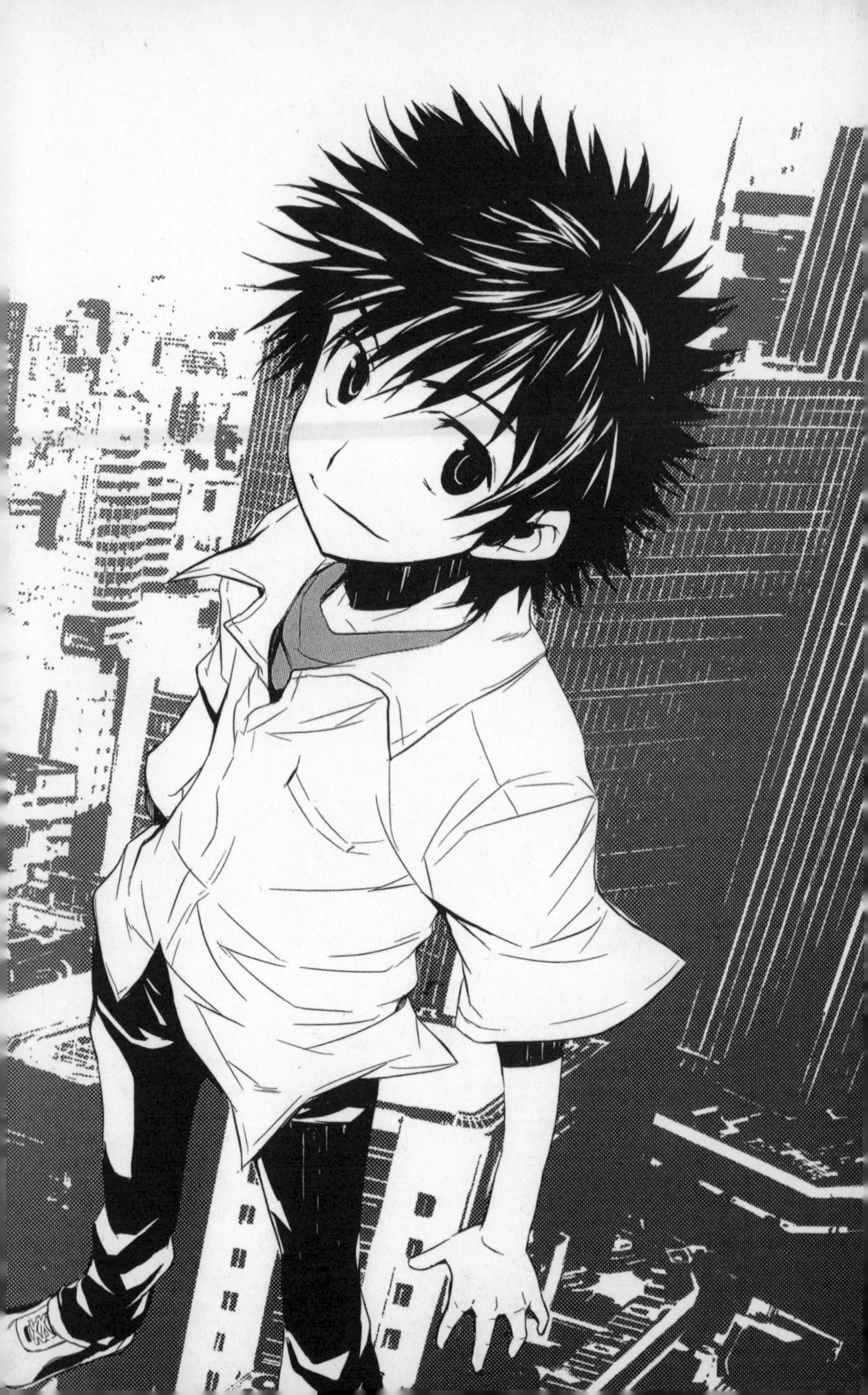

#11
MIKOTO MISAKA

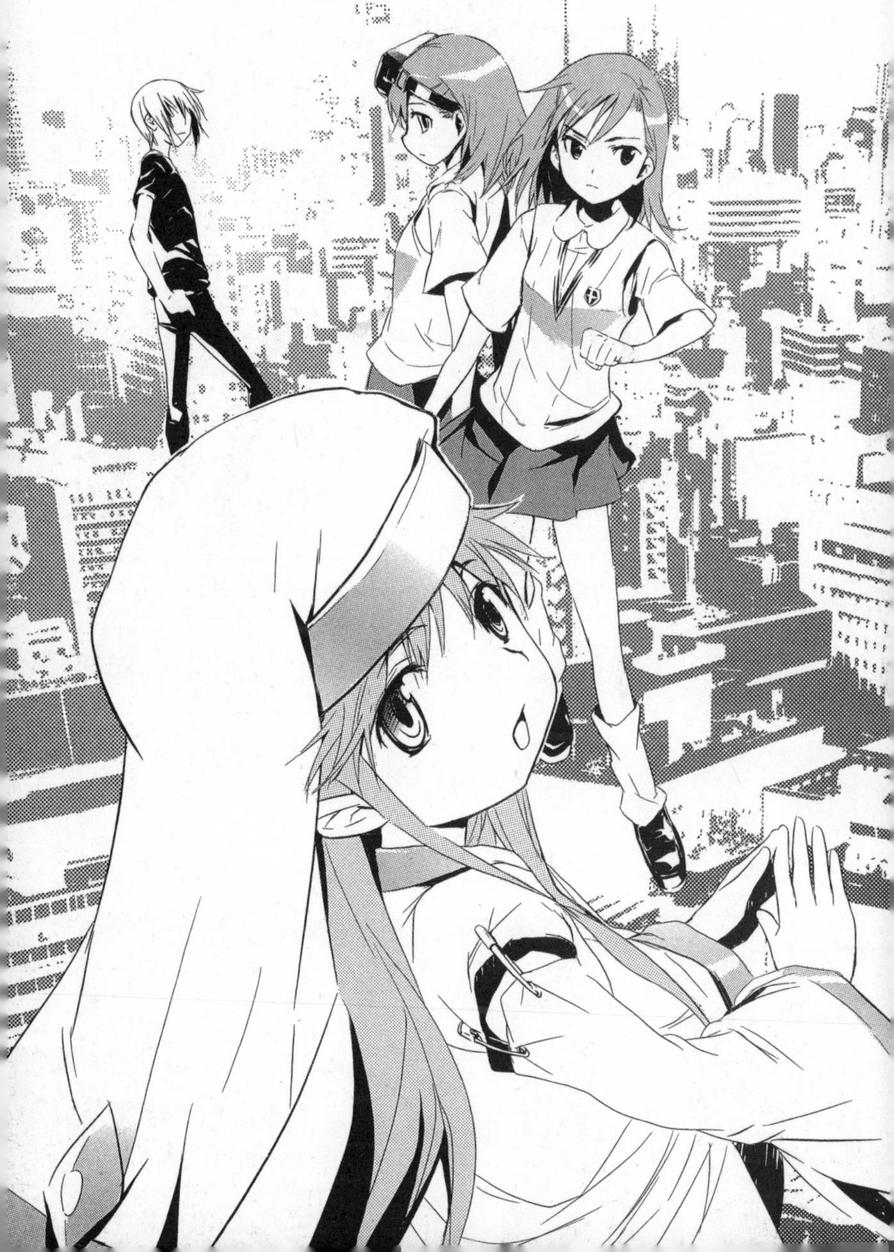

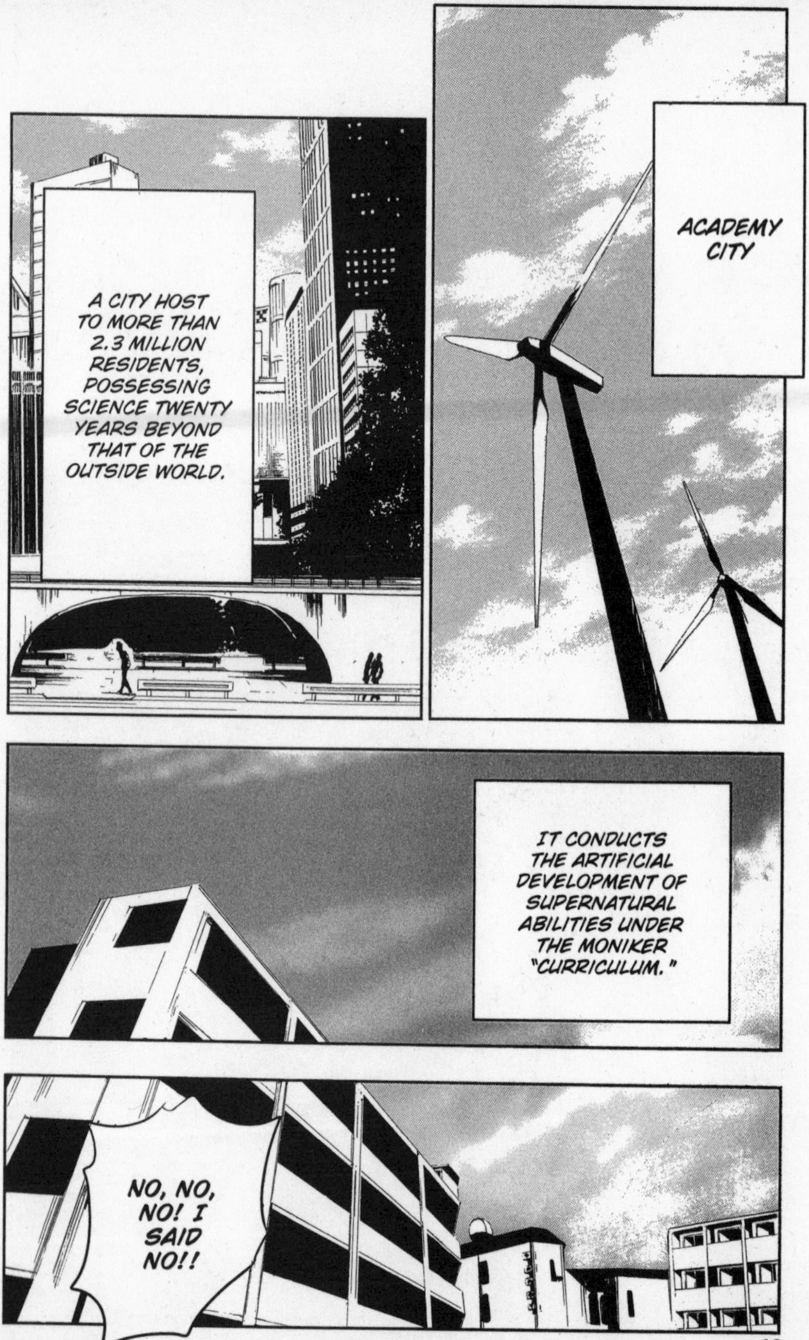
ACADEMY CITY
A CITY HOST TO MORE THAN 2.3 MILLION RESIDENTS, POSSESSING SCIENCE TWENTY YEARS BEYOND THAT OF THE OUTSIDE WORLD.
IT CONDUCTS THE ARTIFICIAL DEVELOPMENT OF SUPERNATURAL ABILITIES UNDER THE MONIKER "CURRICULUM."
NO, NO, NO! I SAID NO!!

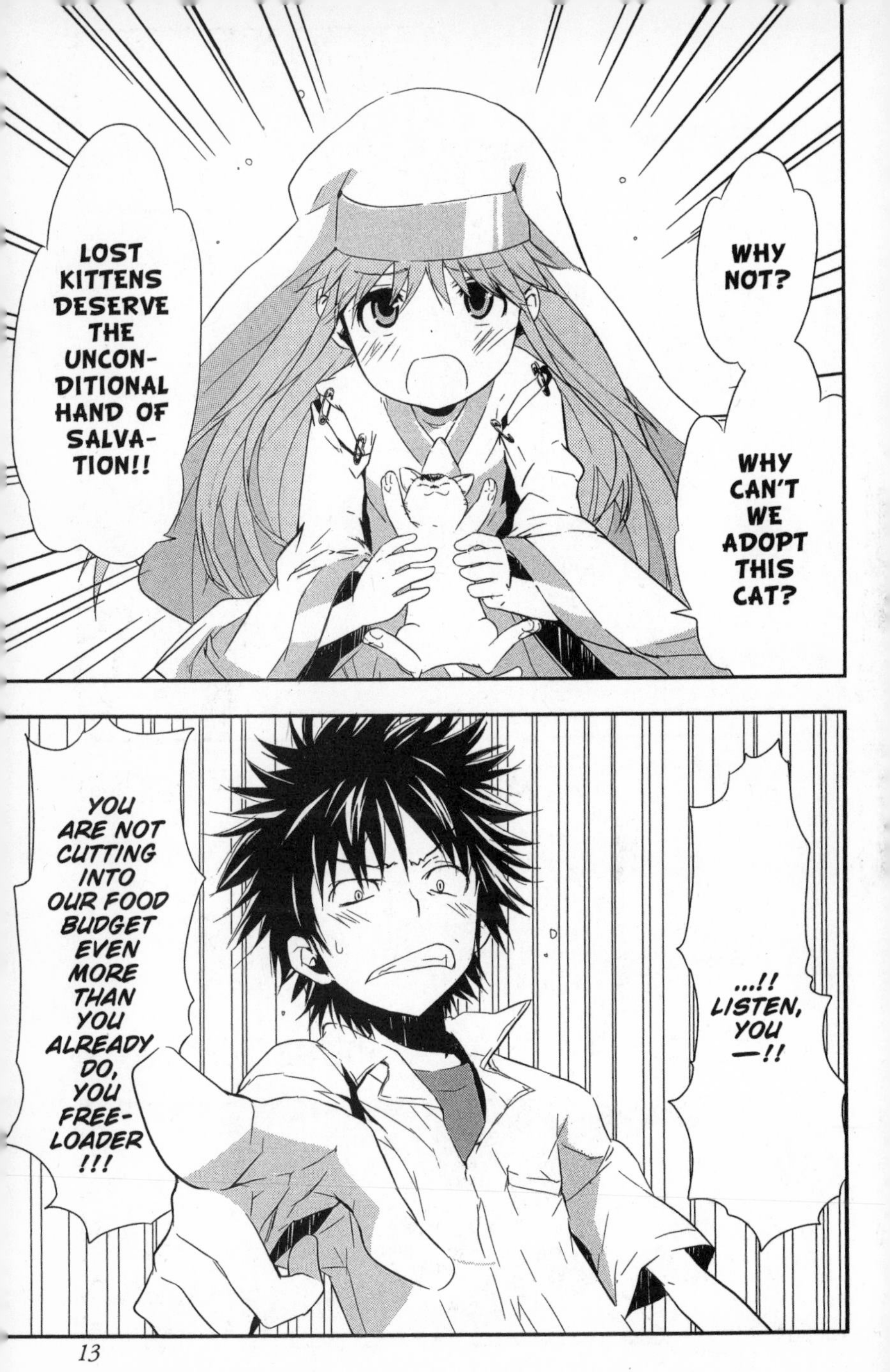
WHY NOT?
WHY CAN'T WE ADOPT THIS CAT?
LOST KITTENS DESERVE THE UNCONDITIONAL HAND OF SALVATION!!
...!! LISTEN, YOU —!!
YOU ARE NOT CUTTING INTO OUR FOOD BUDGET EVEN MORE THAN YOU ALREADY DO, YOU FREELOADER!!!

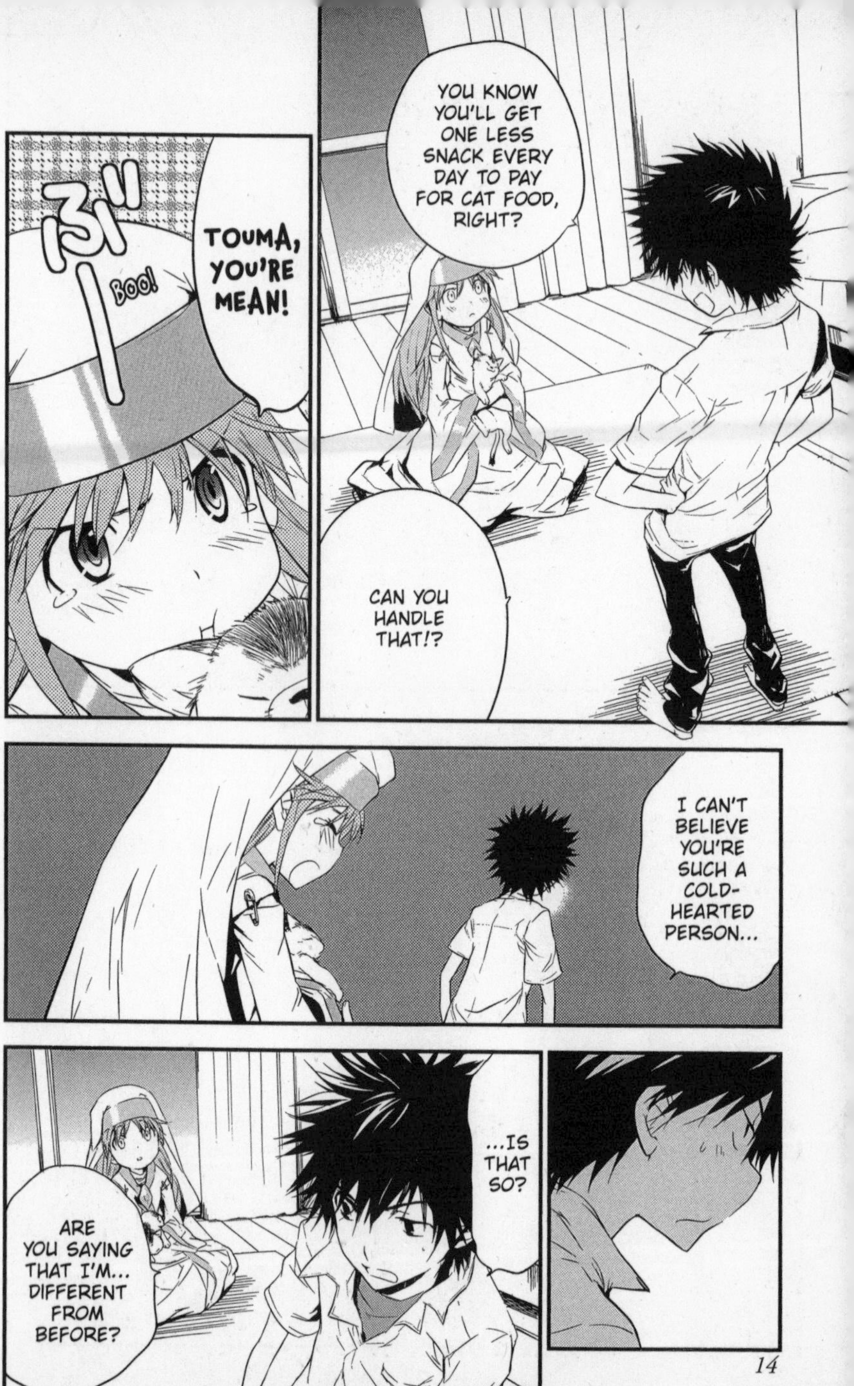
YOU KNOW YOU'LL GET ONE LESS SNACK EVERY DAY TO PAY FOR CAT FOOD, RIGHT?
CAN YOU HANDLE THAT!?
TOUMA, YOU'RE MEAN!
ぶー
BOO!
I CAN'T BELIEVE YOU'RE SUCH A COLD-HEARTED PERSON...
...IS THAT SO?
ARE YOU SAYING THAT I'M... DIFFERENT FROM BEFORE?

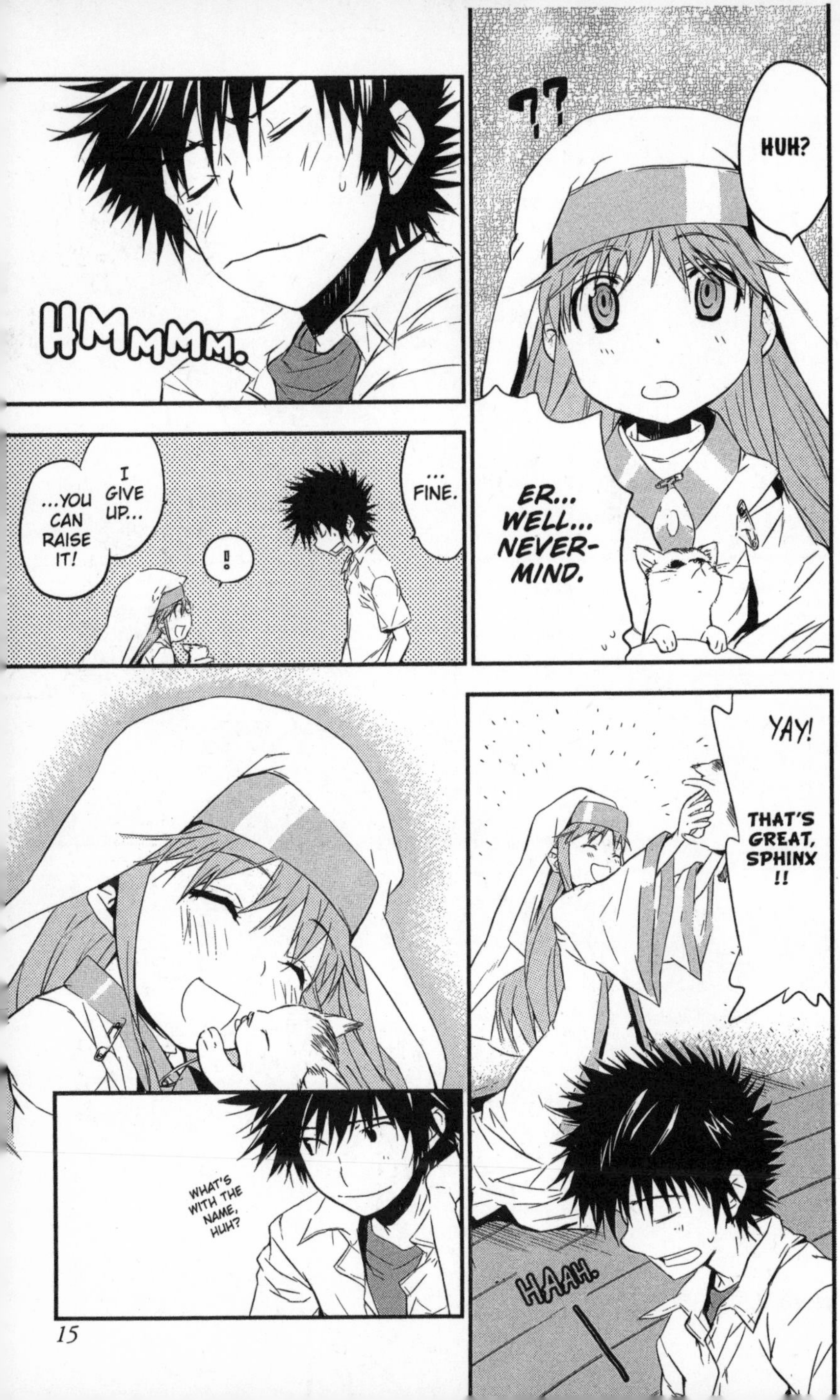
??
HUH?
ER... WELL... NEVER-MIND.
HMMMM.
... FINE.
I GIVE UP...
...YOU CAN RAISE IT!
!
YAY!
THAT'S GREAT, SPHINX!!
HAAH.
WHAT'S WITH THE NAME, HUH?

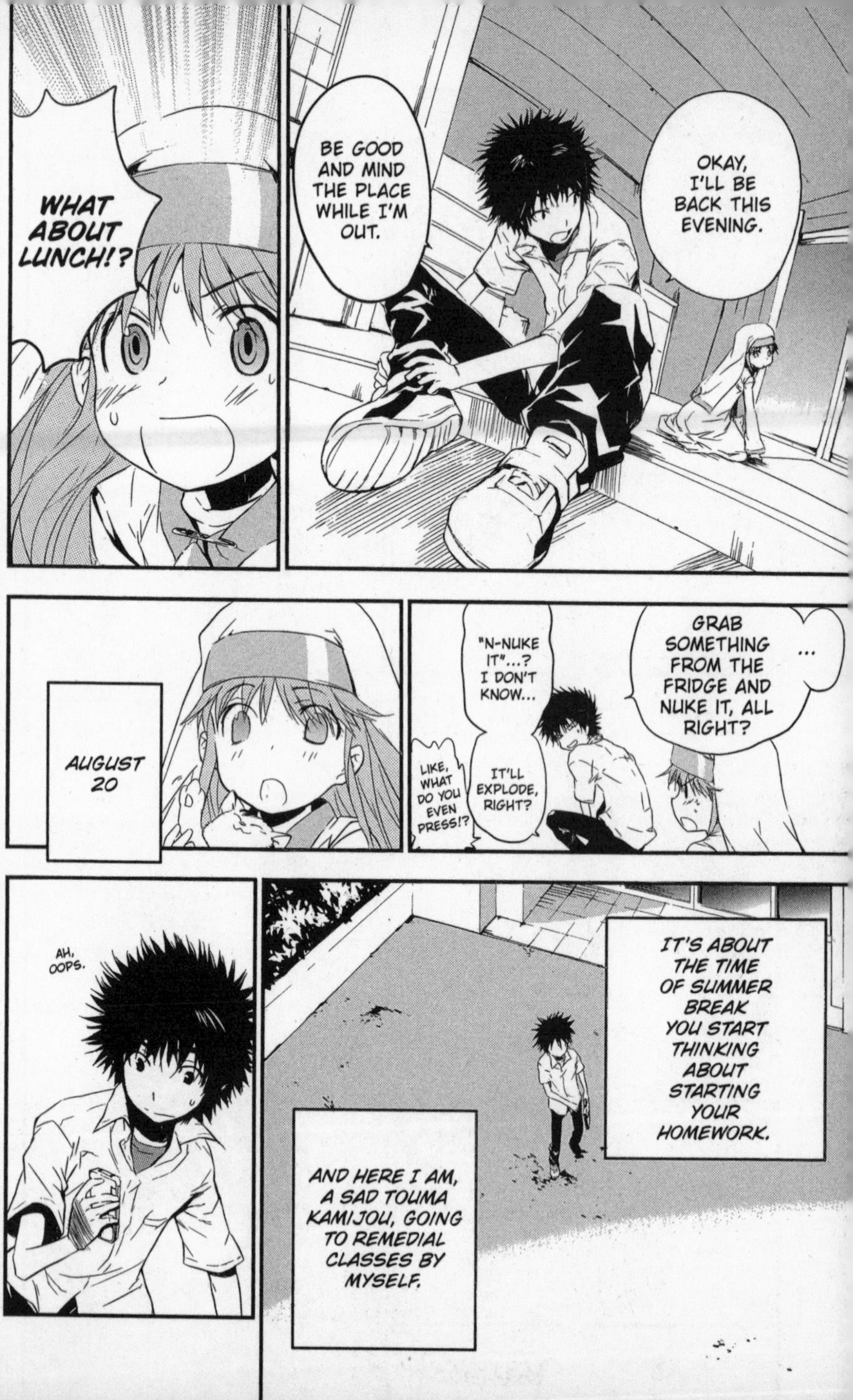
OKAY, I'LL BE BACK THIS EVENING.
BE GOOD AND MIND THE PLACE WHILE I'M OUT.
WHAT ABOUT LUNCH!?
...
GRAB SOMETHING FROM THE FRIDGE AND NUKE IT, ALL RIGHT?
"N-NUKE IT"...? I DON'T KNOW...
IT'LL EXPLODE, RIGHT?
LIKE, WHAT DO YOU EVEN PRESS!?
AUGUST 20
IT'S ABOUT THE TIME OF SUMMER BREAK YOU START THINKING ABOUT STARTING YOUR HOMEWORK.
AND HERE I AM, A SAD TOUMA KAMIJOU, GOING TO REMEDIAL CLASSES BY MYSELF.
AH, OOPS.

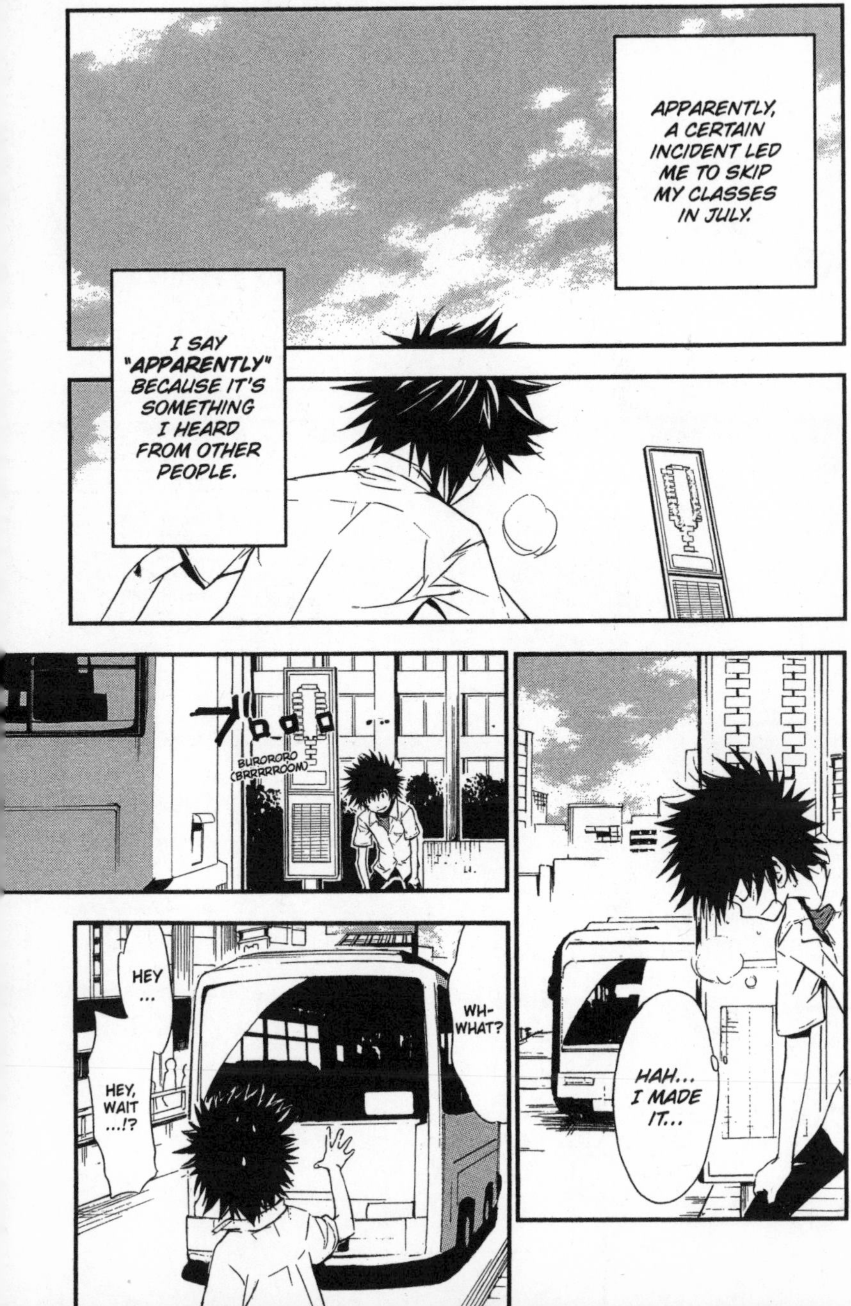
APPARENTLY, A CERTAIN INCIDENT LED ME TO SKIP MY CLASSES IN JULY.
I SAY "APPARENTLY" BECAUSE IT'S SOMETHING I HEARD FROM OTHER PEOPLE.
HAH... I MADE IT...
BUROROROO (BRRRRROOM)
HEY ...
WH-WHAT?
HEY, WAIT ...!?

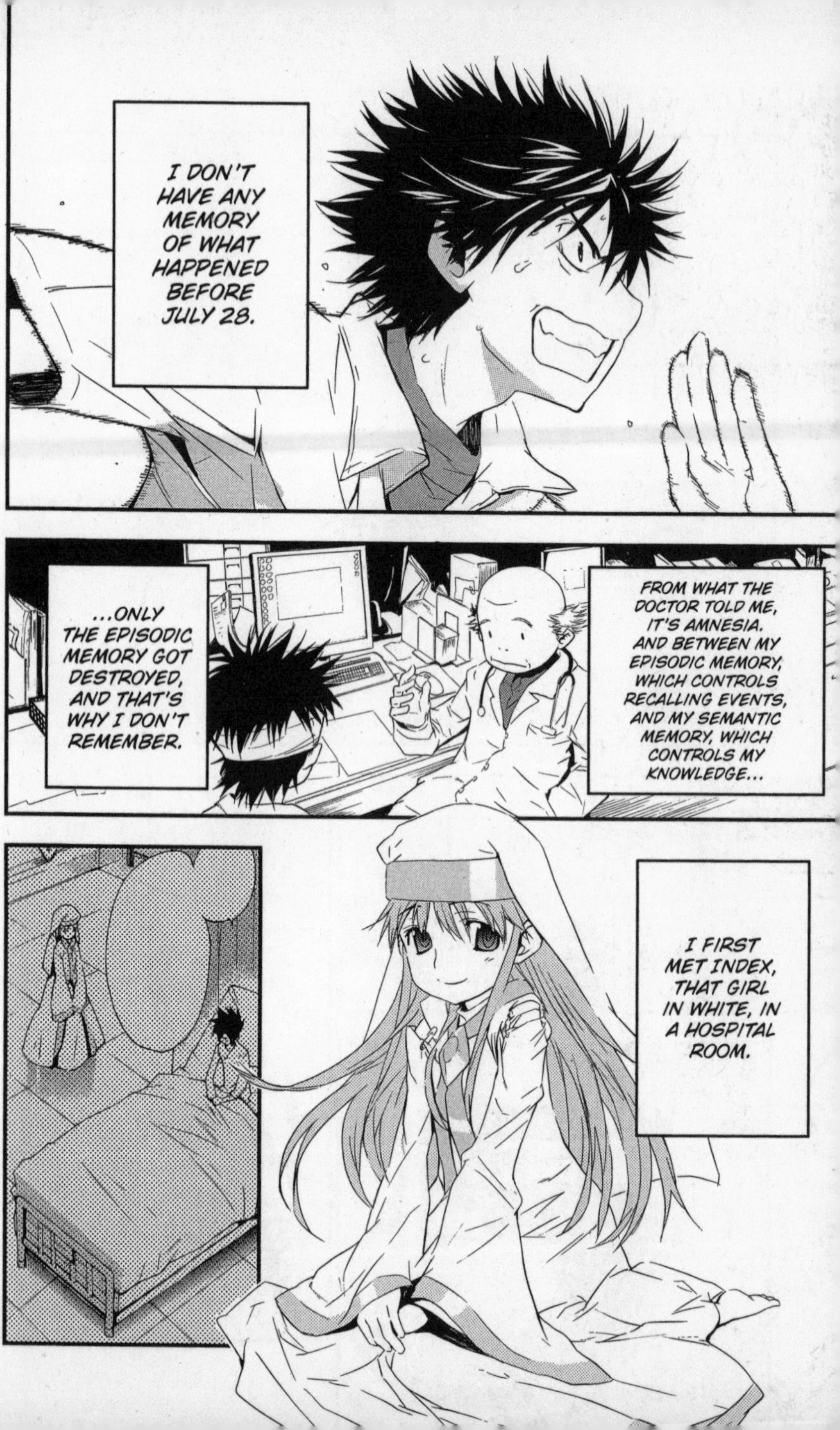
I DON'T HAVE ANY MEMORY OF WHAT HAPPENED BEFORE JULY 28.
FROM WHAT THE DOCTOR TOLD ME, IT'S AMNESIA. AND BETWEEN MY EPISODIC MEMORY, WHICH CONTROLS RECALLING EVENTS, AND MY SEMANTIC MEMORY, WHICH CONTROLS MY KNOWLEDGE...
...ONLY THE EPISODIC MEMORY GOT DESTROYED, AND THAT'S WHY I DON'T REMEMBER.
I FIRST MET INDEX, THAT GIRL IN WHITE, IN A HOSPITAL ROOM.

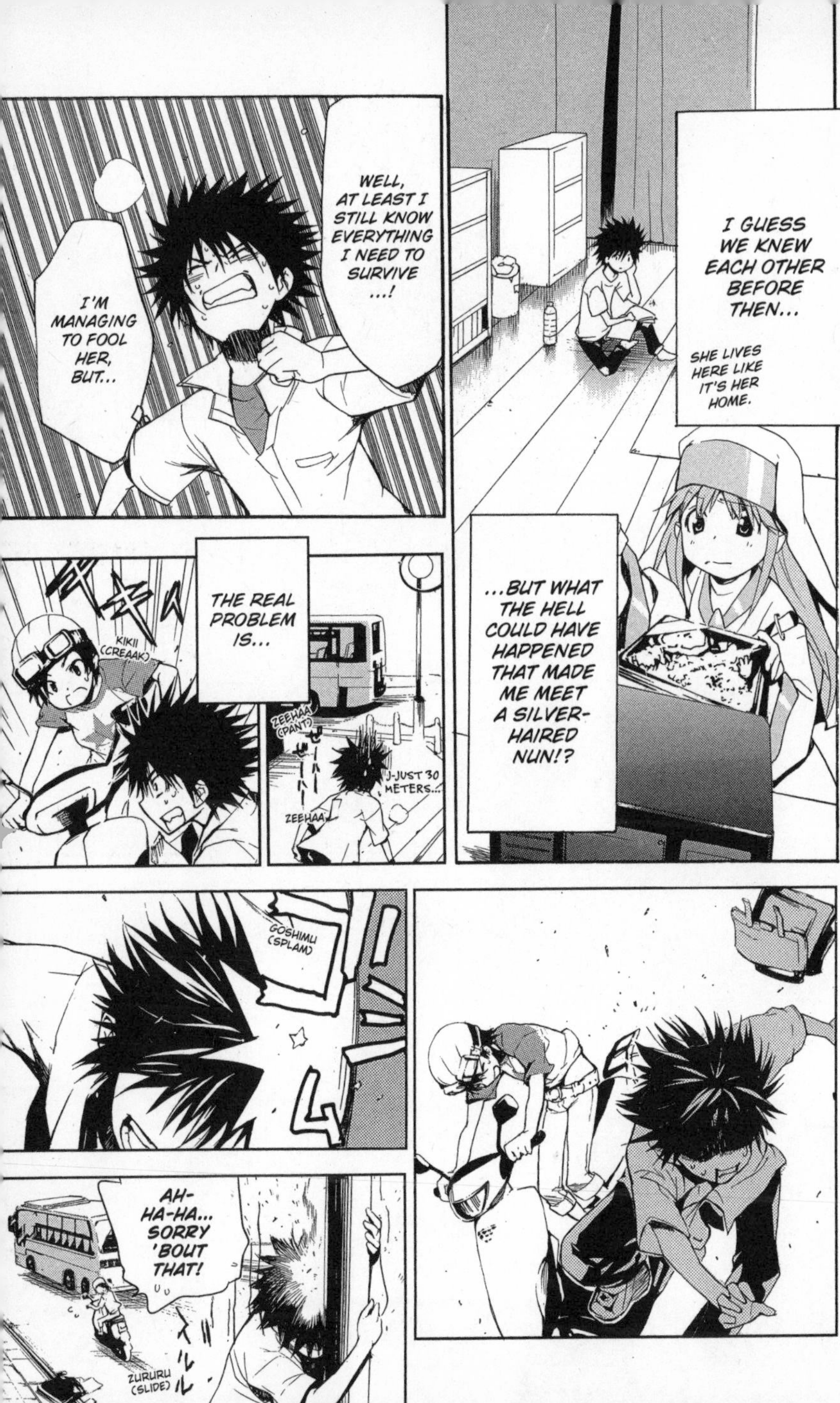
I GUESS WE KNEW EACH OTHER BEFORE THEN...
SHE LIVES HERE LIKE IT'S HER HOME.
...BUT WHAT THE HELL COULD HAVE HAPPENED THAT MADE ME MEET A SILVER-HAIRED NUN!?
WELL, AT LEAST I STILL KNOW EVERYTHING I NEED TO SURVIVE ...!
I'M MANAGING TO FOOL HER, BUT...
THE REAL PROBLEM IS...
ZEEHAA (PANT)
J-JUST 30 METERS...
ZEEHAA
KIKII (CREAAK)
GOSHIMU (SPLAM)
AH-HA-HA... SORRY 'BOUT THAT!
ZURURU (SLIDE)

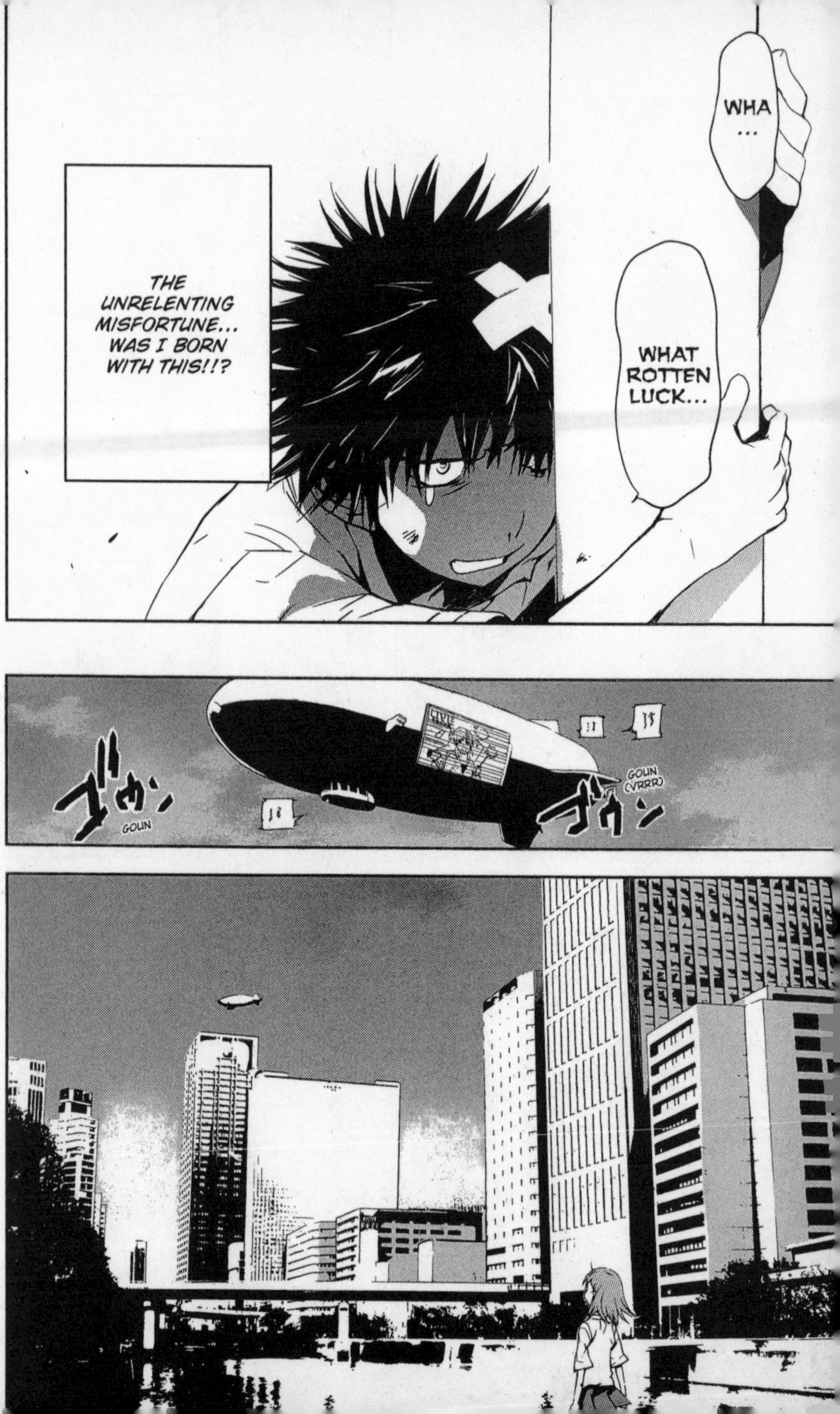
WHA...
WHAT ROTTEN LUCK...
THE UNRELENTING MISFORTUNE... WAS I BORN WITH THIS!!?
GOUN (VRRR)
GOUN

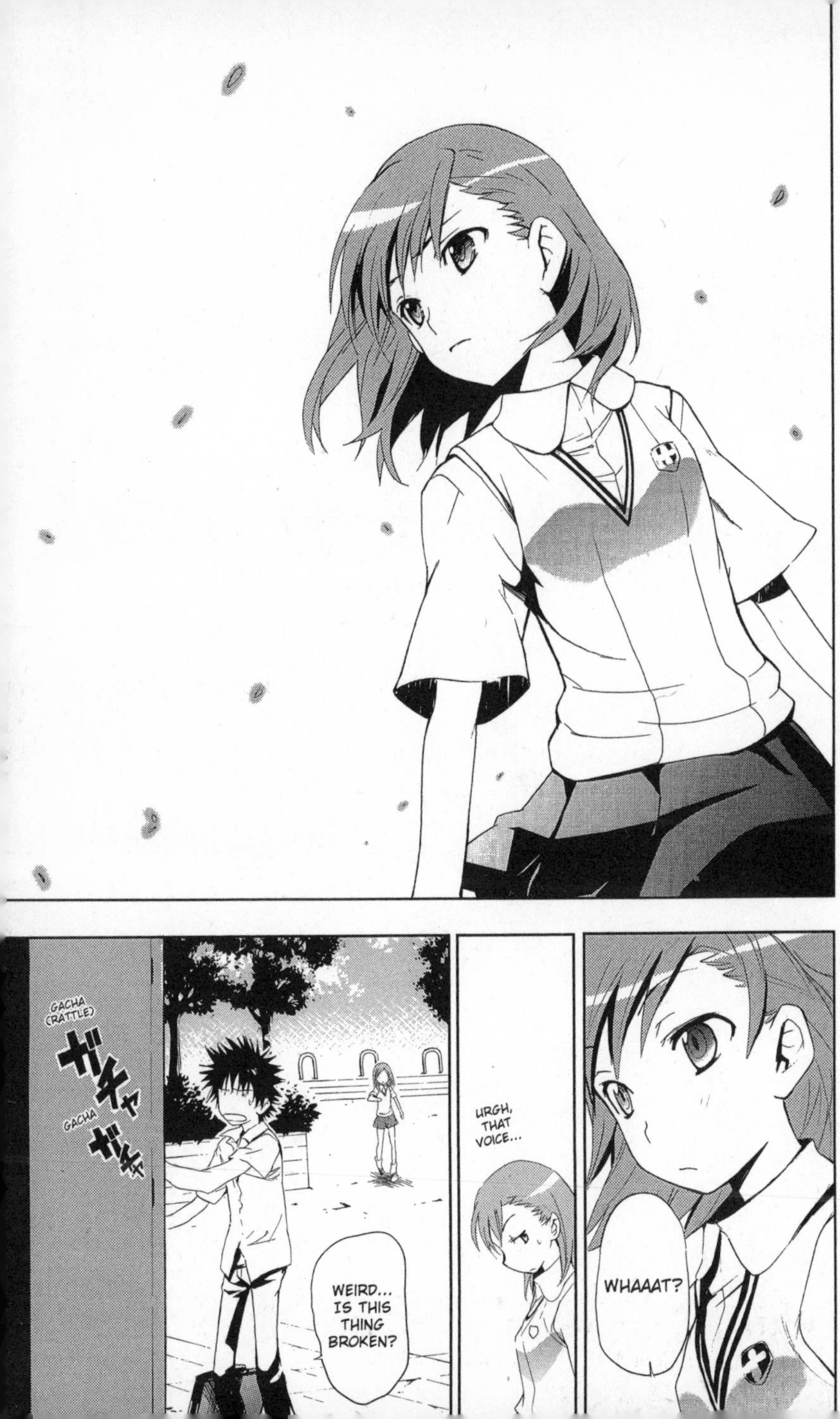
WHAAAT?
URGH, THAT VOICE...
GACHA (RATTLE)
GACHA
WEIRD... IS THIS THING BROKEN?

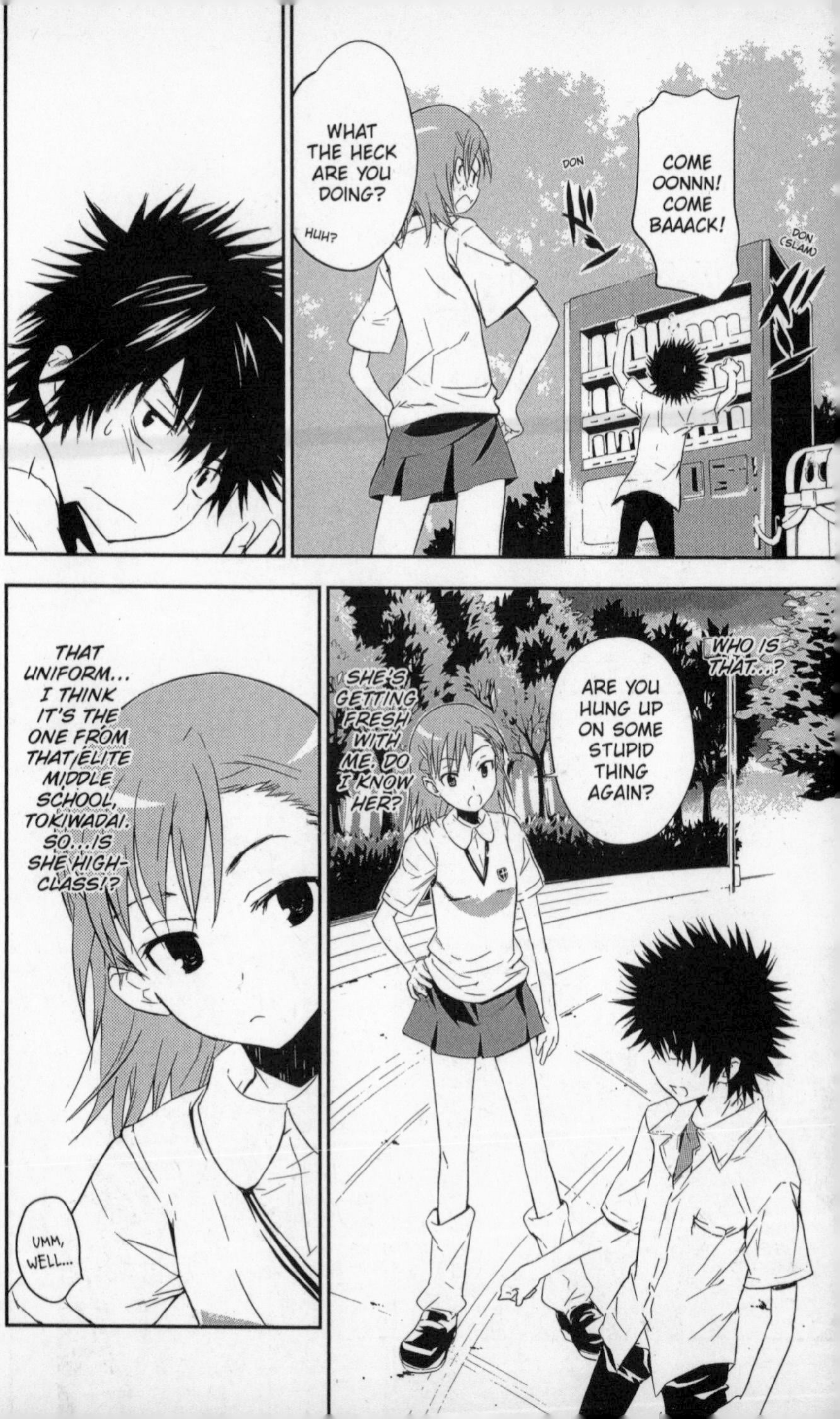
DON (SLAM)
COME OONNN! COME BAAACK!
DON
WHAT THE HECK ARE YOU DOING?
HUH?
WHO IS THAT...?
ARE YOU HUNG UP ON SOME STUPID THING AGAIN?
SHE'S GETTING FRESH WITH ME. DO I KNOW HER?
THAT UNIFORM... I THINK IT'S THE ONE FROM THAT ELITE MIDDLE SCHOOL, TOKIWADAI. SO...IS SHE HIGH-CLASS!?
UMM, WELL...

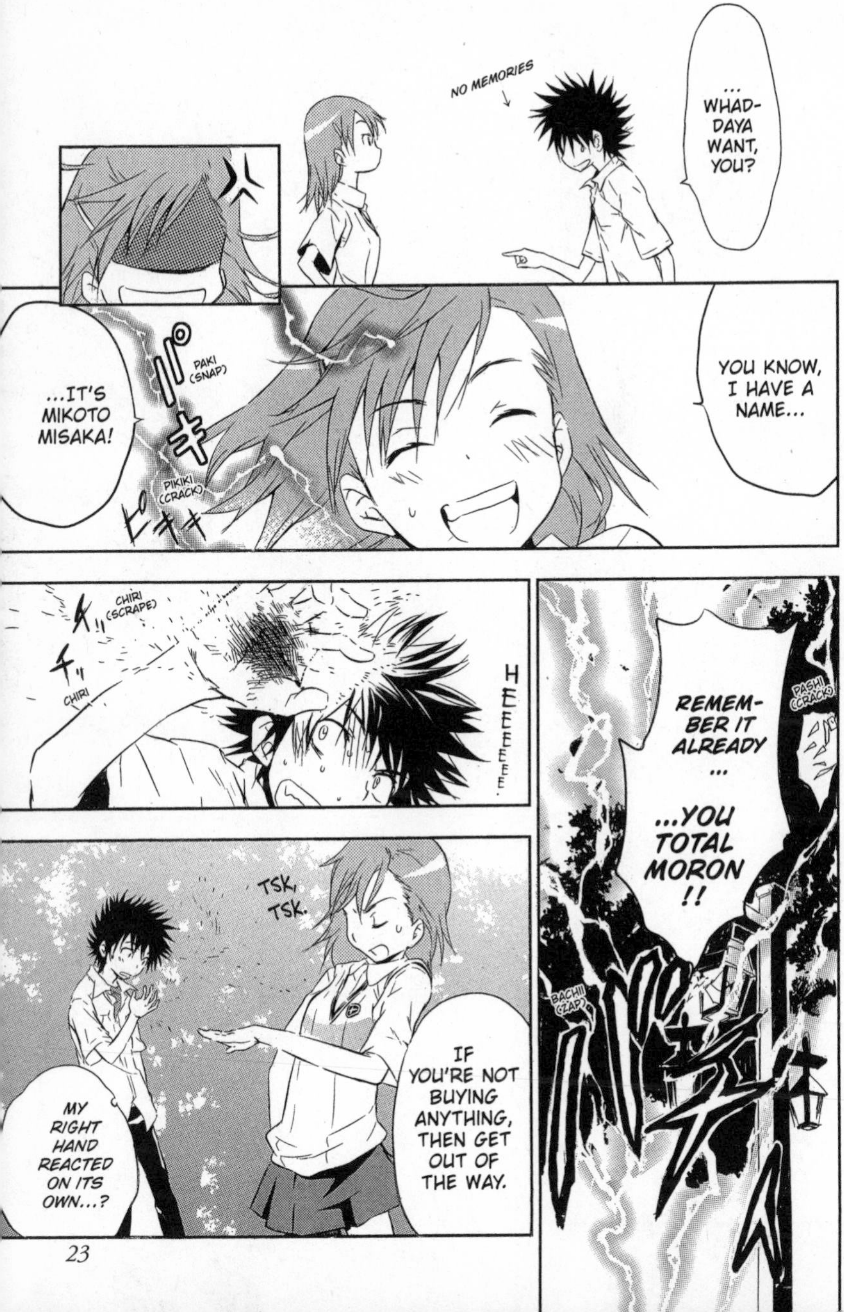
...WHAD-DAYA WANT, YOU?
NO MEMORIES
YOU KNOW, I HAVE A NAME...
PAKI (SNAP)
...IT'S MIKOTO MISAKA!
PIKIKI (CRACK)
REMEM-BER IT ALREADY ...
...YOU TOTAL MORON !!
PASHI (CRACK)
BACHII (ZAP)
CHIRI (SCRAPE)
CHIRI
HEEEEEEE.
TSK, TSK.
IF YOU'RE NOT BUYING ANYTHING, THEN GET OUT OF THE WAY.
MY RIGHT HAND REACTED ON ITS OWN...?

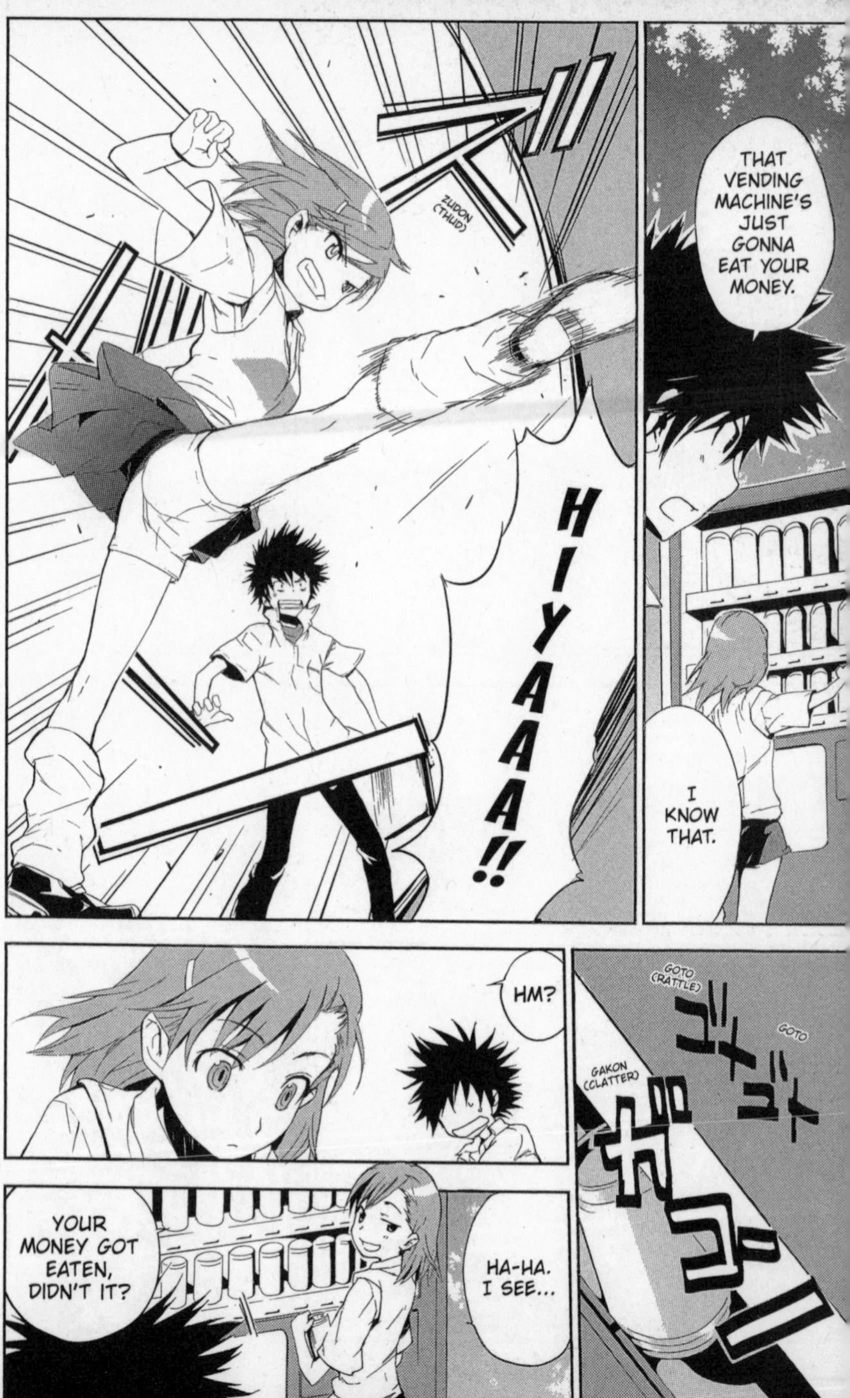
THAT VENDING MACHINE'S JUST GONNA EAT YOUR MONEY.
I KNOW THAT.
ZUDON (THUD)
HIYAAAA!!
GOTO (RATTLE)
GOTO
GAKON (CLATTER)
HM?
HA-HA. I SEE...
YOUR MONEY GOT EATEN, DIDN'T IT?

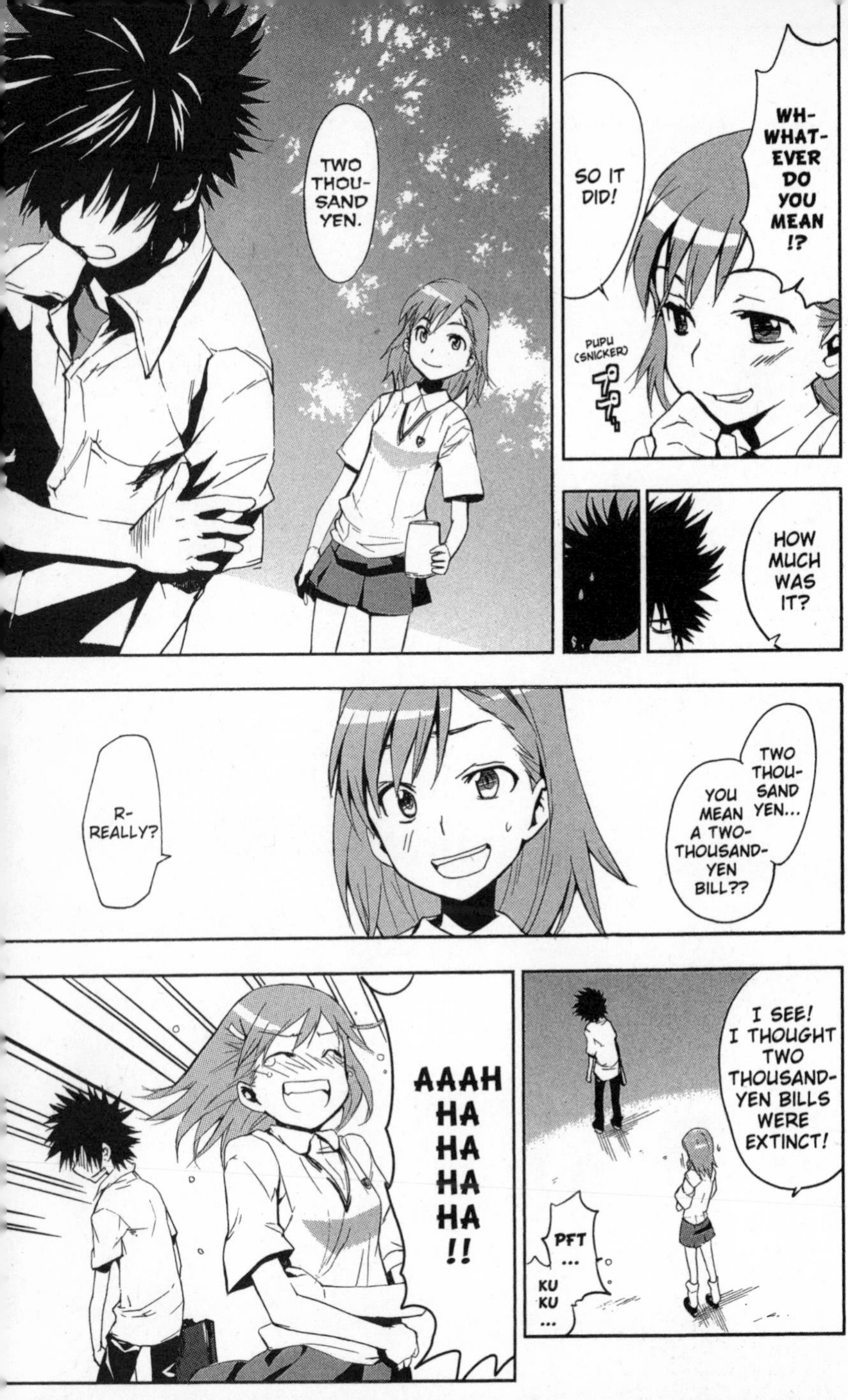
WH-WHAT-EVER DO YOU MEAN!?
SO IT DID!
PUPU (SNICKER)
HOW MUCH WAS IT?
TWO THOU-SAND YEN.
TWO THOU-SAND YEN...
YOU MEAN A TWO-THOUSAND-YEN BILL??
R-REALLY?
I SEE! I THOUGHT TWO THOUSAND-YEN BILLS WERE EXTINCT!
PFT...
KU KU...
AAAH HA HA HA HA!!

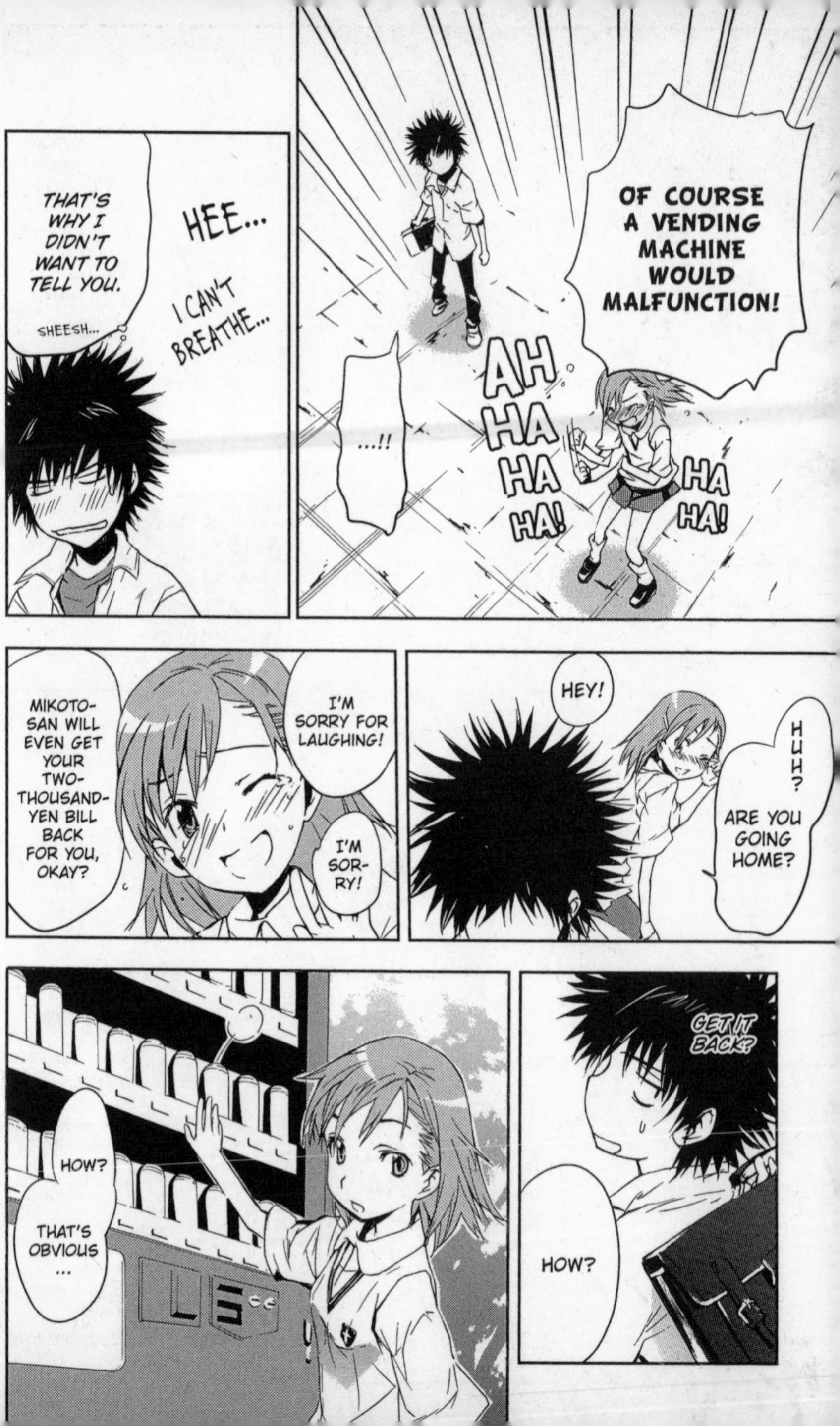
OF COURSE A VENDING MACHINE WOULD MALFUNCTION!
AH HA HA HA!
HA HA!
...!!
HEE...
I CAN'T BREATHE...
THAT'S WHY I DIDN'T WANT TO TELL YOU.
SHEESH...
HEY!
HUH?
ARE YOU GOING HOME?
I'M SORRY FOR LAUGHING!
I'M SOR-RY!
MIKOTO-SAN WILL EVEN GET YOUR TWO-THOUSAND-YEN BILL BACK FOR YOU, OKAY?
GET IT BACK?
HOW?
HOW?
THAT'S OBVIOUS ...

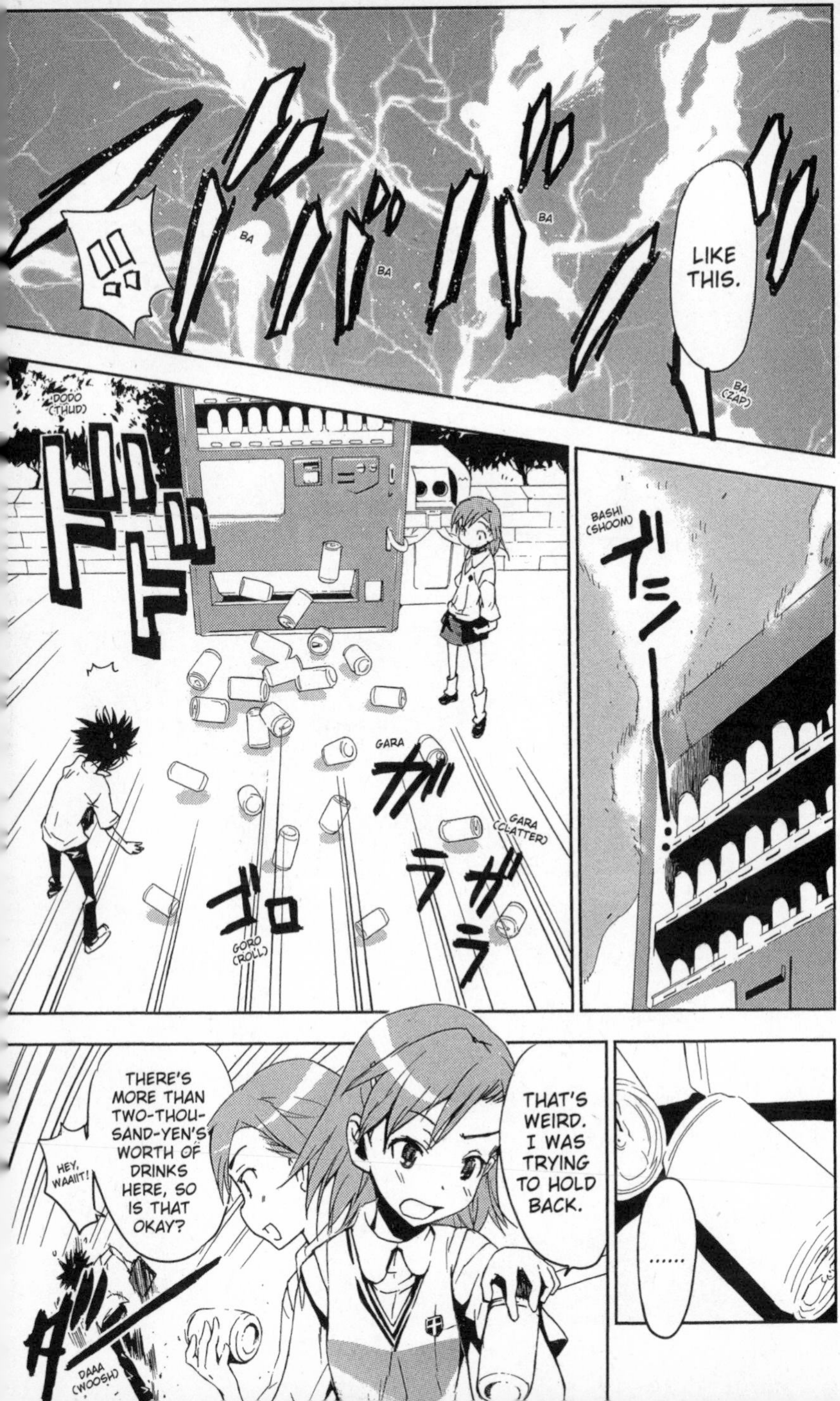
LIKE THIS.
BA (ZAP)
BA
BA
BA
BASHI (SHOOM)
DODO (THUD)
GARA
GARA (CLATTER)
GORO (ROLL)
......
THAT'S WEIRD. I WAS TRYING TO HOLD BACK.
THERE'S MORE THAN TWO-THOUSAND-YEN'S WORTH OF DRINKS HERE, SO IS THAT OKAY?
HEY, WAAIIT!
DAAA (WOOSH)

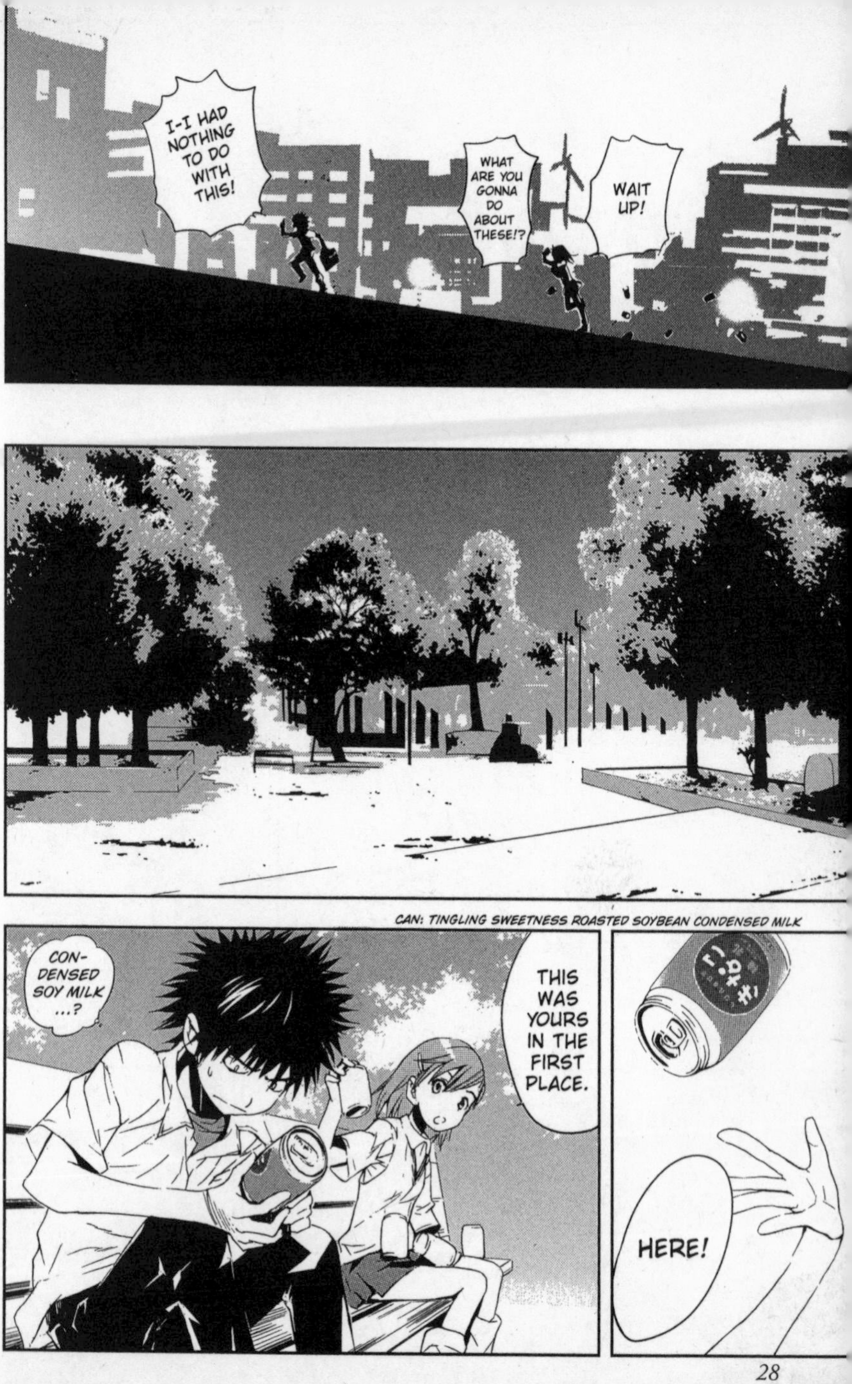
WAIT UP!
WHAT ARE YOU GONNA DO ABOUT THESE!?
I-I HAD NOTHING TO DO WITH THIS!
CAN: TINGLING SWEETNESS ROASTED SOYBEAN CONDENSED MILK
HERE!
THIS WAS YOURS IN THE FIRST PLACE.
CON-DENSED SOY MILK ...?

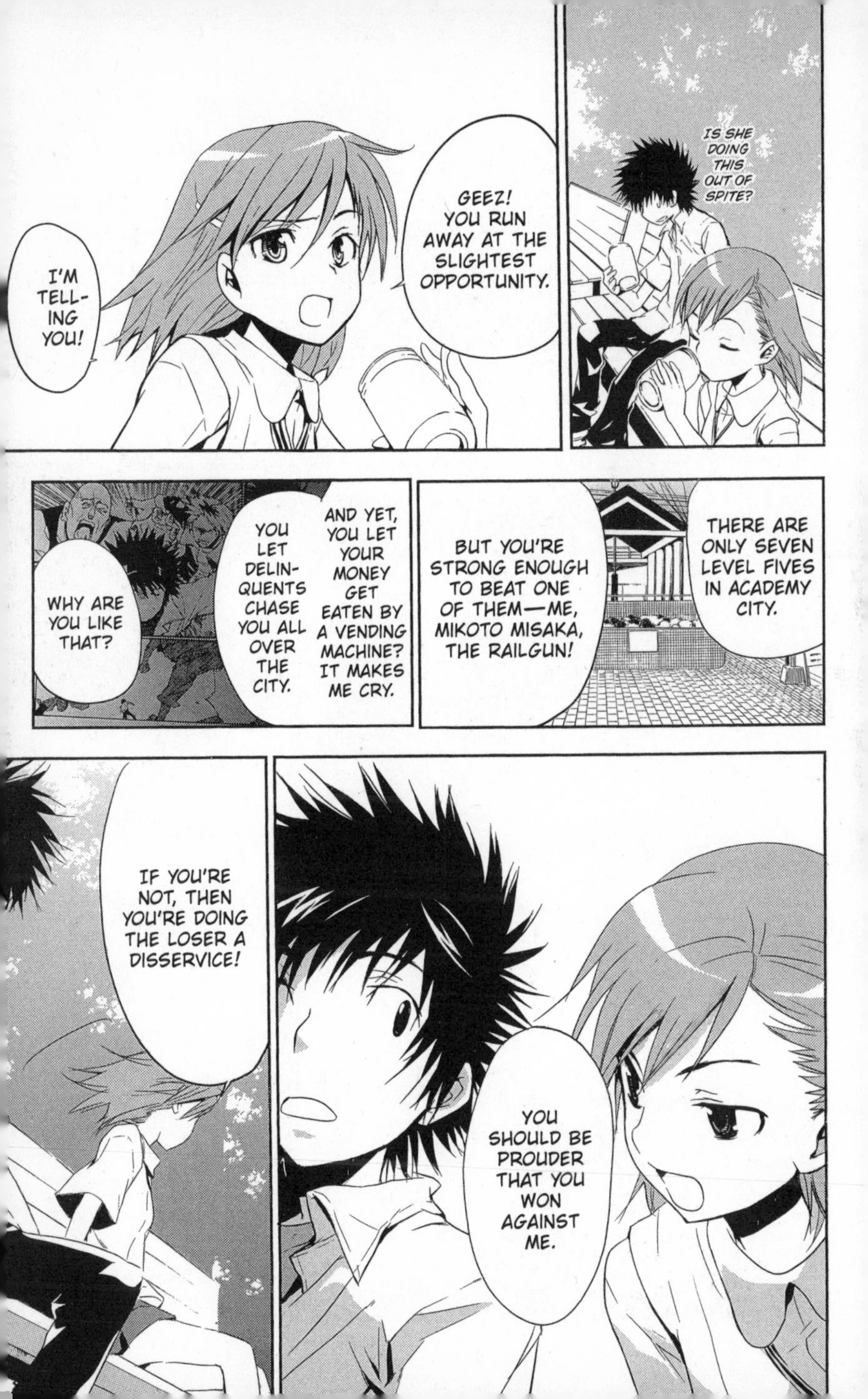
IS SHE DOING THIS OUT OF SPITE?
GEEZ! YOU RUN AWAY AT THE SLIGHTEST OPPORTUNITY.
I'M TELL-ING YOU!
THERE ARE ONLY SEVEN LEVEL FIVES IN ACADEMY CITY.
BUT YOU'RE STRONG ENOUGH TO BEAT ONE OF THEM—ME, MIKOTO MISAKA, THE RAILGUN!
AND YET, YOU LET YOUR MONEY GET EATEN BY A VENDING MACHINE? IT MAKES ME CRY.
YOU LET DELIN-QUENTS CHASE YOU ALL OVER THE CITY.
WHY ARE YOU LIKE THAT?
YOU SHOULD BE PROUDER THAT YOU WON AGAINST ME.
IF YOU'RE NOT, THEN YOU'RE DOING THE LOSER A DISSERVICE!

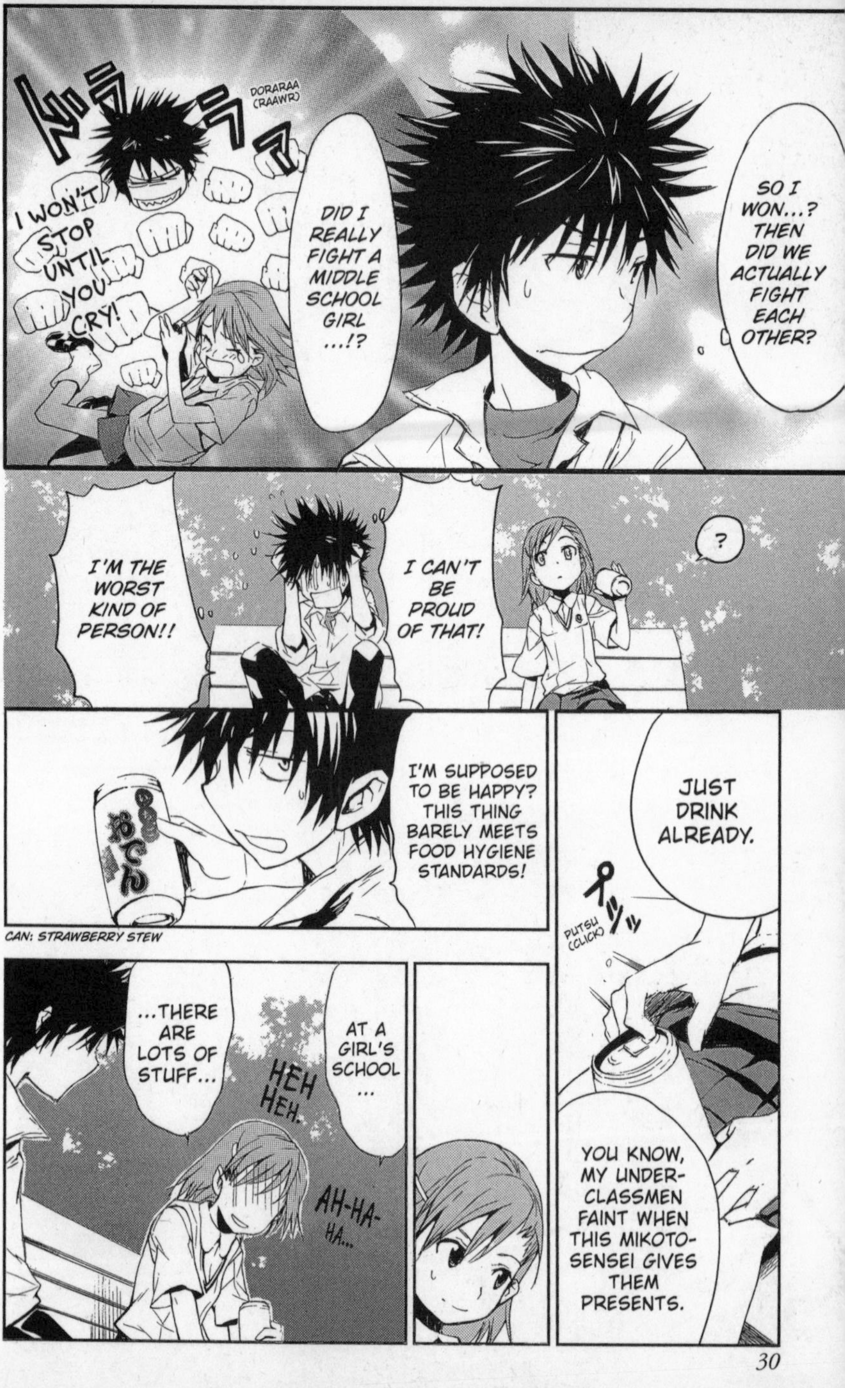
SO I WON...? THEN DID WE ACTUALLY FIGHT EACH OTHER?
DID I REALLY FIGHT A MIDDLE SCHOOL GIRL ...!?
DORARAA (RAAWR)
I WON'T STOP UNTIL YOU CRY!
?
I CAN'T BE PROUD OF THAT!
I'M THE WORST KIND OF PERSON!!
JUST DRINK ALREADY.
PUTSU (CLICK)
YOU KNOW, MY UNDER-CLASSMEN FAINT WHEN THIS MIKOTO-SENSEI GIVES THEM PRESENTS.
I'M SUPPOSED TO BE HAPPY? THIS THING BARELY MEETS FOOD HYGIENE STANDARDS!
CAN: STRAWBERRY STEW
AT A GIRL'S SCHOOL ...
...THERE ARE LOTS OF STUFF...
HEH HEH.
AH-HA-HA...

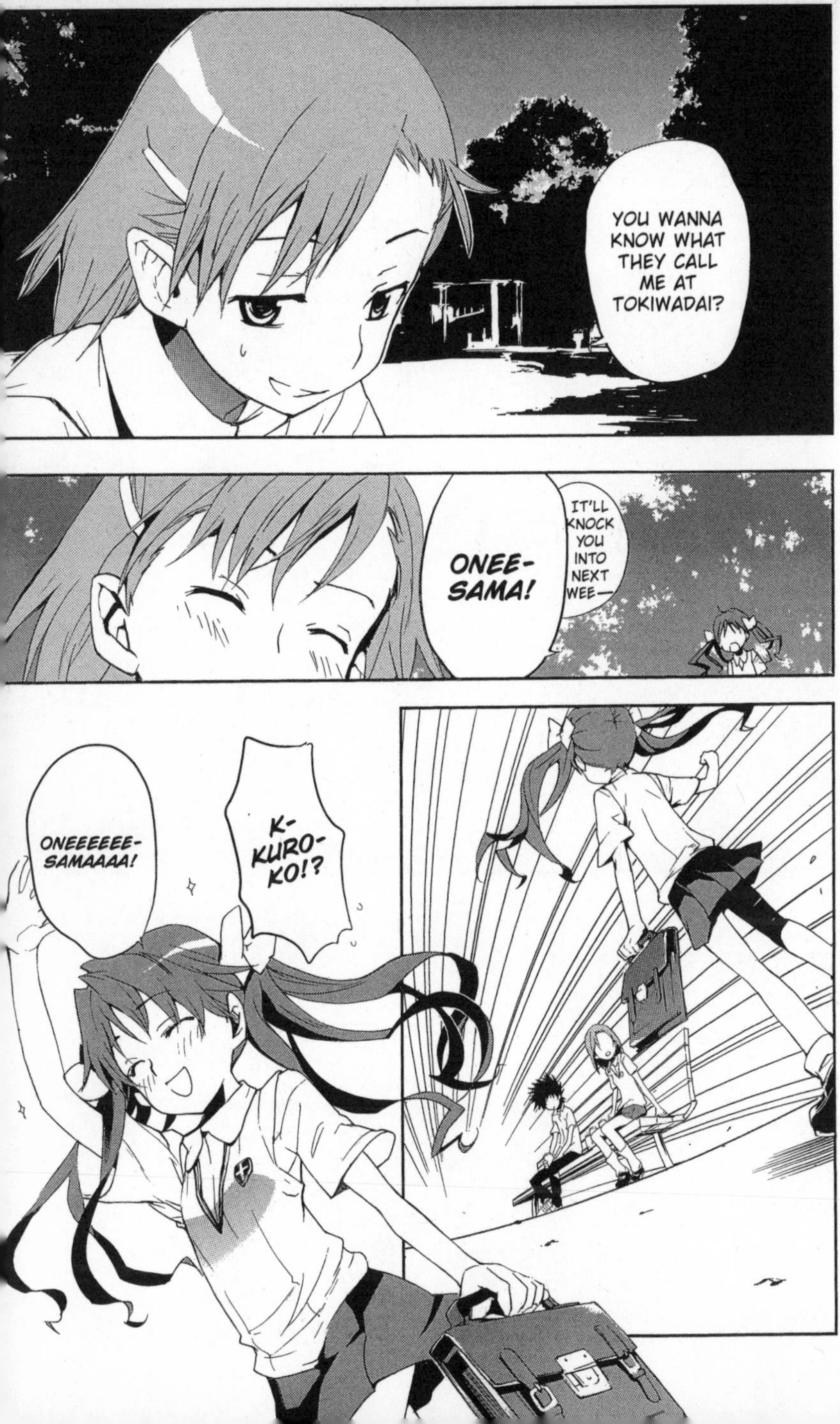
YOU WANNA KNOW WHAT THEY CALL ME AT TOKIWADAI?
IT'LL KNOCK YOU INTO NEXT WEE—
ONEE-SAMA!
K-KURO-KO!?
ONEEEEEE-SAMAAAA!

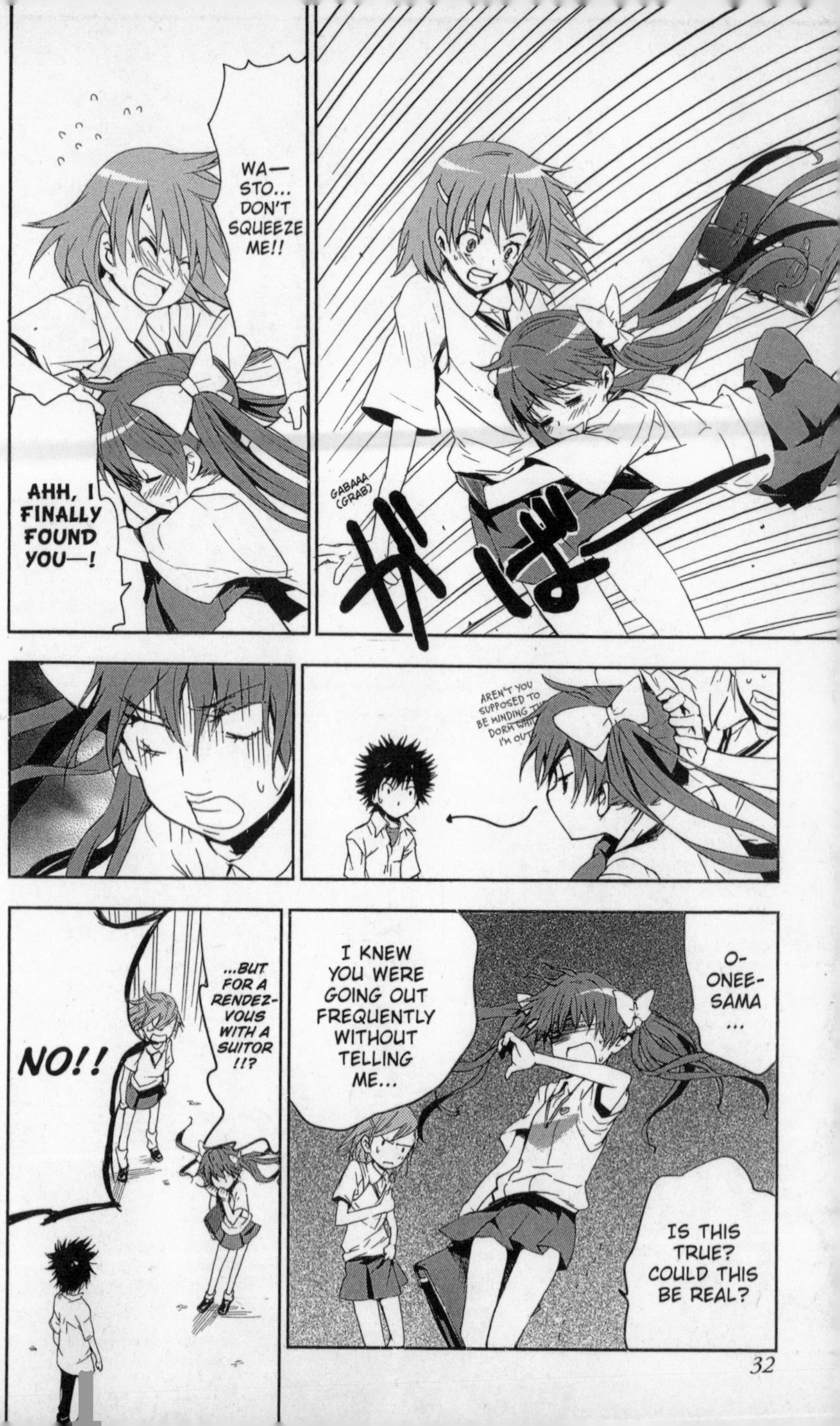

GABAAA (GRAB)
がばー
WA— STO... DON'T SQUEEZE ME!!
AHH, I FINALLY FOUND YOU—!
AREN'T YOU SUPPOSED TO BE MINDING TH DORM WHI I'M OUT
O-ONEE-SAMA ...
I KNEW YOU WERE GOING OUT FREQUENTLY WITHOUT TELLING ME...
IS THIS TRUE? COULD THIS BE REAL?
...BUT FOR A RENDEZVOUS WITH A SUITOR !!?
NO!!

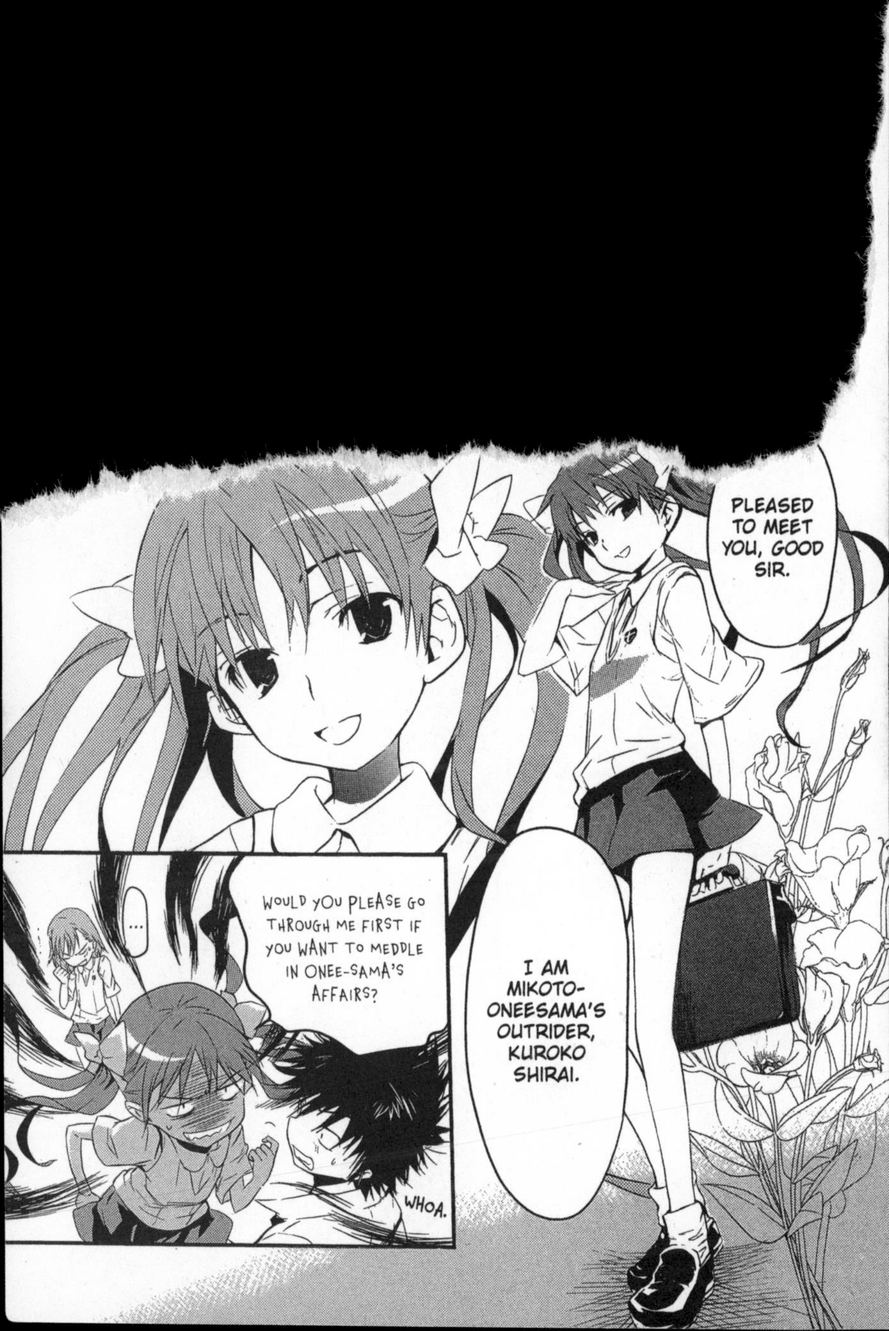
PLEASED TO MEET YOU, GOOD SIR.
I AM MIKOTO-ONEESAMA'S OUTRIDER, KUROKO SHIRAI.
WOULD YOU PLEASE GO THROUGH ME FIRST IF YOU WANT TO MEDDLE IN ONEE-SAMA'S AFFAIRS?
...
WHOA.

[redacted]

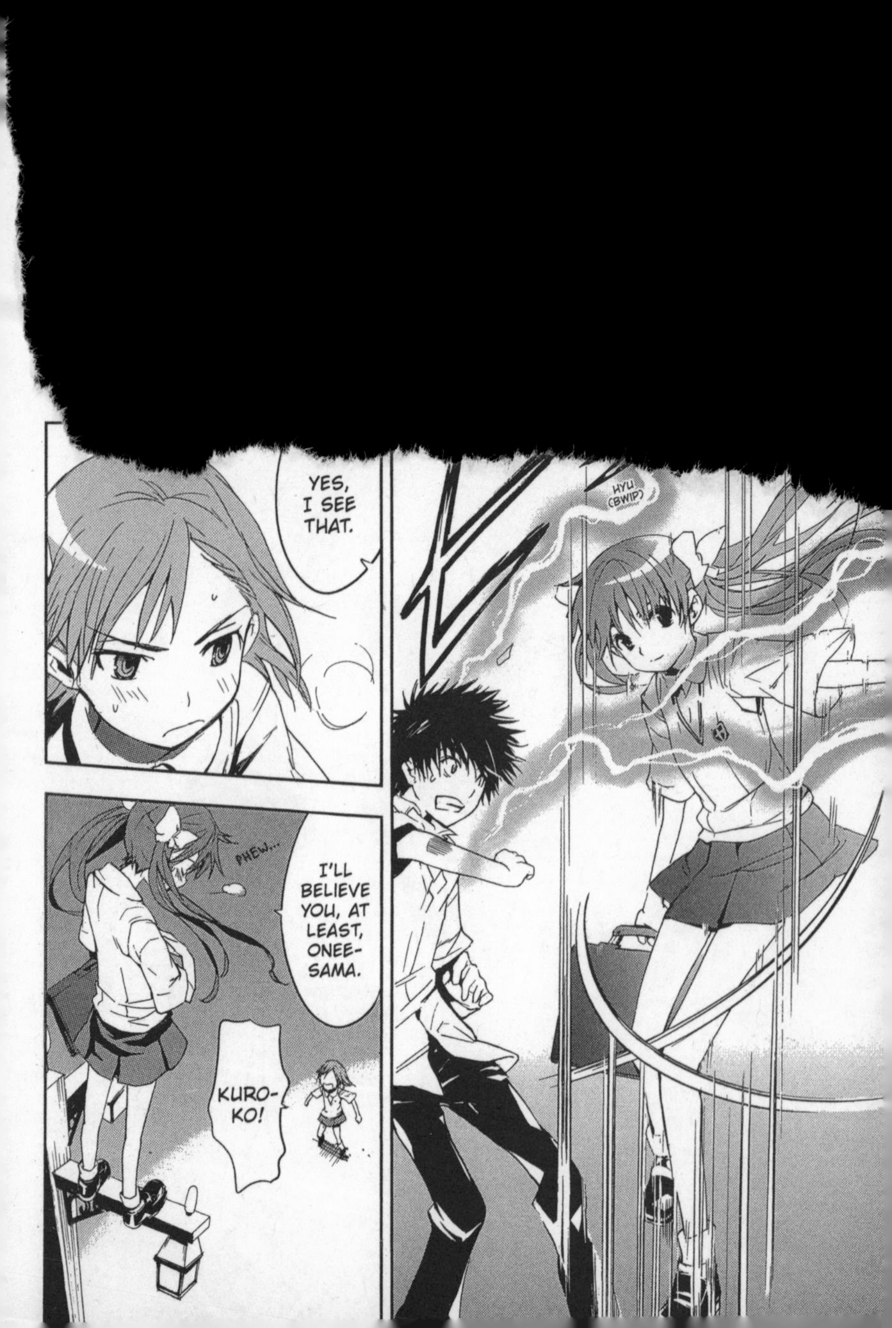
HYU (BWIP)
YES, I SEE THAT.
PHEW...
I'LL BELIEVE YOU, AT LEAST, ONEE-SAMA.
KURO-KO!

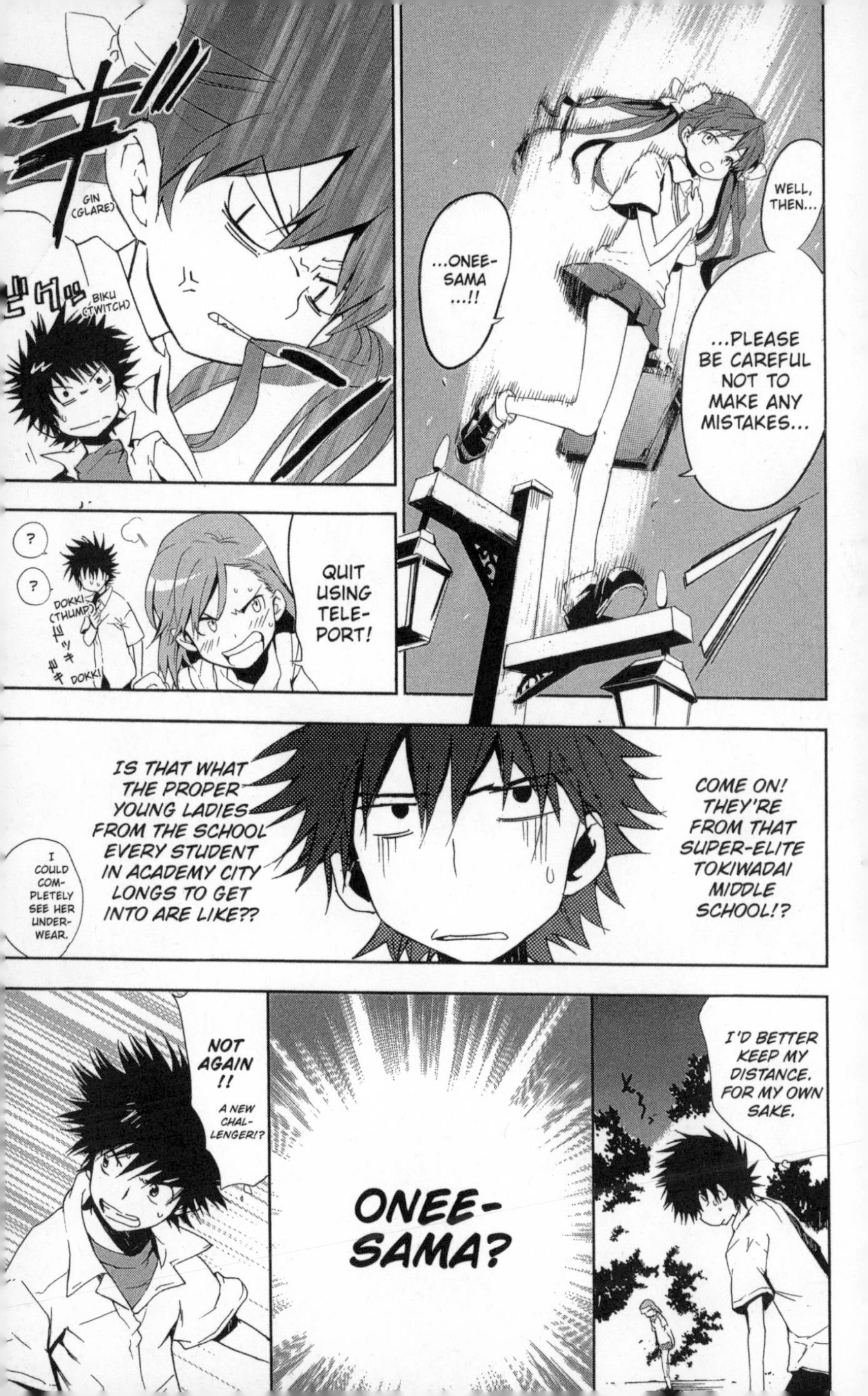
WELL, THEN...
...PLEASE BE CAREFUL NOT TO MAKE ANY MISTAKES...
...ONEE-SAMA ...!!
GIN (GLARE)
BIKU (TWITCH)
QUIT USING TELE-PORT!
?
?
DOKKI (THUMP)
DOKKI
COME ON! THEY'RE FROM THAT SUPER-ELITE TOKIWADAI MIDDLE SCHOOL!?
IS THAT WHAT THE PROPER YOUNG LADIES FROM THE SCHOOL EVERY STUDENT IN ACADEMY CITY LONGS TO GET INTO ARE LIKE??
I COULD COM-PLETELY SEE HER UNDER-WEAR.
I'D BETTER KEEP MY DISTANCE. FOR MY OWN SAKE.
ONEE-SAMA?
NOT AGAIN!!
A NEW CHAL-LENGER!?

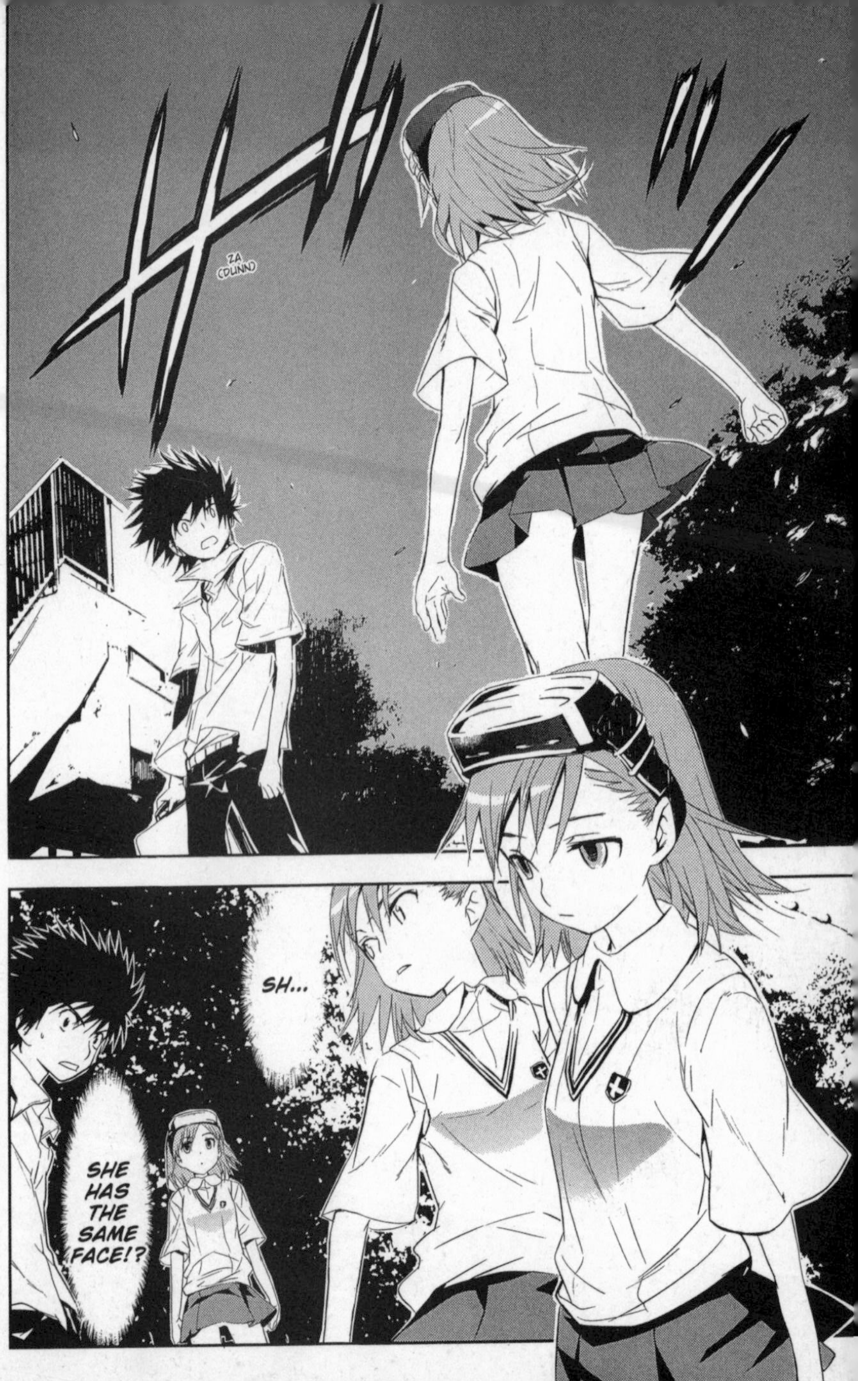
ZA (DUNN)
SH...
SHE HAS THE SAME FACE!?

A
Certain
Magical
Index

ασοβιδα

しびれる甘さ

きなこ
練乳

旨みとコクの
ねっとりクリーミー製法

国産大豆使用

TINGLING SWEETNESS
ROASTED SOYBEAN CONDENSED MILK
RICHNESS AND FLAVOR PROCESSED INTO A STICKY
CREAMINESS
USES DOMESTIC SOYBEANS

いちご
おでん
たっぷり果肉入り

STRAWBERRY STEW: PACKED FULL OF FRUIT SKIN

#12 LITTLE SISTER

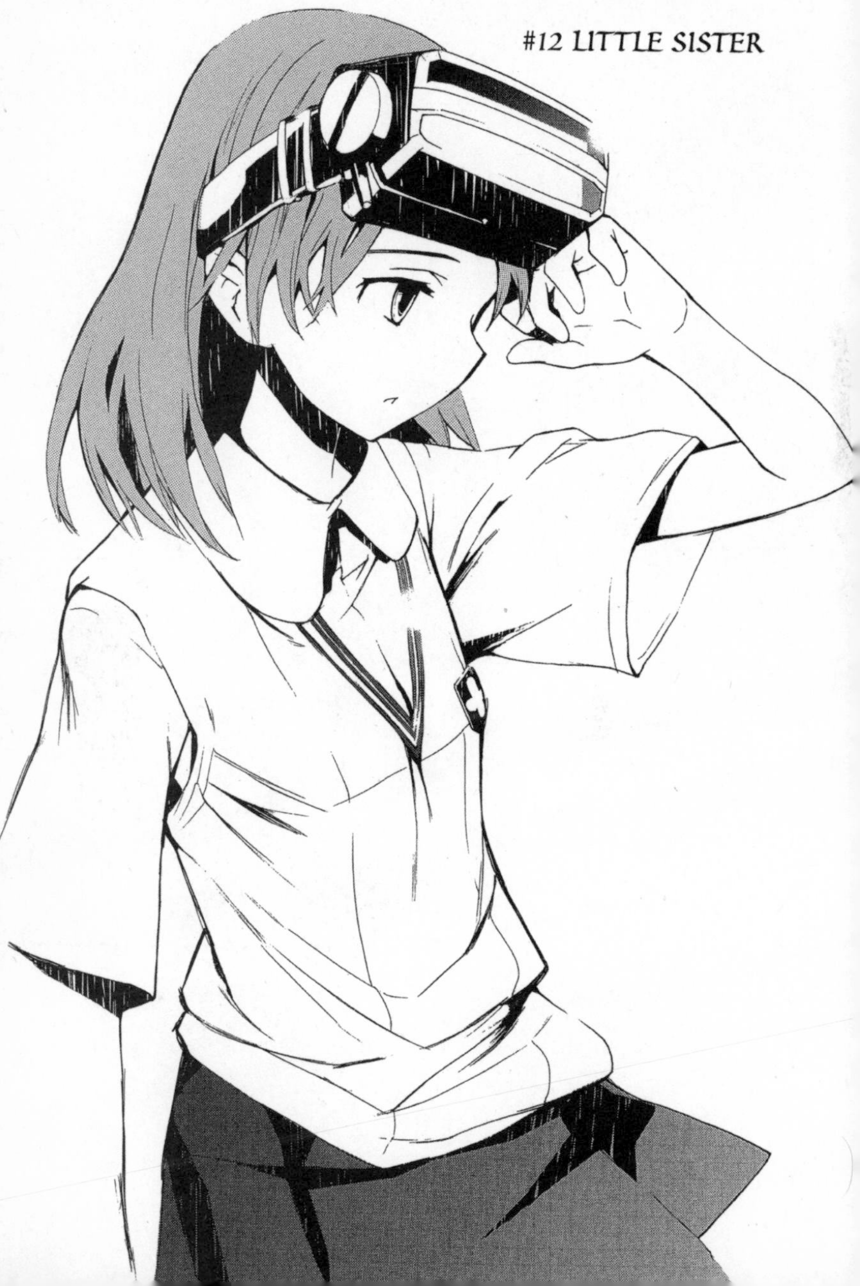

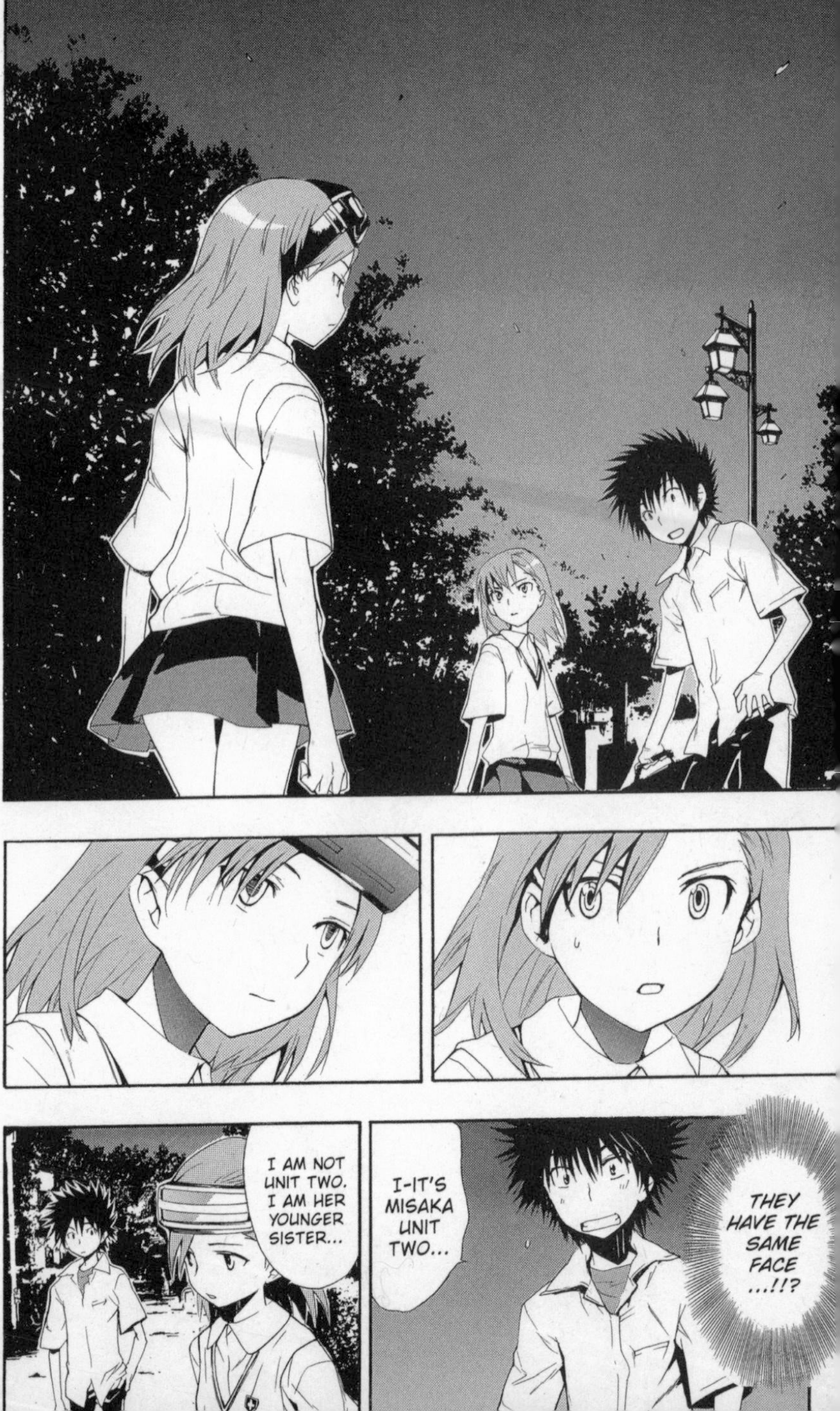
THEY HAVE THE SAME FACE ...!!?
I-IT'S MISAKA UNIT TWO...
I AM NOT UNIT TWO. I AM HER YOUNGER SISTER...

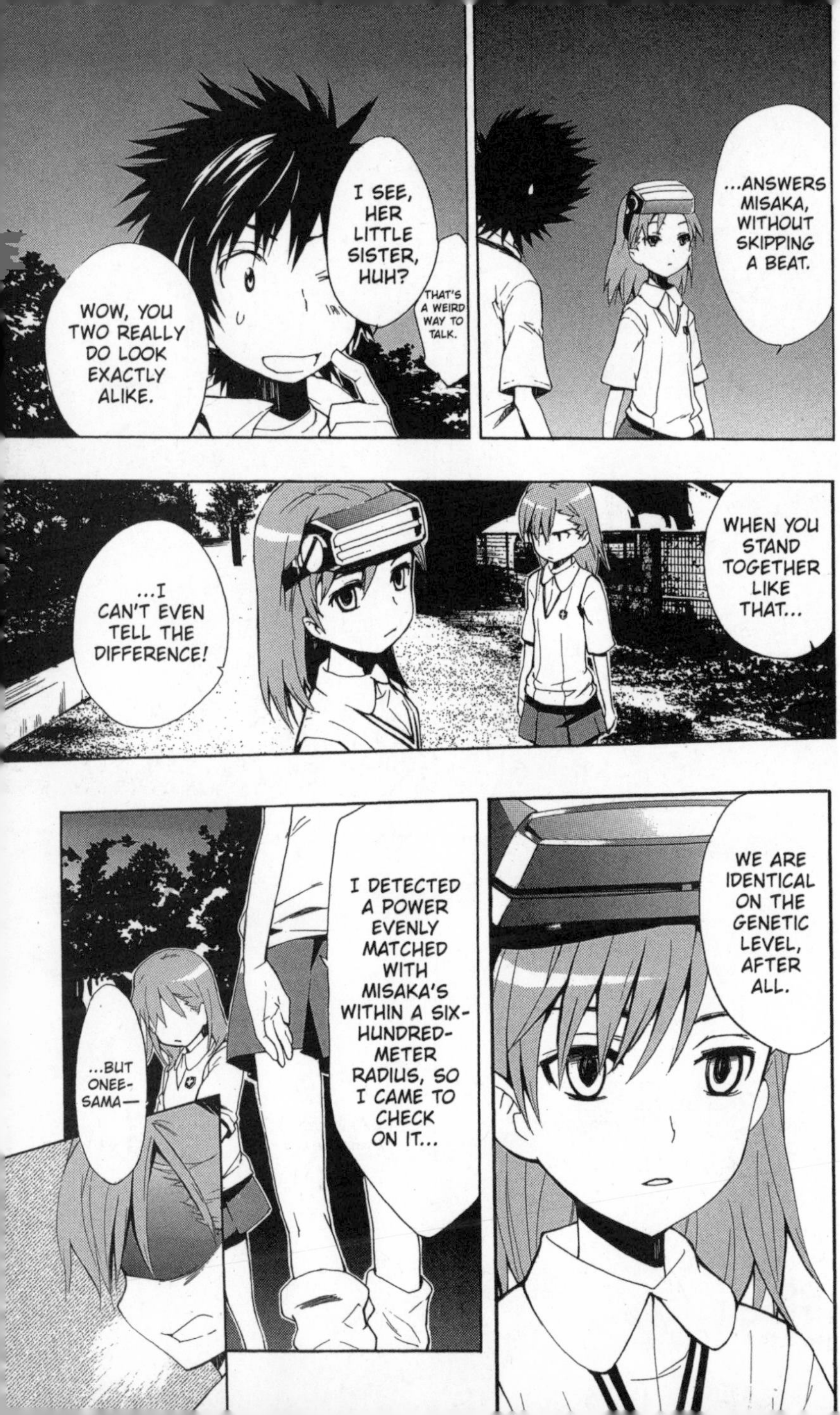
...ANSWERS MISAKA, WITHOUT SKIPPING A BEAT.
I SEE, HER LITTLE SISTER, HUH?
THAT'S A WEIRD WAY TO TALK.
WOW, YOU TWO REALLY DO LOOK EXACTLY ALIKE.
WHEN YOU STAND TOGETHER LIKE THAT...
...I CAN'T EVEN TELL THE DIFFERENCE!
WE ARE IDENTICAL ON THE GENETIC LEVEL, AFTER ALL.
I DETECTED A POWER EVENLY MATCHED WITH MISAKA'S WITHIN A SIX-HUNDRED-METER RADIUS, SO I CAME TO CHECK ON IT...
...BUT ONEE-SAMA—

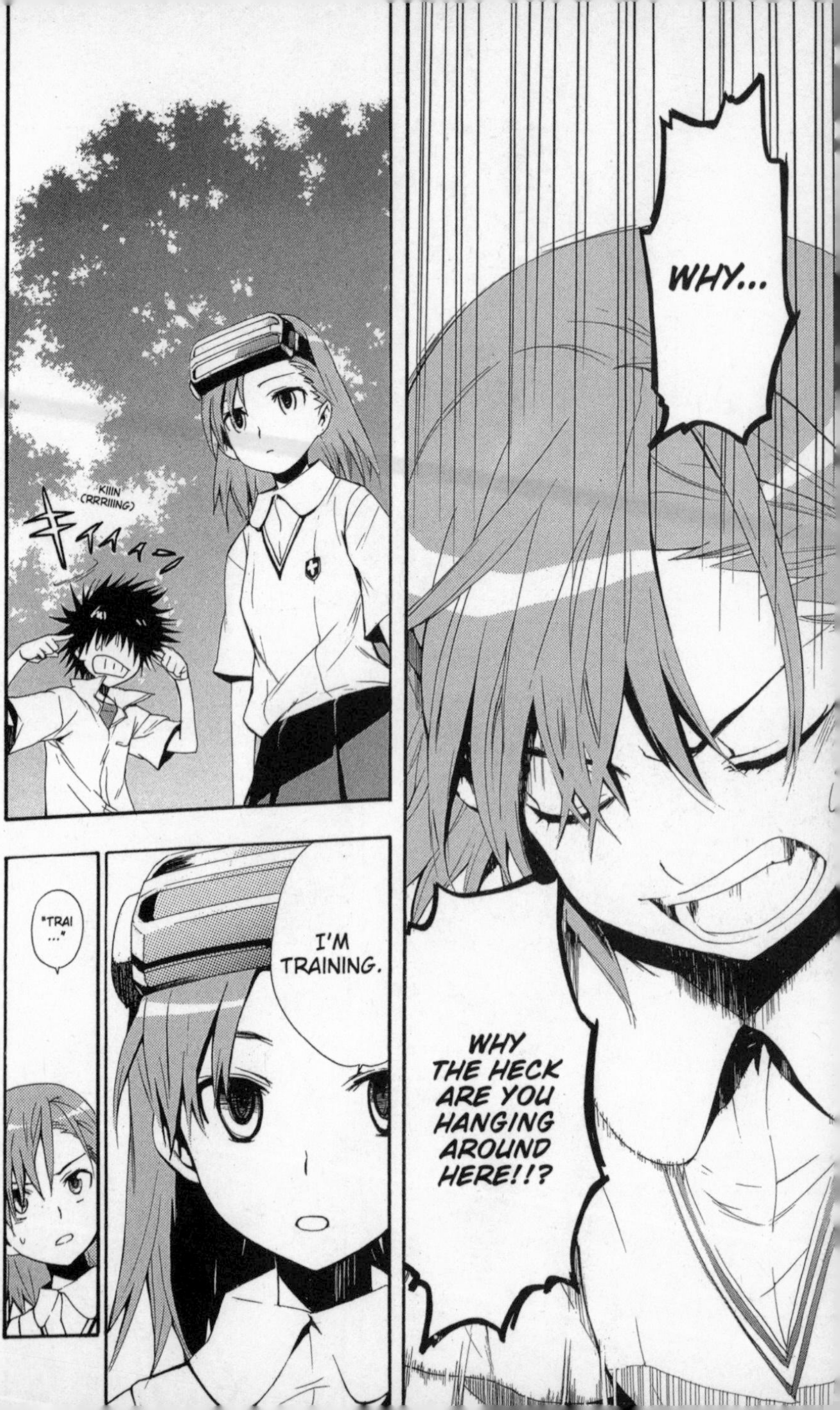
WHY...
WHY THE HECK ARE YOU HANGING AROUND HERE!!?
KIIN (RRRIIING)
I'M TRAINING.
"TRAI ..."

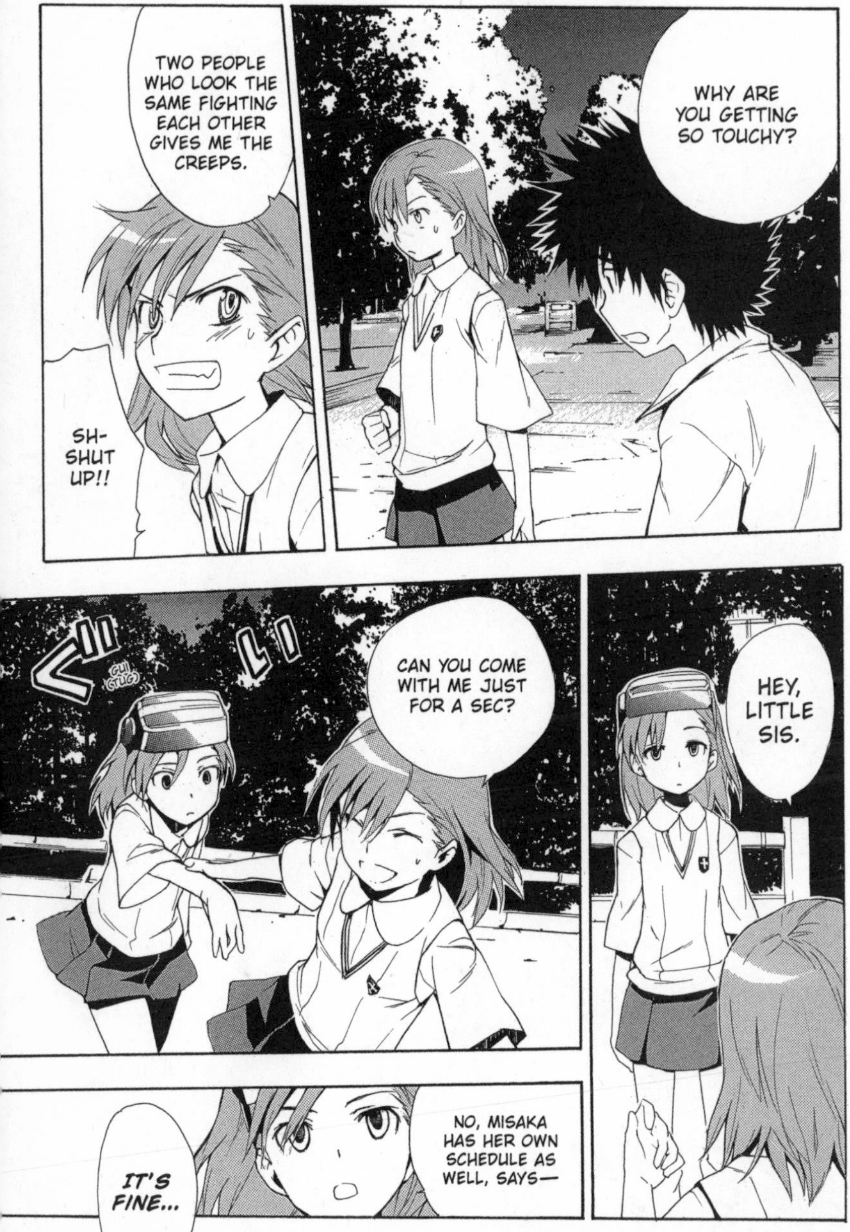
WHY ARE YOU GETTING SO TOUCHY?
TWO PEOPLE WHO LOOK THE SAME FIGHTING EACH OTHER GIVES ME THE CREEPS.
SH-SHUT UP!!
HEY, LITTLE SIS.
CAN YOU COME WITH ME JUST FOR A SEC?
GUI (TUG)
NO, MISAKA HAS HER OWN SCHEDULE AS WELL, SAYS—
IT'S FINE...

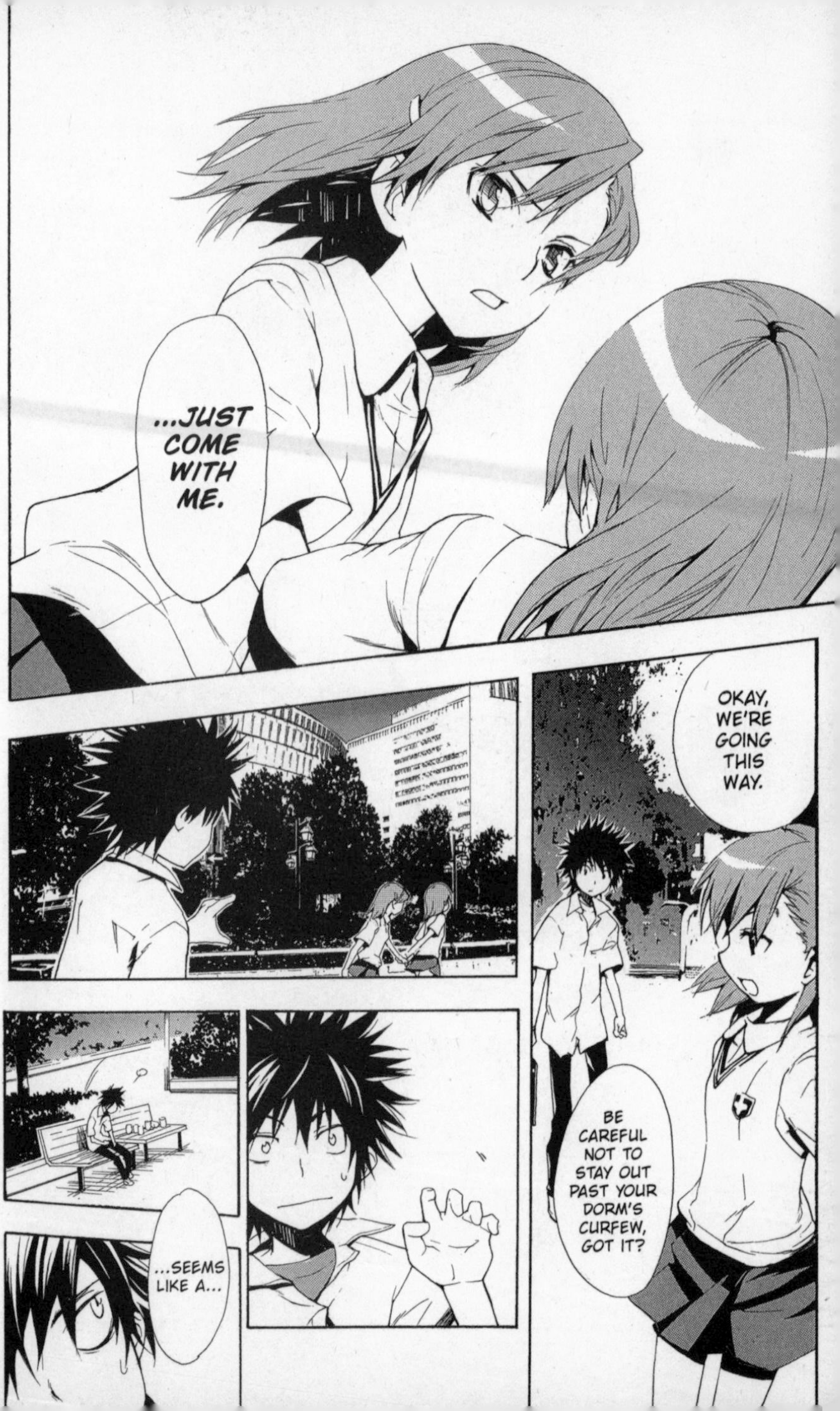
...JUST COME WITH ME.
OKAY, WE'RE GOING THIS WAY.
BE CAREFUL NOT TO STAY OUT PAST YOUR DORM'S CURFEW, GOT IT?
...SEEMS LIKE A...

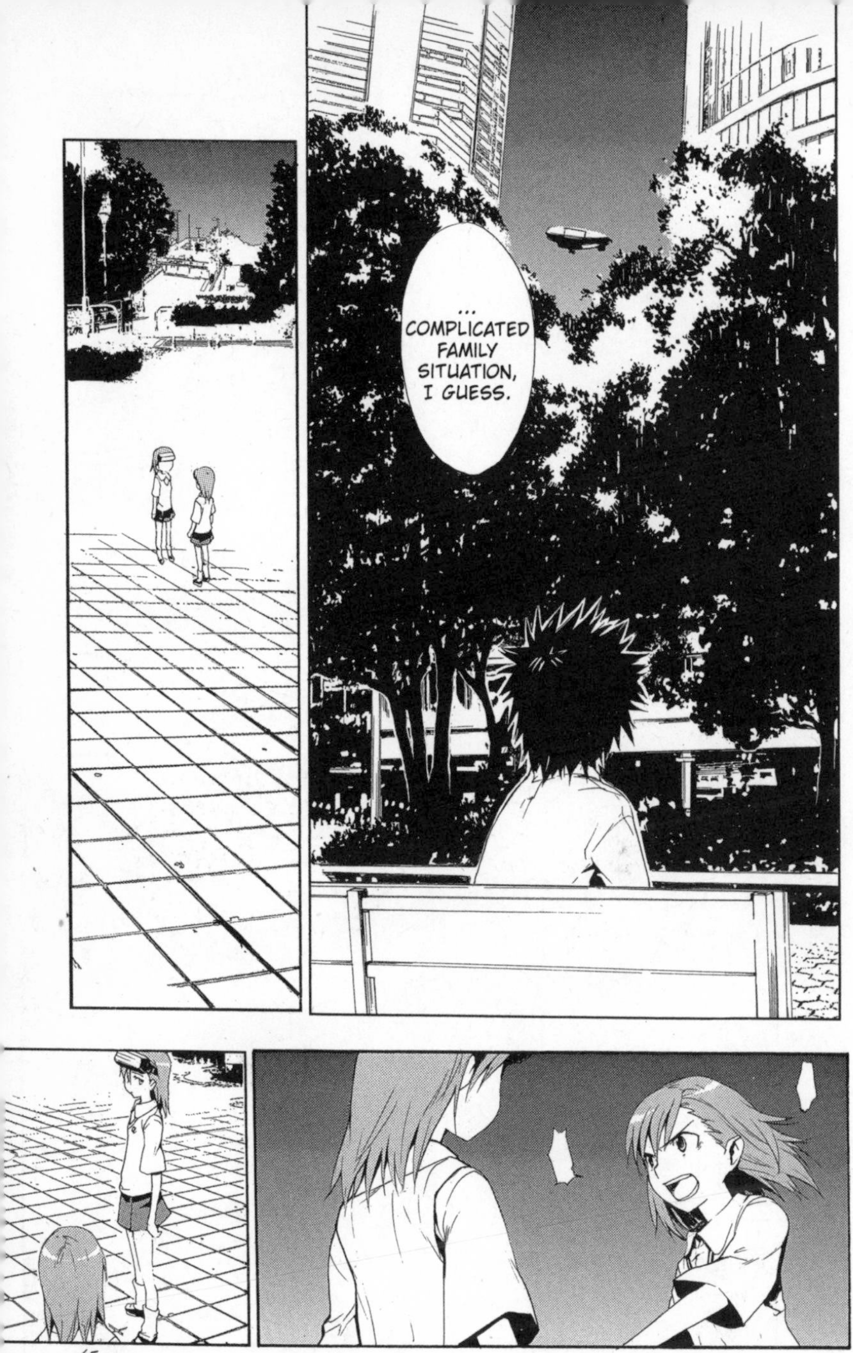
...
COMPLICATED FAMILY SITUATION, I GUESS.

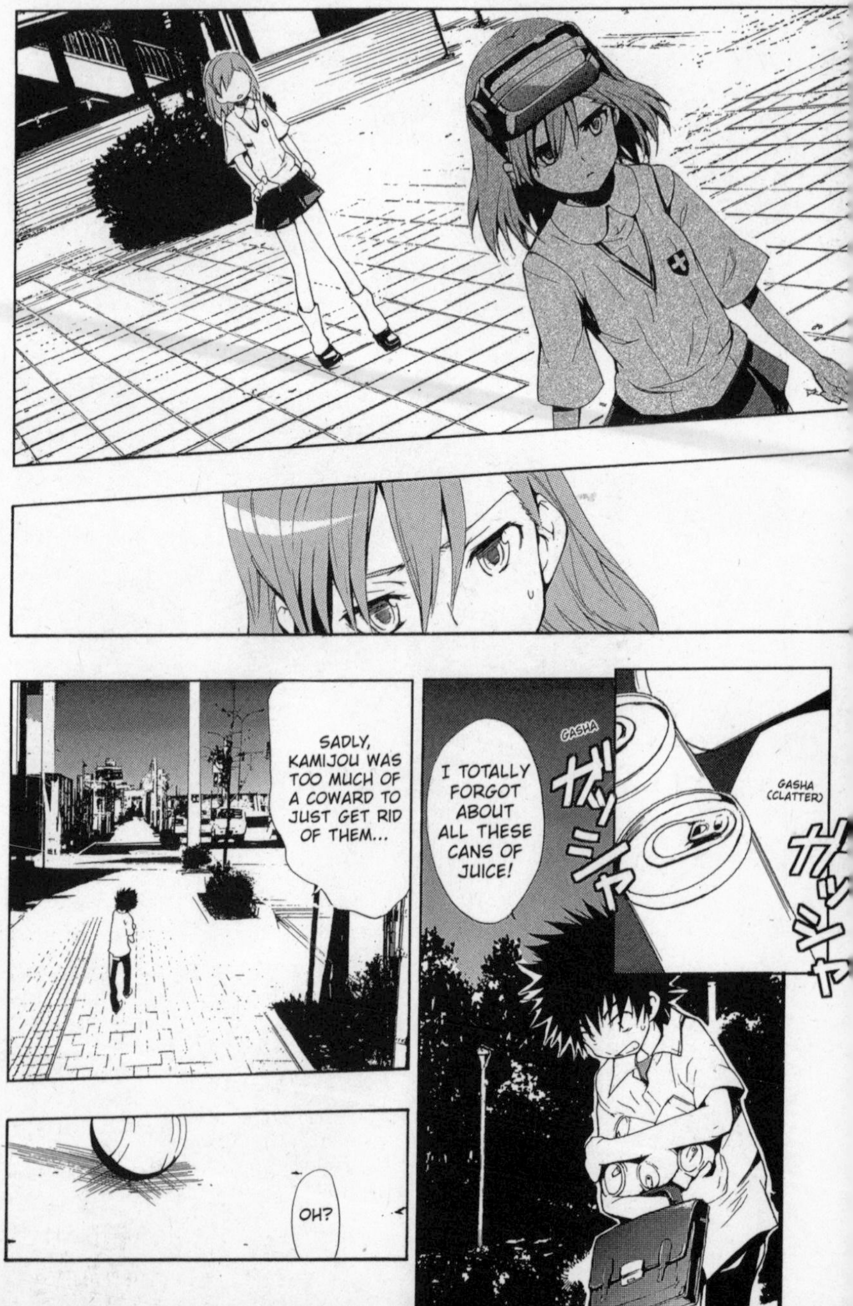
GASHA
(CLATTER)
ガッシャ
GASHA
ガッシャ
I TOTALLY FORGOT ABOUT ALL THESE CANS OF JUICE!
SADLY, KAMIJOU WAS TOO MUCH OF A COWARD TO JUST GET RID OF THEM...
OH?

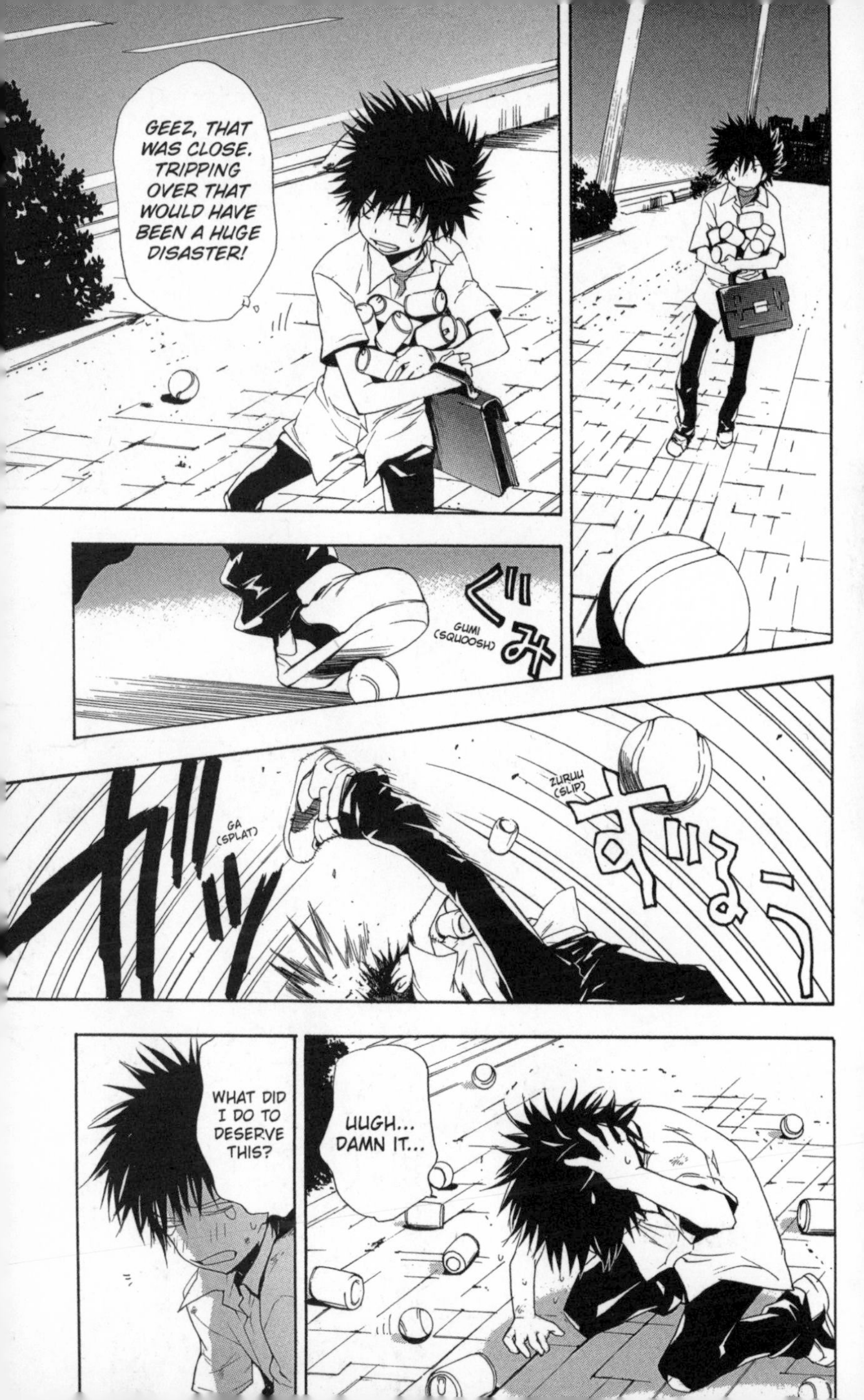
GEEZ, THAT WAS CLOSE. TRIPPING OVER THAT WOULD HAVE BEEN A HUGE DISASTER!
ぐみ
GUMI (SQUOOSH)
ずるーっ
ZURUU (SLIP)
ガッ
GA (SPLAT)
UUGH... DAMN IT...
WHAT DID I DO TO DESERVE THIS?

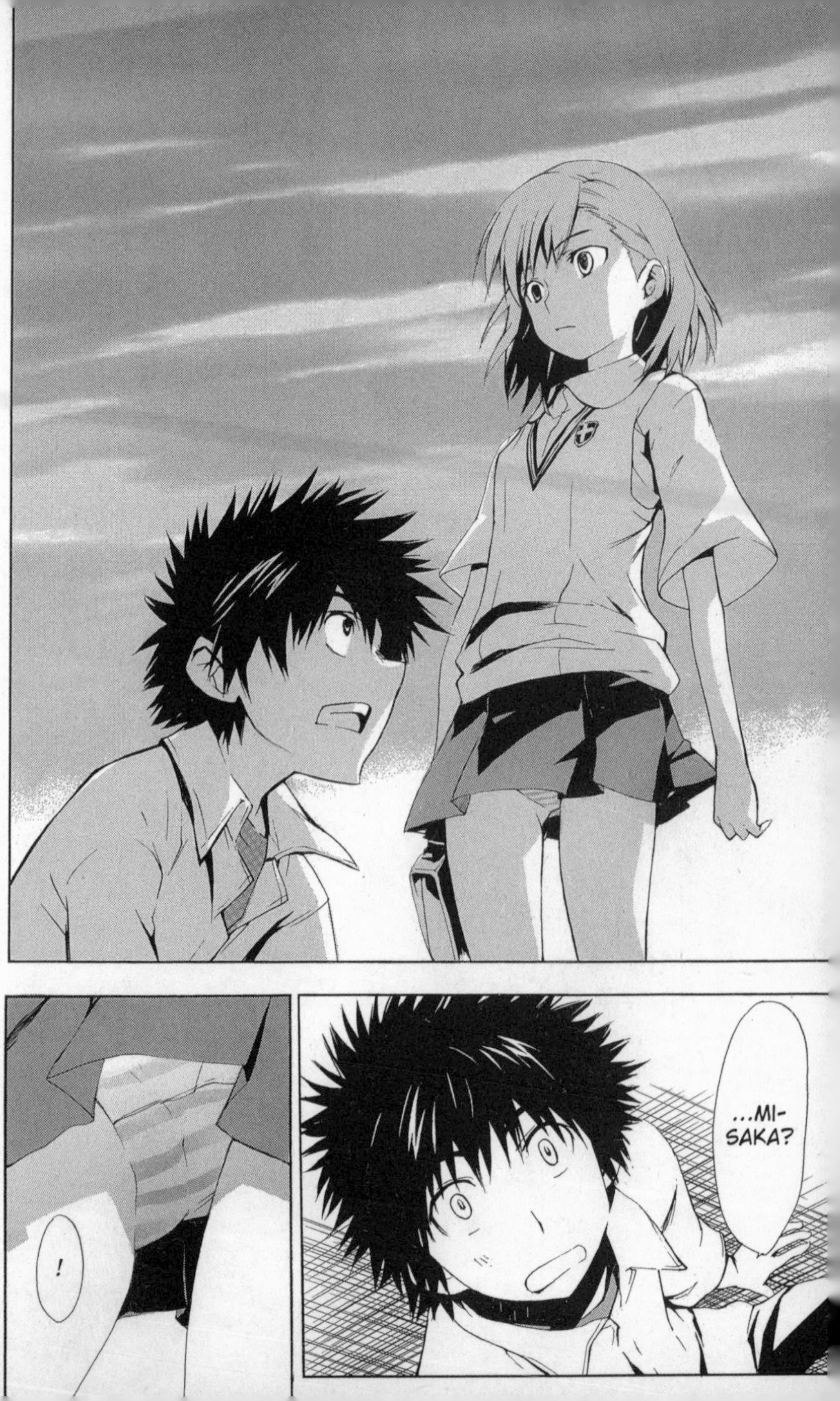
...MI-
SAKA?
!

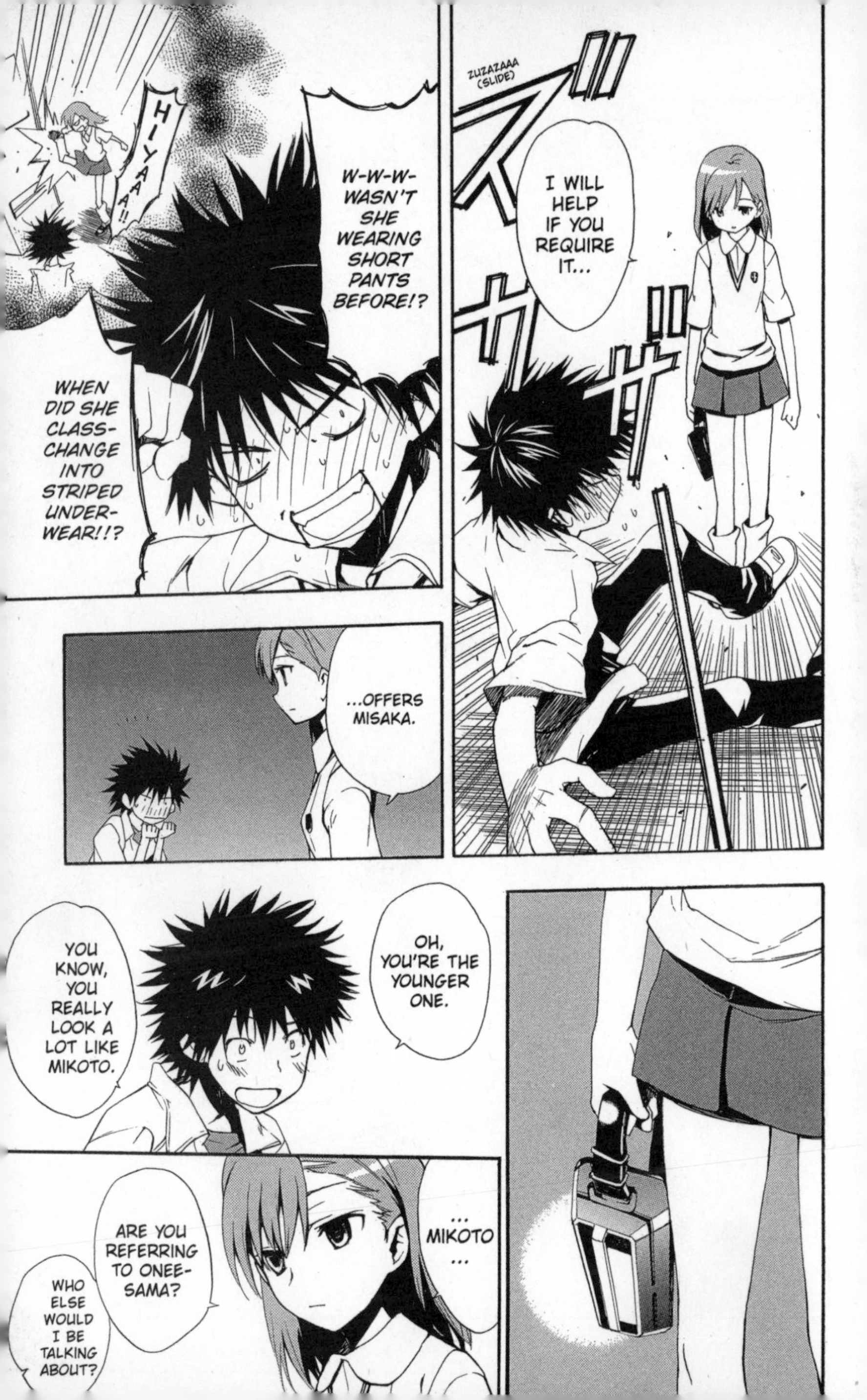
ZUZAZAAA (SLIDE)
I WILL HELP IF YOU REQUIRE IT...
HIYAAAA!!
W-W-W-WASN'T SHE WEARING SHORT PANTS BEFORE!?
WHEN DID SHE CLASS-CHANGE INTO STRIPED UNDERWEAR!!?
...OFFERS MISAKA.
OH, YOU'RE THE YOUNGER ONE.
YOU KNOW, YOU REALLY LOOK A LOT LIKE MIKOTO.
...MIKOTO...
ARE YOU REFERRING TO ONEE-SAMA?
WHO ELSE WOULD I BE TALKING ABOUT?

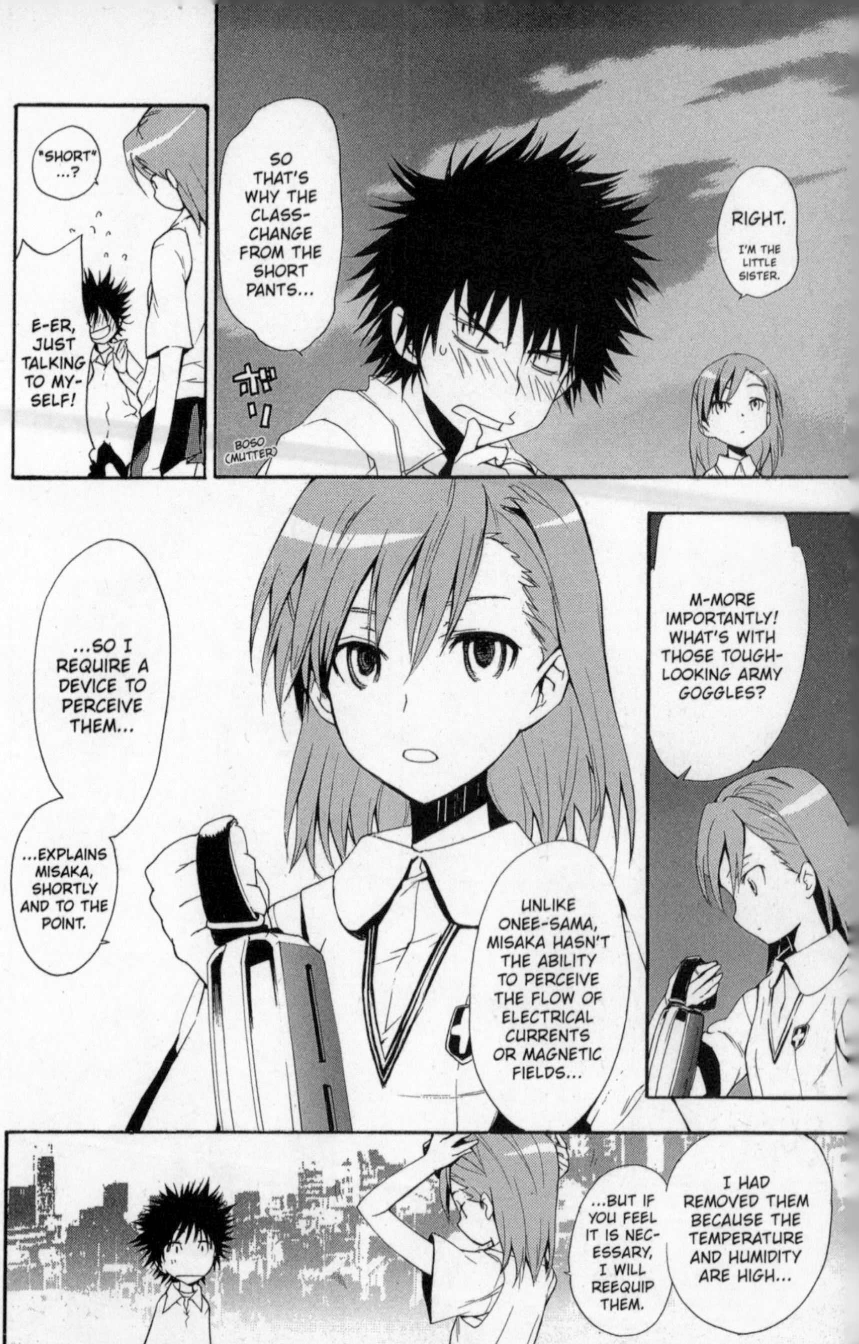
RIGHT.
I'M THE LITTLE SISTER.
SO THAT'S WHY THE CLASS-CHANGE FROM THE SHORT PANTS...
BOSO (MUTTER)
"SHORT" ...?
E-ER, JUST TALKING TO MY-SELF!
M-MORE IMPORTANTLY! WHAT'S WITH THOSE TOUGH-LOOKING ARMY GOGGLES?
UNLIKE ONEE-SAMA, MISAKA HASN'T THE ABILITY TO PERCEIVE THE FLOW OF ELECTRICAL CURRENTS OR MAGNETIC FIELDS...
...SO I REQUIRE A DEVICE TO PERCEIVE THEM...
...EXPLAINS MISAKA, SHORTLY AND TO THE POINT.
I HAD REMOVED THEM BECAUSE THE TEMPERATURE AND HUMIDITY ARE HIGH...
...BUT IF YOU FEEL IT IS NEC-ESSARY, I WILL REEQUIP THEM.

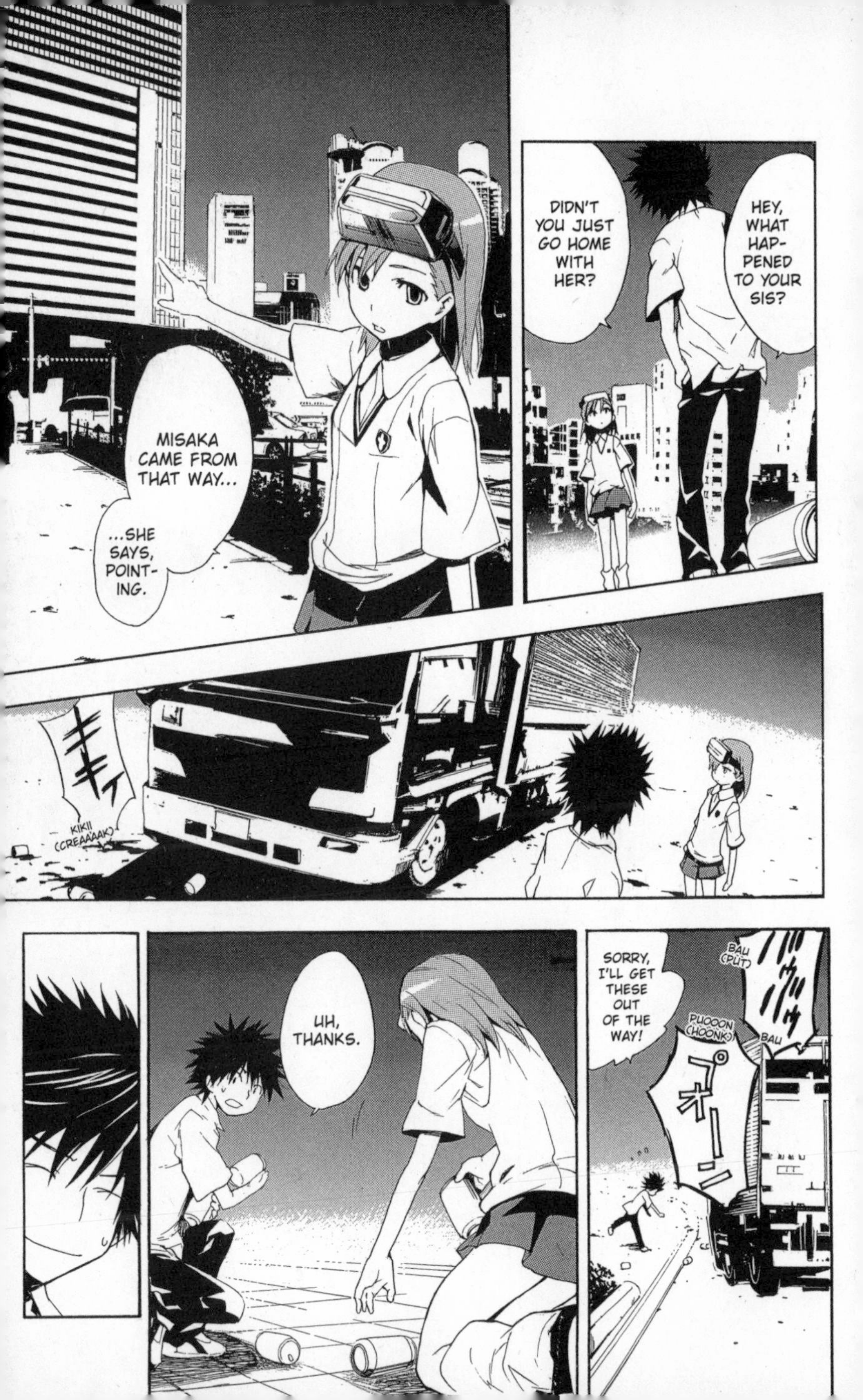
HEY, WHAT HAP-PENED TO YOUR SIS?
DIDN'T YOU JUST GO HOME WITH HER?
MISAKA CAME FROM THAT WAY...
...SHE SAYS, POINT-ING.
KIKII (CREAAAK)
BAU (PUT)
SORRY, I'LL GET THESE OUT OF THE WAY!
PUOOON (HOONK)
BAU
UH, THANKS.

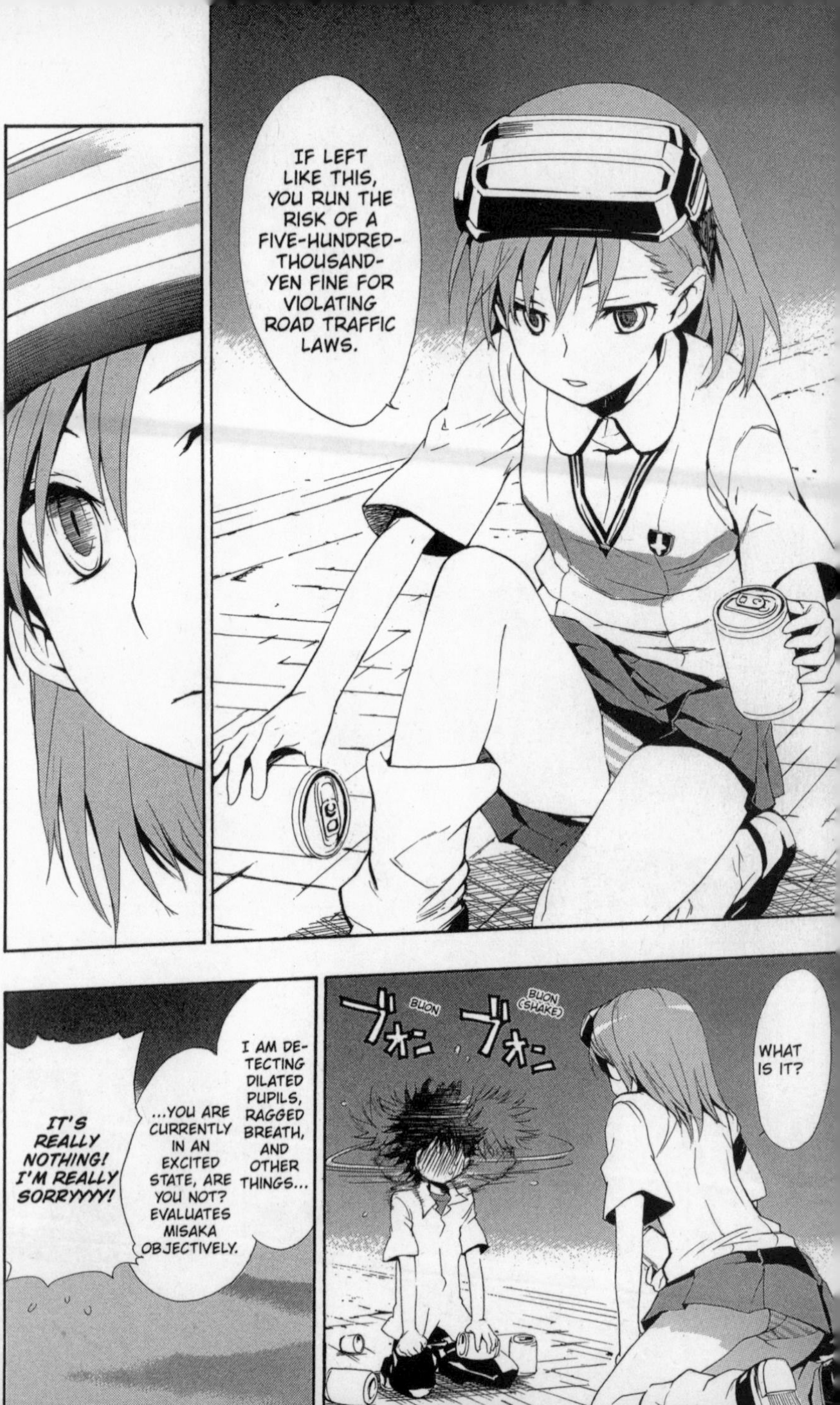
IF LEFT LIKE THIS, YOU RUN THE RISK OF A FIVE-HUNDRED-THOUSAND-YEN FINE FOR VIOLATING ROAD TRAFFIC LAWS.
WHAT IS IT?
ブオン
BUON (SHAKE)
ブオン
BUON
I AM DETECTING DILATED PUPILS, RAGGED BREATH, AND OTHER THINGS...
...YOU ARE CURRENTLY IN AN EXCITED STATE, ARE YOU NOT? EVALUATES MISAKA OBJECTIVELY.
IT'S REALLY NOTHING! I'M REALLY SORRYYYY!

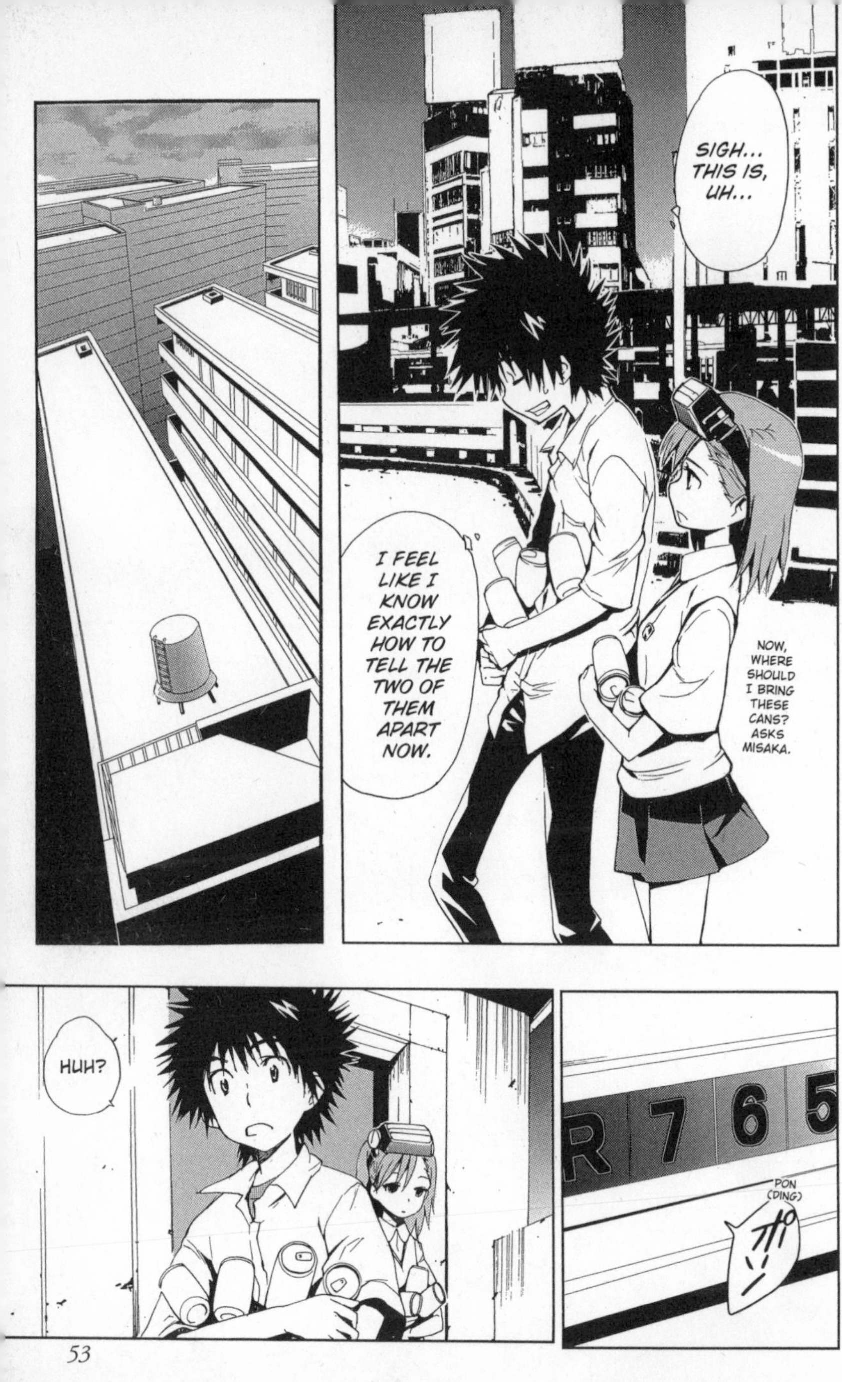
SIGH... THIS IS, UH...
I FEEL LIKE I KNOW EXACTLY HOW TO TELL THE TWO OF THEM APART NOW.
NOW, WHERE SHOULD I BRING THESE CANS? ASKS MISAKA.
R765
PON (DING)
HUH?

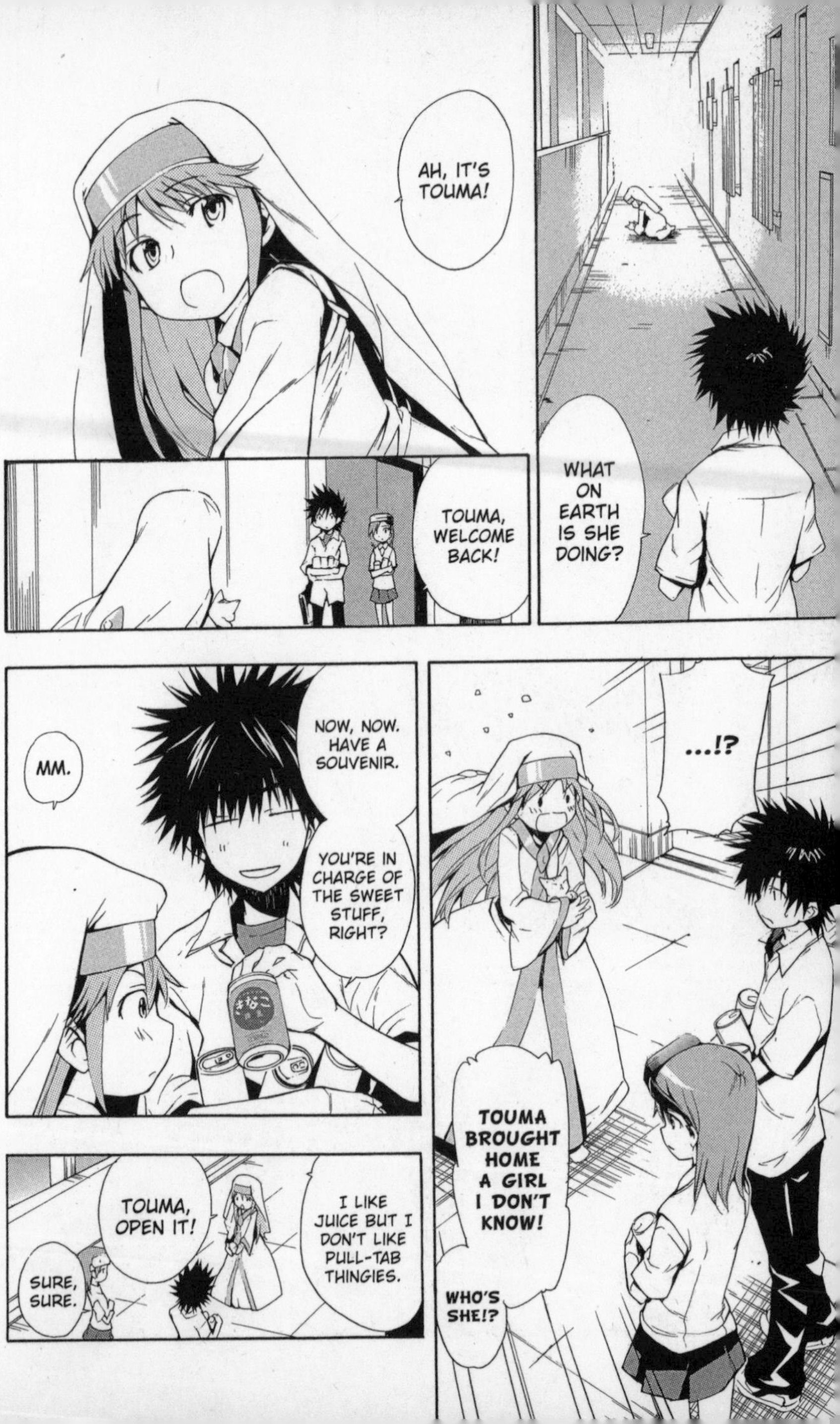
WHAT ON EARTH IS SHE DOING?
AH, IT'S TOUMA!
TOUMA, WELCOME BACK!
...!?
TOUMA BROUGHT HOME A GIRL I DON'T KNOW!
WHO'S SHE!?
NOW, NOW. HAVE A SOUVENIR.
YOU'RE IN CHARGE OF THE SWEET STUFF, RIGHT?
MM.
I LIKE JUICE BUT I DON'T LIKE PULL-TAB THINGIES.
TOUMA, OPEN IT!
SURE, SURE.

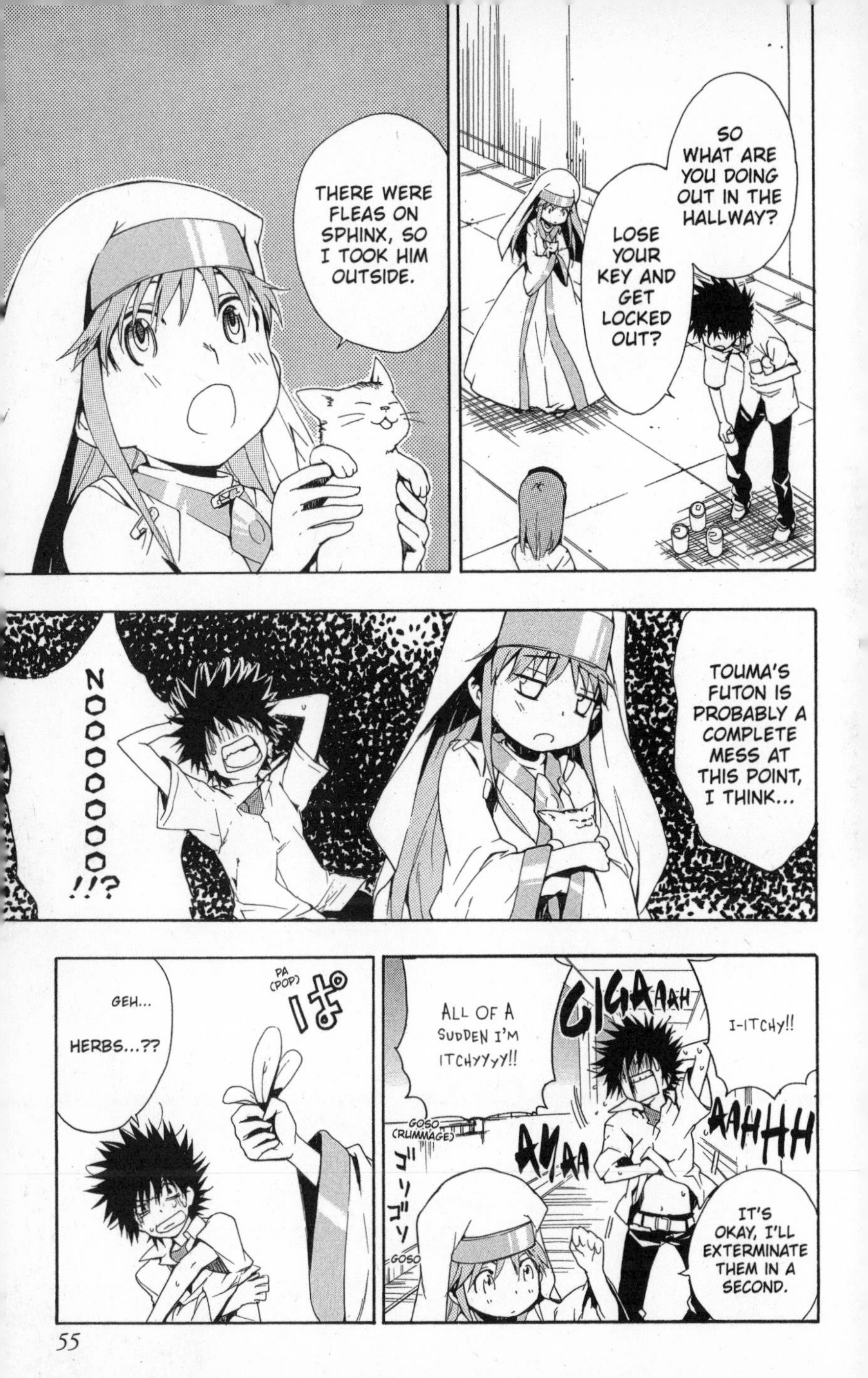
SO WHAT ARE YOU DOING OUT IN THE HALLWAY?
LOSE YOUR KEY AND GET LOCKED OUT?
THERE WERE FLEAS ON SPHINX, SO I TOOK HIM OUTSIDE.
TOUMA'S FUTON IS PROBABLY A COMPLETE MESS AT THIS POINT, I THINK...
NOOOOOOOOO!!?
GIGAAAH
I-ITCHY!!
ALL OF A SUDDEN I'M ITCHYYYY!!
AAHHH
AAAAA
GOSO (RUMMAGE)
ゴソゴソ
GOSO
IT'S OKAY, I'LL EXTERMINATE THEM IN A SECOND.
PA (POP)
ぱ
GEH...
HERBS...??

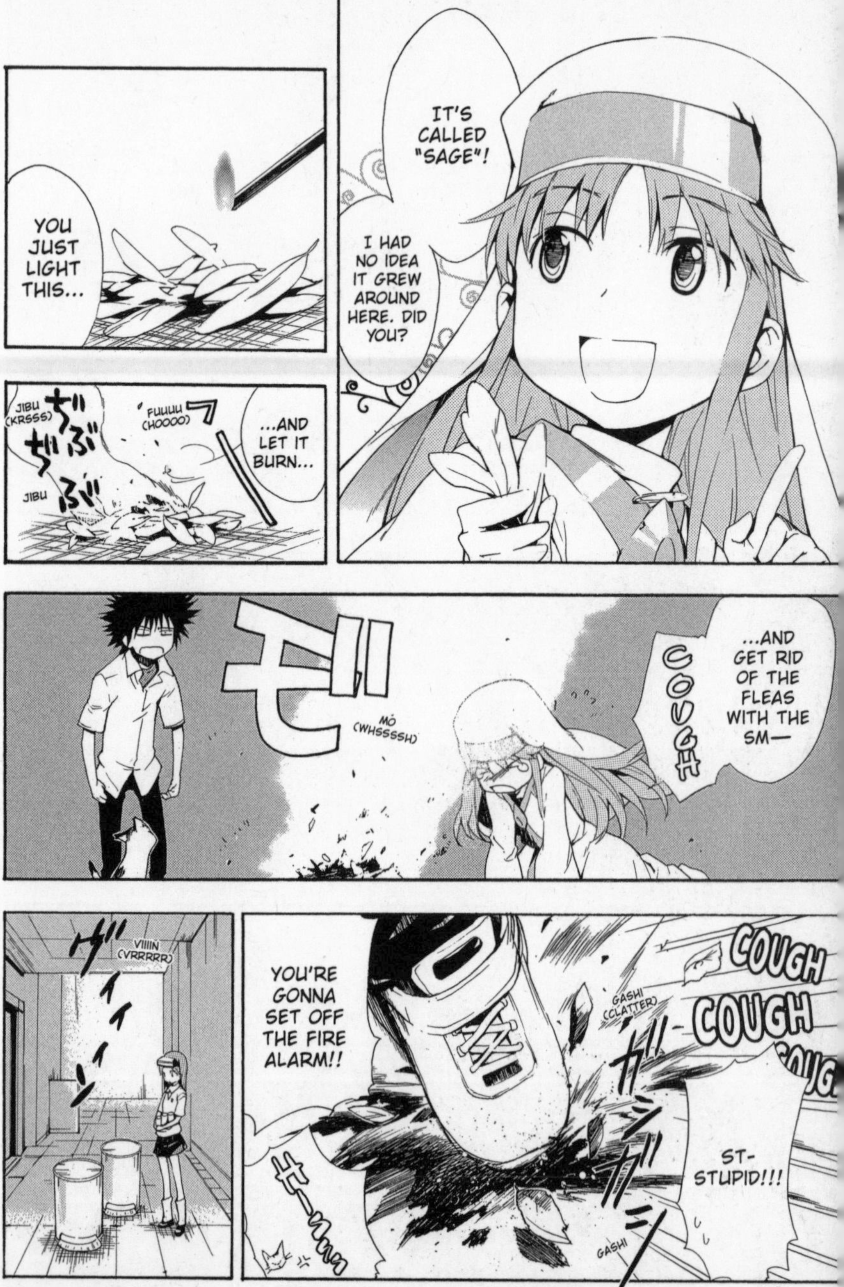
IT'S CALLED "SAGE"!
I HAD NO IDEA IT GREW AROUND HERE. DID YOU?
YOU JUST LIGHT THIS...
JIBU (KRSSS)
JIBU
FUUUU (HOOOO)
...AND LET IT BURN...
...AND GET RID OF THE FLEAS WITH THE SM—
COUGH
MO (WHSSSSH)
COUGH
COUGH
GASHI (CLATTER)
YOU'RE GONNA SET OFF THE FIRE ALARM!!
ST- STUPID!!!
GASHI
VIIIN (VRRRRR)

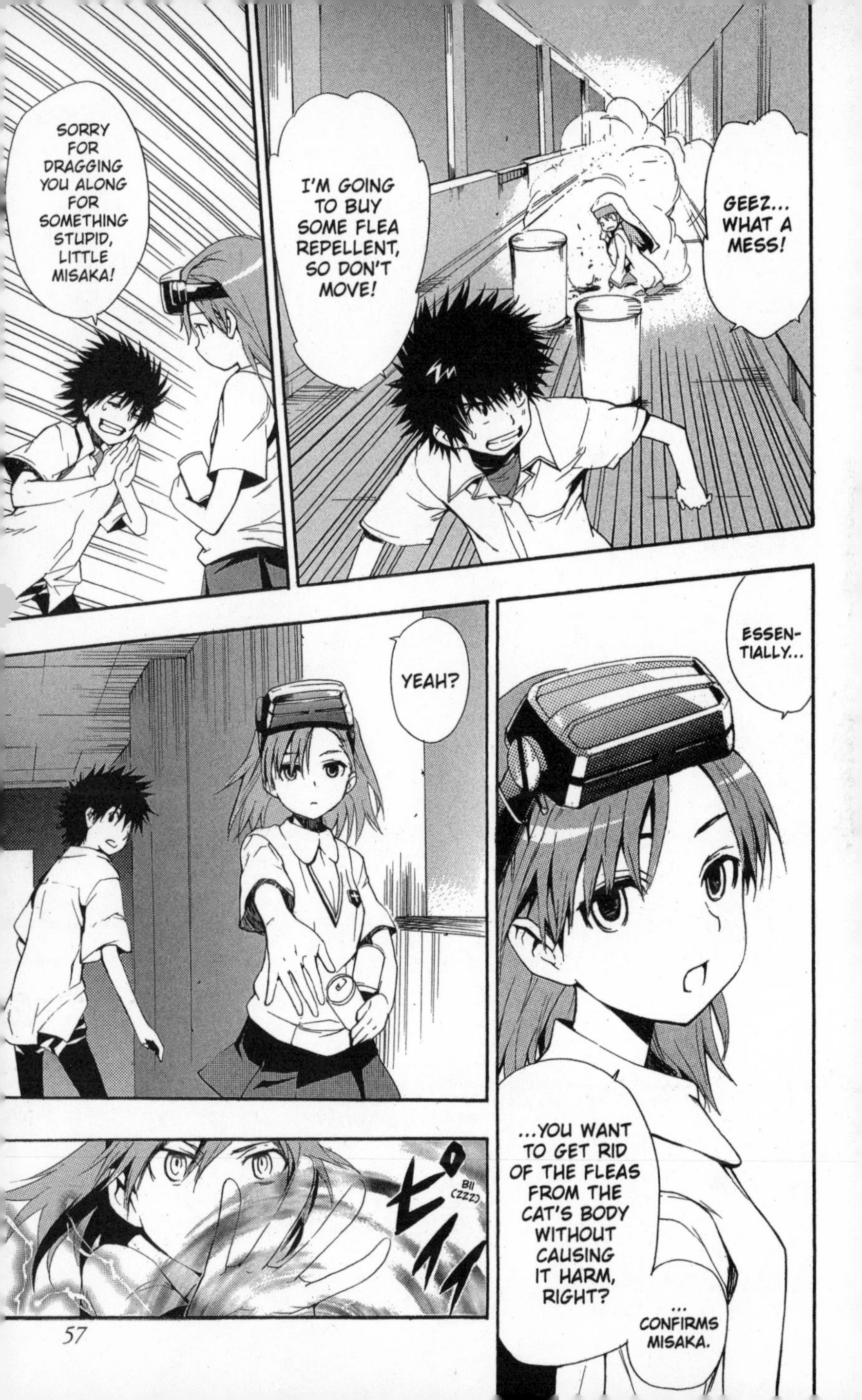
GEEZ... WHAT A MESS!
I'M GOING TO BUY SOME FLEA REPELLENT, SO DON'T MOVE!
SORRY FOR DRAGGING YOU ALONG FOR SOMETHING STUPID, LITTLE MISAKA!
ESSEN-TIALLY...
...YOU WANT TO GET RID OF THE FLEAS FROM THE CAT'S BODY WITHOUT CAUSING IT HARM, RIGHT?
... CONFIRMS MISAKA.
YEAH?
BII (ZZZ)

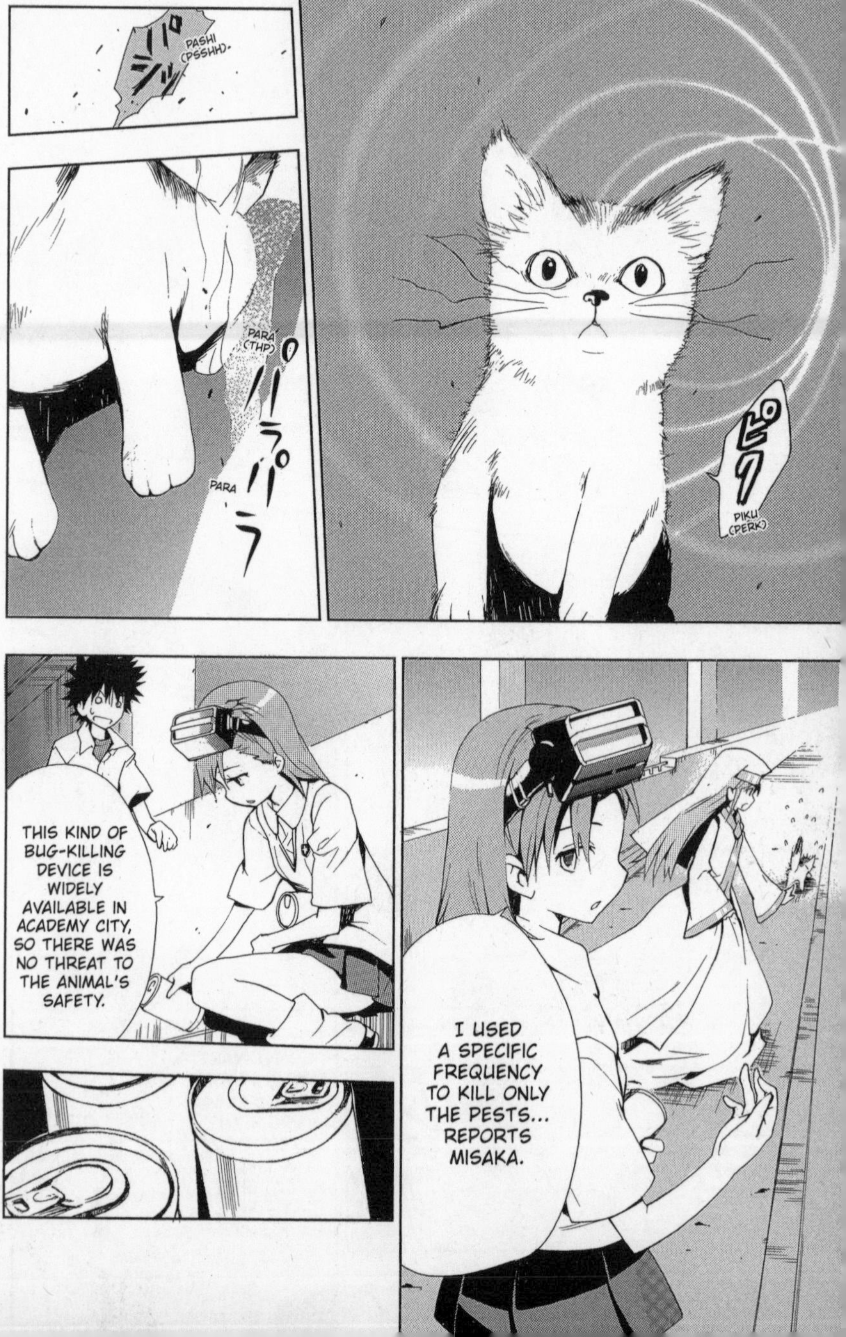
PIKU (PERK)
PASHI (PSSHH)
PARA (THP)
PARA
I USED A SPECIFIC FREQUENCY TO KILL ONLY THE PESTS... REPORTS MISAKA.
THIS KIND OF BUG-KILLING DEVICE IS WIDELY AVAILABLE IN ACADEMY CITY, SO THERE WAS NO THREAT TO THE ANIMAL'S SAFETY.

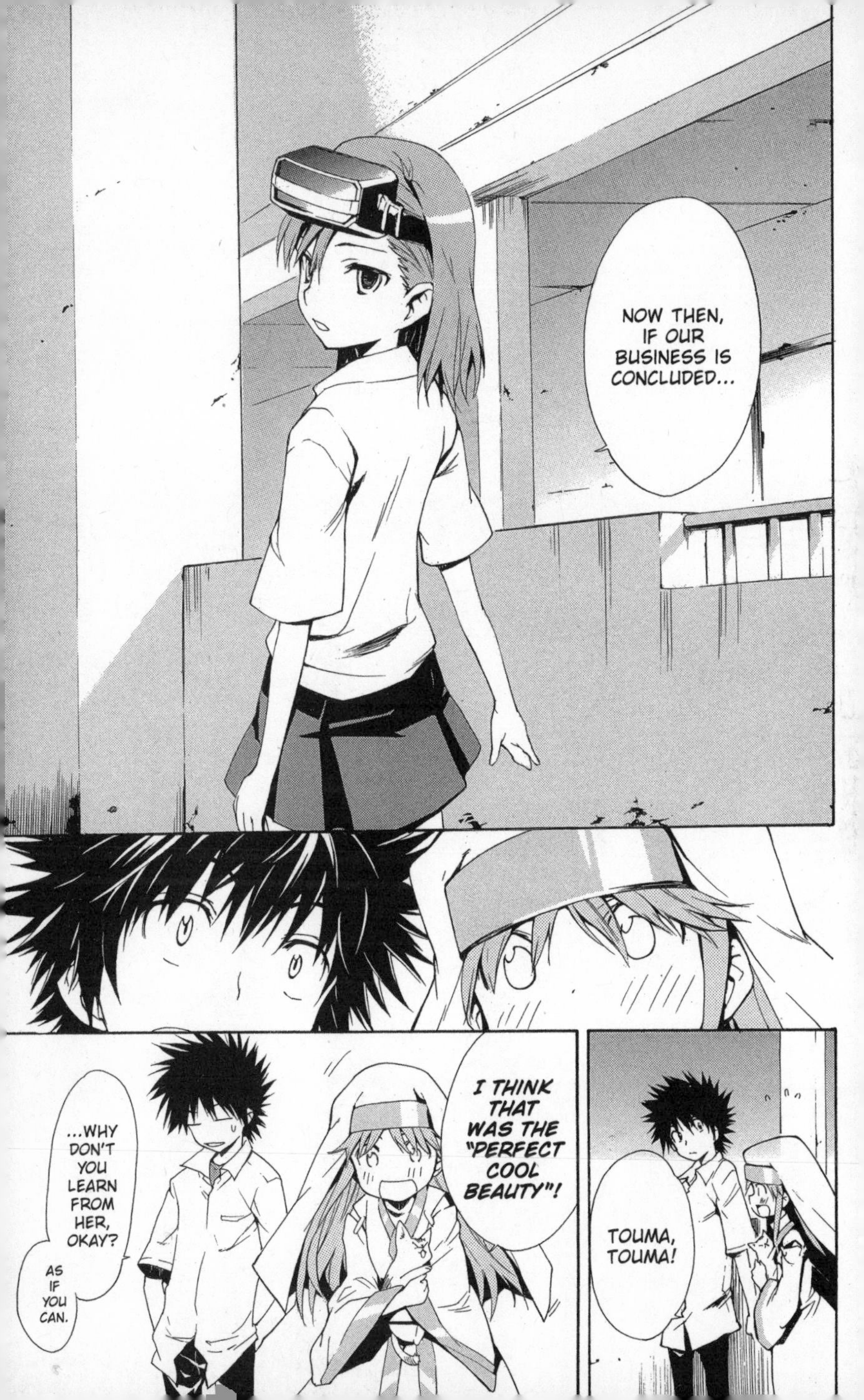
NOW THEN, IF OUR BUSINESS IS CONCLUDED...
TOUMA, TOUMA!
I THINK THAT WAS THE "PERFECT COOL BEAUTY"!
...WHY DON'T YOU LEARN FROM HER, OKAY?
AS IF YOU CAN.

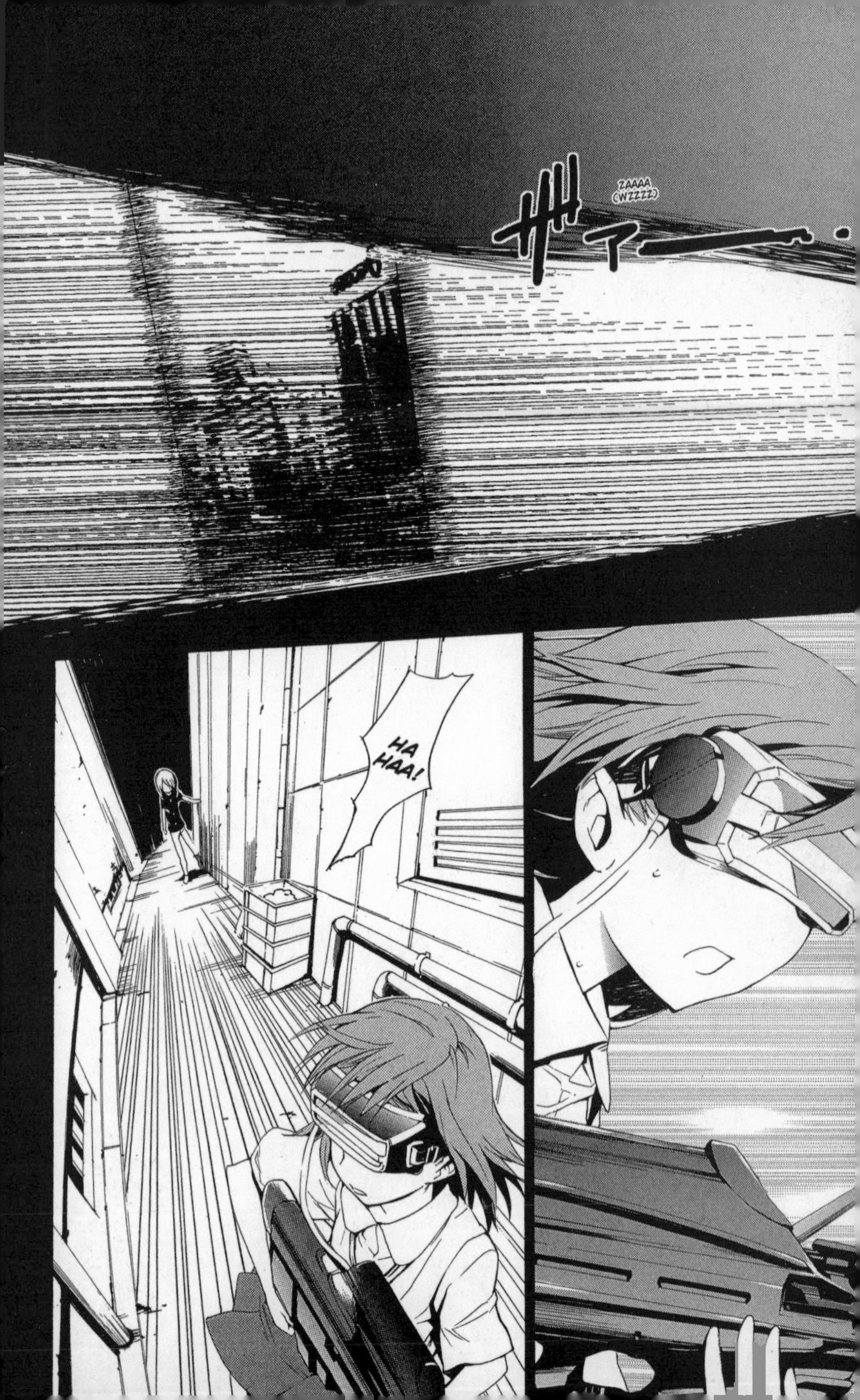
ザァーー・・
ZAAAA
(WZZZZ)
HA HAA!

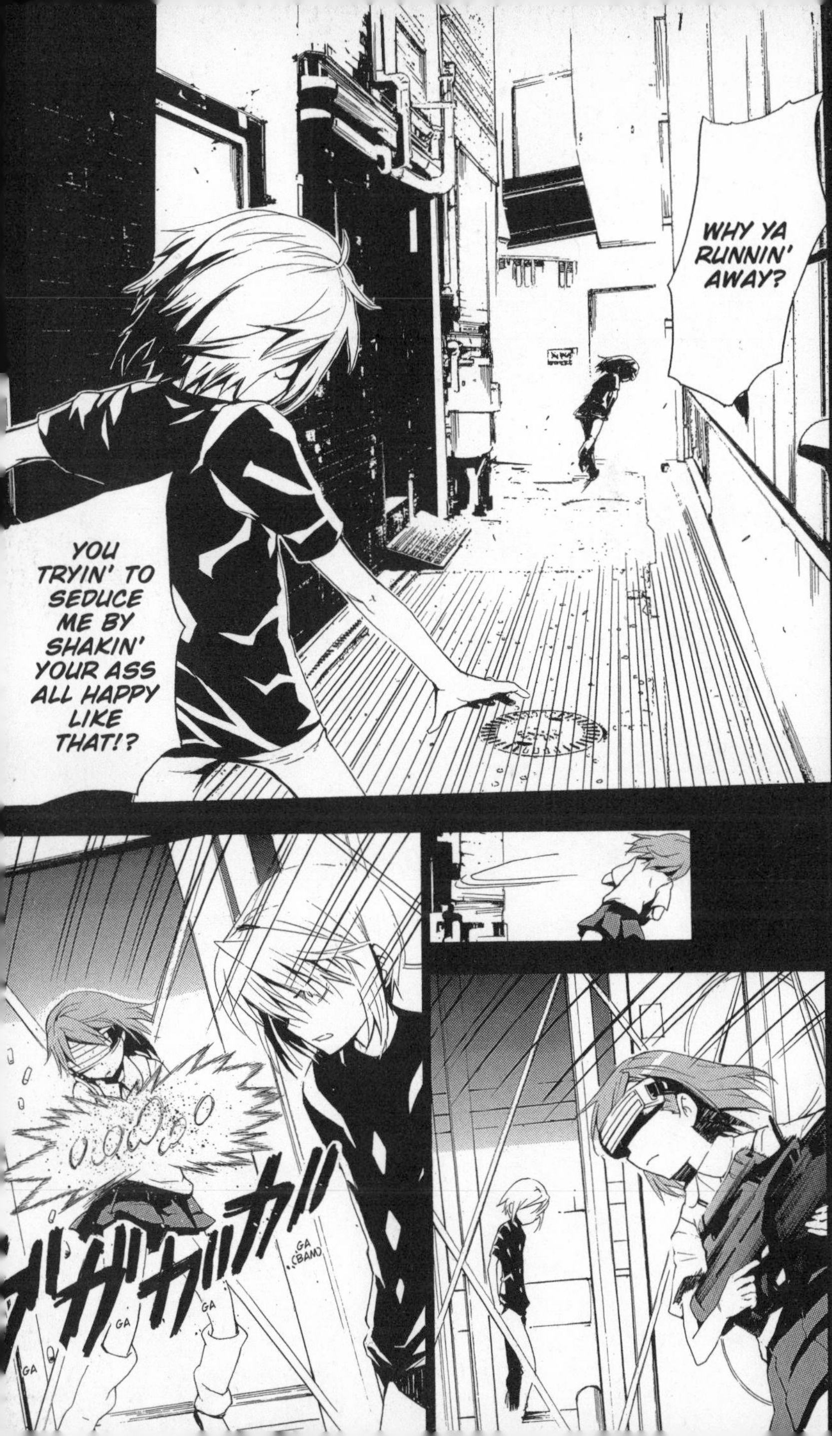
WHY YA RUNNIN' AWAY?
YOU TRYIN' TO SEDUCE ME BY SHAKIN' YOUR ASS ALL HAPPY LIKE THAT!?
GA (BAM)
GA
GA
GA

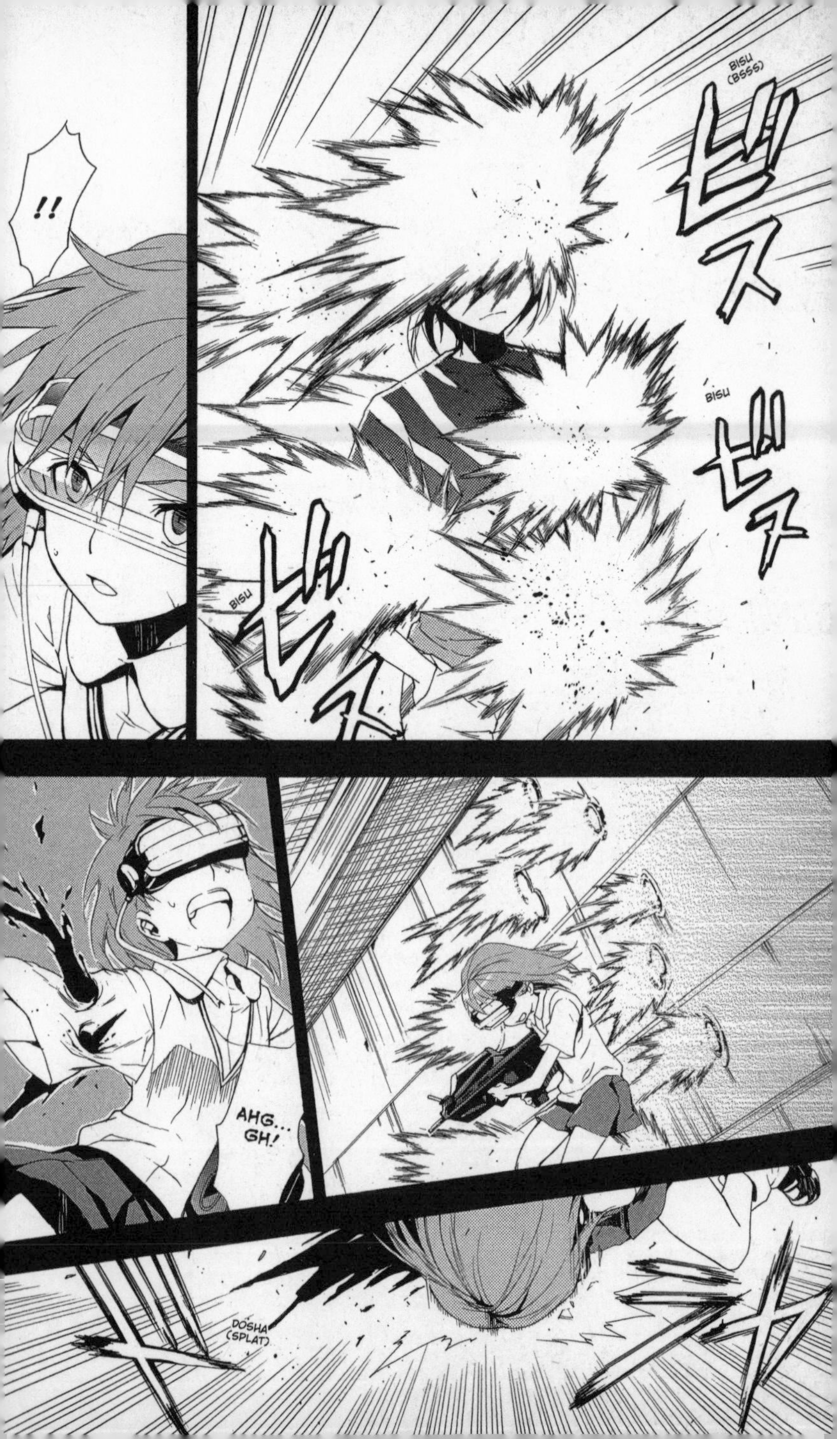
BISU (BSSS)
BISU
BISU
!!
AHG... GH!
DOSHA (SPLAT)

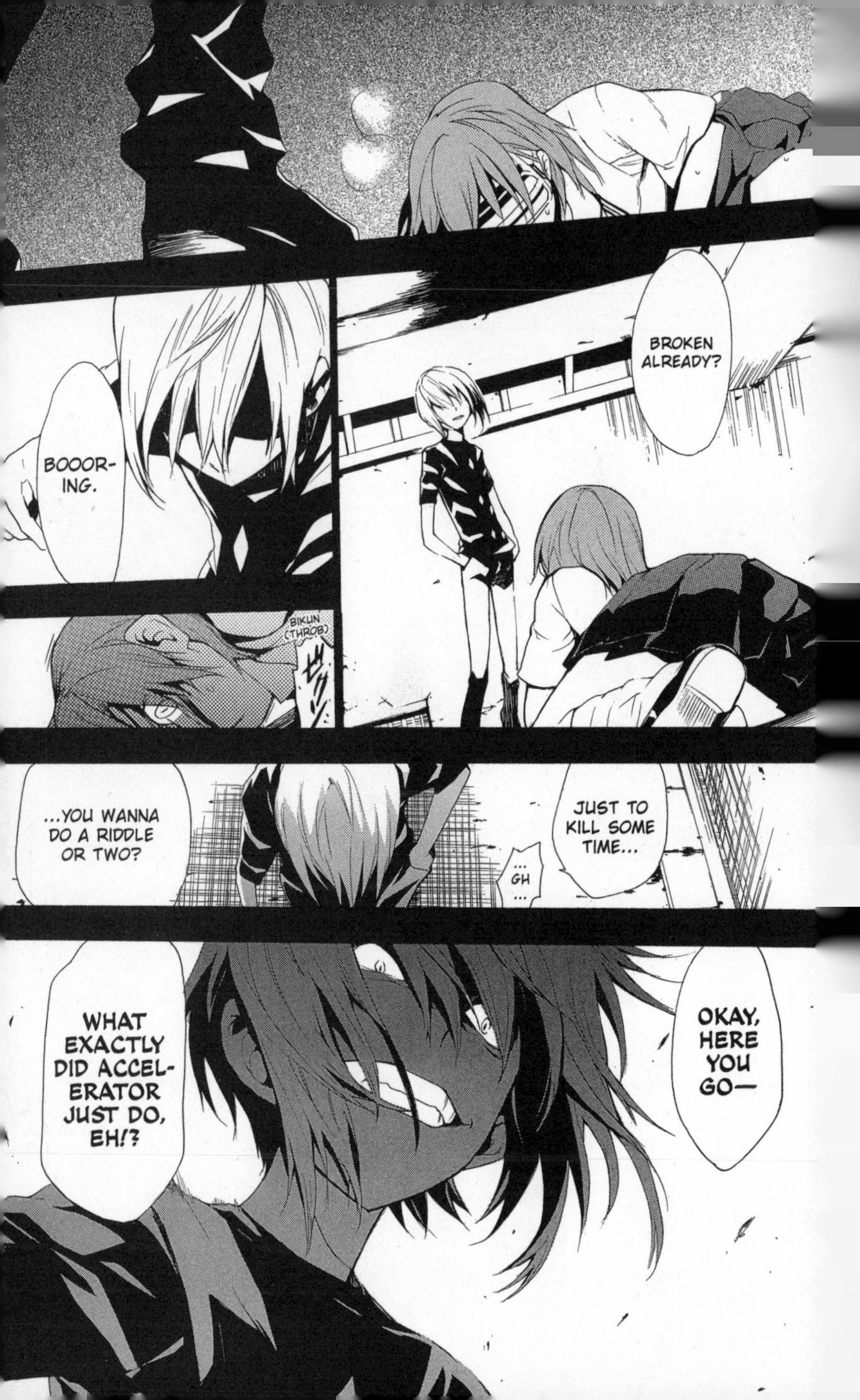
BROKEN ALREADY?
BOOOR-ING.
BIKUN (THROB)
JUST TO KILL SOME TIME...
...GH...
...YOU WANNA DO A RIDDLE OR TWO?
OKAY, HERE YOU GO—
WHAT EXACTLY DID ACCEL-ERATOR JUST DO, EH!?

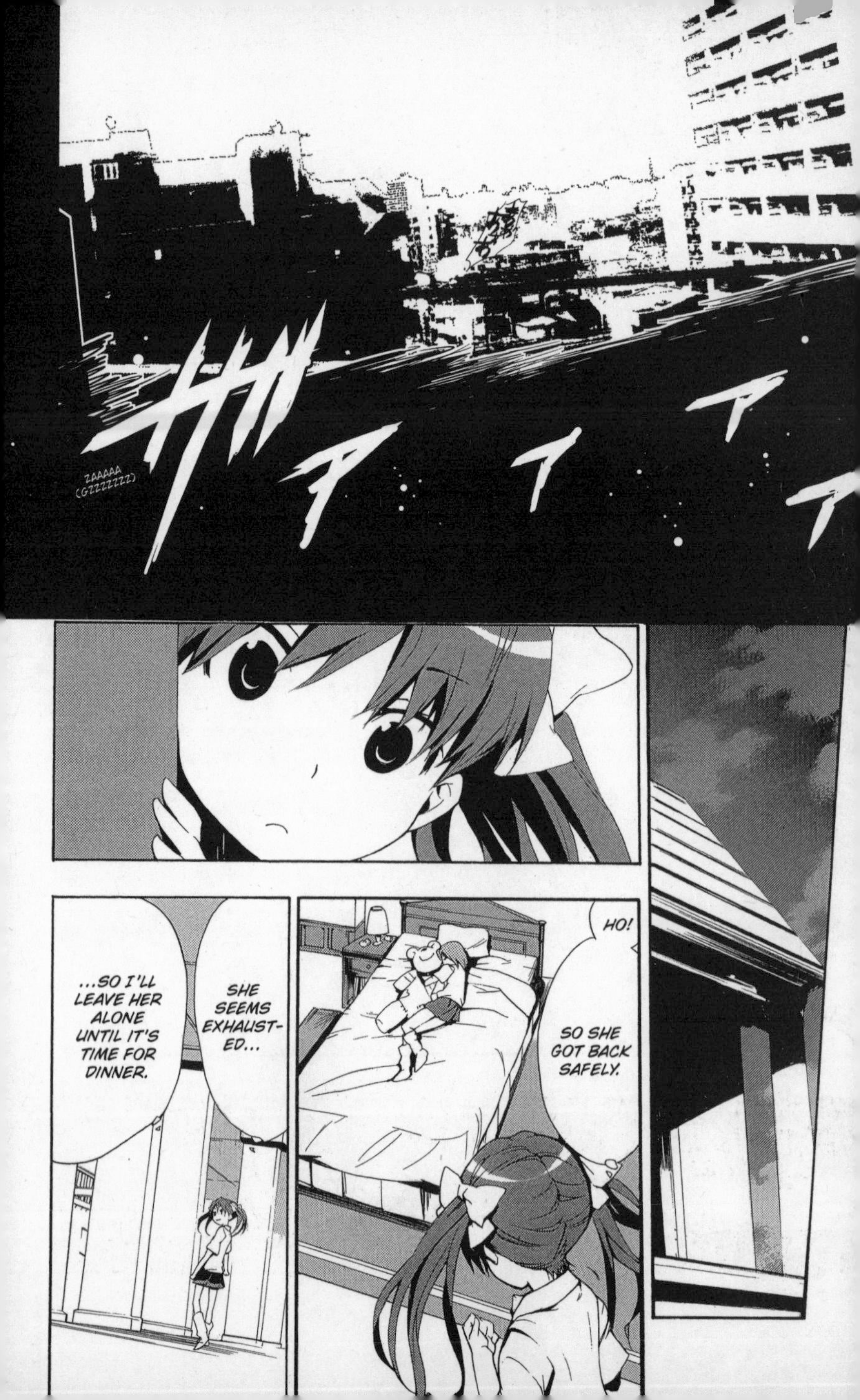
ZAAAAA (GZZZZZZZ)
HO!
SO SHE GOT BACK SAFELY.
SHE SEEMS EXHAUST-ED...
...SO I'LL LEAVE HER ALONE UNTIL IT'S TIME FOR DINNER.

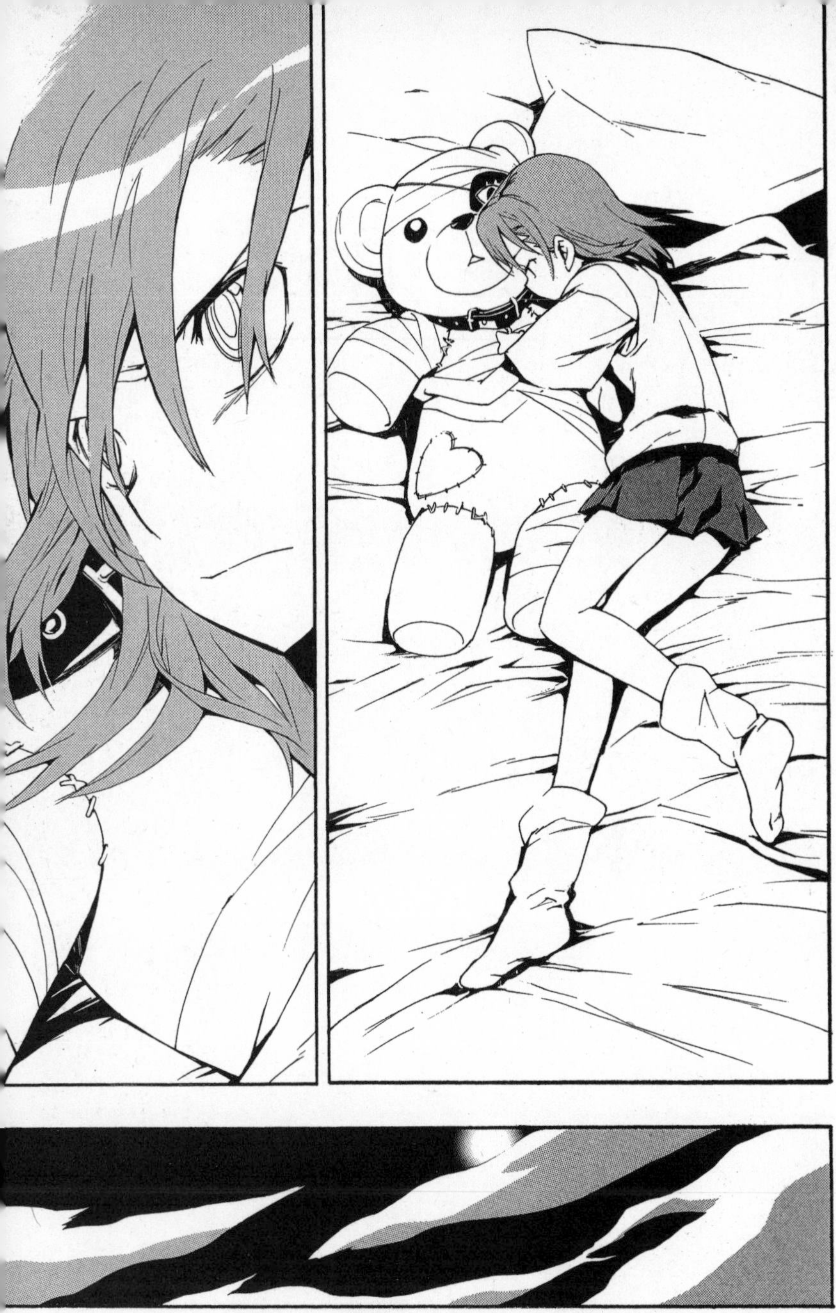

A Certain Magical Index

#13 THE STRONGEST SUPERPOWER

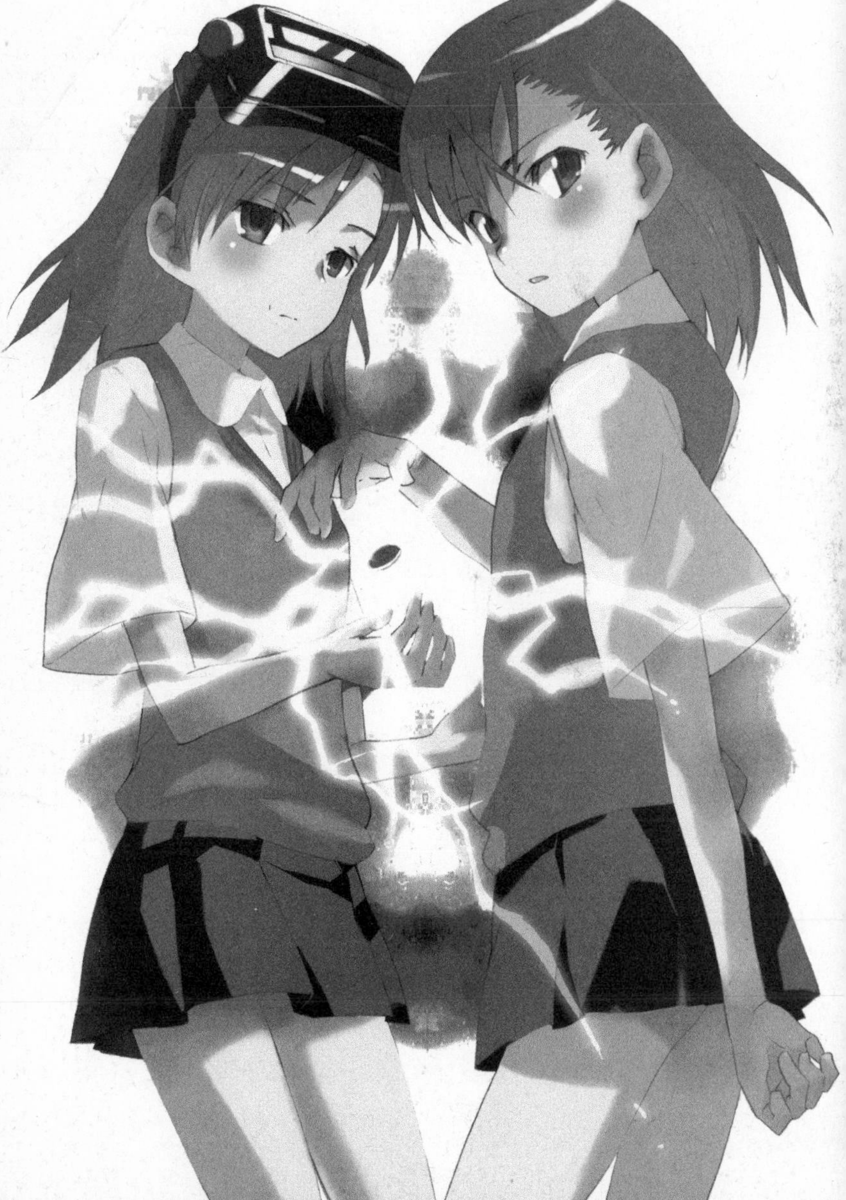

A Certain Magical Index

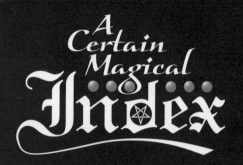

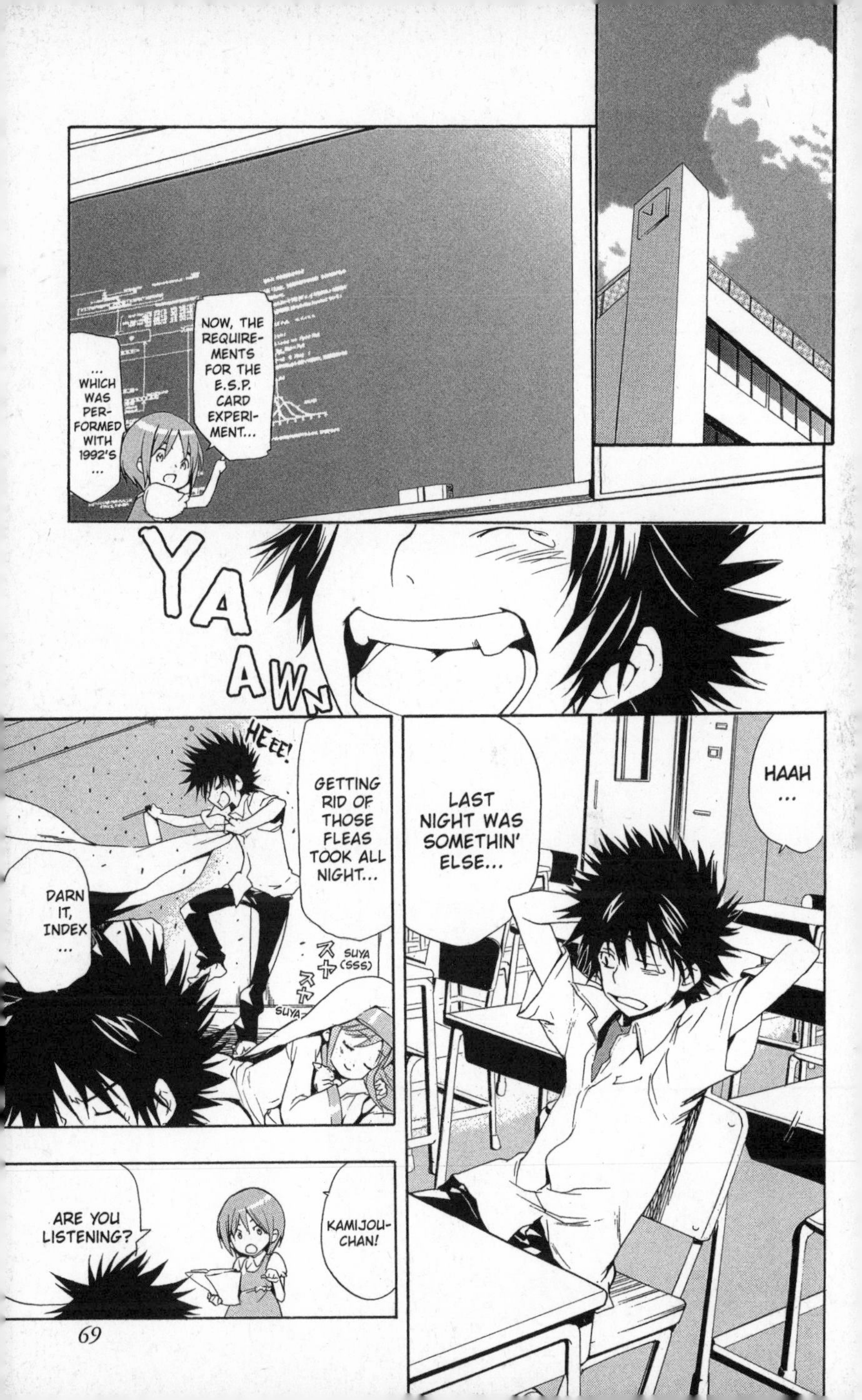
NOW, THE REQUIREMENTS FOR THE E.S.P. CARD EXPERIMENT...
... WHICH WAS PERFORMED WITH 1992'S ...
YAAWN
HAAH ...
LAST NIGHT WAS SOMETHIN' ELSE...
HEEE!
GETTING RID OF THOSE FLEAS TOOK ALL NIGHT...
SUYA (SSS)
SUYA
DARN IT, INDEX ...
KAMIJOU-CHAN!
ARE YOU LISTENING?

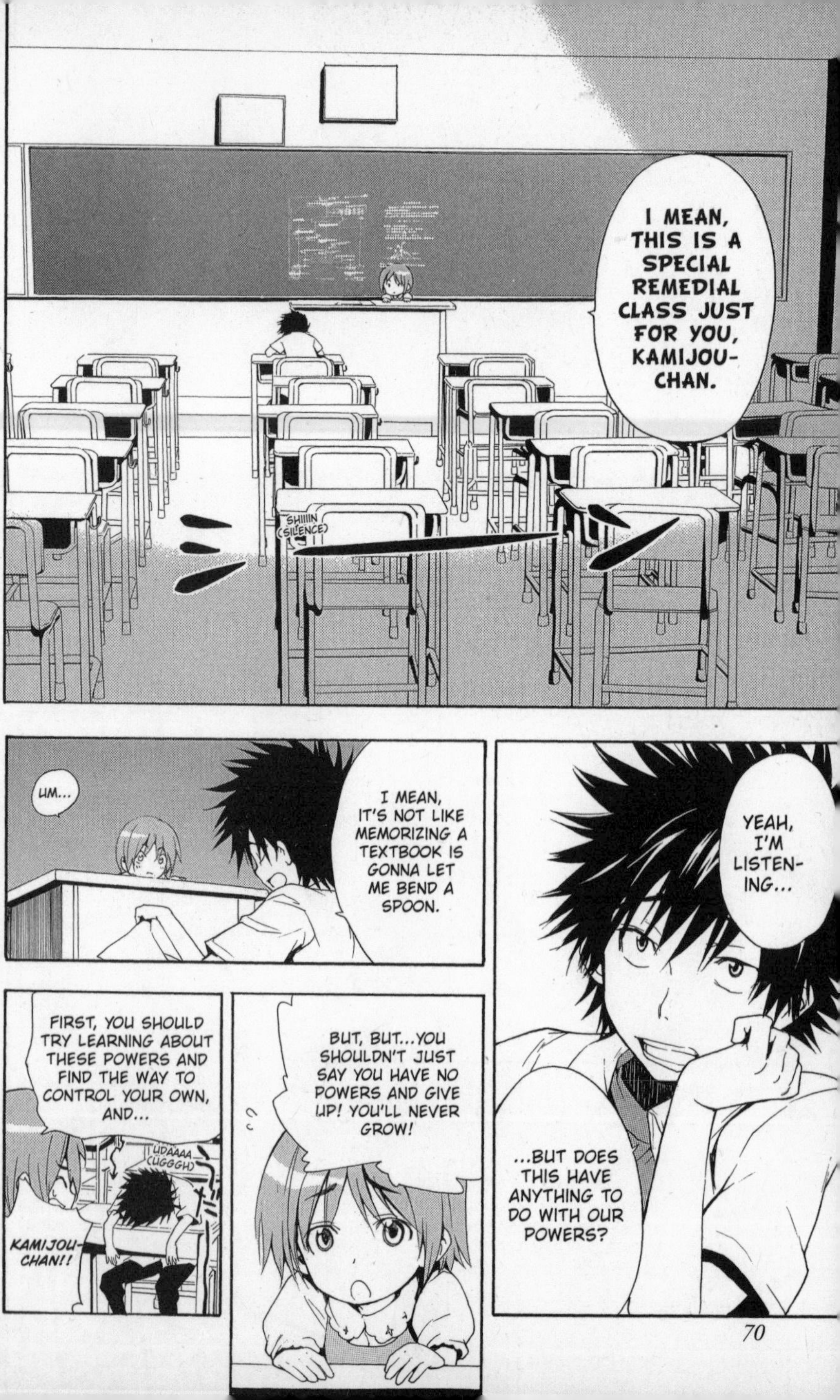
I MEAN, THIS IS A SPECIAL REMEDIAL CLASS JUST FOR YOU, KAMIJOU-CHAN.
SHIIIIN (SILENCE)
YEAH, I'M LISTEN-ING...
...BUT DOES THIS HAVE ANYTHING TO DO WITH OUR POWERS?
I MEAN, IT'S NOT LIKE MEMORIZING A TEXTBOOK IS GONNA LET ME BEND A SPOON.
UM...
BUT, BUT...YOU SHOULDN'T JUST SAY YOU HAVE NO POWERS AND GIVE UP! YOU'LL NEVER GROW!
FIRST, YOU SHOULD TRY LEARNING ABOUT THESE POWERS AND FIND THE WAY TO CONTROL YOUR OWN, AND...
UDAAAA (UGGGH)
KAMIJOU-CHAN!!

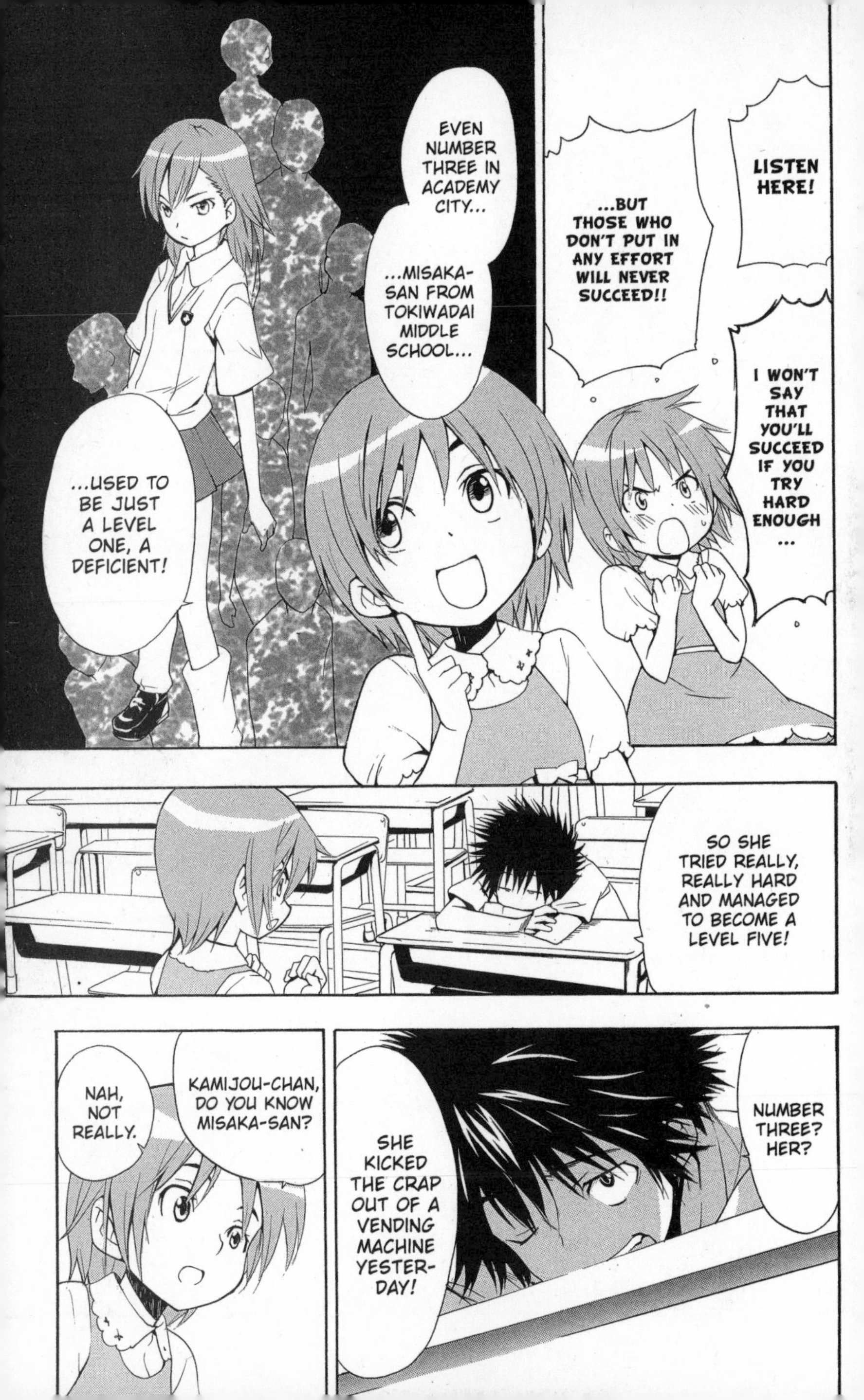
LISTEN HERE!
I WON'T SAY THAT YOU'LL SUCCEED IF YOU TRY HARD ENOUGH...
...BUT THOSE WHO DON'T PUT IN ANY EFFORT WILL NEVER SUCCEED!!
EVEN NUMBER THREE IN ACADEMY CITY...
...MISAKA-SAN FROM TOKIWADAI MIDDLE SCHOOL...
...USED TO BE JUST A LEVEL ONE, A DEFICIENT!
SO SHE TRIED REALLY, REALLY HARD AND MANAGED TO BECOME A LEVEL FIVE!
NUMBER THREE? HER?
SHE KICKED THE CRAP OUT OF A VENDING MACHINE YESTER-DAY!
KAMIJOU-CHAN, DO YOU KNOW MISAKA-SAN?
NAH, NOT REALLY.

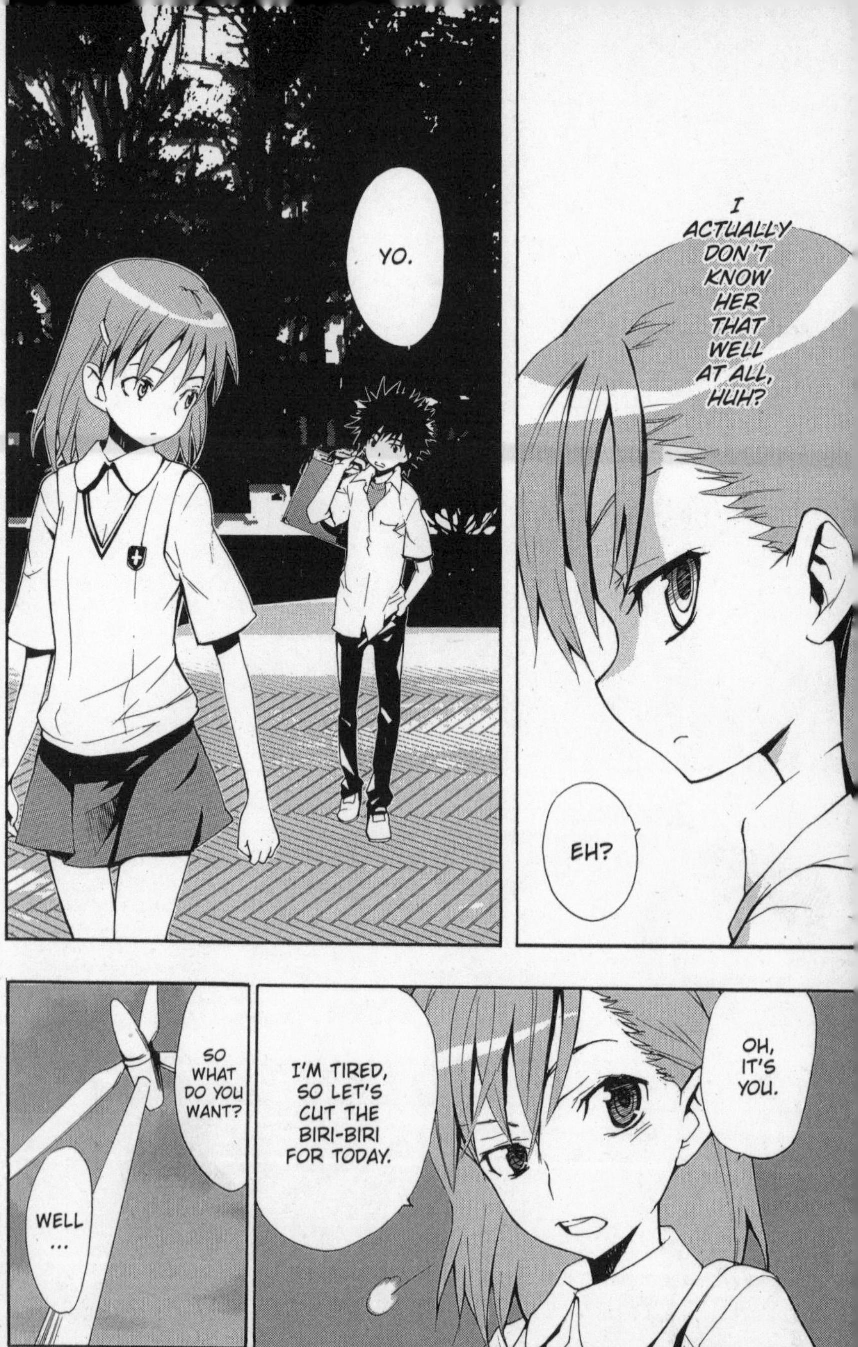
I ACTUALLY DON'T KNOW HER THAT WELL AT ALL, HUH?
EH?
YO.
OH, IT'S YOU.
I'M TIRED, SO LET'S CUT THE BIRI-BIRI FOR TODAY.
SO WHAT DO YOU WANT?
WELL ...

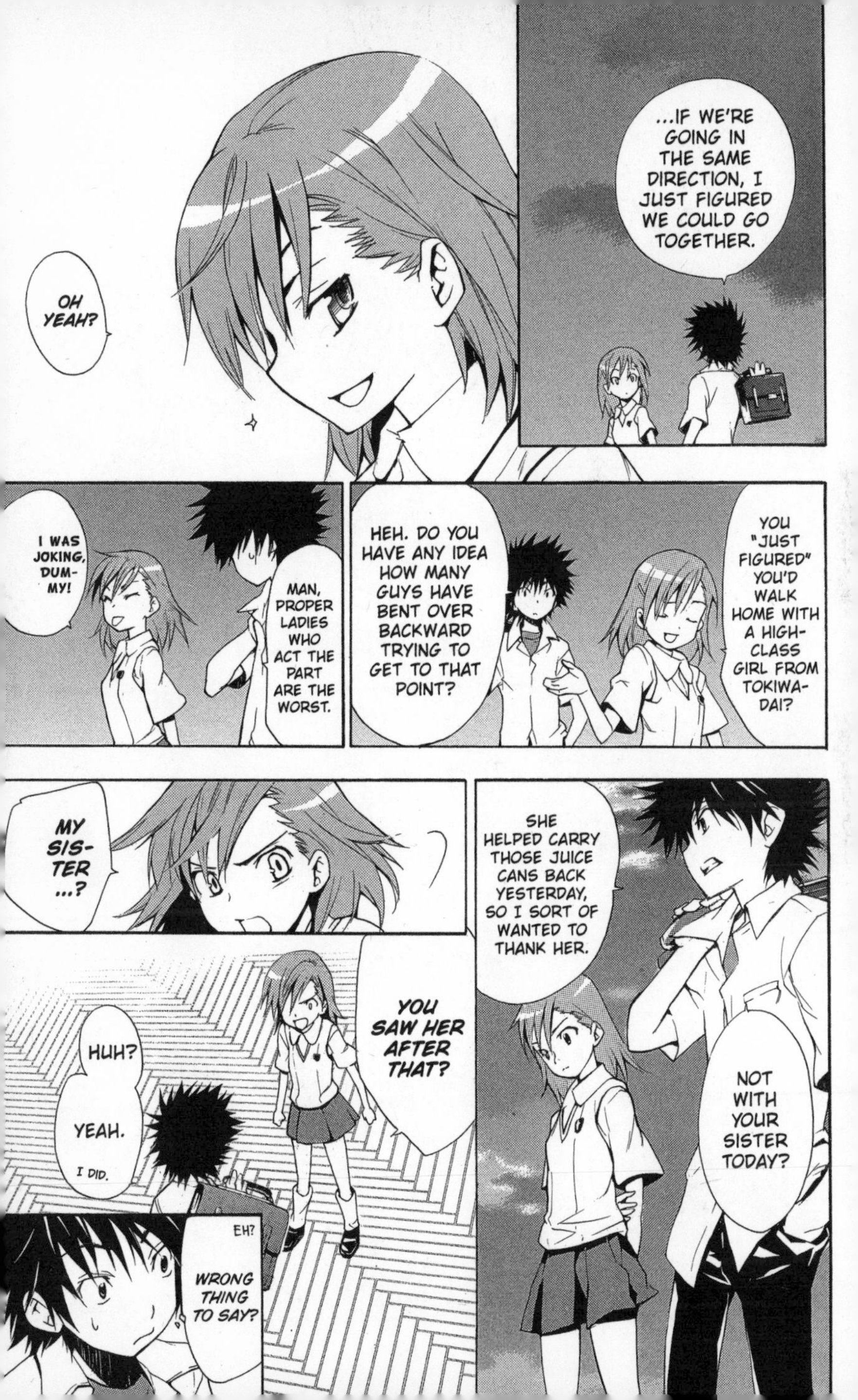
...IF WE'RE GOING IN THE SAME DIRECTION, I JUST FIGURED WE COULD GO TOGETHER.
OH YEAH?
YOU "JUST FIGURED" YOU'D WALK HOME WITH A HIGH-CLASS GIRL FROM TOKIWA-DAI?
HEH. DO YOU HAVE ANY IDEA HOW MANY GUYS HAVE BENT OVER BACKWARD TRYING TO GET TO THAT POINT?
MAN, PROPER LADIES WHO ACT THE PART ARE THE WORST.
I WAS JOKING, DUM-MY!
NOT WITH YOUR SISTER TODAY?
SHE HELPED CARRY THOSE JUICE CANS BACK YESTERDAY, SO I SORT OF WANTED TO THANK HER.
MY SIS-TER ...?
YOU SAW HER AFTER THAT?
HUH?
YEAH.
I DID.
EH?
WRONG THING TO SAY?

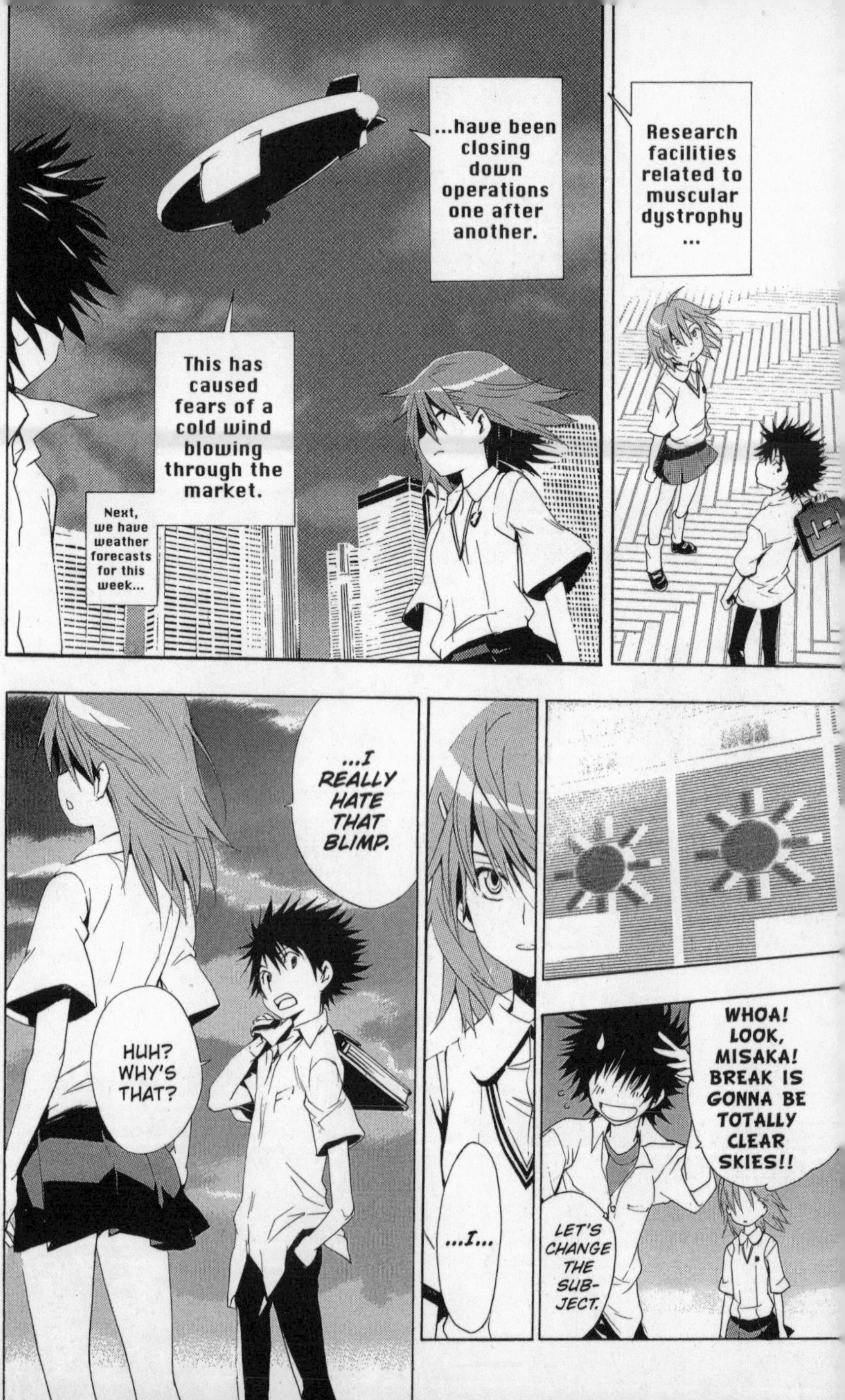
Research facilities related to muscular dystrophy ...
...have been closing down operations one after another.
This has caused fears of a cold wind blowing through the market.
Next, we have weather forecasts for this week...
WHOA! LOOK, MISAKA! BREAK IS GONNA BE TOTALLY CLEAR SKIES!!
LET'S CHANGE THE SUB-JECT.
...I...
...I REALLY HATE THAT BLIMP.
HUH? WHY'S THAT?

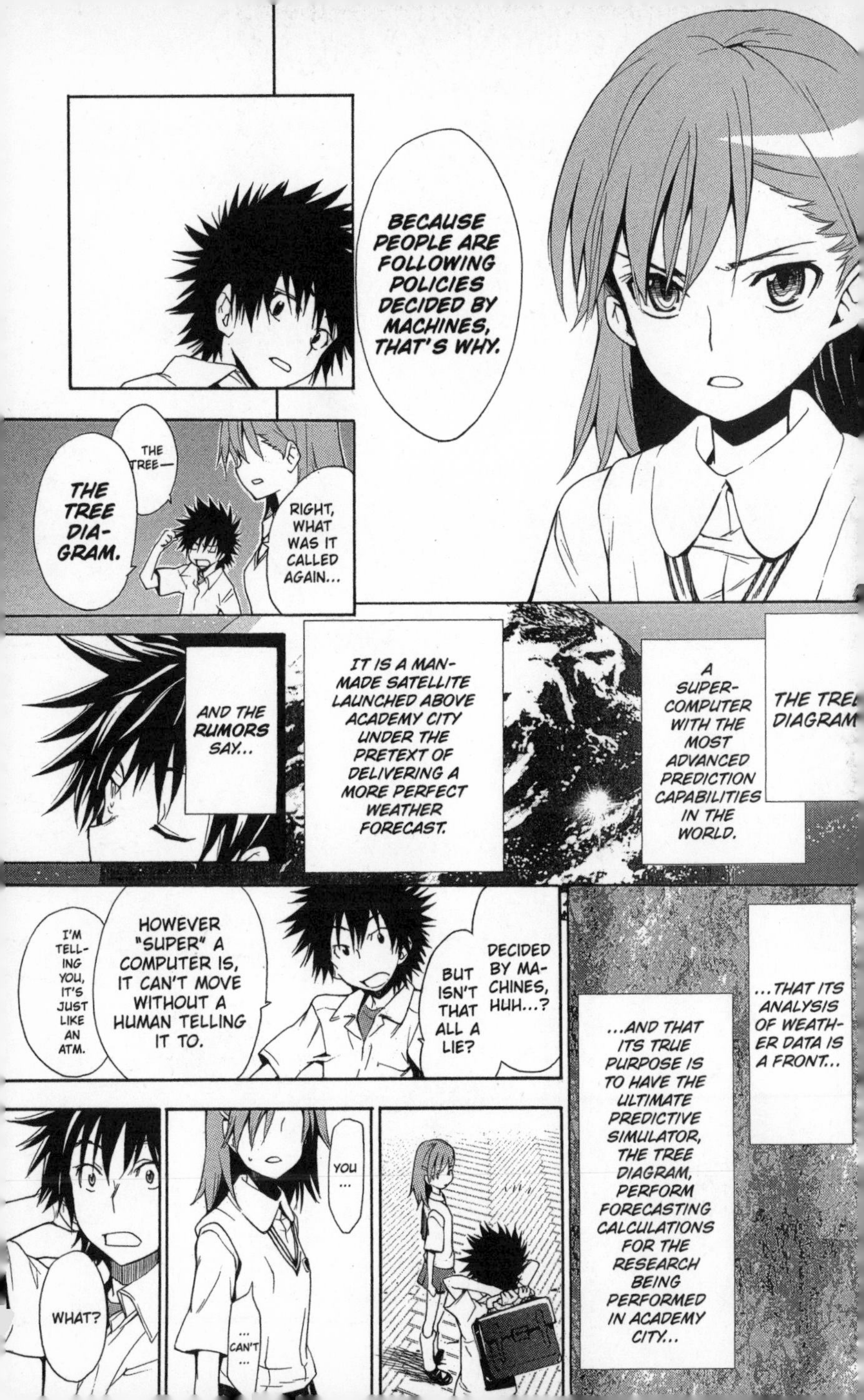
BECAUSE PEOPLE ARE FOLLOWING POLICIES DECIDED BY MACHINES, THAT'S WHY.
RIGHT, WHAT WAS IT CALLED AGAIN...
THE TREE—
THE TREE DIAGRAM.
THE TREE DIAGRAM
A SUPER-COMPUTER WITH THE MOST ADVANCED PREDICTION CAPABILITIES IN THE WORLD.
IT IS A MAN-MADE SATELLITE LAUNCHED ABOVE ACADEMY CITY UNDER THE PRETEXT OF DELIVERING A MORE PERFECT WEATHER FORECAST.
AND THE RUMORS SAY...
...THAT ITS ANALYSIS OF WEATHER DATA IS A FRONT...
...AND THAT ITS TRUE PURPOSE IS TO HAVE THE ULTIMATE PREDICTIVE SIMULATOR, THE TREE DIAGRAM, PERFORM FORECASTING CALCULATIONS FOR THE RESEARCH BEING PERFORMED IN ACADEMY CITY...
DECIDED BY MACHINES, HUH...?
BUT ISN'T THAT ALL A LIE?
HOWEVER "SUPER" A COMPUTER IS, IT CAN'T MOVE WITHOUT A HUMAN TELLING IT TO.
I'M TELLING YOU, IT'S JUST LIKE AN ATM.
YOU ...
... CAN'T ...
WHAT?

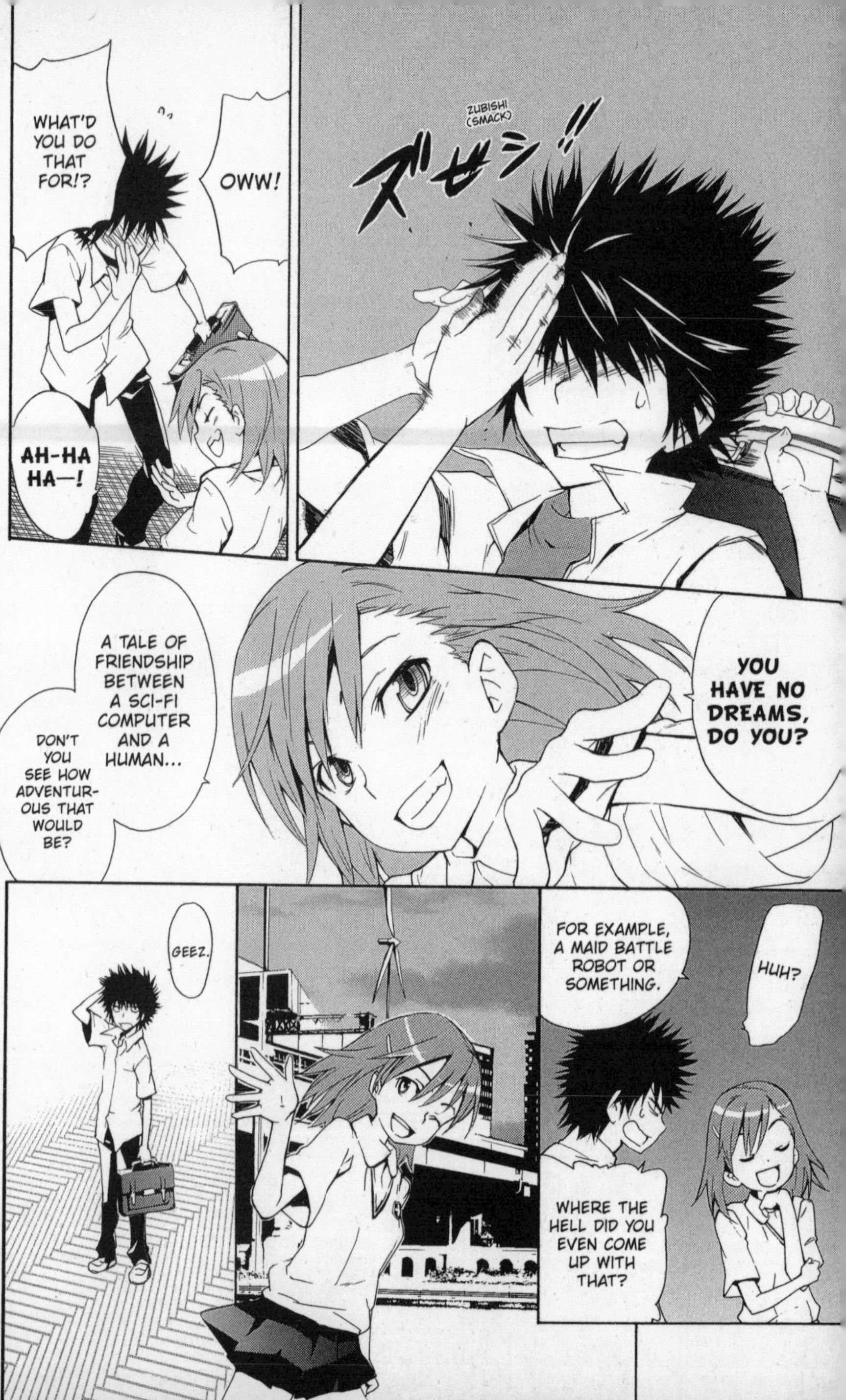
ZUBISHI (SMACK)
ズビシ!!
OWW!
WHAT'D YOU DO THAT FOR!?
AH-HA HA—!
YOU HAVE NO DREAMS, DO YOU?
A TALE OF FRIENDSHIP BETWEEN A SCI-FI COMPUTER AND A HUMAN...
DON'T YOU SEE HOW ADVENTUR-OUS THAT WOULD BE?
FOR EXAMPLE, A MAID BATTLE ROBOT OR SOMETHING.
HUH?
WHERE THE HELL DID YOU EVEN COME UP WITH THAT?
GEEZ.

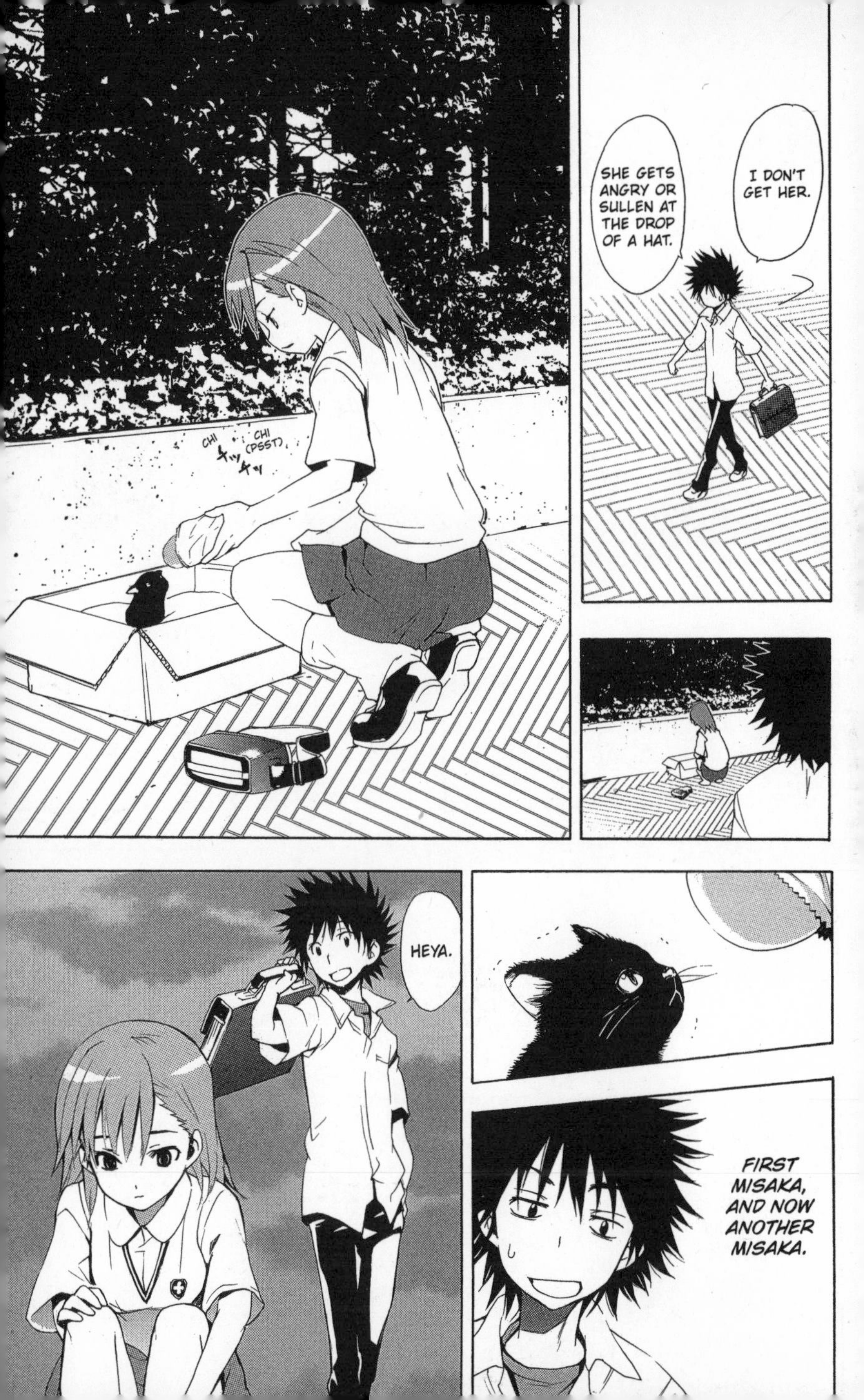
I DON'T GET HER.
SHE GETS ANGRY OR SULLEN AT THE DROP OF A HAT.
CHI CHI (PSST)
FIRST MISAKA, AND NOW ANOTHER MISAKA.
HEYA.

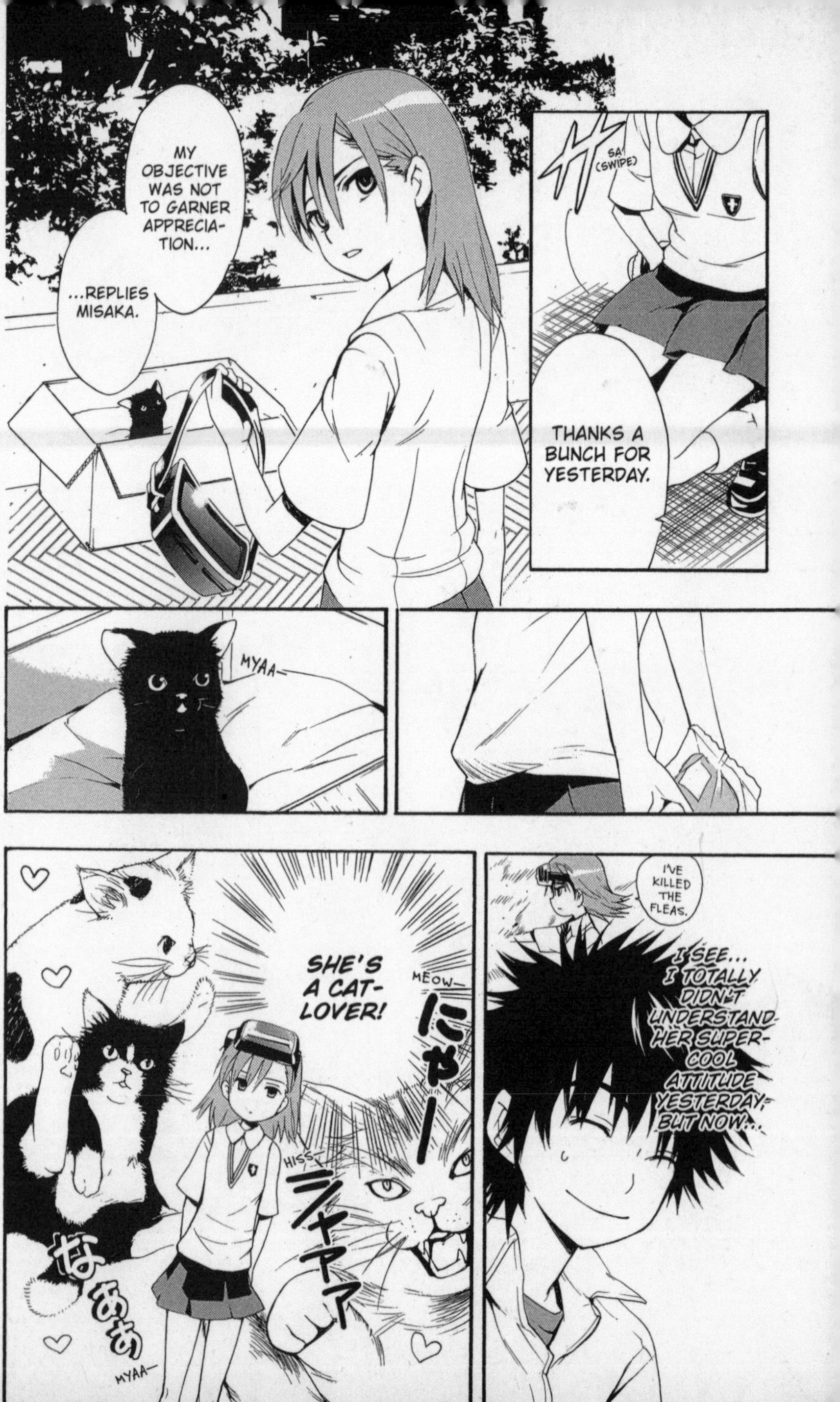
SA (SWIPE)
THANKS A BUNCH FOR YESTERDAY.
MY OBJECTIVE WAS NOT TO GARNER APPRECIATION...
...REPLIES MISAKA.
MYAA—
I'VE KILLED THE FLEAS.
I SEE... I TOTALLY DIDN'T UNDERSTAND HER SUPER-COOL ATTITUDE YESTERDAY, BUT NOW...
MEOW—
にゃー
SHE'S A CAT-LOVER!
HISS—
シャアア
なあぁ
MYAA—

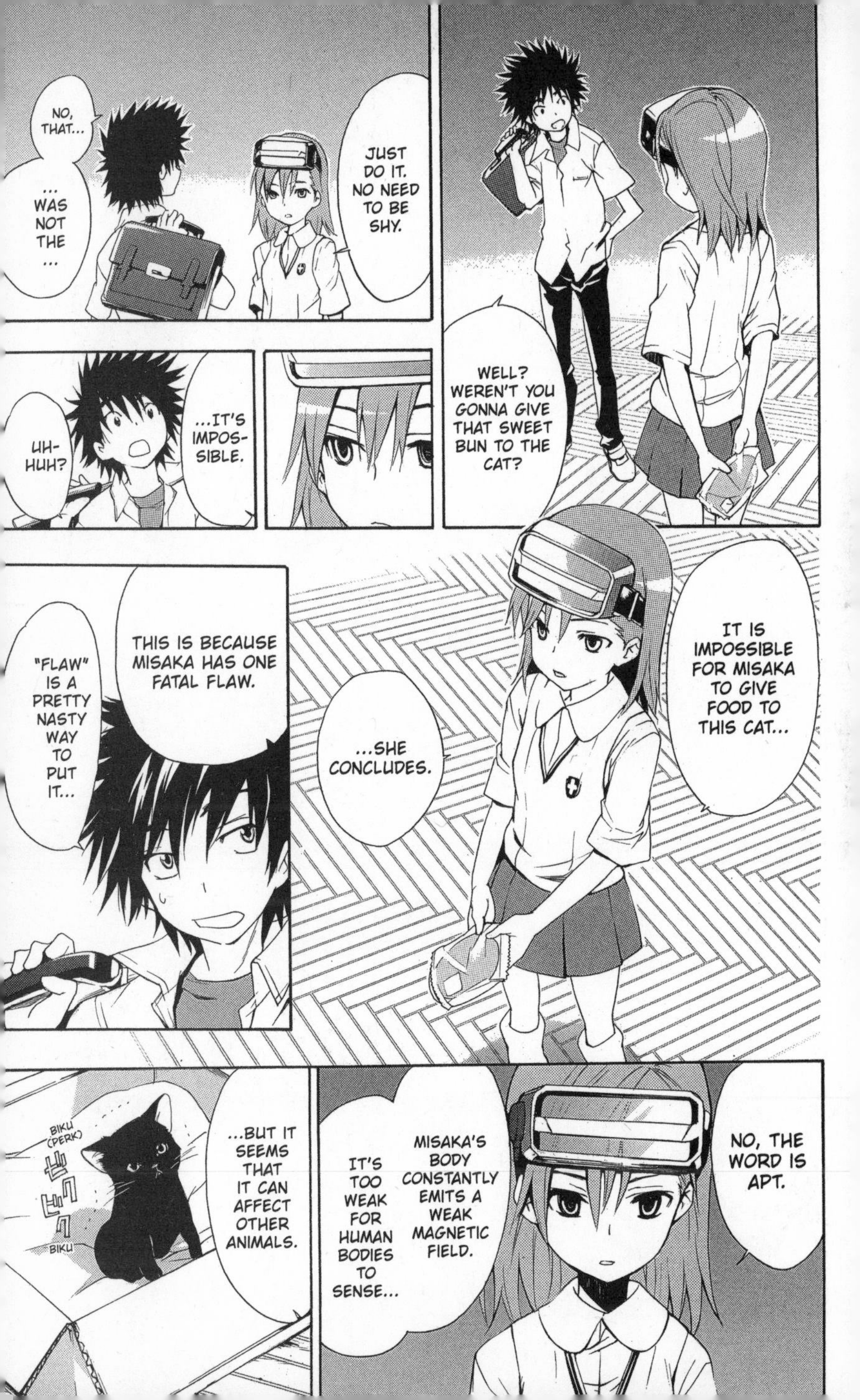
WELL? WEREN'T YOU GONNA GIVE THAT SWEET BUN TO THE CAT?
JUST DO IT. NO NEED TO BE SHY.
NO, THAT...
...WAS NOT THE...
...IT'S IMPOSSIBLE.
UH-HUH?
IT IS IMPOSSIBLE FOR MISAKA TO GIVE FOOD TO THIS CAT...
...SHE CONCLUDES.
THIS IS BECAUSE MISAKA HAS ONE FATAL FLAW.
"FLAW" IS A PRETTY NASTY WAY TO PUT IT...
NO, THE WORD IS APT.
MISAKA'S BODY CONSTANTLY EMITS A WEAK MAGNETIC FIELD.
IT'S TOO WEAK FOR HUMAN BODIES TO SENSE...
...BUT IT SEEMS THAT IT CAN AFFECT OTHER ANIMALS.
BIKU (PERK)
BIKU

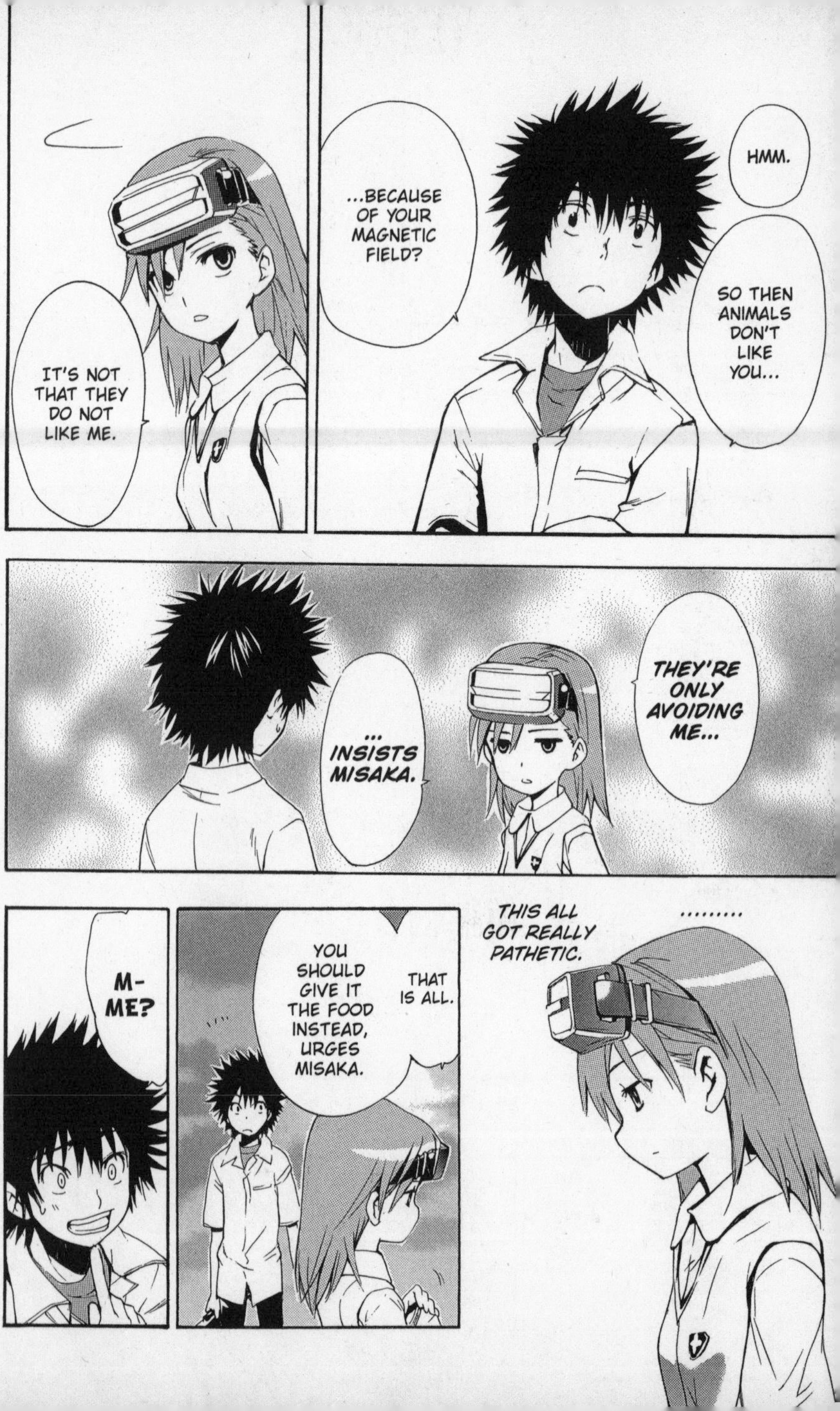
HMM.
SO THEN ANIMALS DON'T LIKE YOU...
...BECAUSE OF YOUR MAGNETIC FIELD?
IT'S NOT THAT THEY DO NOT LIKE ME.
THEY'RE ONLY AVOIDING ME...
...INSISTS MISAKA.
....
THIS ALL GOT REALLY PATHETIC.
THAT IS ALL.
YOU SHOULD GIVE IT THE FOOD INSTEAD, URGES MISAKA.
M-ME?

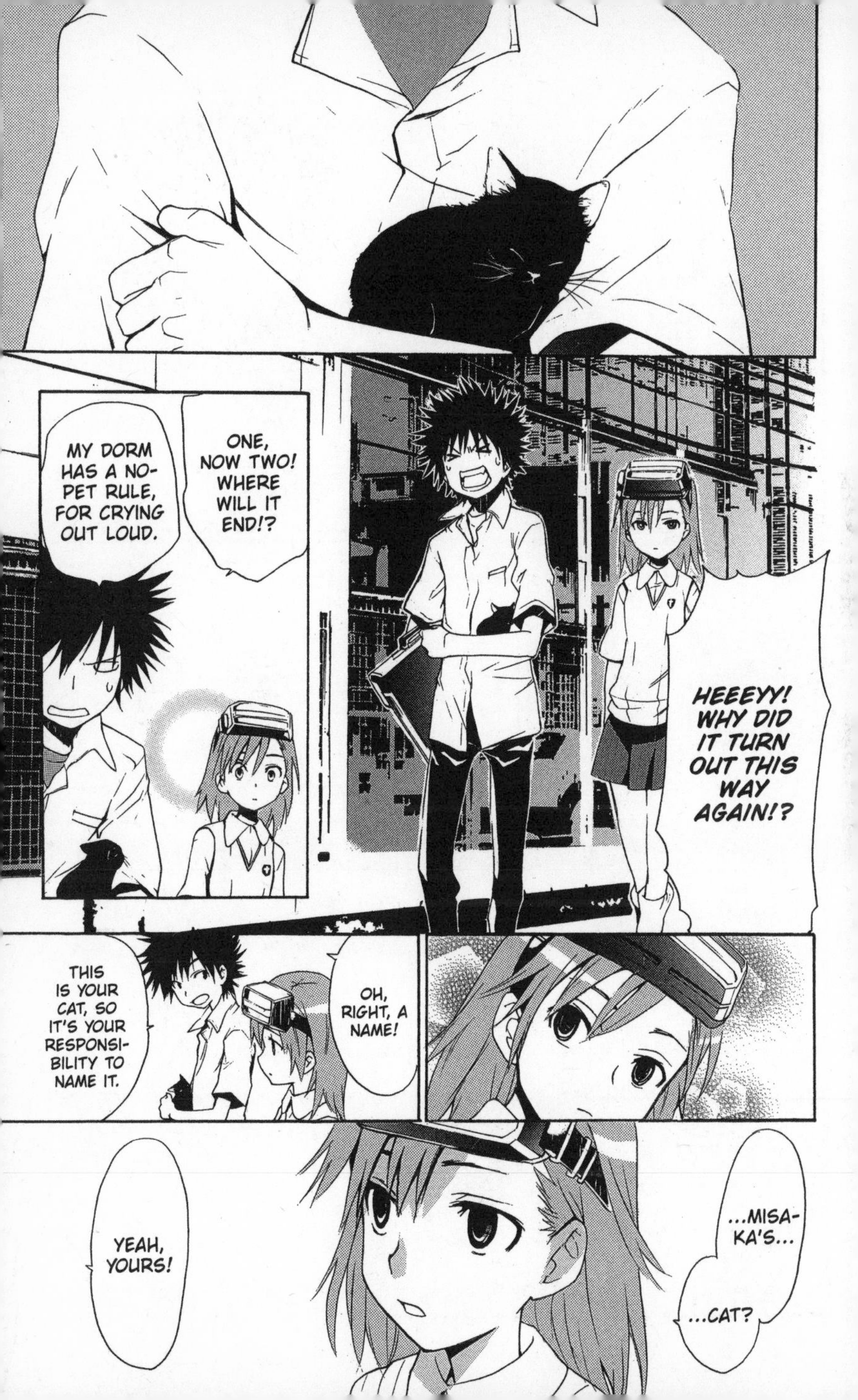
HEEEYY! WHY DID IT TURN OUT THIS WAY AGAIN!?
ONE, NOW TWO! WHERE WILL IT END!?
MY DORM HAS A NO-PET RULE, FOR CRYING OUT LOUD.
OH, RIGHT, A NAME!
THIS IS YOUR CAT, SO IT'S YOUR RESPONSI-BILITY TO NAME IT.
...MISA-KA'S...
...CAT?
YEAH, YOURS!

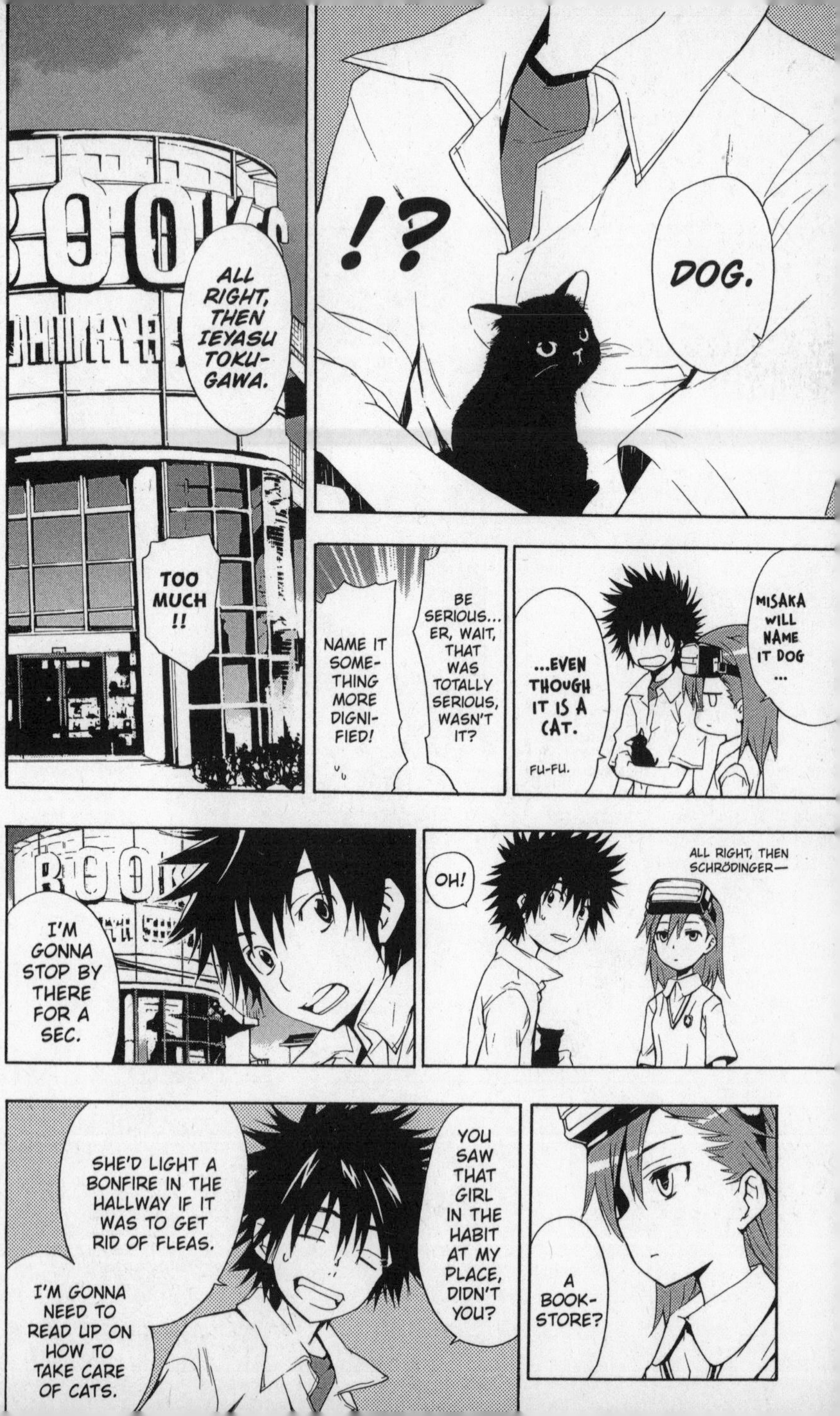
DOG.
!?
MISAKA WILL NAME IT DOG ...
...EVEN THOUGH IT IS A CAT.
FU-FU.
BE SERIOUS... ER, WAIT, THAT WAS TOTALLY SERIOUS, WASN'T IT?
NAME IT SOMETHING MORE DIGNIFIED!
ALL RIGHT, THEN IEYASU TOKUGAWA.
TOO MUCH!!
ALL RIGHT, THEN SCHRÖDINGER—
OH!
I'M GONNA STOP BY THERE FOR A SEC.
A BOOKSTORE?
YOU SAW THAT GIRL IN THE HABIT AT MY PLACE, DIDN'T YOU?
SHE'D LIGHT A BONFIRE IN THE HALLWAY IF IT WAS TO GET RID OF FLEAS.
I'M GONNA NEED TO READ UP ON HOW TO TAKE CARE OF CATS.

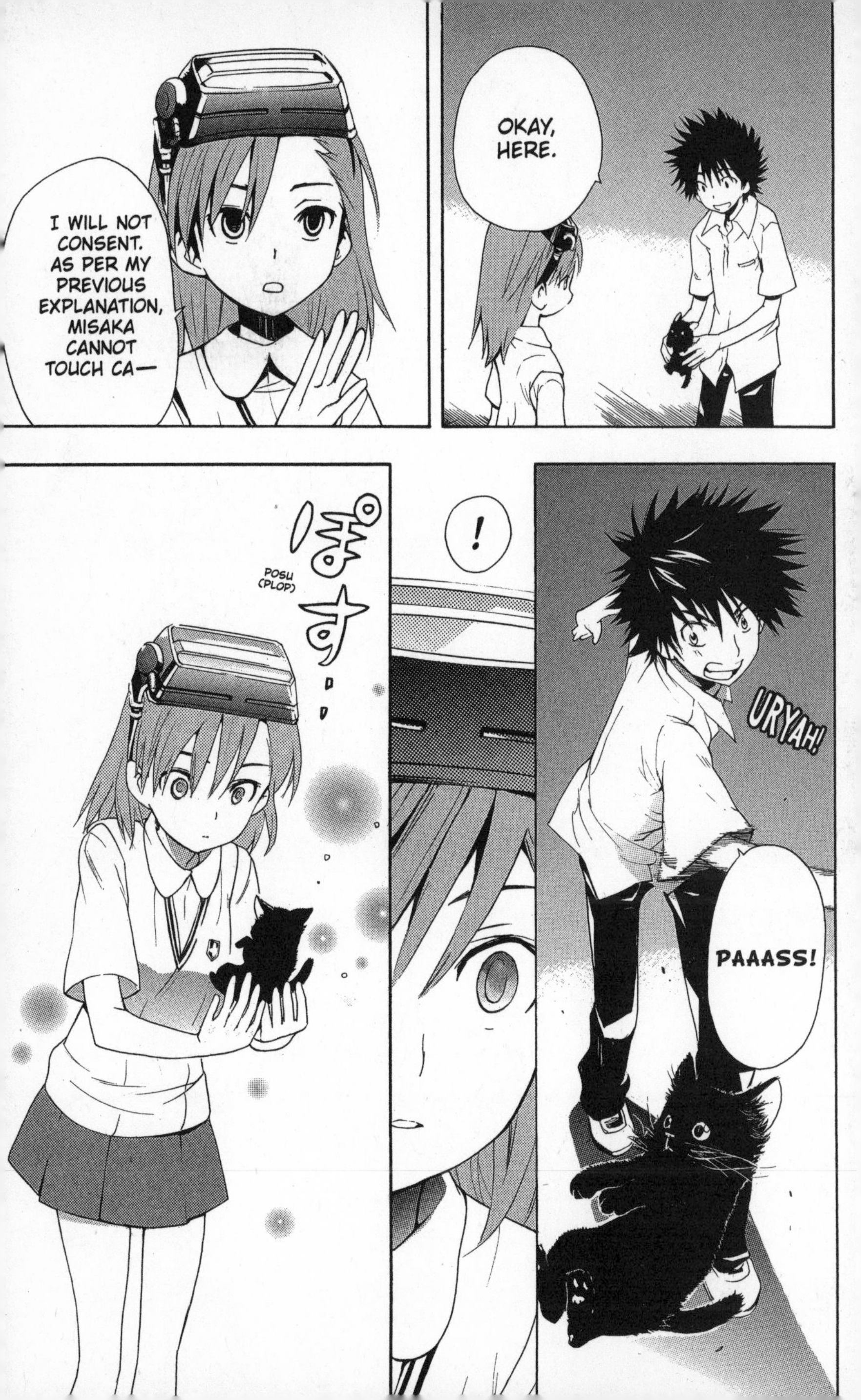
OKAY, HERE.
I WILL NOT CONSENT. AS PER MY PREVIOUS EXPLANATION, MISAKA CANNOT TOUCH CA—
URYAH!
PAAASS!
!
ぽす
POSU (PLOP)

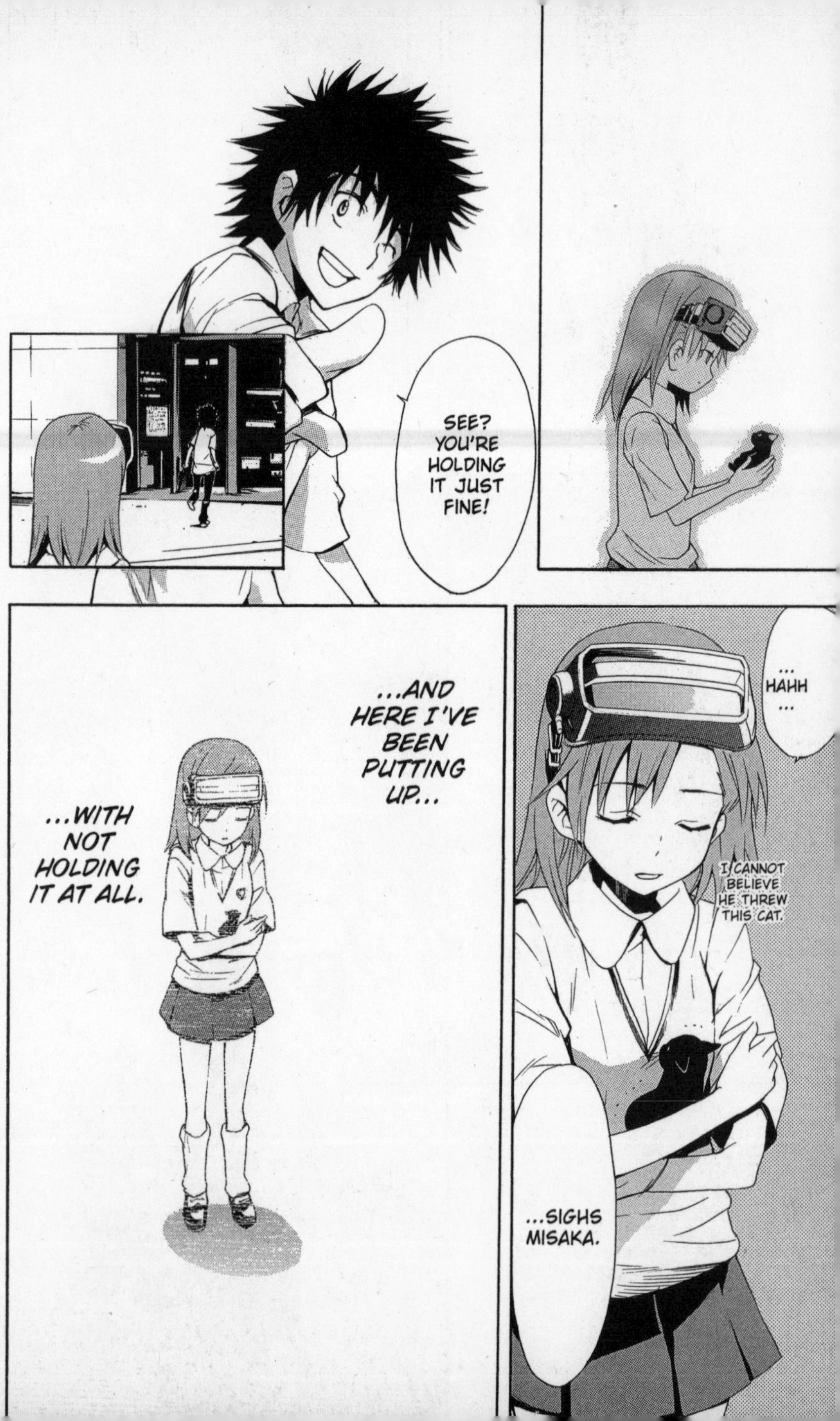
SEE? YOU'RE HOLDING IT JUST FINE!
...HAHH...
I CANNOT BELIEVE HE THREW THIS CAT.
...SIGHS MISAKA.
...AND HERE I'VE BEEN PUTTING UP...
...WITH NOT HOLDING IT AT ALL.

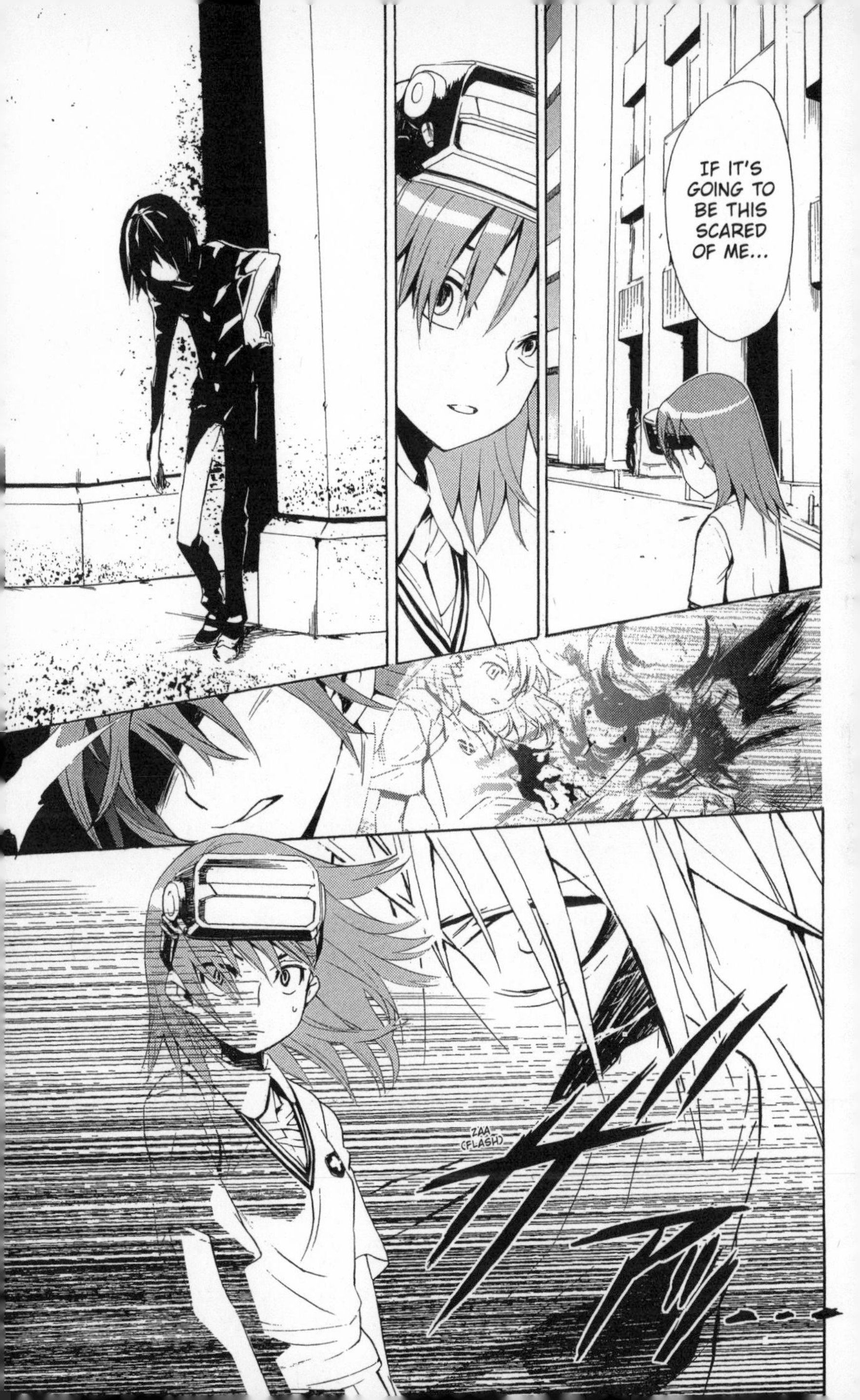
IF IT'S GOING TO BE THIS SCARED OF ME...
ZAA (FLASH)

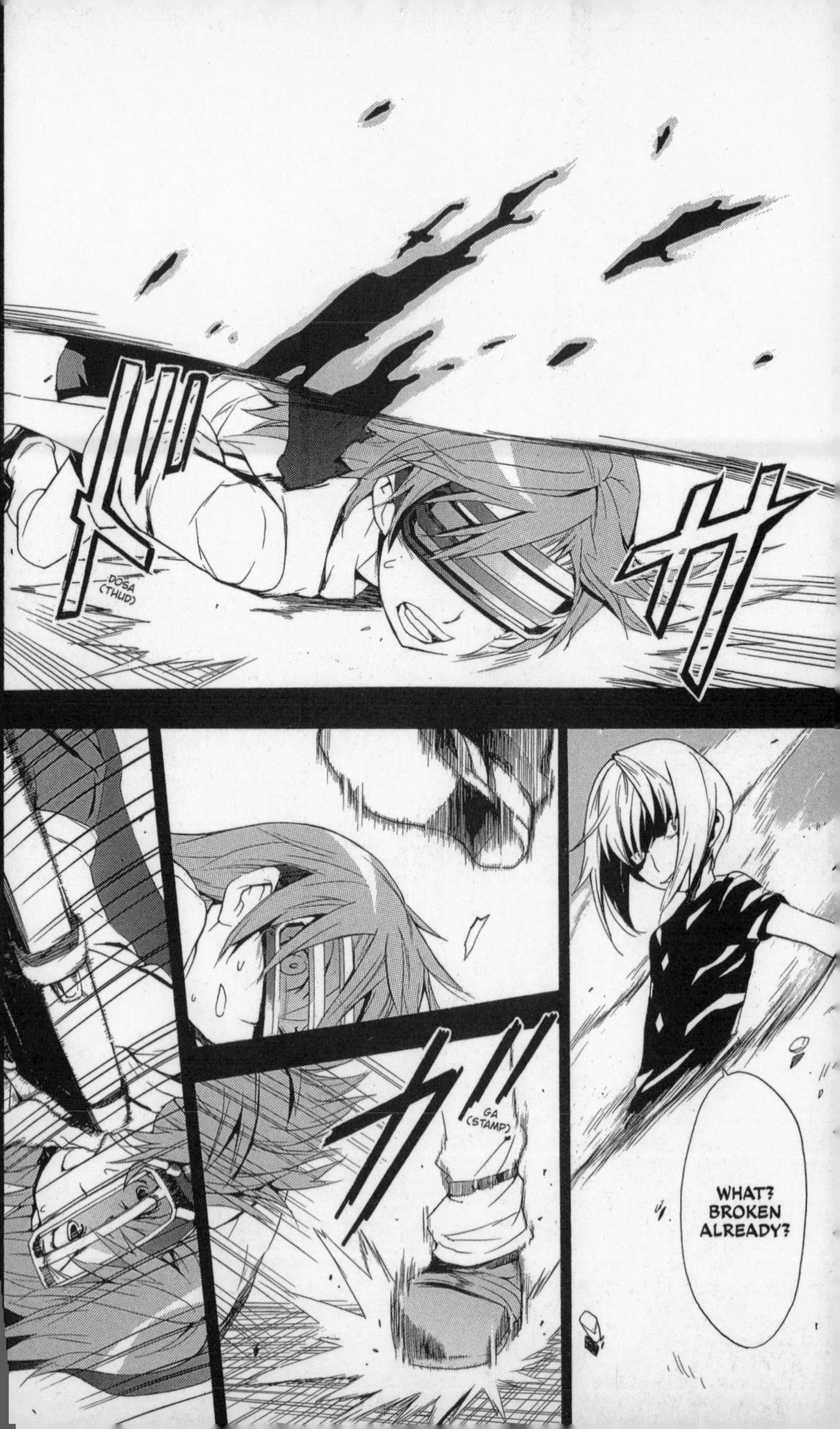
DOSA (THUD)
GA (STAMP)
WHAT? BROKEN ALREADY?

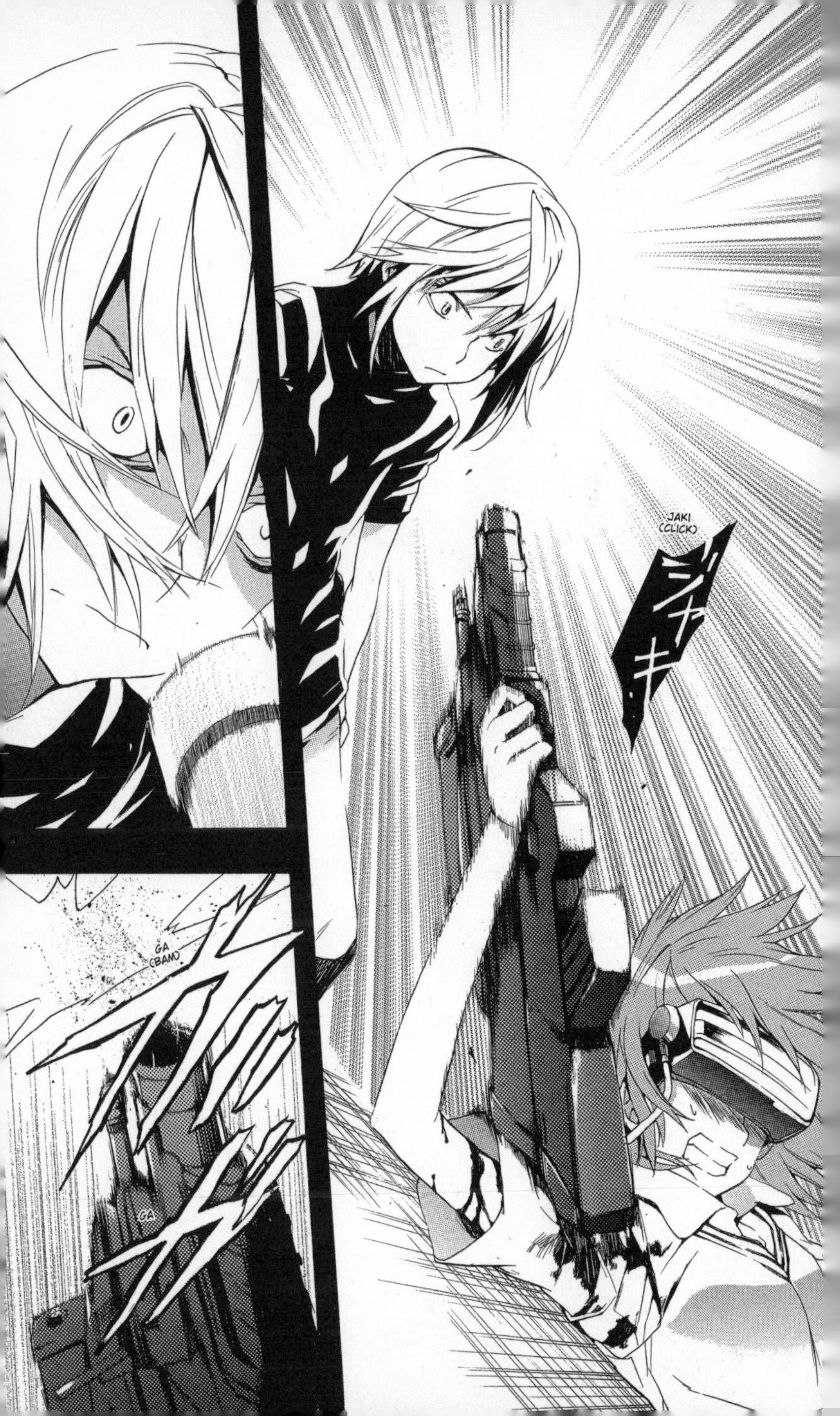
JAKI (CLICK)
ジャキ
GA (BAM)
GA

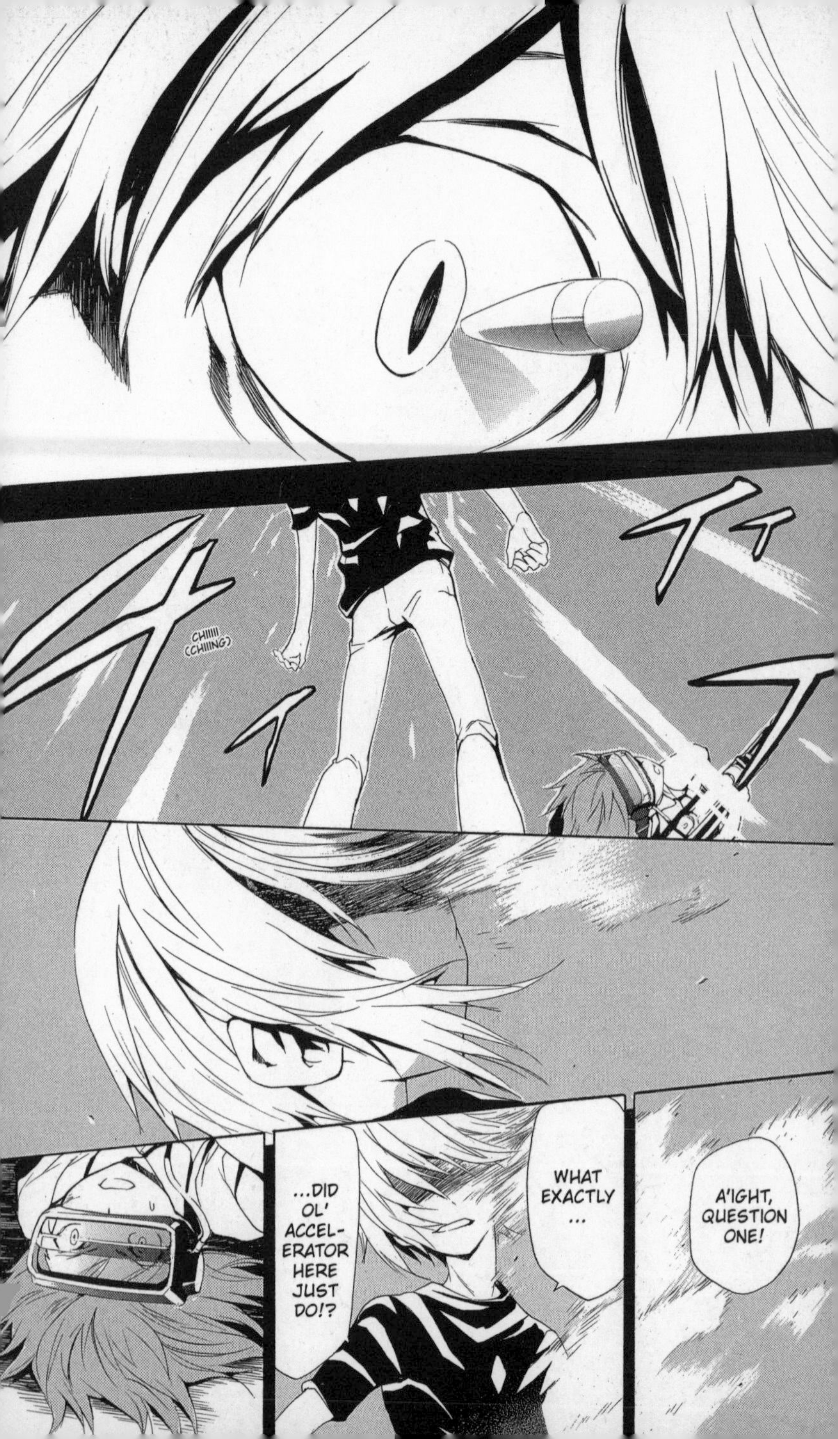
CHIIIII
(CHIIING)
A'IGHT, QUESTION ONE!
WHAT EXACTLY ...
...DID OL' ACCEL-ERATOR HERE JUST DO!?

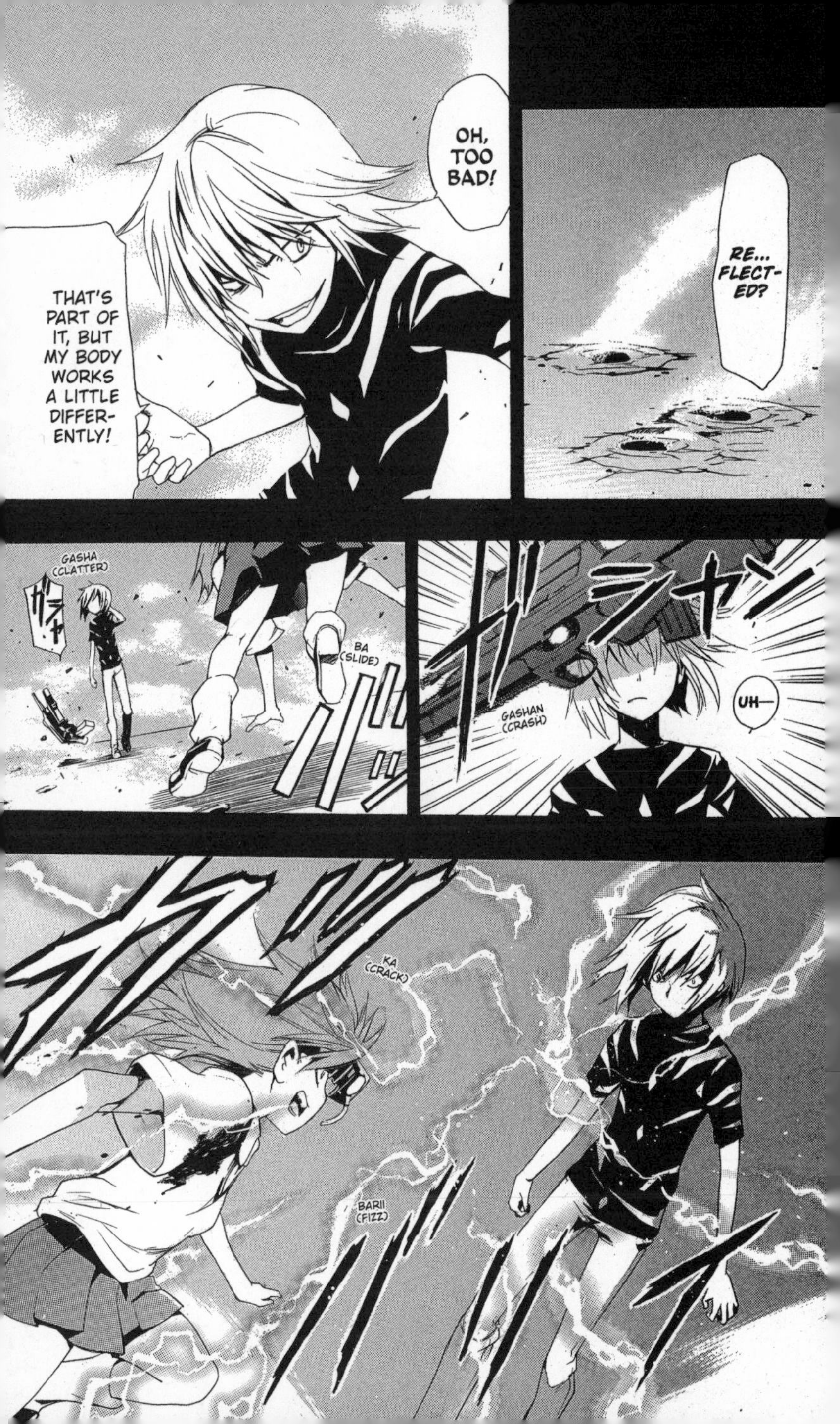
RE... FLECTED?
OH, TOO BAD!
THAT'S PART OF IT, BUT MY BODY WORKS A LITTLE DIFFERENTLY!
GASHAN (CRASH)
UH—
BA (SLIDE)
GASHA (CLATTER)
KA (CRACK)
BARII (FIZZ)

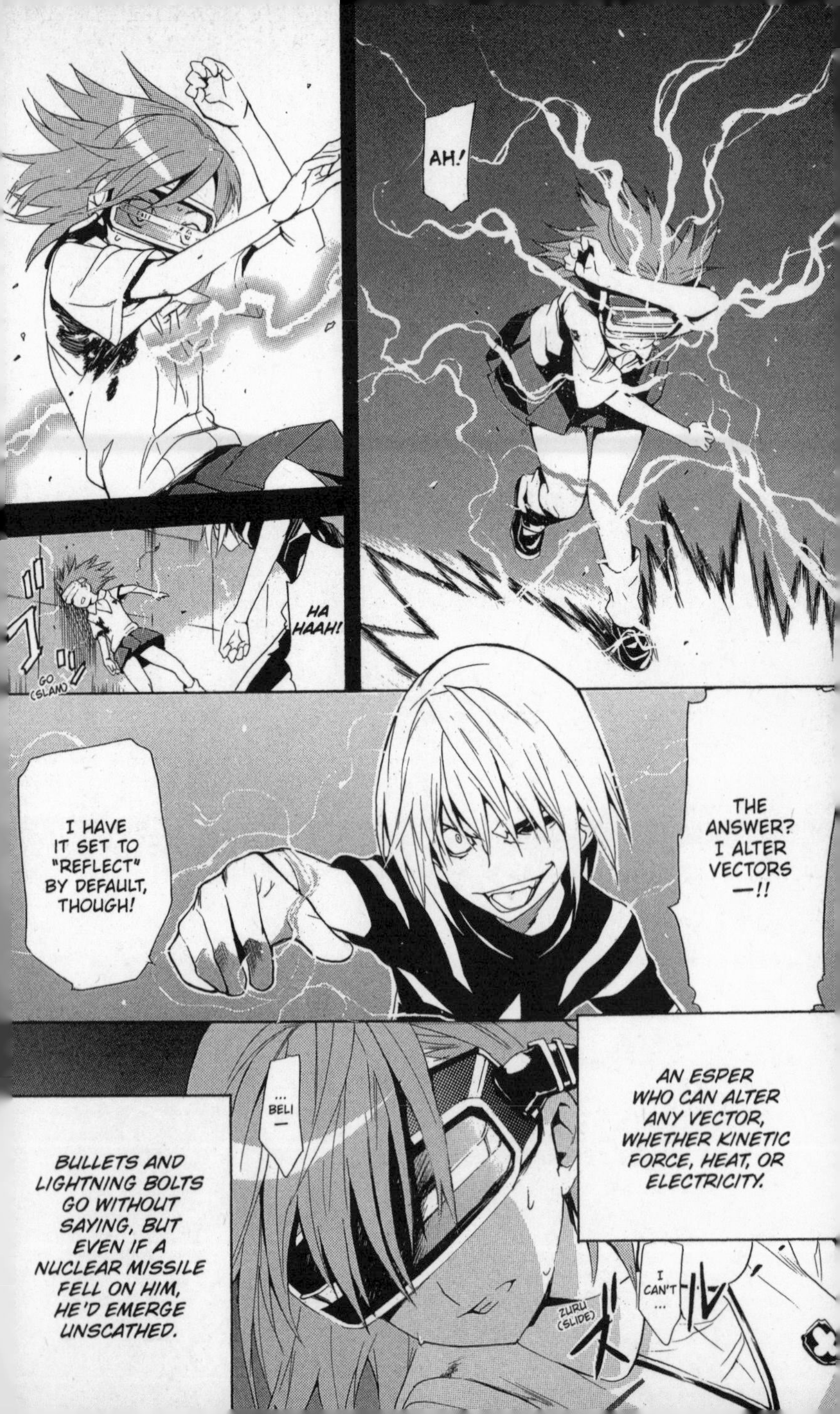
AH!
HA HAAH!
GO (SLAM)
THE ANSWER? I ALTER VECTORS —!!
I HAVE IT SET TO "REFLECT" BY DEFAULT, THOUGH!
AN ESPER WHO CAN ALTER ANY VECTOR, WHETHER KINETIC FORCE, HEAT, OR ELECTRICITY.
I CAN'T ...
ZURU (SLIDE)
... BELI —
BULLETS AND LIGHTNING BOLTS GO WITHOUT SAYING, BUT EVEN IF A NUCLEAR MISSILE FELL ON HIM, HE'D EMERGE UNSCATHED.

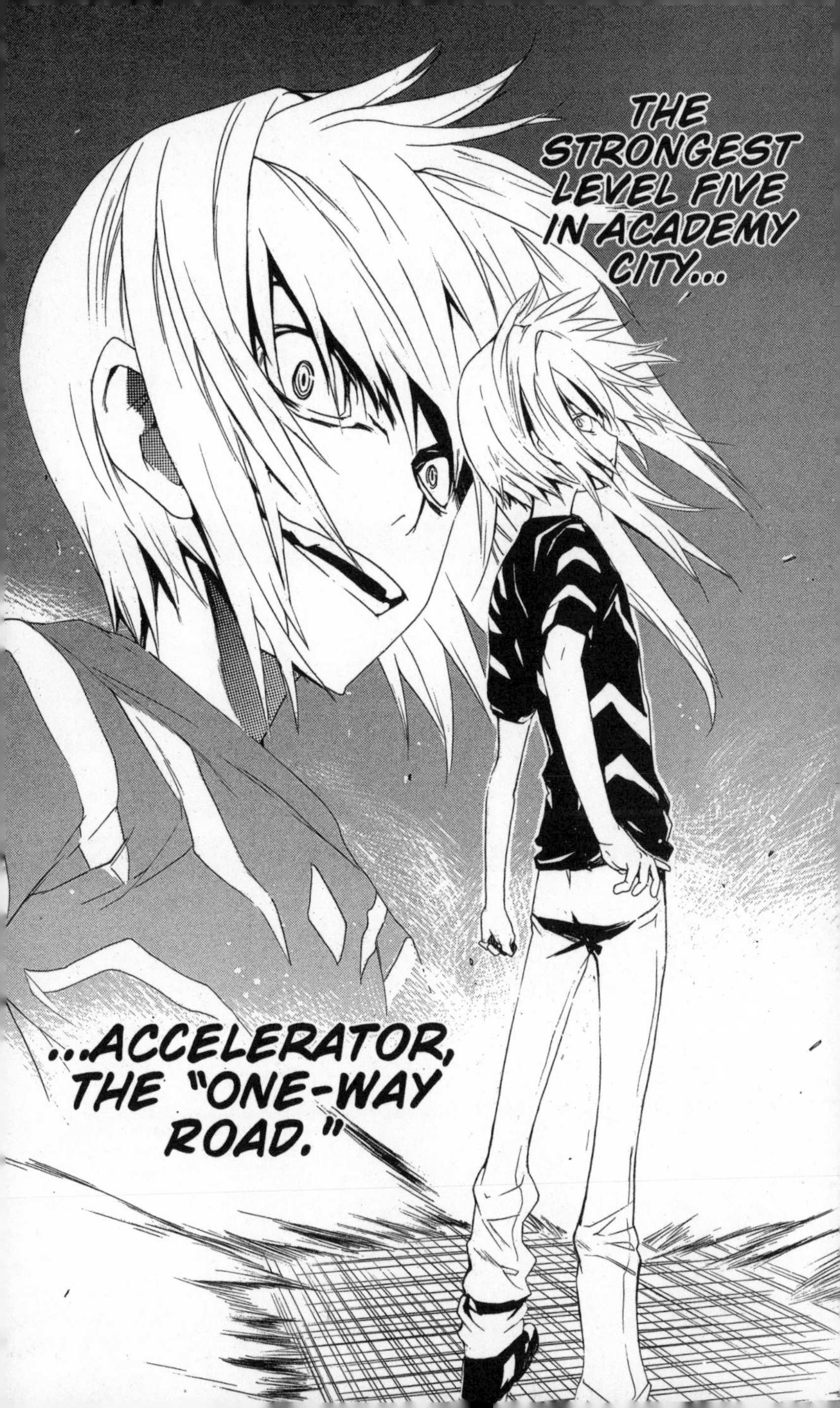
THE STRONGEST LEVEL FIVE IN ACADEMY CITY...
...ACCELERATOR, THE "ONE-WAY ROAD."

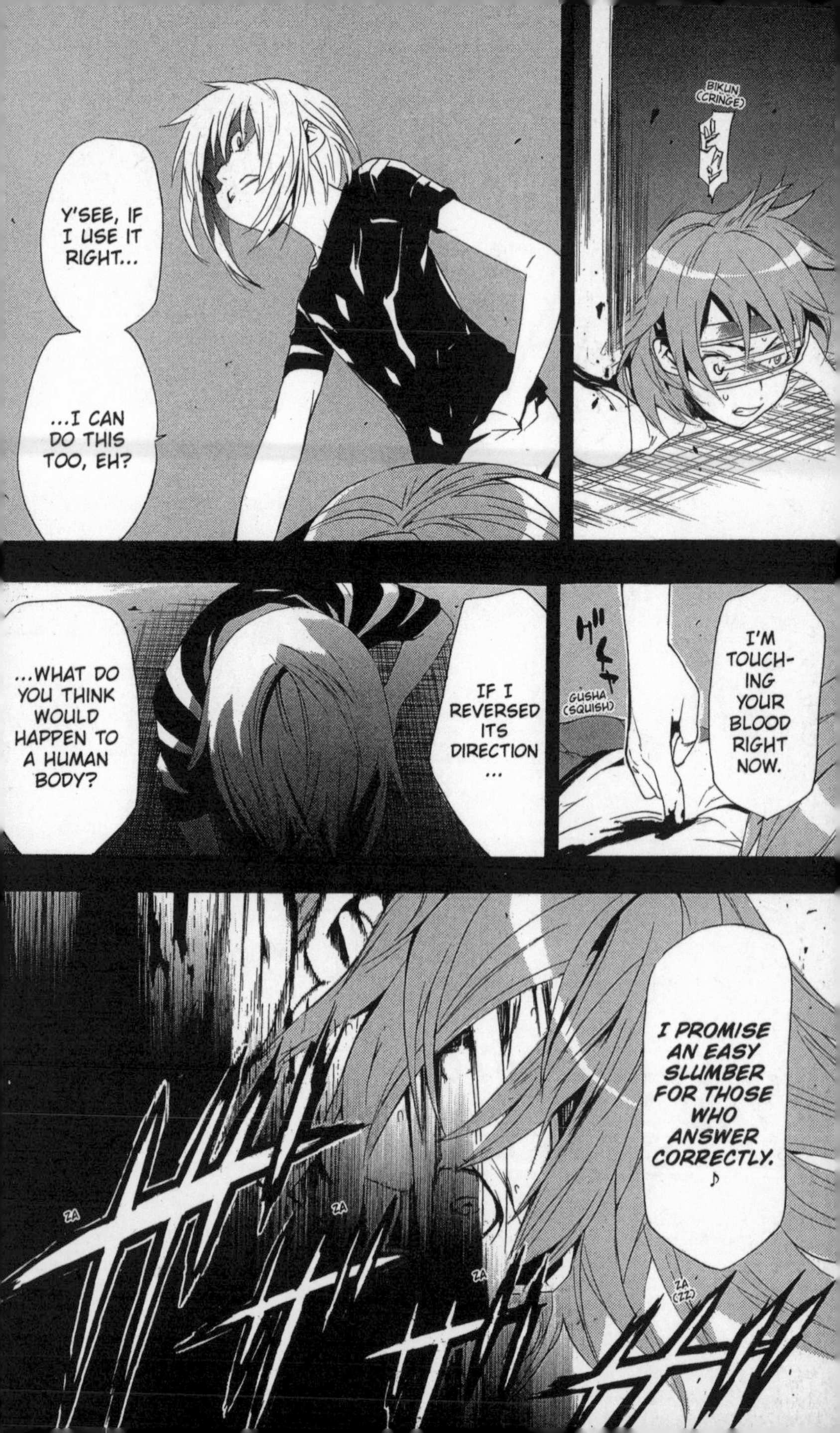
BIKUN (CRINGE)
Y'SEE, IF I USE IT RIGHT...
...I CAN DO THIS TOO, EH?
GUSHA (SQUISH)
I'M TOUCHING YOUR BLOOD RIGHT NOW.
IF I REVERSED ITS DIRECTION ...
...WHAT DO YOU THINK WOULD HAPPEN TO A HUMAN BODY?
I PROMISE AN EASY SLUMBER FOR THOSE WHO ANSWER CORRECTLY. ♪
ZA
ZA
ZA
ZA (ZZ)

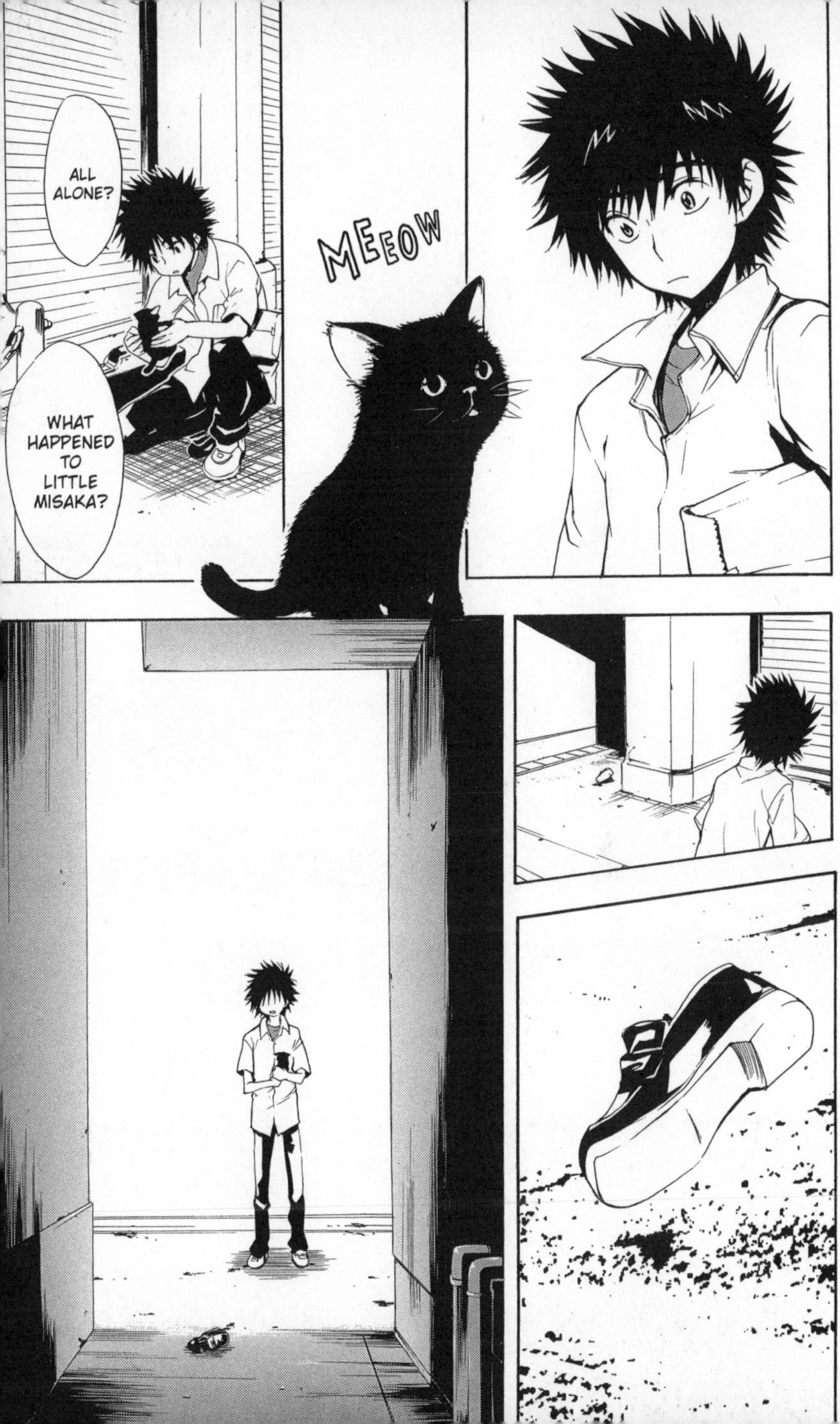
MEEOW
ALL ALONE?
WHAT HAPPENED TO LITTLE MISAKA?

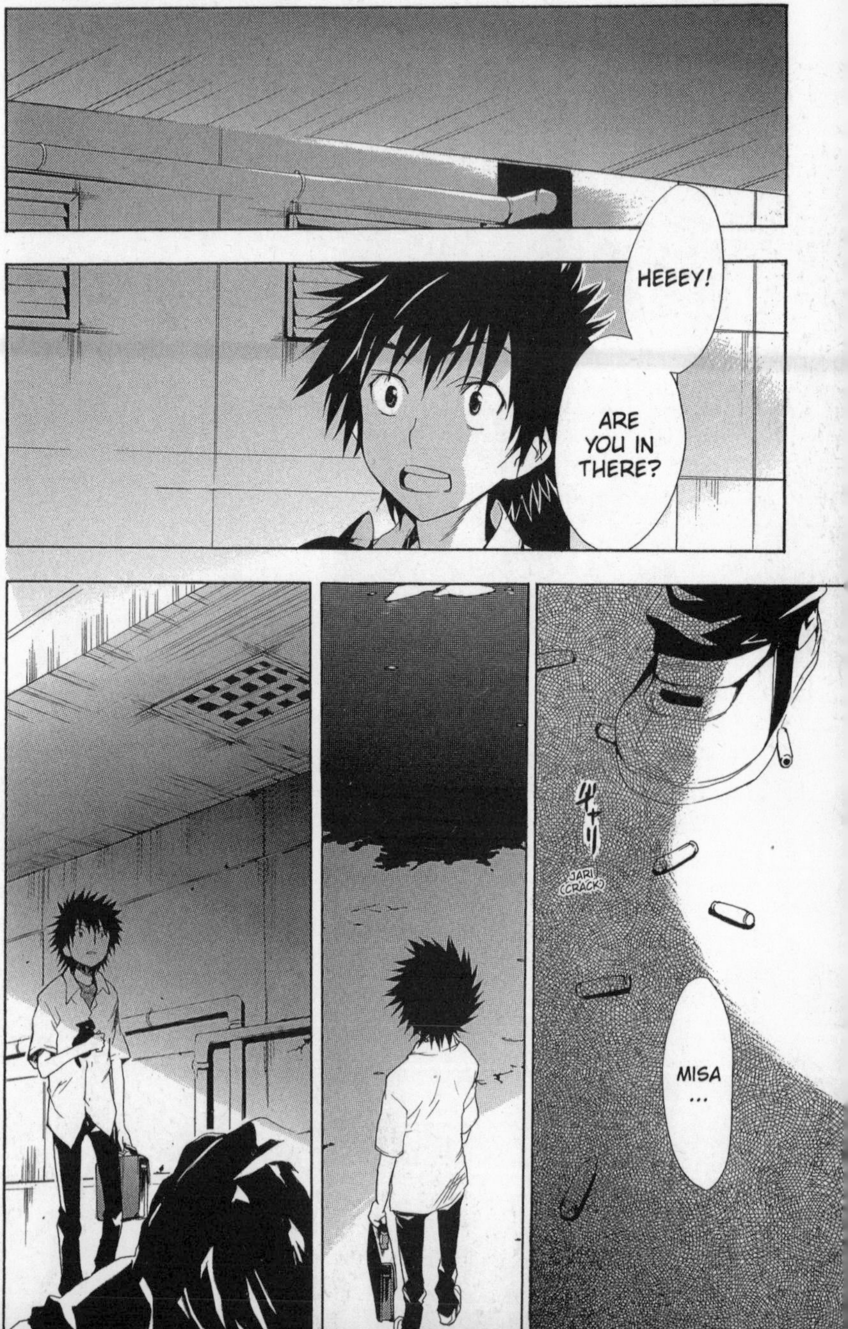
HEEEY!
ARE YOU IN THERE?
MISA ...
JARI (CRACK)

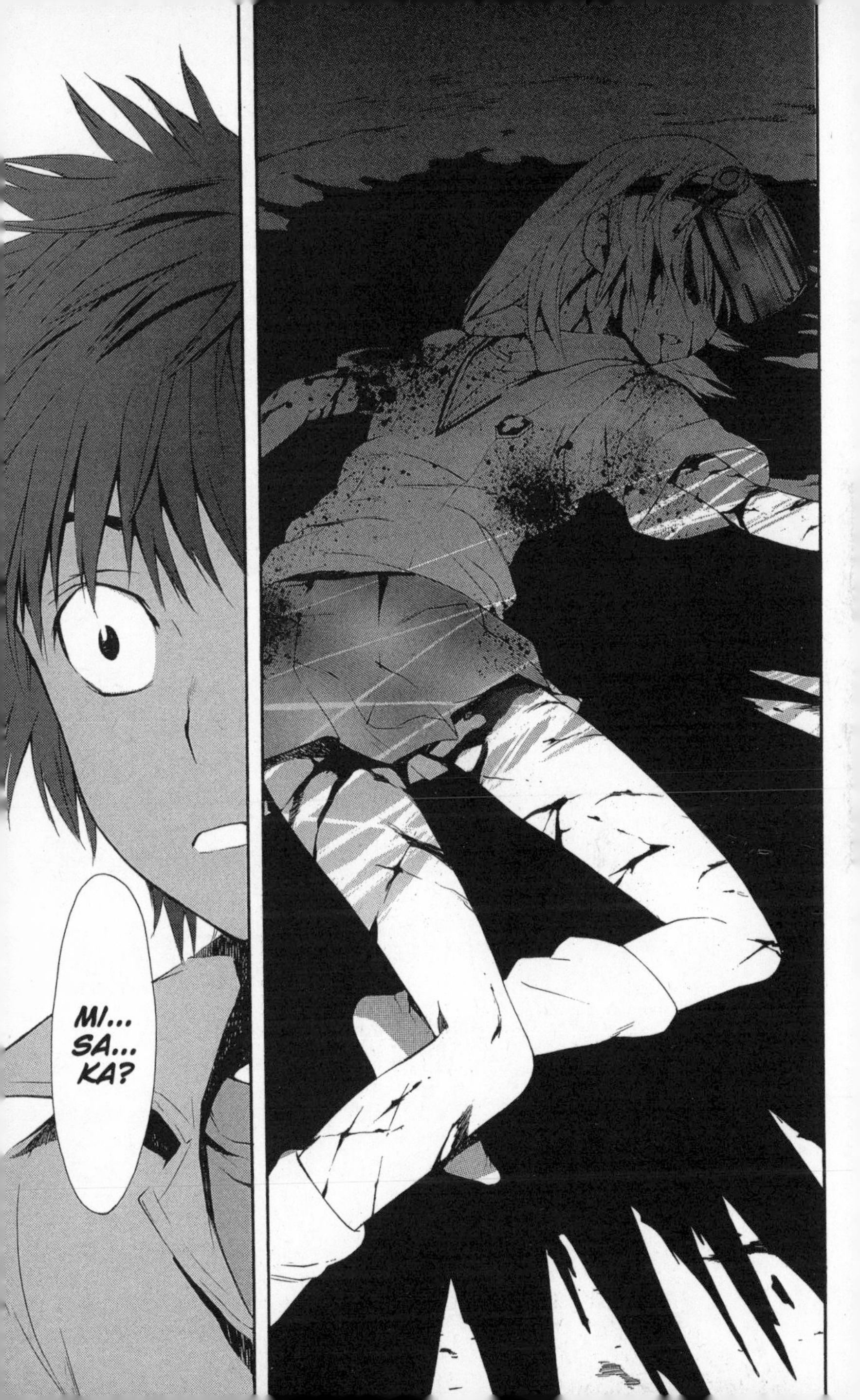
MI... SA... KA?

A Certain Magical Index

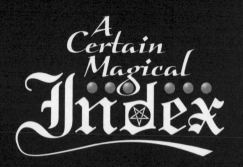

#14 SISTERS

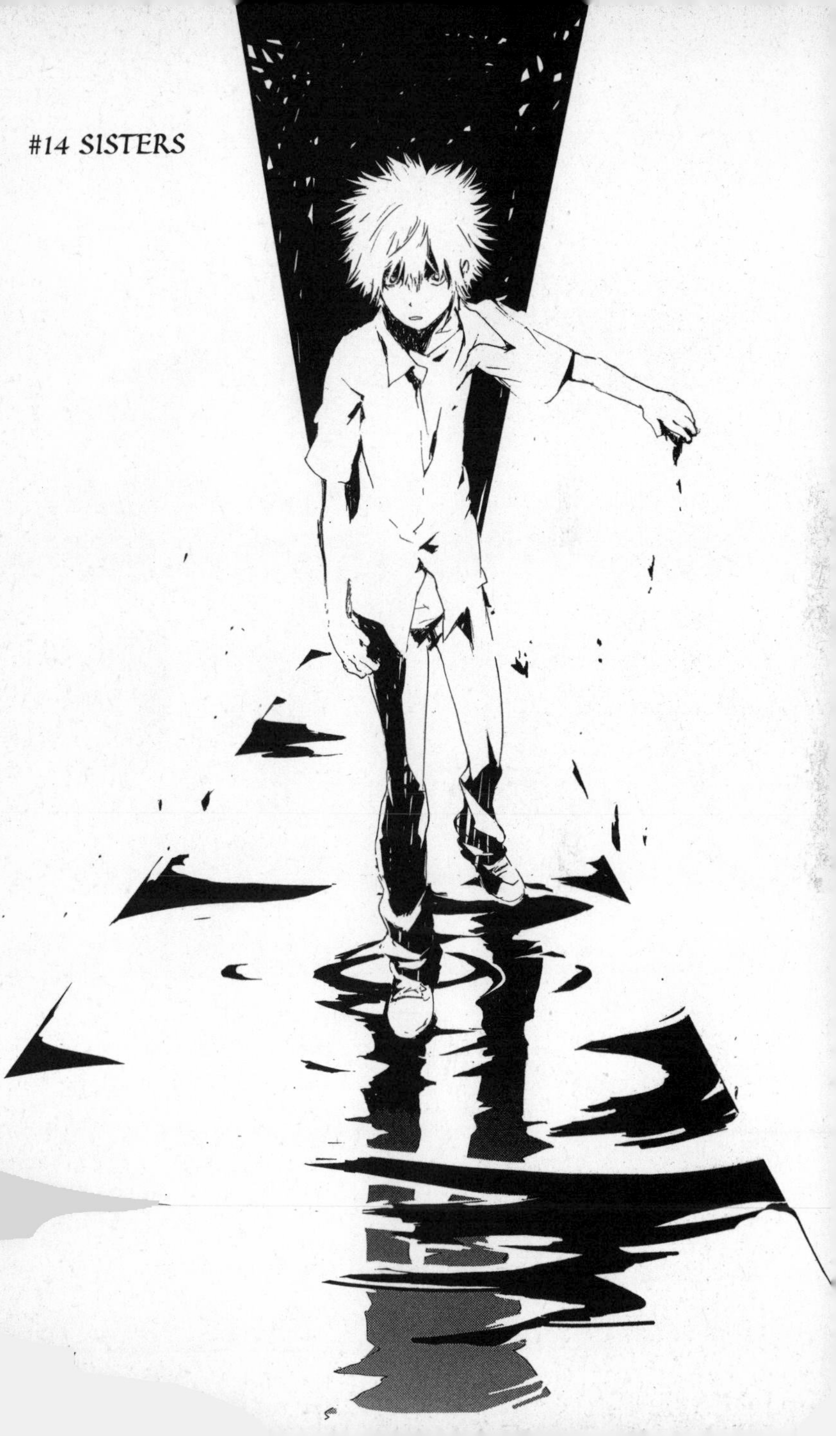

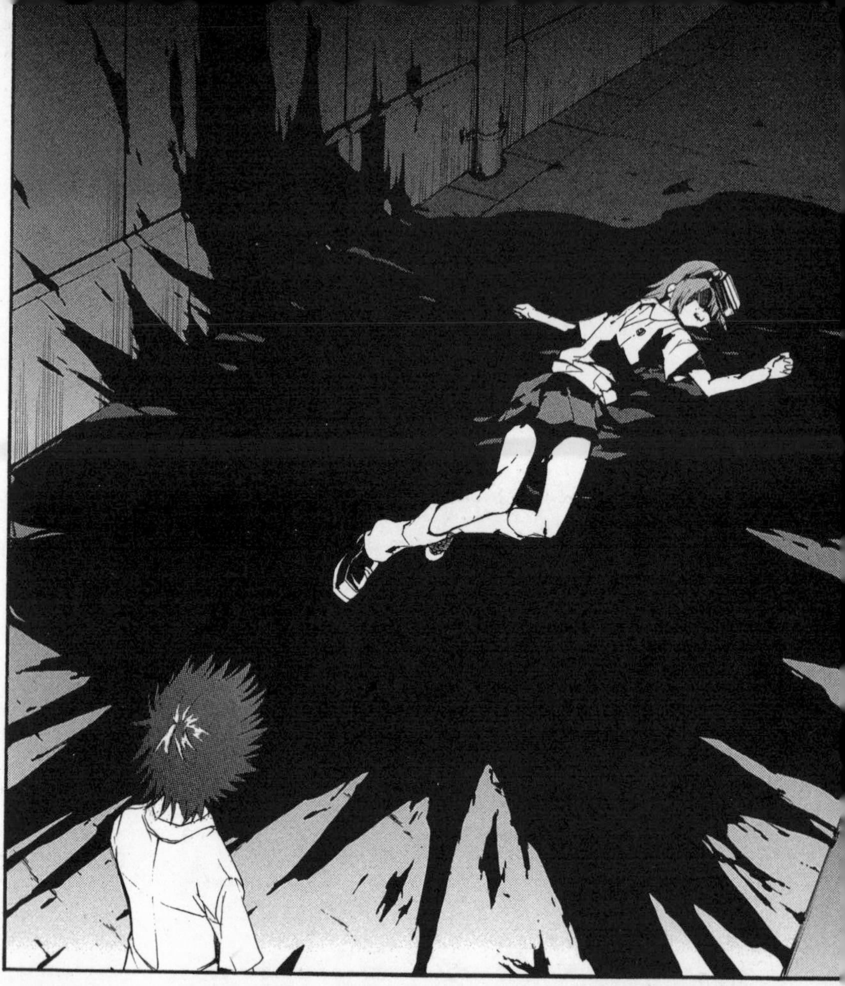

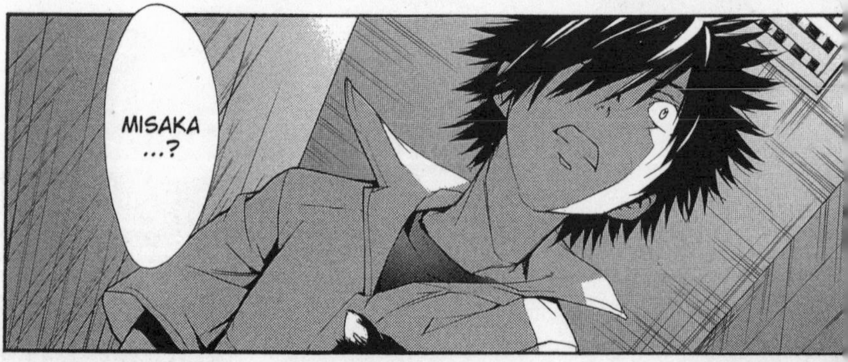
MISAKA
...?

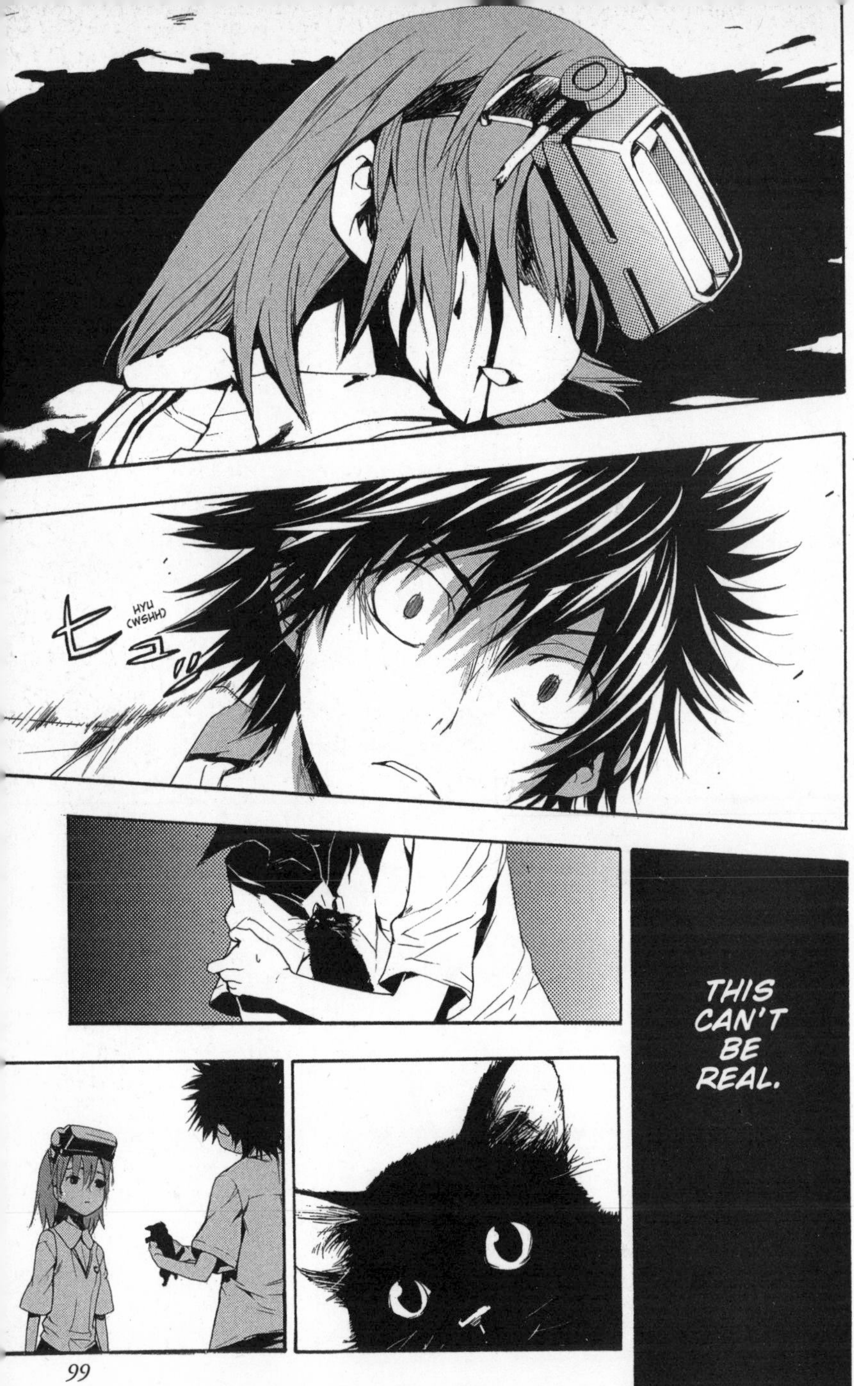
HYU (WSHH)
THIS CAN'T BE REAL.

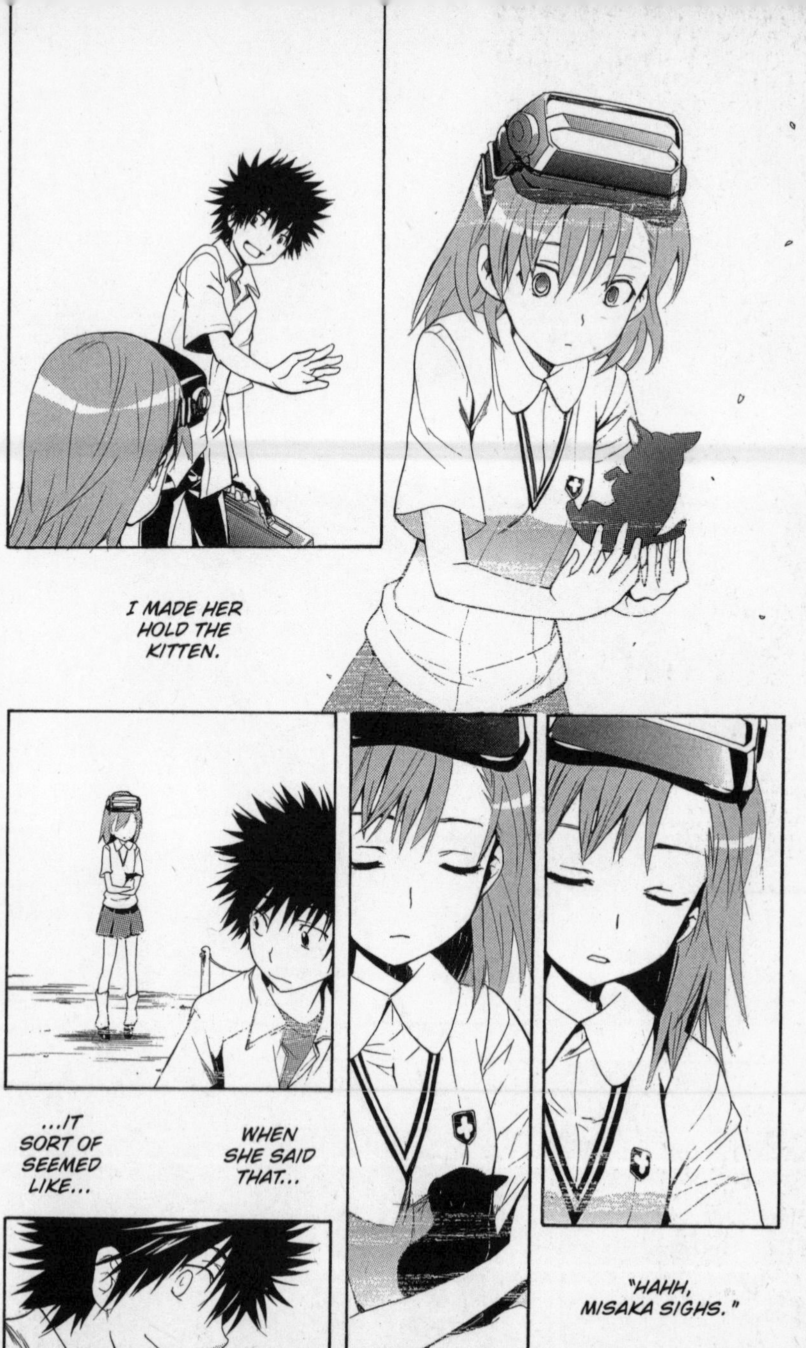
I MADE HER HOLD THE KITTEN.
"HAHH, MISAKA SIGHS."
WHEN SHE SAID THAT...
...IT SORT OF SEEMED LIKE...

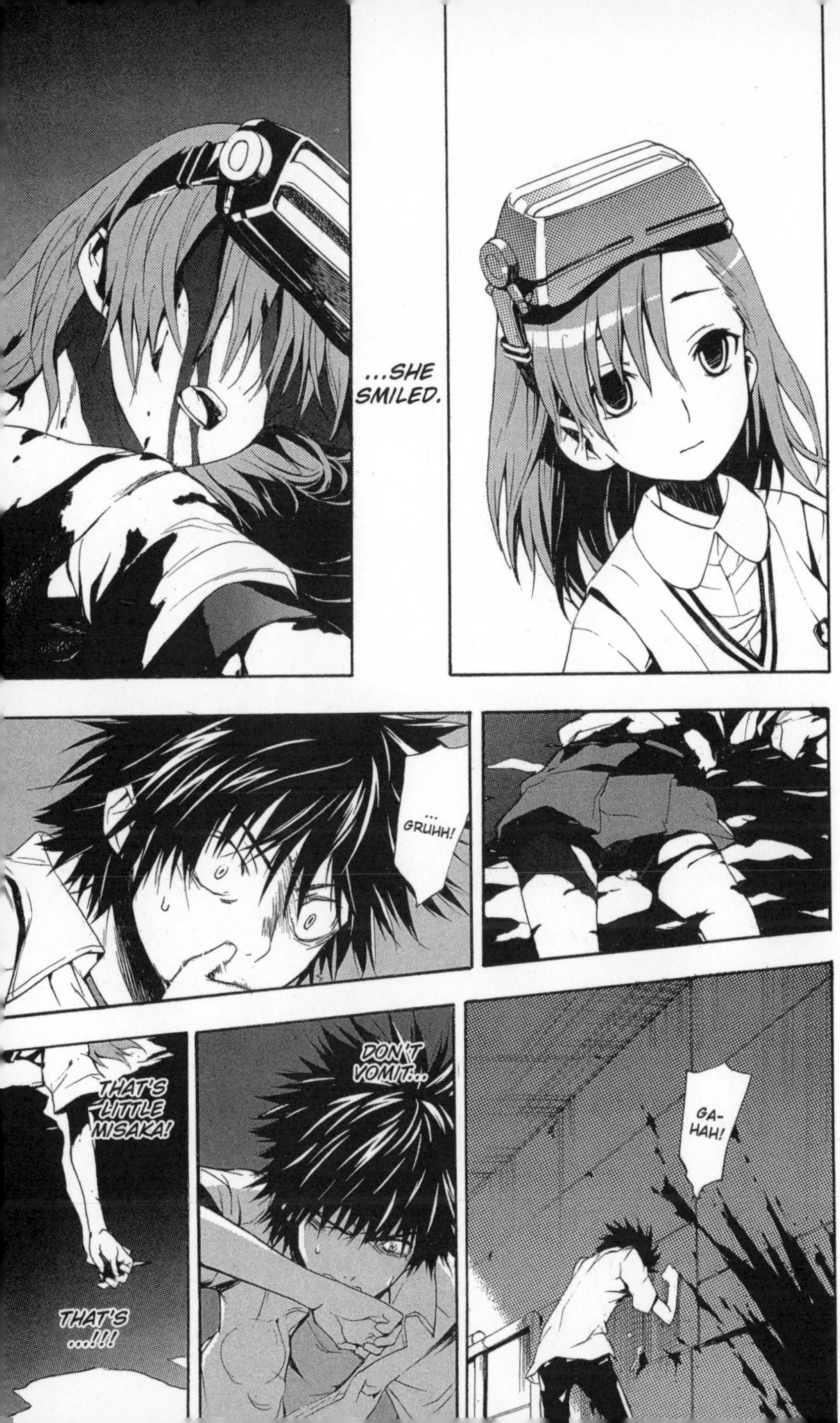
...SHE SMILED.
... GRUHH!
GA-HAH!
DON'T VOMIT...
THAT'S LITTLE MISAKA!
THAT'S ...!!!

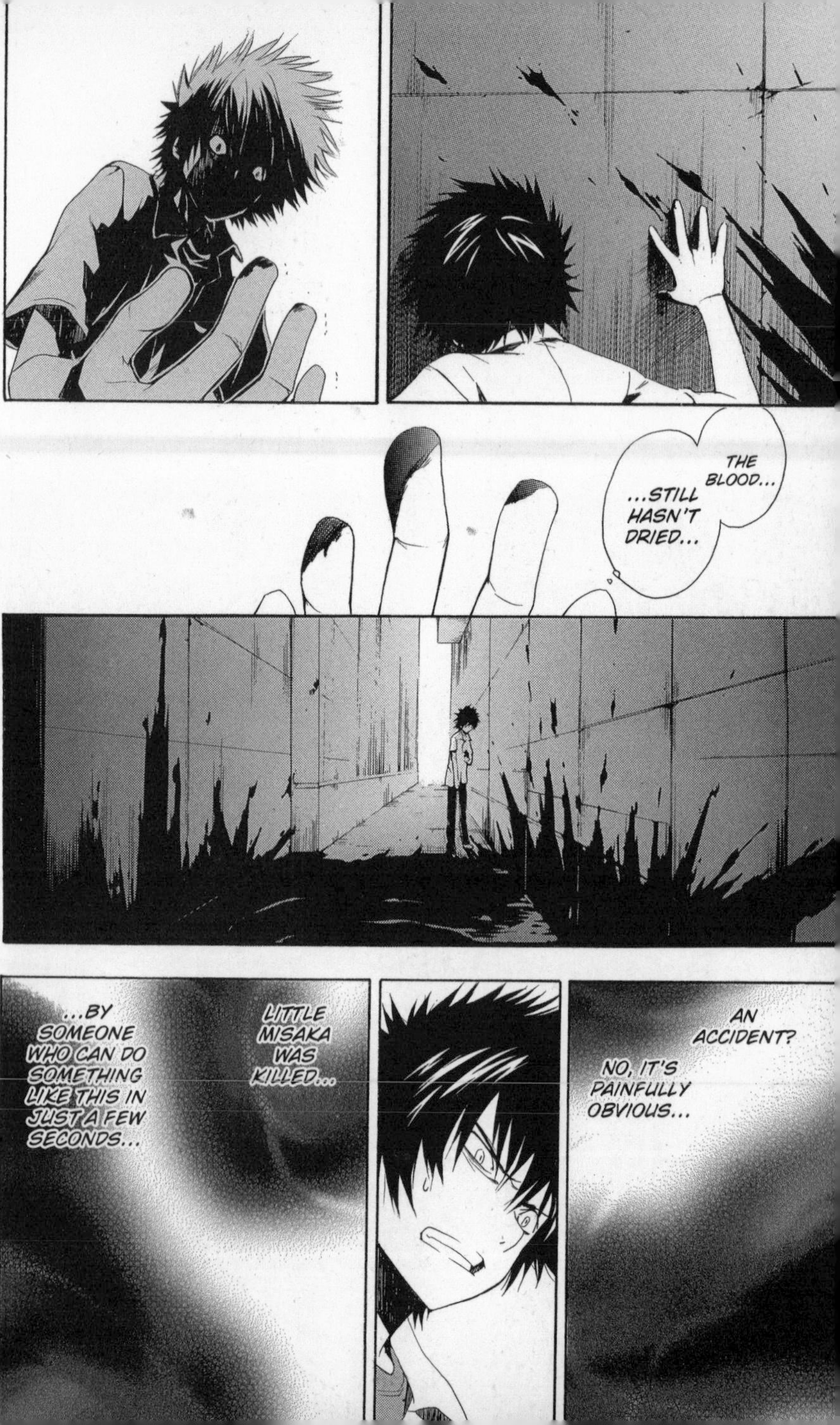
THE BLOOD... ...STILL HASN'T DRIED...
AN ACCIDENT?
NO, IT'S PAINFULLY OBVIOUS...
LITTLE MISAKA WAS KILLED...
...BY SOMEONE WHO CAN DO SOMETHING LIKE THIS IN JUST A FEW SECONDS...

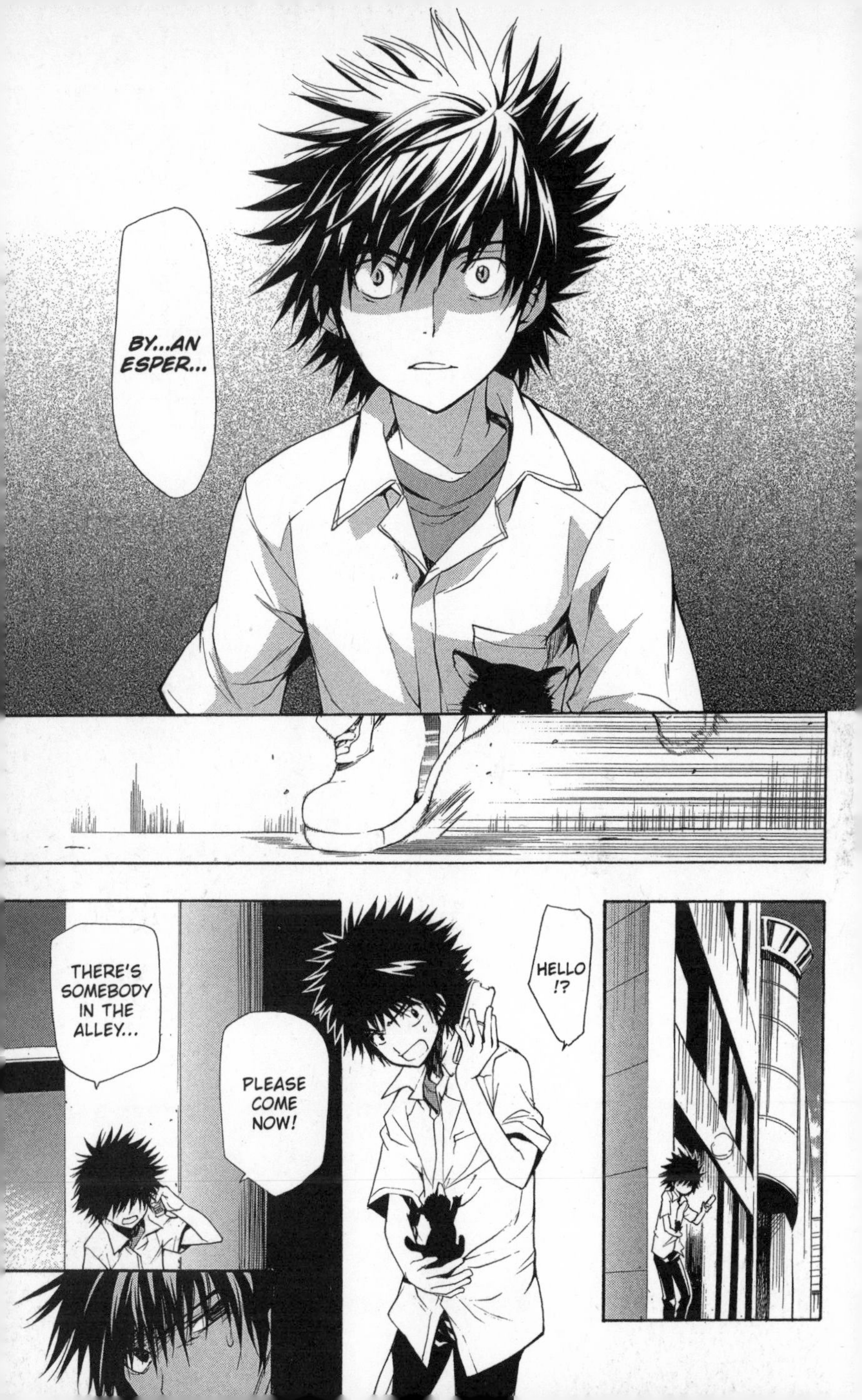
BY...AN ESPER...
HELLO !?
PLEASE COME NOW!
THERE'S SOMEBODY IN THE ALLEY...

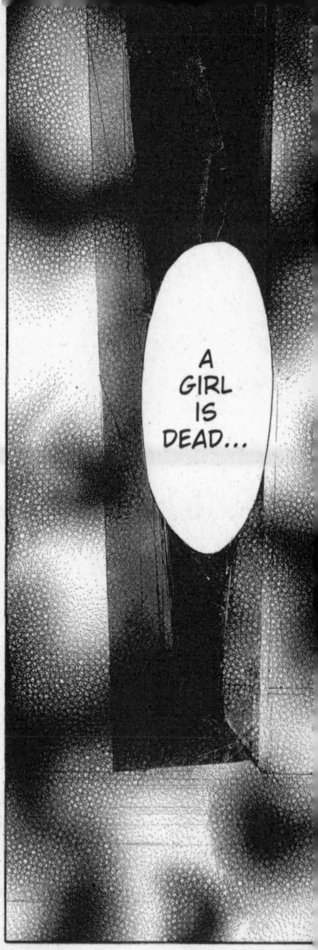
A GIRL IS DEAD...
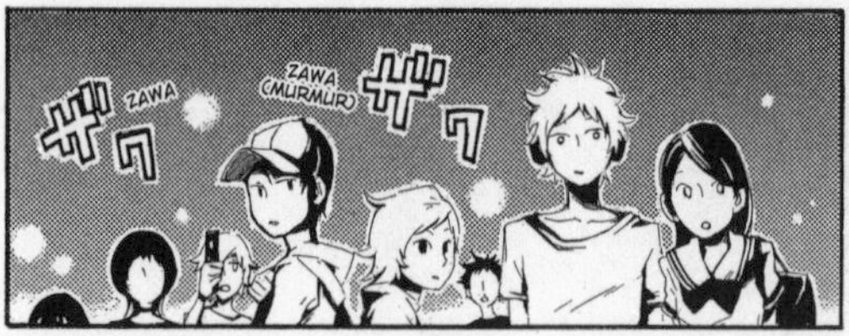
ZAWA (MURMUR)
ZAWA
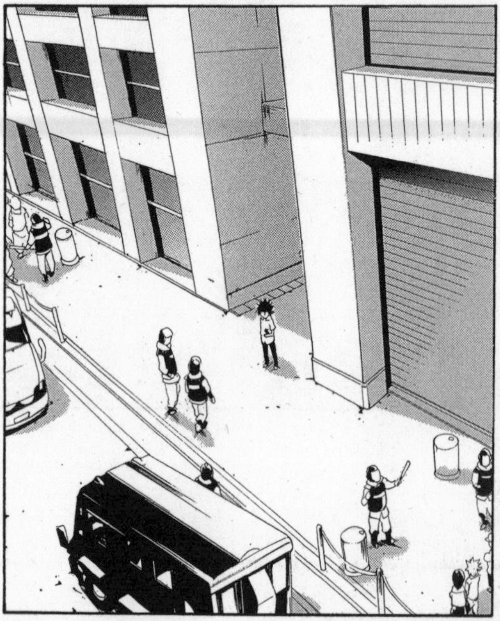
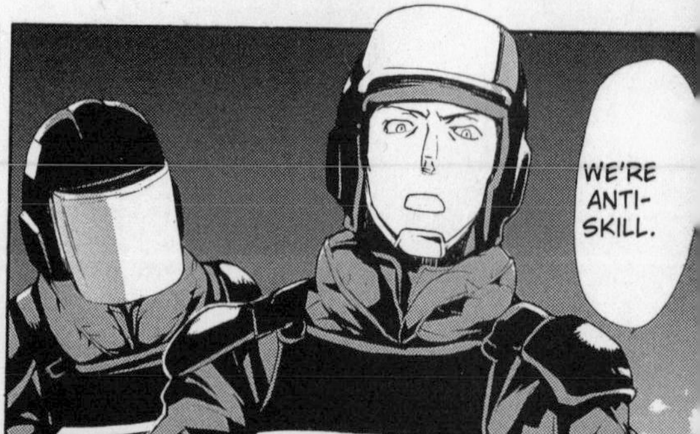
WE'RE ANTI-SKILL.
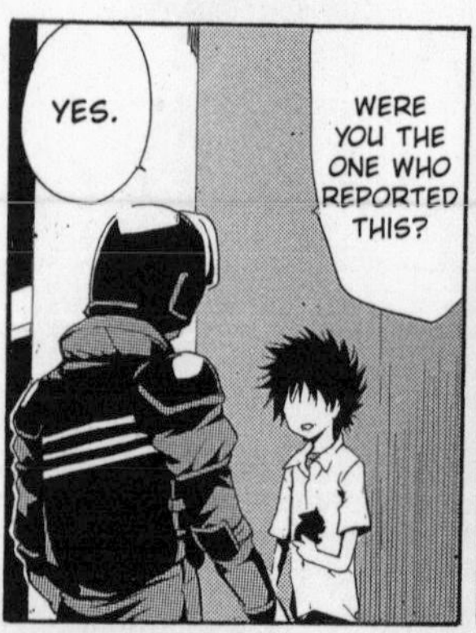
WERE YOU THE ONE WHO REPORTED THIS?
YES.

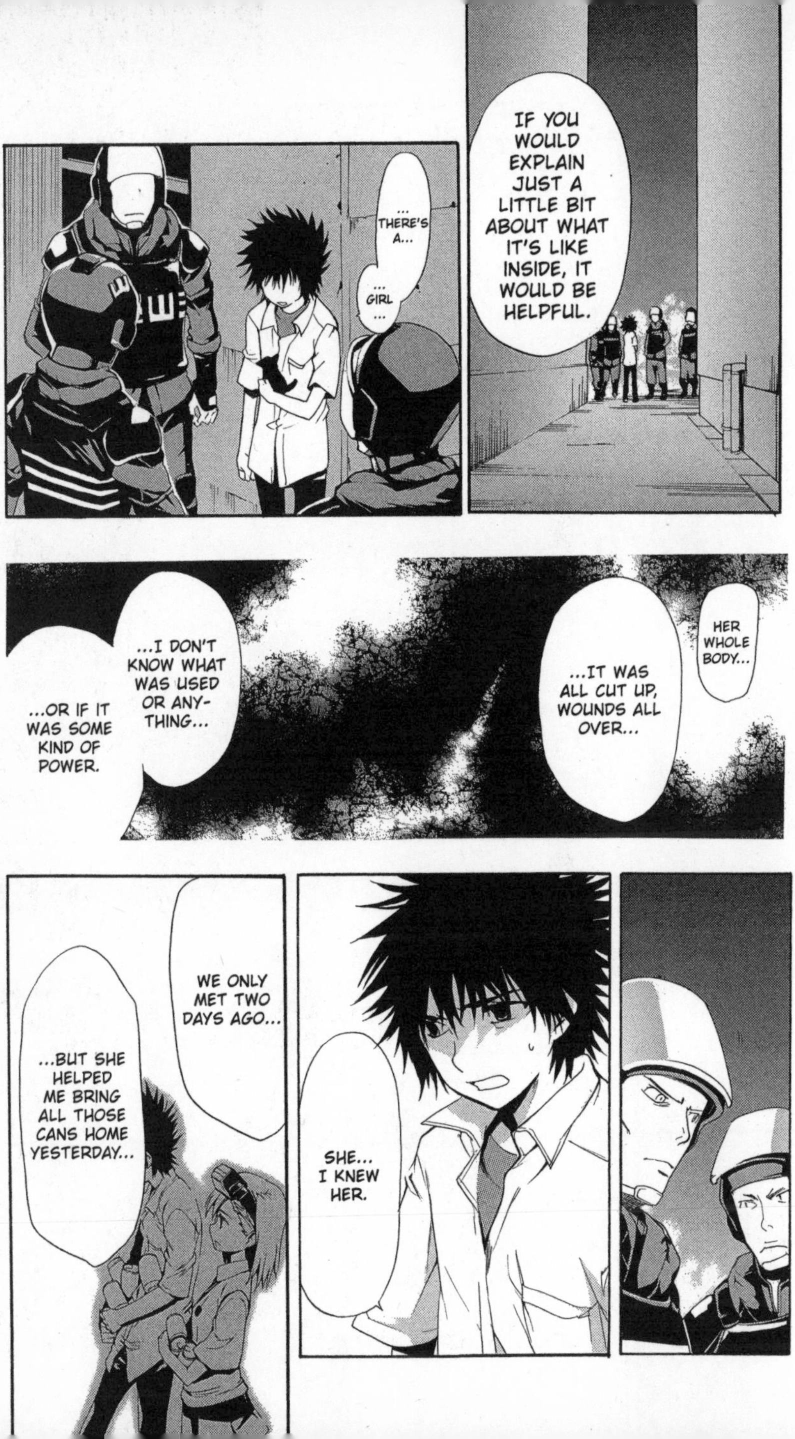
IF YOU WOULD EXPLAIN JUST A LITTLE BIT ABOUT WHAT IT'S LIKE INSIDE, IT WOULD BE HELPFUL.
...THERE'S A...
...GIRL...
HER WHOLE BODY...
...IT WAS ALL CUT UP, WOUNDS ALL OVER...
...I DON'T KNOW WHAT WAS USED OR ANY-THING...
...OR IF IT WAS SOME KIND OF POWER.
SHE... I KNEW HER.
WE ONLY MET TWO DAYS AGO...
...BUT SHE HELPED ME BRING ALL THOSE CANS HOME YESTERDAY...

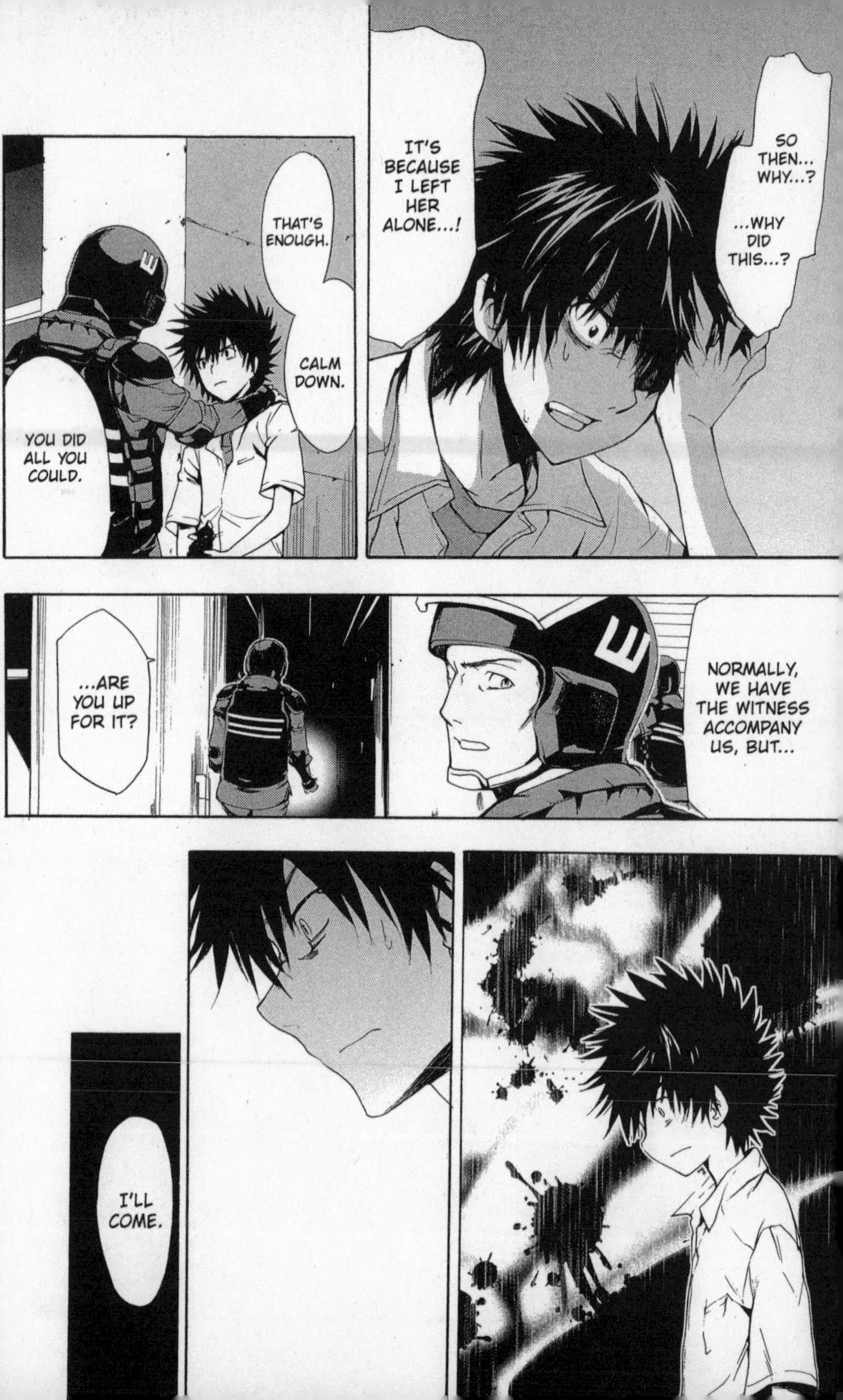
SO THEN... WHY...?
...WHY DID THIS...?
IT'S BECAUSE I LEFT HER ALONE...!
THAT'S ENOUGH.
CALM DOWN.
YOU DID ALL YOU COULD.
NORMALLY, WE HAVE THE WITNESS ACCOMPANY US, BUT...
...ARE YOU UP FOR IT?
I'LL COME.

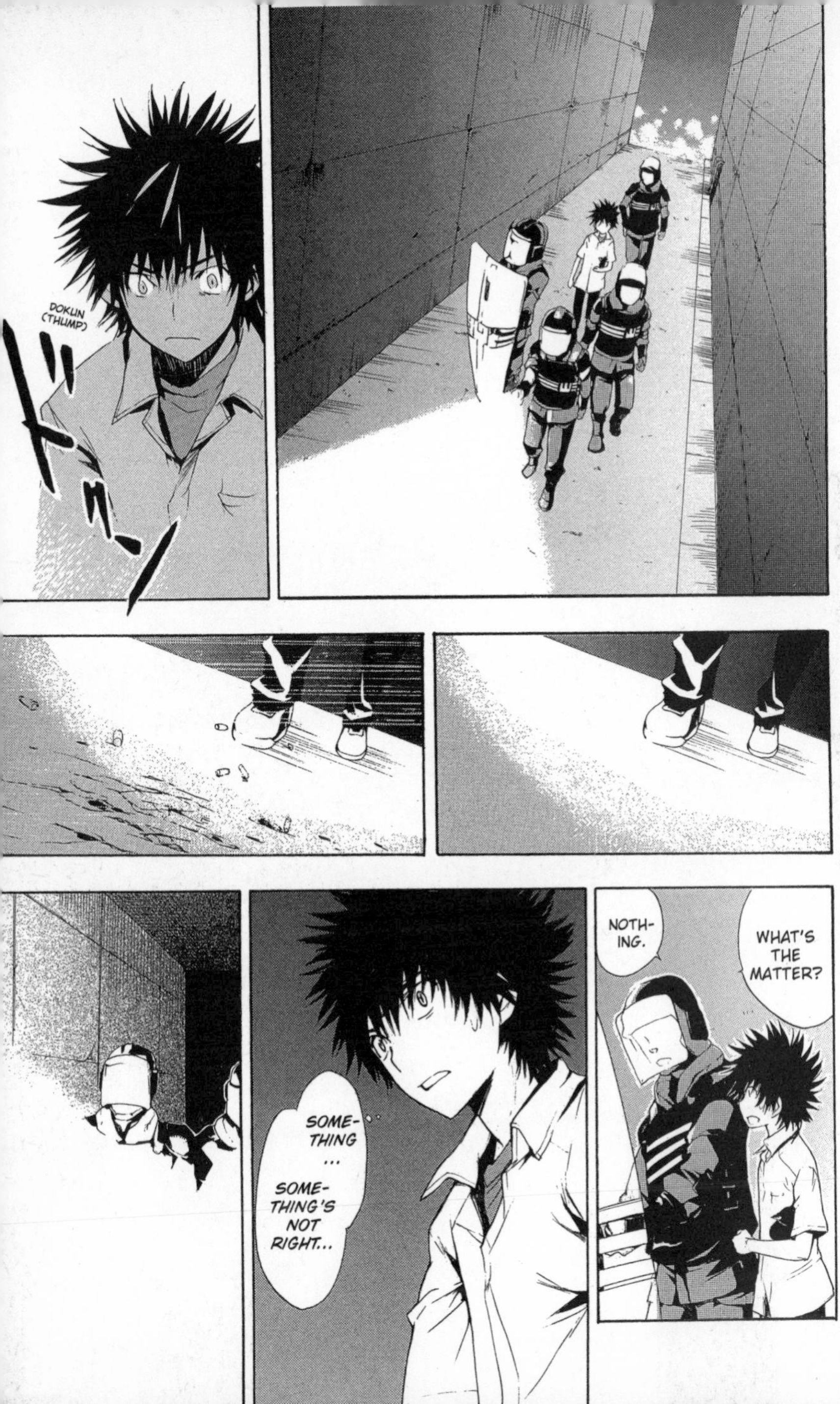
DOKUN (THUMP)
WHAT'S THE MATTER?
NOTH-ING.
SOME-THING... SOME-THING'S NOT RIGHT...

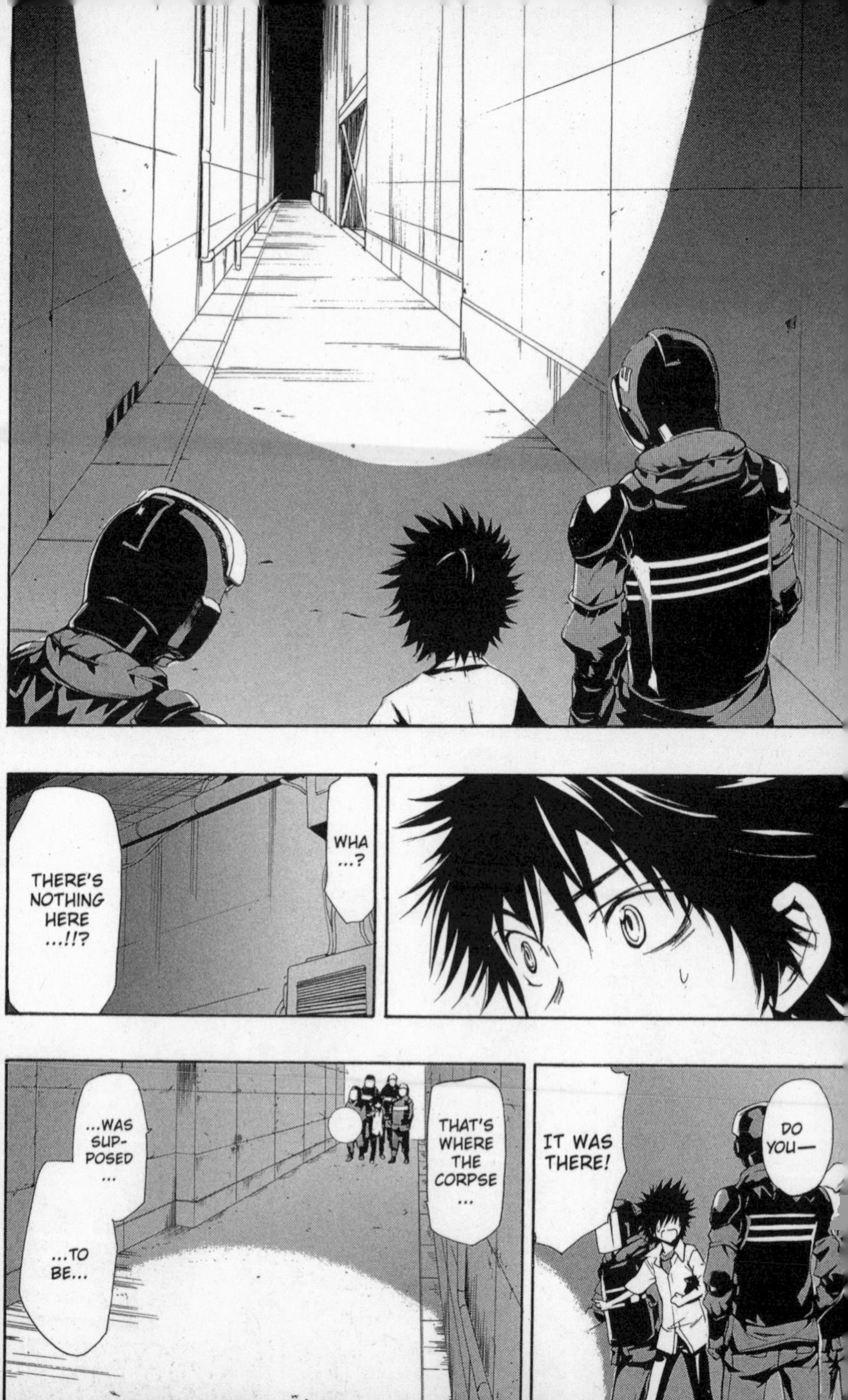
WHA...?
THERE'S NOTHING HERE...!!?
DO YOU—
IT WAS THERE!
THAT'S WHERE THE CORPSE...
...WAS SUP-POSED...
...TO BE...

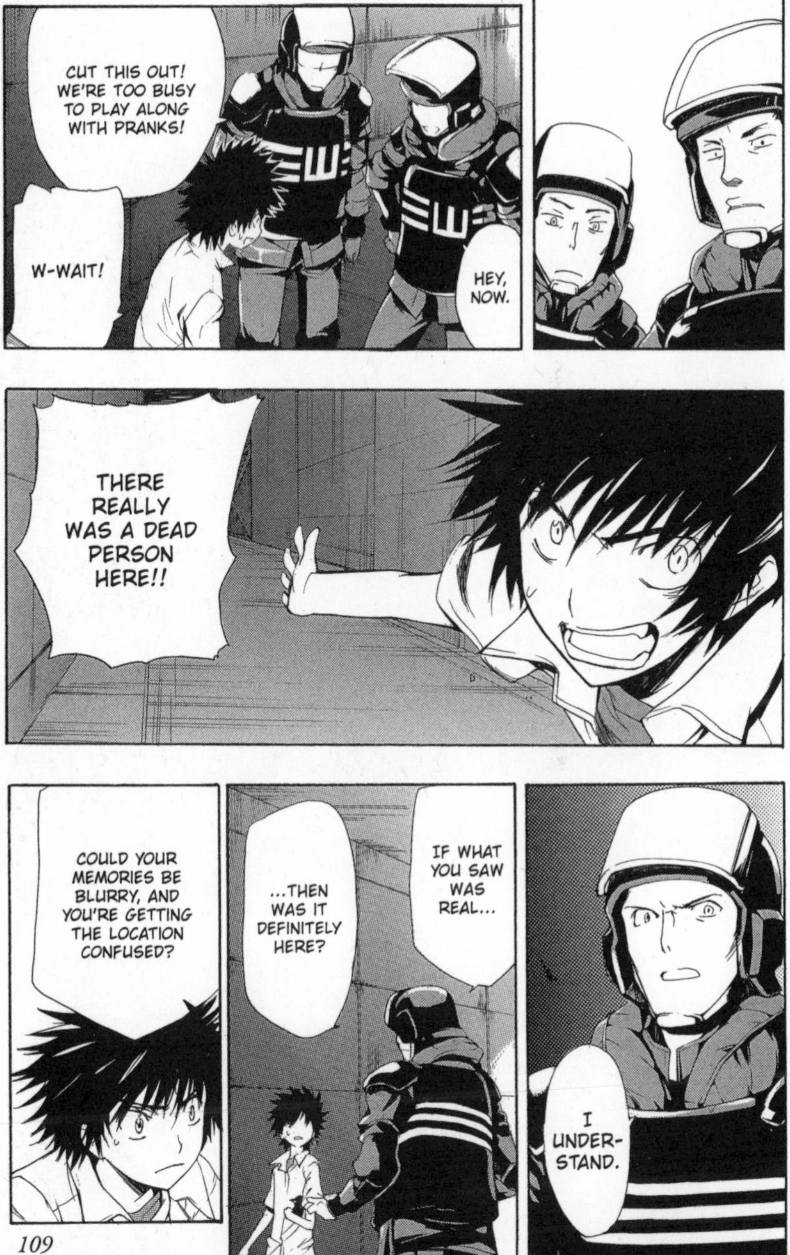
HEY, NOW.
CUT THIS OUT! WE'RE TOO BUSY TO PLAY ALONG WITH PRANKS!
W-WAIT!
THERE REALLY WAS A DEAD PERSON HERE!!
I UNDER-STAND.
IF WHAT YOU SAW WAS REAL...
...THEN WAS IT DEFINITELY HERE?
COULD YOUR MEMORIES BE BLURRY, AND YOU'RE GETTING THE LOCATION CONFUSED?

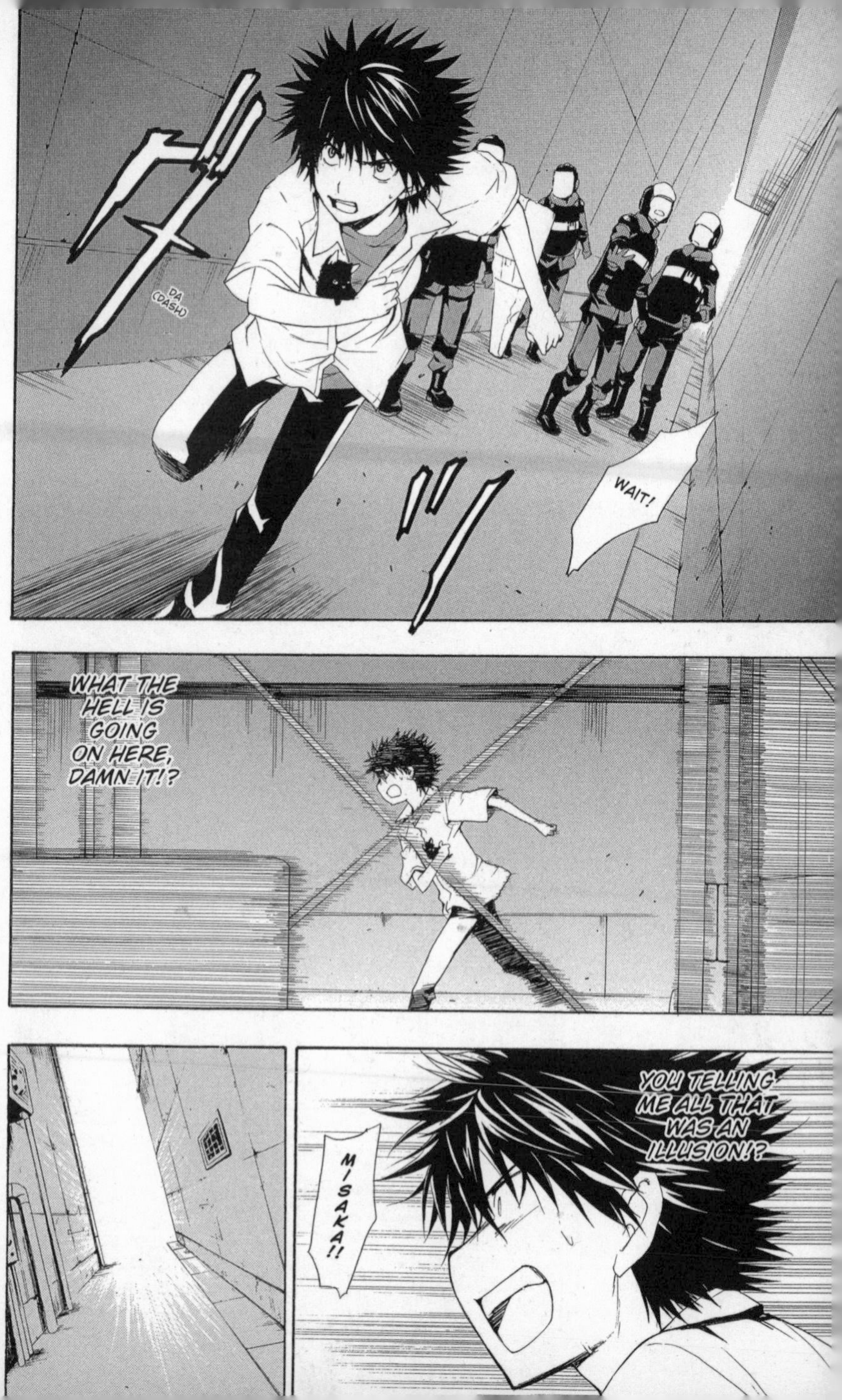
WAIT!
DA (DASH)
WHAT THE HELL IS GOING ON HERE, DAMN IT!?
YOU TELLING ME ALL THAT WAS AN ILLUSION!?
MISAKA!!

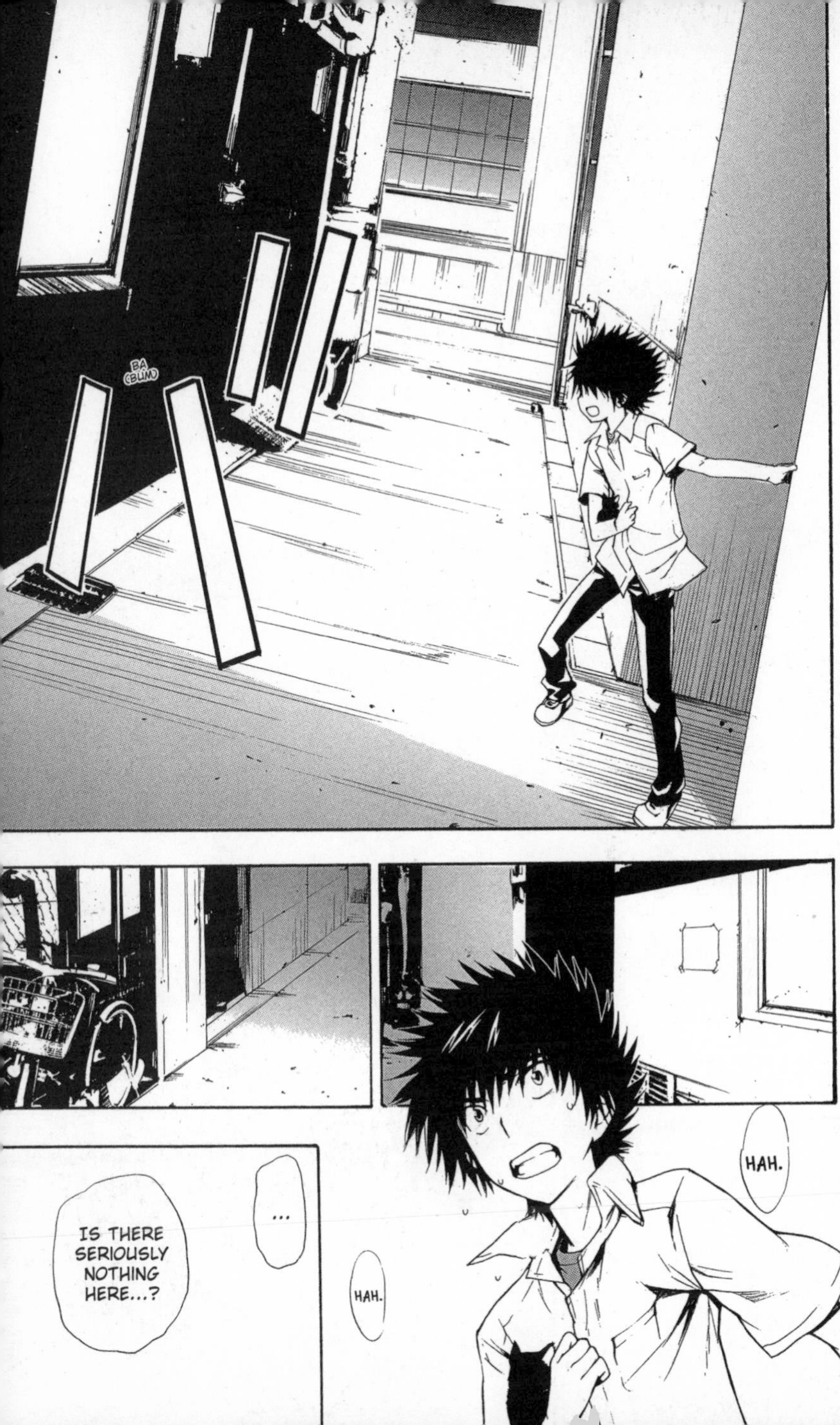
BA
(BUM)
HAH.
HAH.
...
IS THERE SERIOUSLY NOTHING HERE...?

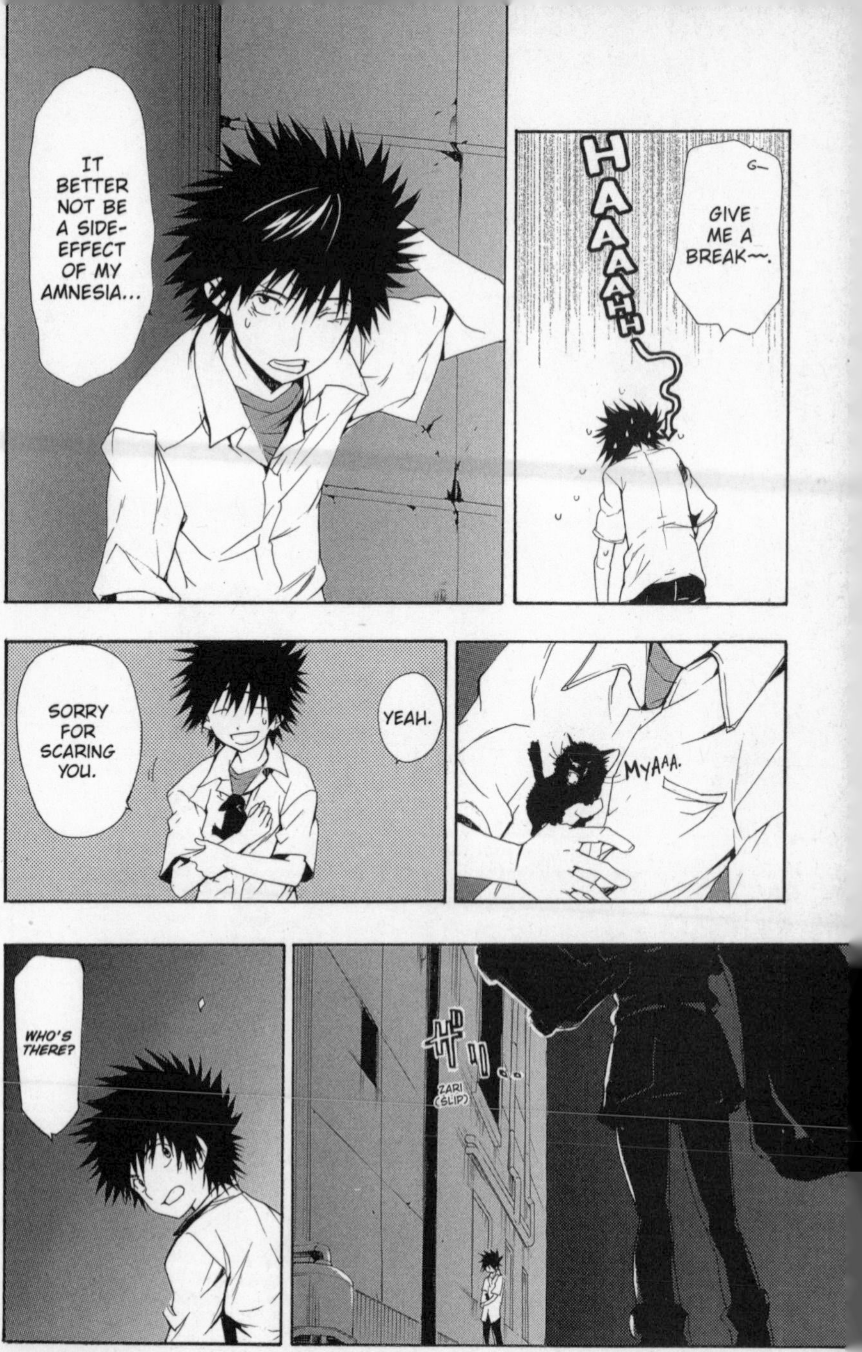
G—
GIVE ME A BREAK~~.
HAAAAH
IT BETTER NOT BE A SIDE-EFFECT OF MY AMNESIA...
MYAAA.
YEAH.
SORRY FOR SCARING YOU.
ザリ..
ZARI (SLIP)
WHO'S THERE?

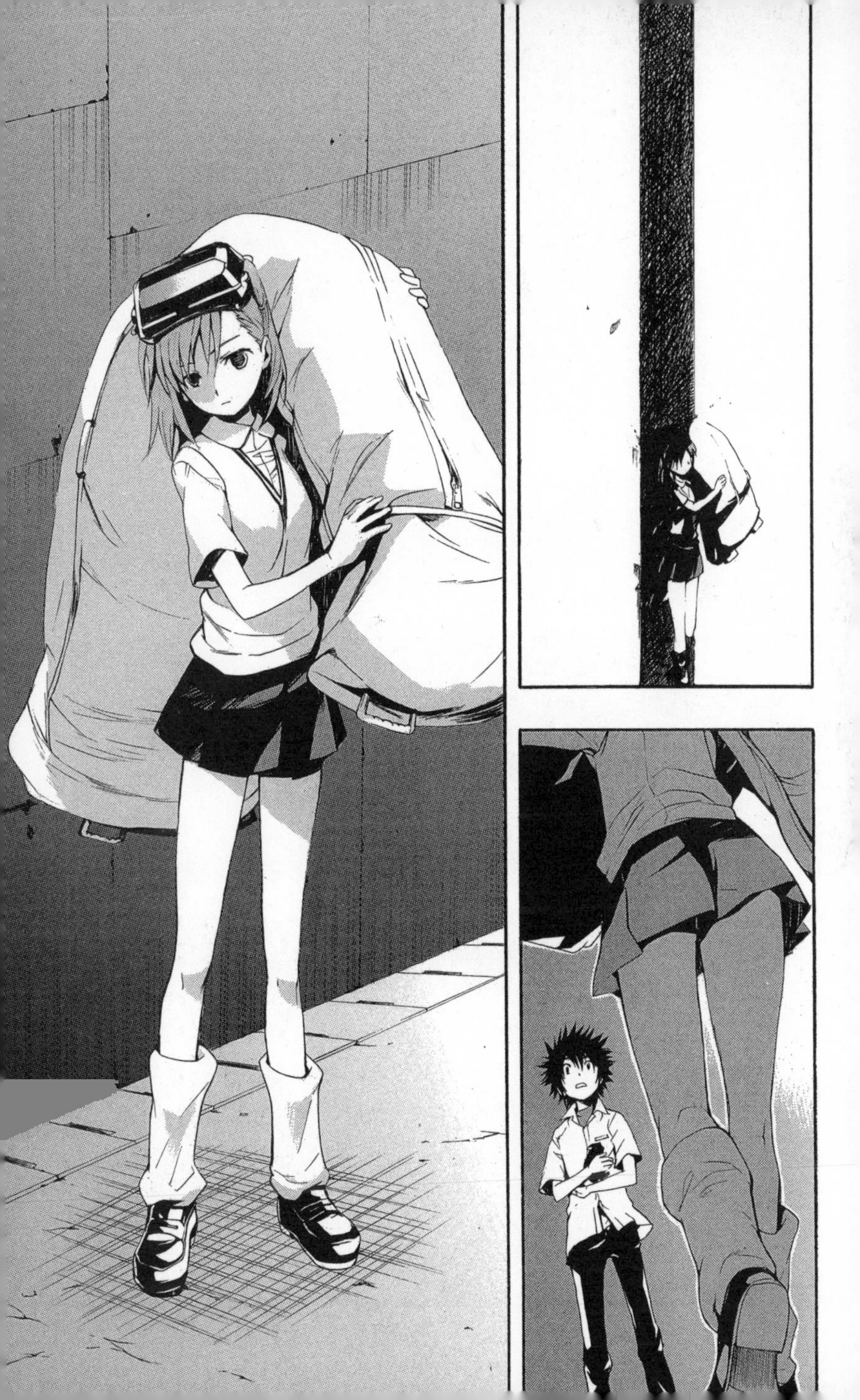

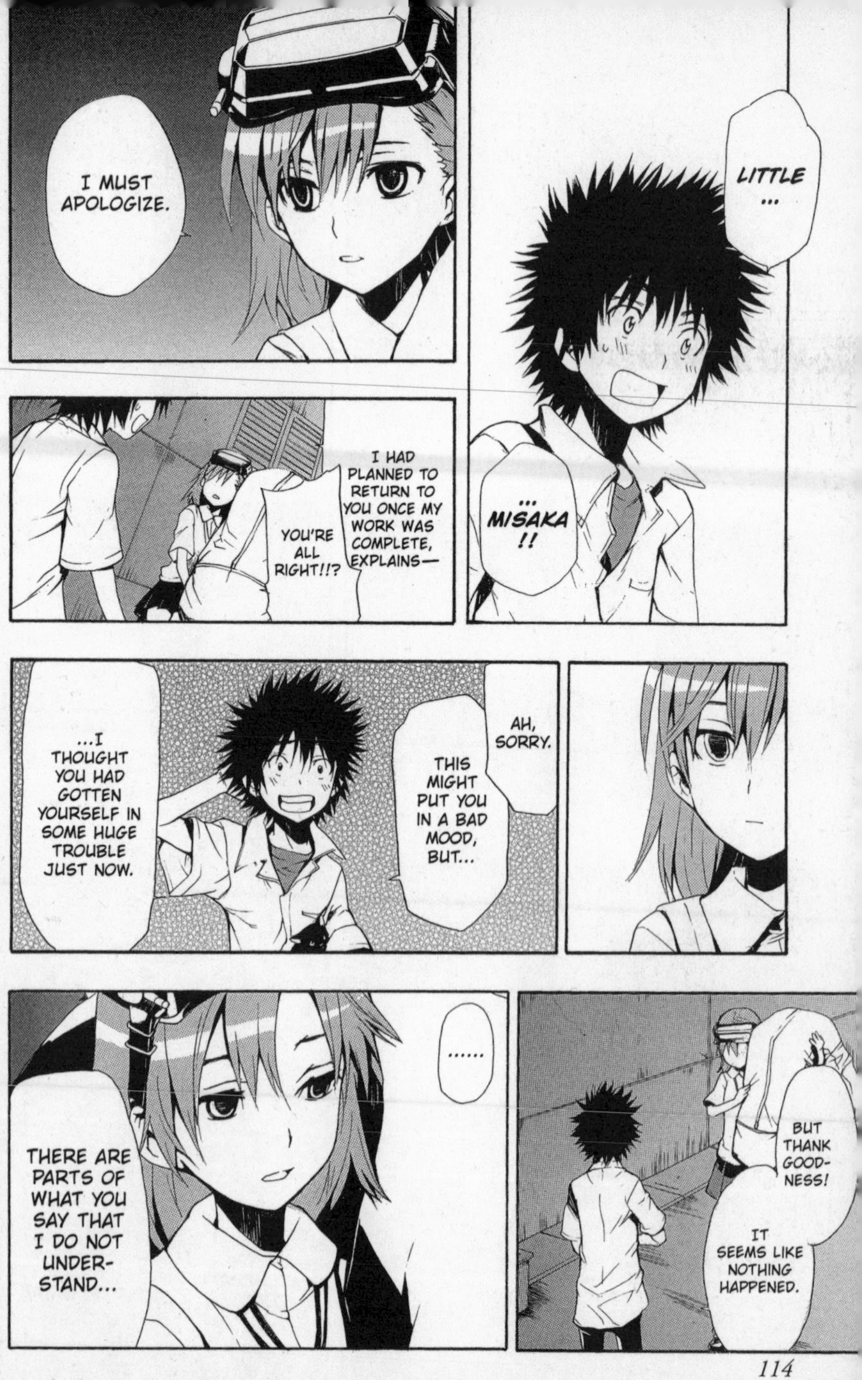
LITTLE ...
... MISAKA !!
I MUST APOLOGIZE.
I HAD PLANNED TO RETURN TO YOU ONCE MY WORK WAS COMPLETE, EXPLAINS—
YOU'RE ALL RIGHT!!?
AH, SORRY.
THIS MIGHT PUT YOU IN A BAD MOOD, BUT...
...I THOUGHT YOU HAD GOTTEN YOURSELF IN SOME HUGE TROUBLE JUST NOW.
BUT THANK GOOD-NESS!
IT SEEMS LIKE NOTHING HAPPENED.
......
THERE ARE PARTS OF WHAT YOU SAY THAT I DO NOT UNDER-STAND...

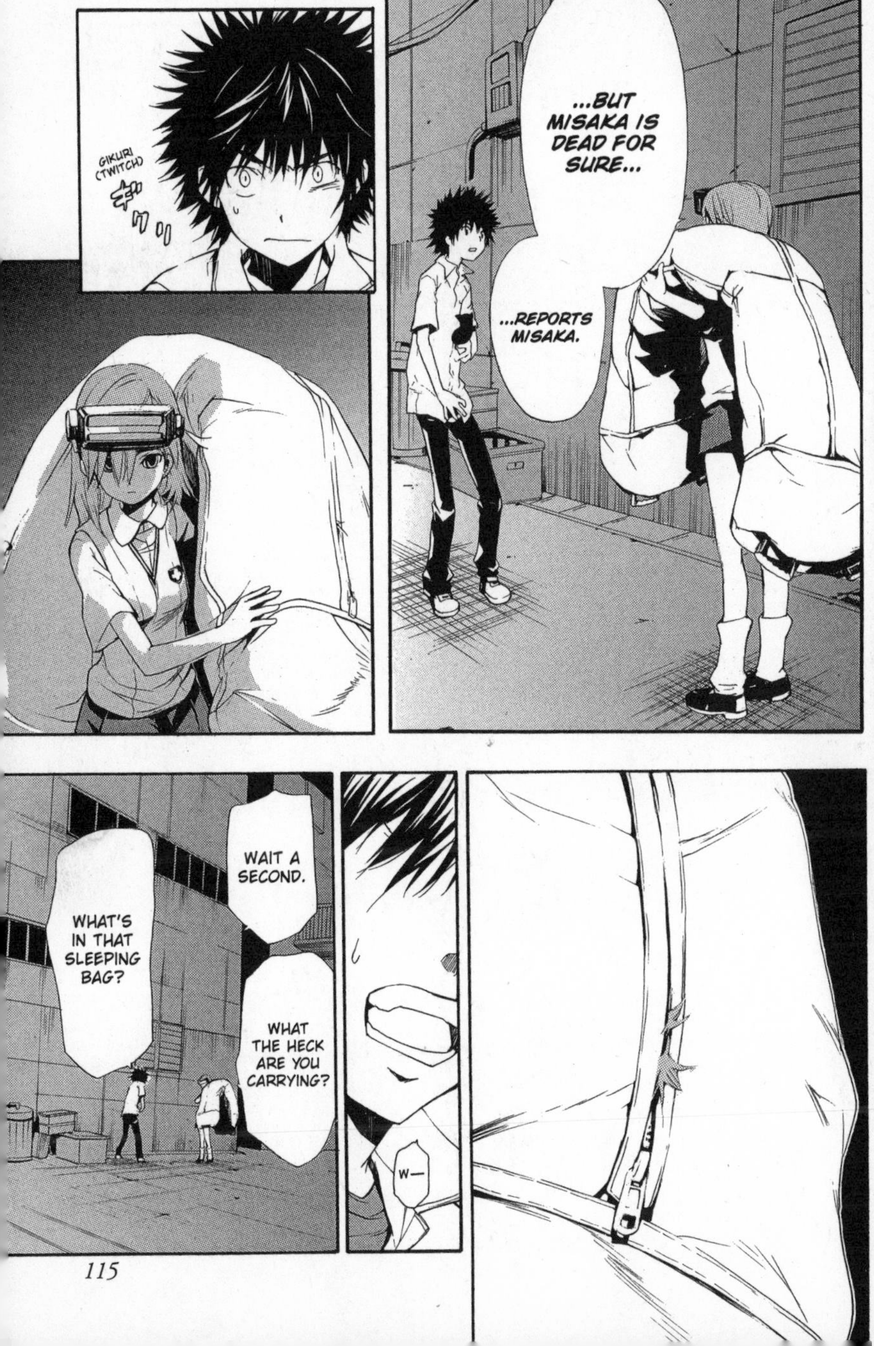
...BUT MISAKA IS DEAD FOR SURE...
...REPORTS MISAKA.
GIKURI (TWITCH)
WAIT A SECOND.
WHAT'S IN THAT SLEEPING BAG?
WHAT THE HECK ARE YOU CARRYING?
W—

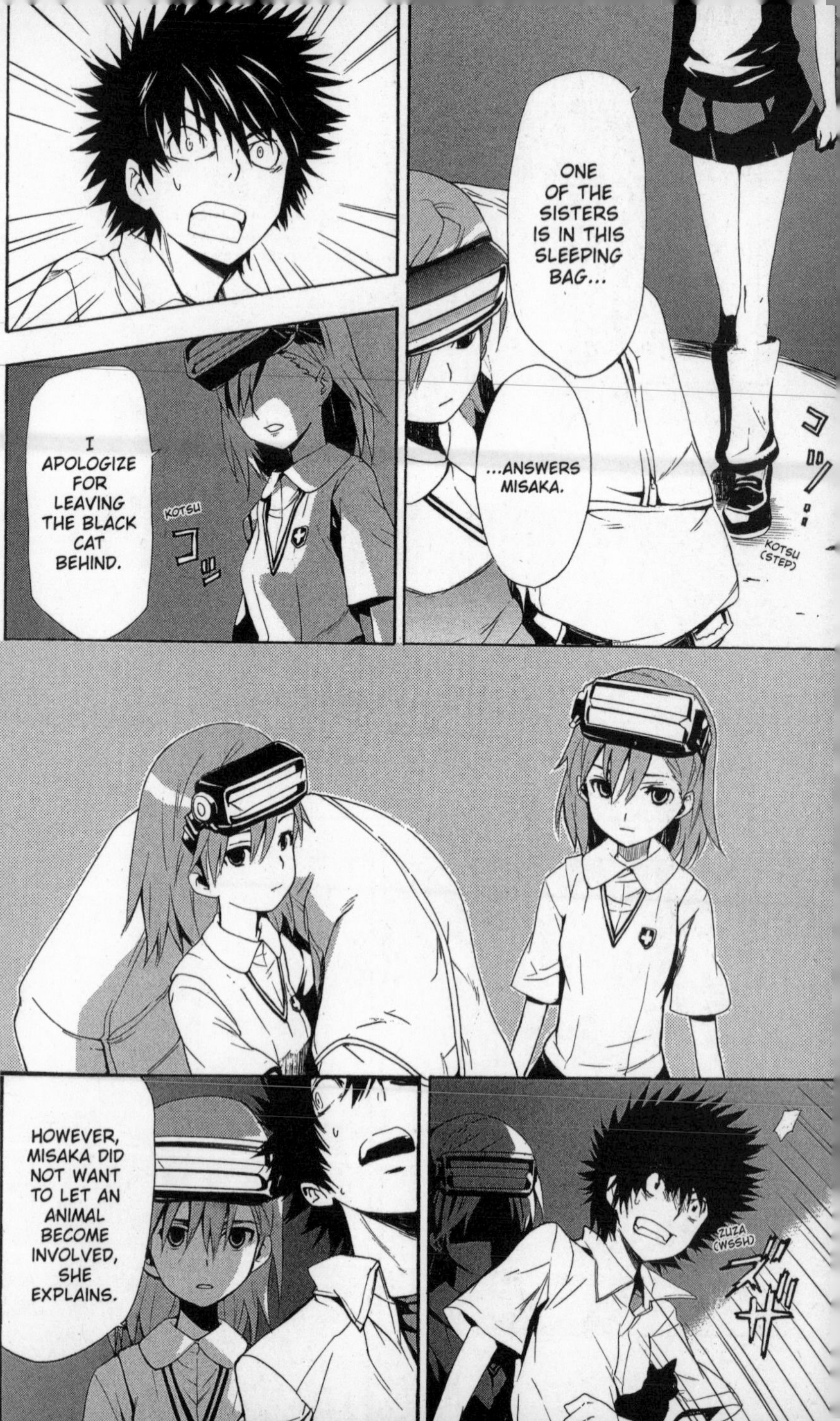
ONE OF THE SISTERS IS IN THIS SLEEPING BAG...
...ANSWERS MISAKA.
KOTSU (STEP)
I APOLOGIZE FOR LEAVING THE BLACK CAT BEHIND.
KOTSU
ZUZA (WSSH)
HOWEVER, MISAKA DID NOT WANT TO LET AN ANIMAL BECOME INVOLVED, SHE EXPLAINS.

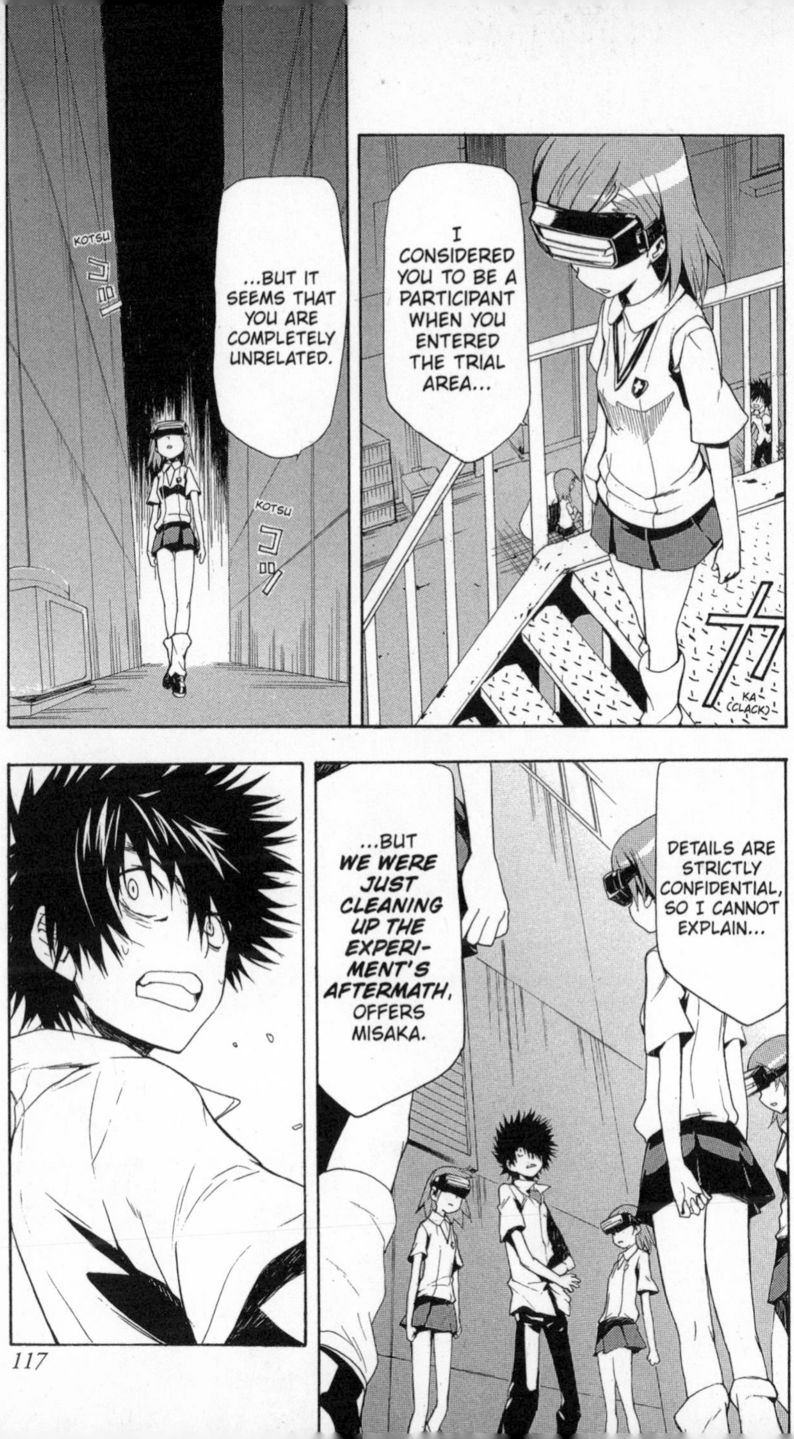

I CONSIDERED YOU TO BE A PARTICIPANT WHEN YOU ENTERED THE TRIAL AREA...
KA (CLACK)
...BUT IT SEEMS THAT YOU ARE COMPLETELY UNRELATED.
KOTSU
KOTSU
DETAILS ARE STRICTLY CONFIDENTIAL, SO I CANNOT EXPLAIN...
...BUT ***WE WERE JUST CLEANING UP THE EXPERIMENT'S AFTERMATH,*** OFFERS MISAKA.

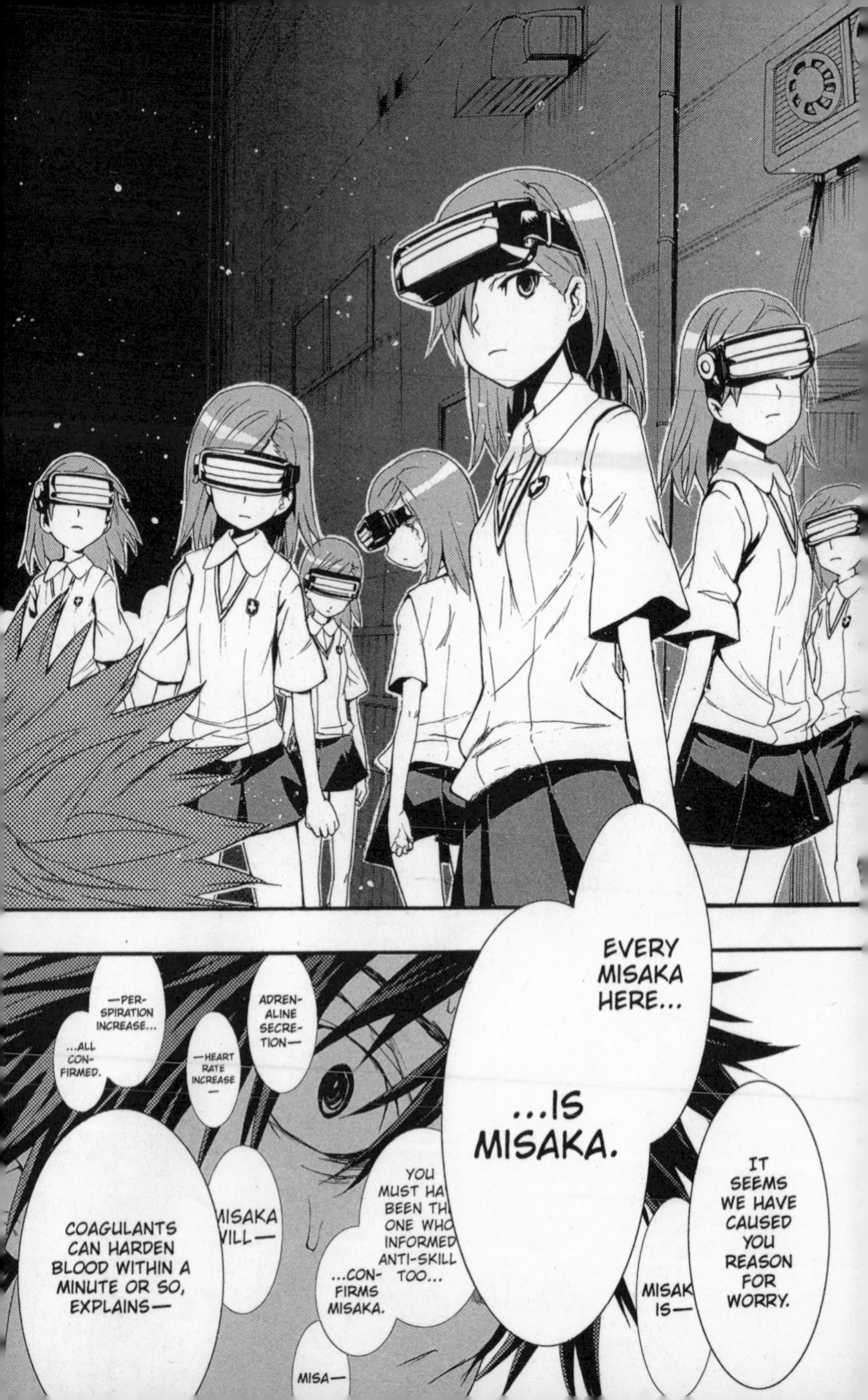
EVERY MISAKA HERE...
...IS MISAKA.
IT SEEMS WE HAVE CAUSED YOU REASON FOR WORRY.
MISAK IS—
ADREN-ALINE SECRE-TION—
YOU MUST HAV BEEN TH ONE WHO INFORMED ANTI-SKILL TOO...
...CON-FIRMS MISAKA.
—HEART RATE INCREASE—
—PER-SPIRATION INCREASE...
...ALL CON-FIRMED.
MISAKA WILL—
COAGULANTS CAN HARDEN BLOOD WITHIN A MINUTE OR SO, EXPLAINS—
MISA—

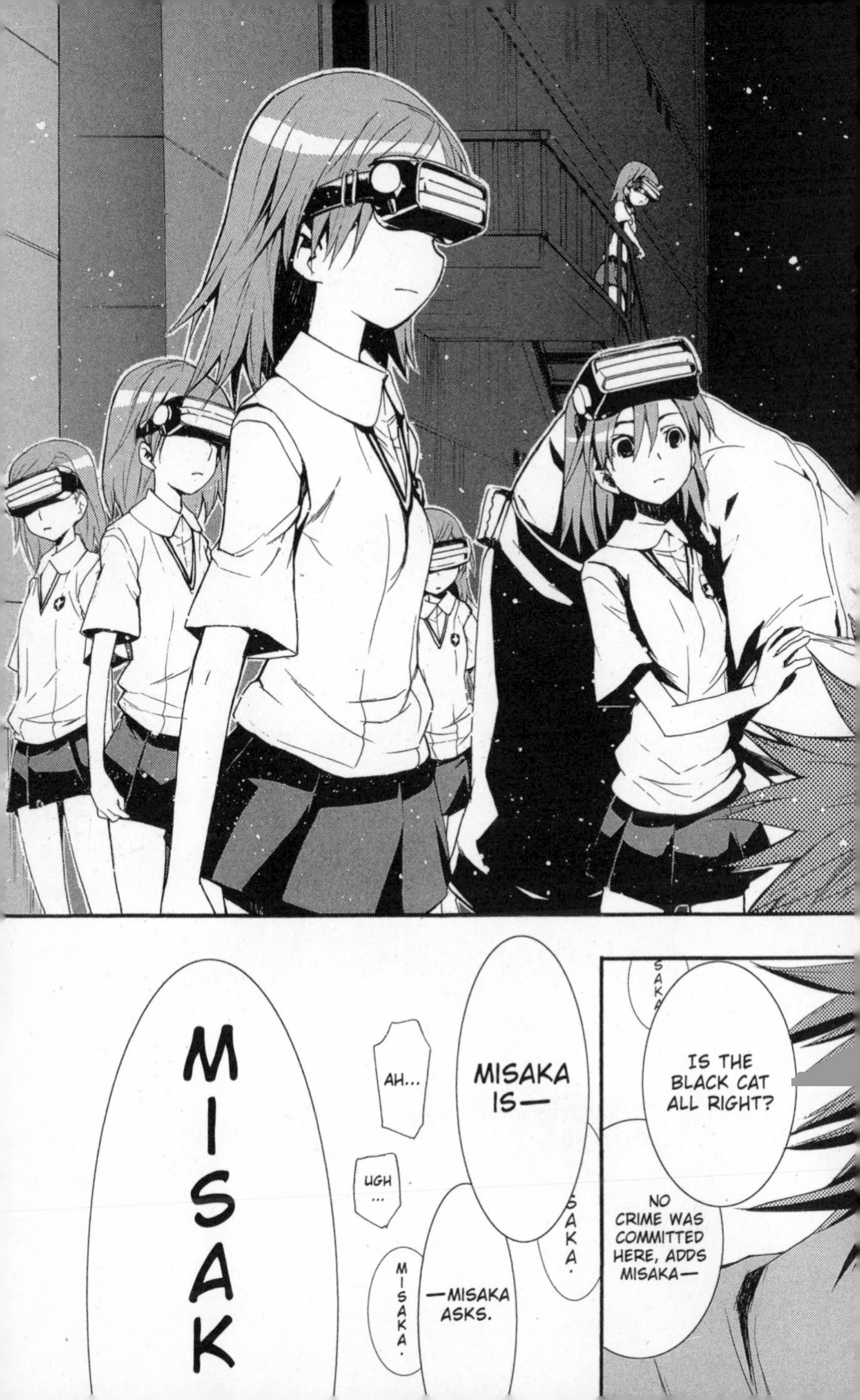
IS THE BLACK CAT ALL RIGHT?
NO CRIME WAS COMMITTED HERE, ADDS MISAKA—
MISAKA IS—
SAKA.
AH...
UGH...
—MISAKA ASKS.
MISAKA.
MISAK

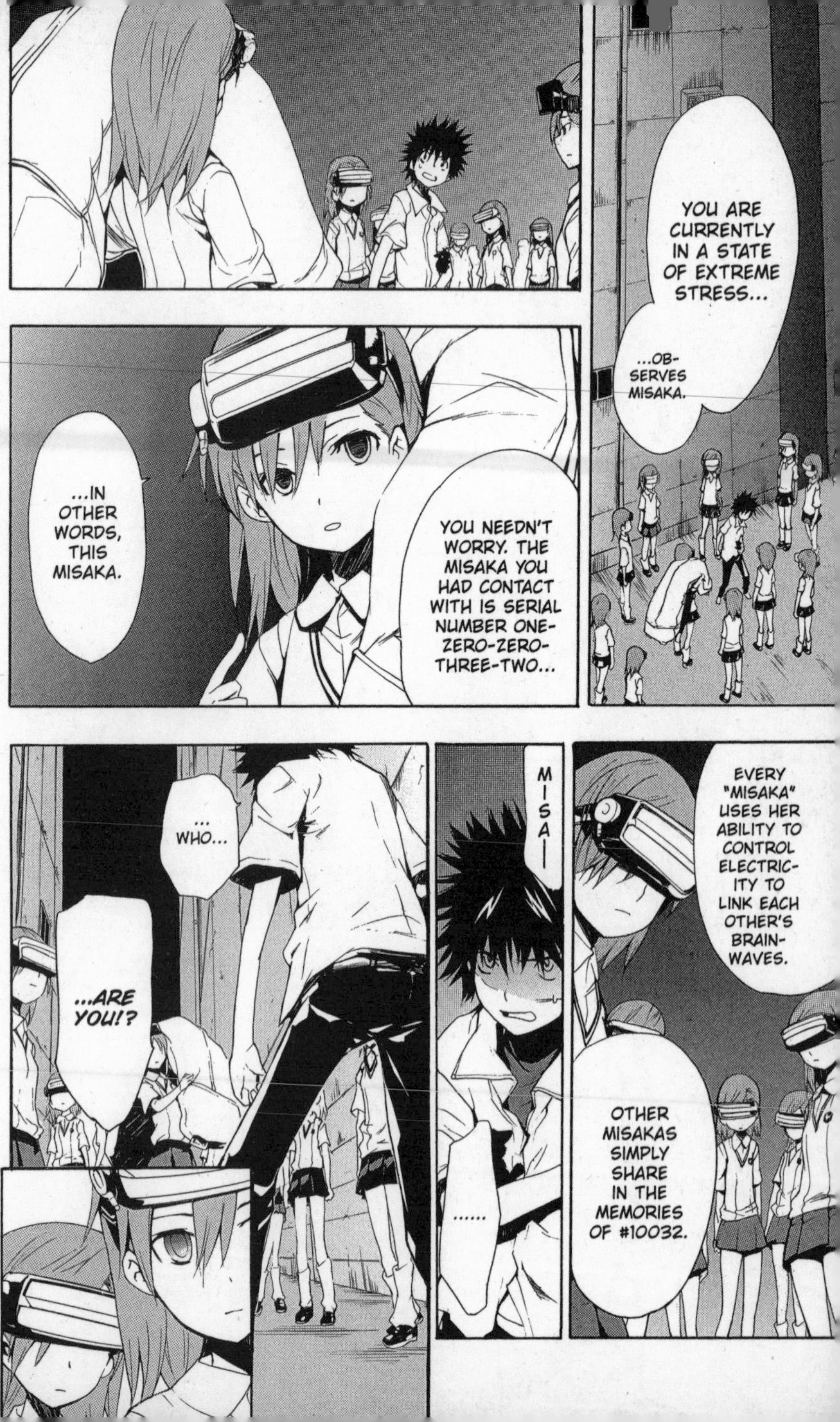
YOU ARE CURRENTLY IN A STATE OF EXTREME STRESS...
...OB-SERVES MISAKA.
YOU NEEDN'T WORRY. THE MISAKA YOU HAD CONTACT WITH IS SERIAL NUMBER ONE-ZERO-ZERO-THREE-TWO...
...IN OTHER WORDS, THIS MISAKA.
EVERY "MISAKA" USES HER ABILITY TO CONTROL ELECTRICITY TO LINK EACH OTHER'S BRAINWAVES.
OTHER MISAKAS SIMPLY SHARE IN THE MEMORIES OF #10032.
MISA—
......
... WHO...
...ARE YOU!?

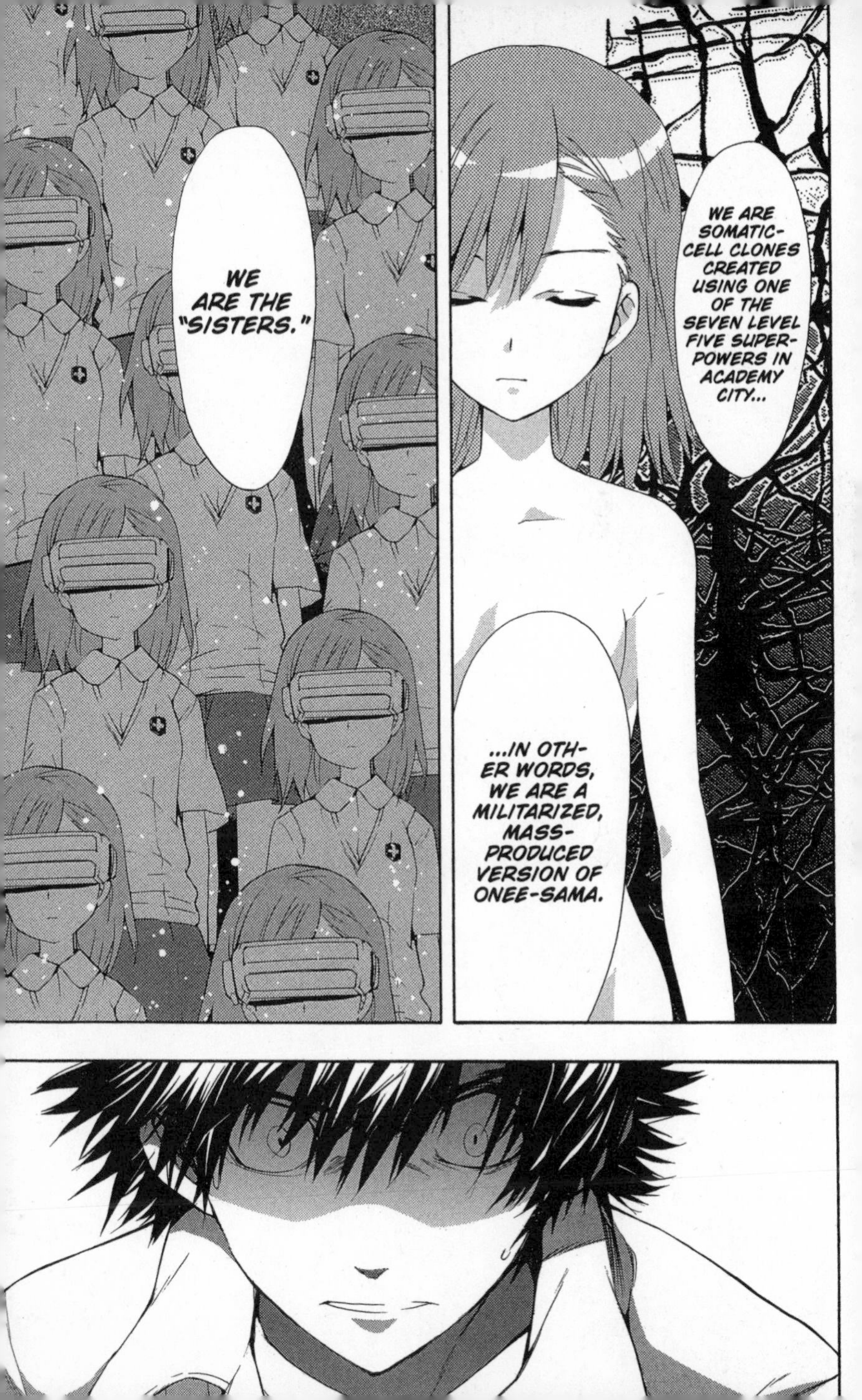
WE ARE SOMATIC-CELL CLONES CREATED USING ONE OF THE SEVEN LEVEL FIVE SUPER-POWERS IN ACADEMY CITY...
...IN OTH-ER WORDS, WE ARE A MILITARIZED, MASS-PRODUCED VERSION OF ONEE-SAMA.
WE ARE THE "SISTERS."

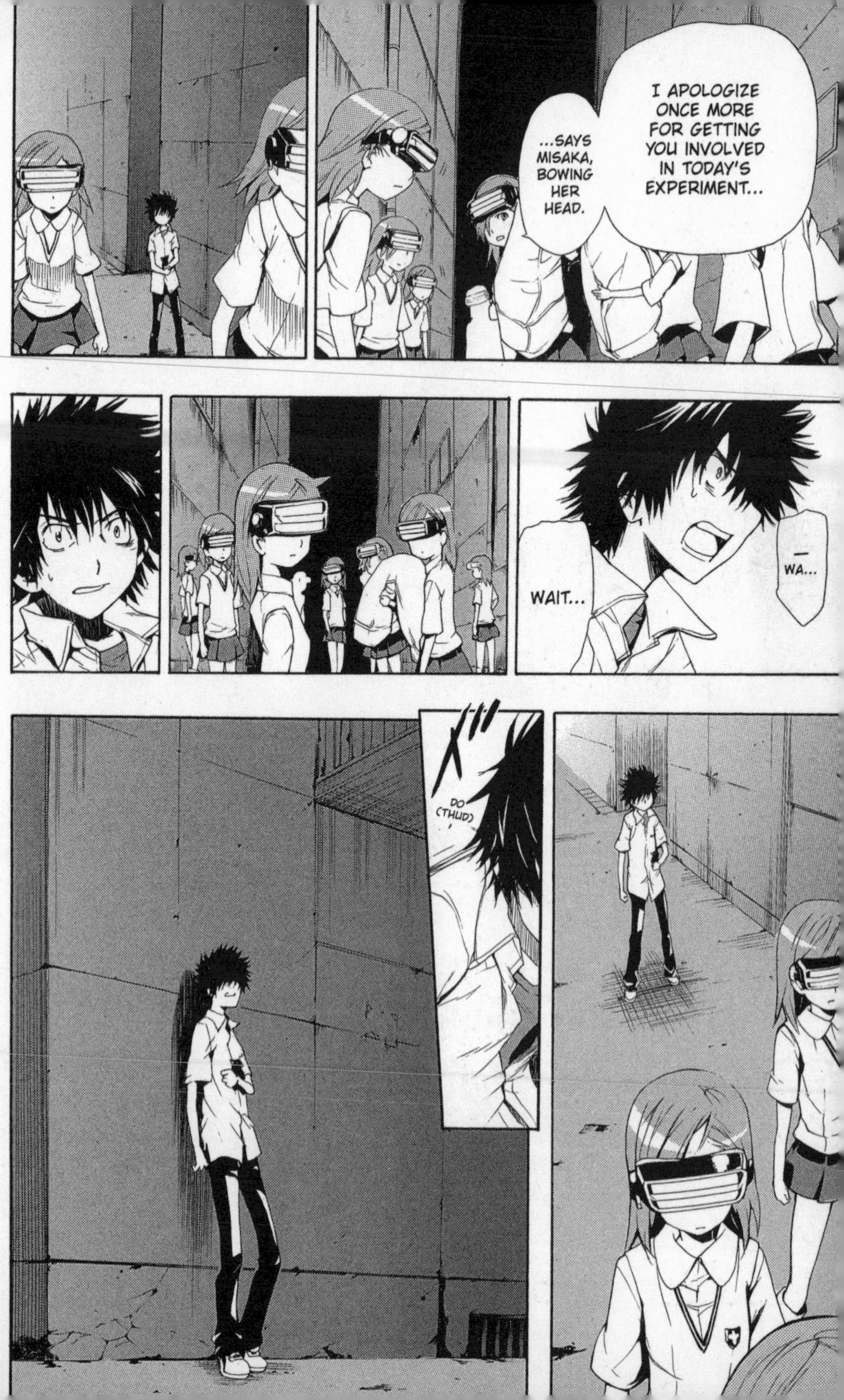
I APOLOGIZE ONCE MORE FOR GETTING YOU INVOLVED IN TODAY'S EXPERIMENT...
...SAYS MISAKA, BOWING HER HEAD.
—WA...
WAIT...
DO (THUD)

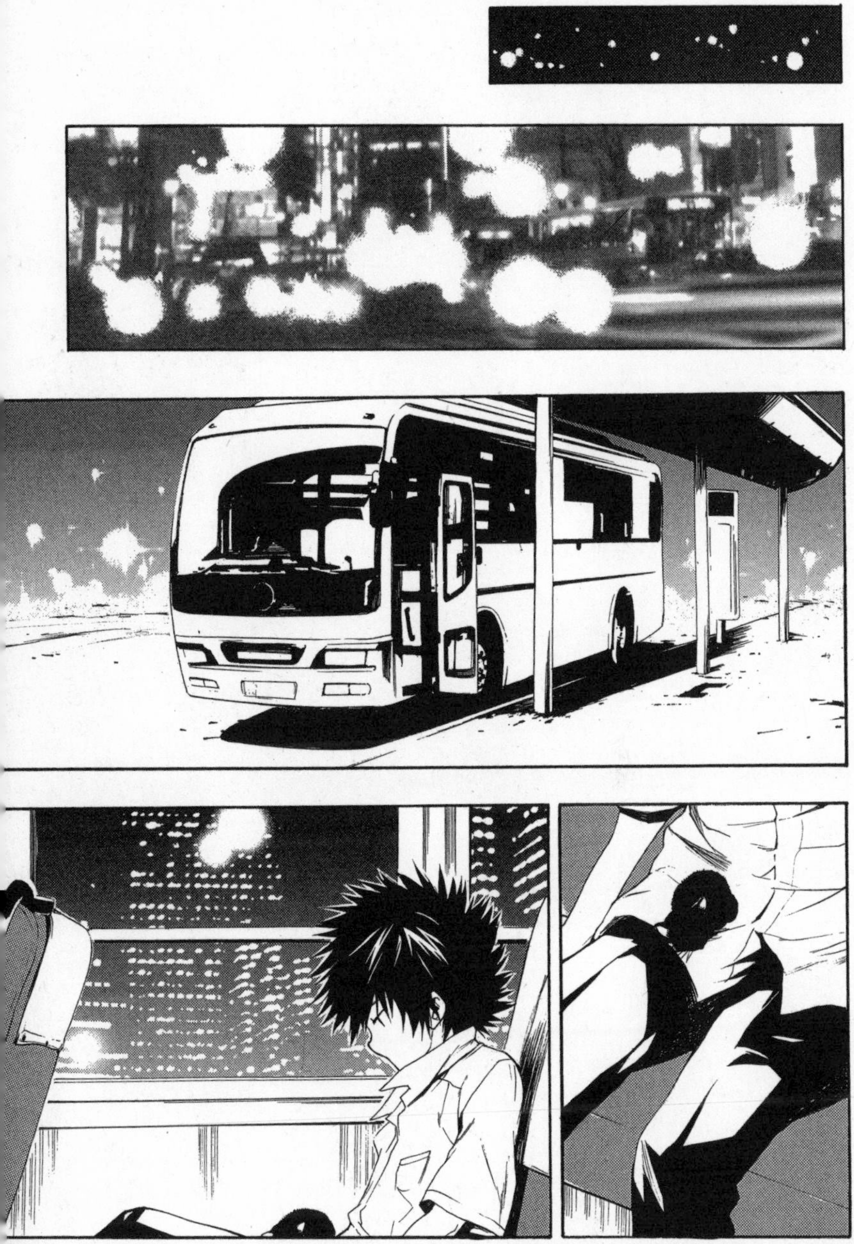

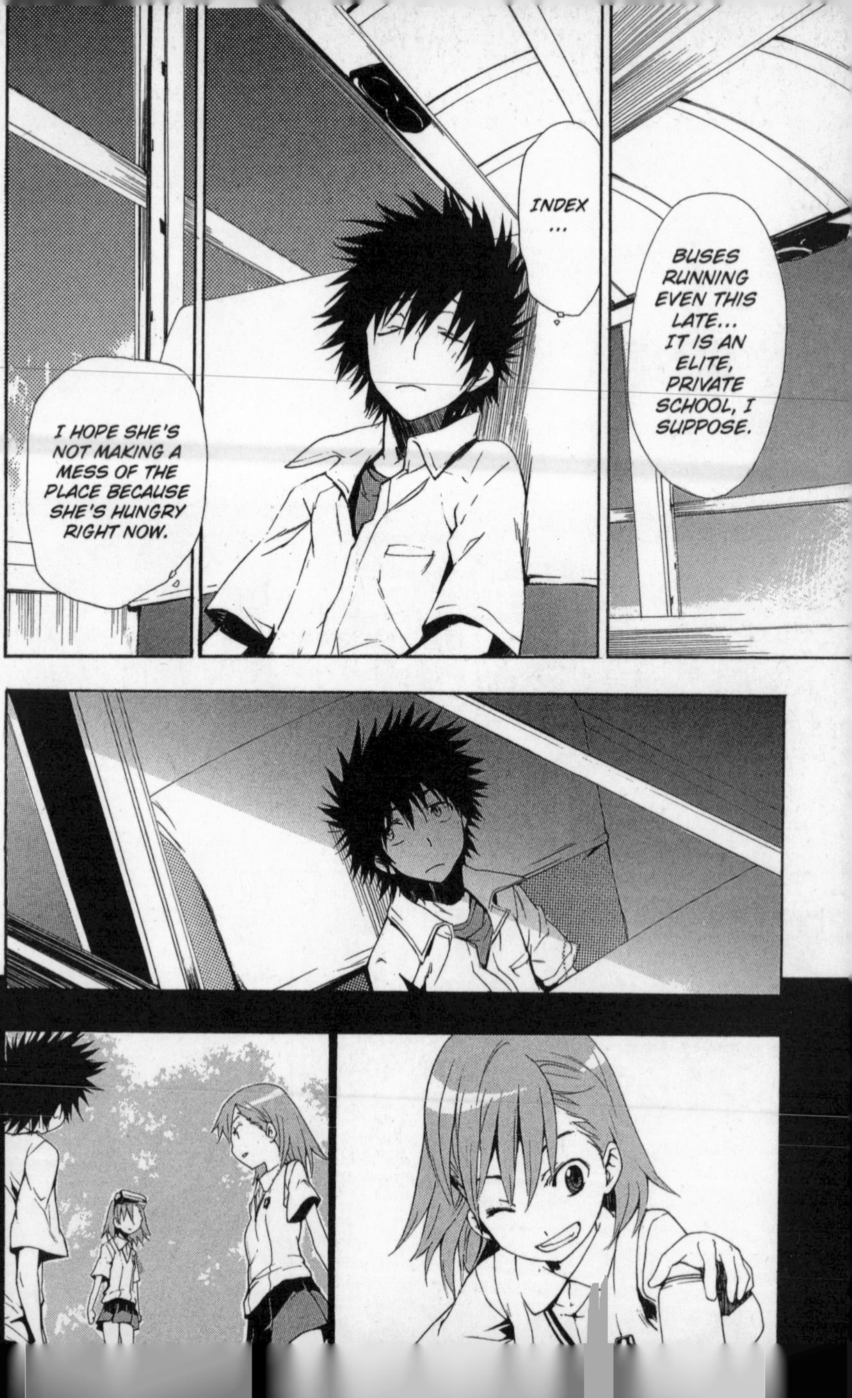
BUSES RUNNING EVEN THIS LATE... IT IS AN ELITE, PRIVATE SCHOOL, I SUPPOSE.
INDEX ...
I HOPE SHE'S NOT MAKING A MESS OF THE PLACE BECAUSE SHE'S HUNGRY RIGHT NOW.

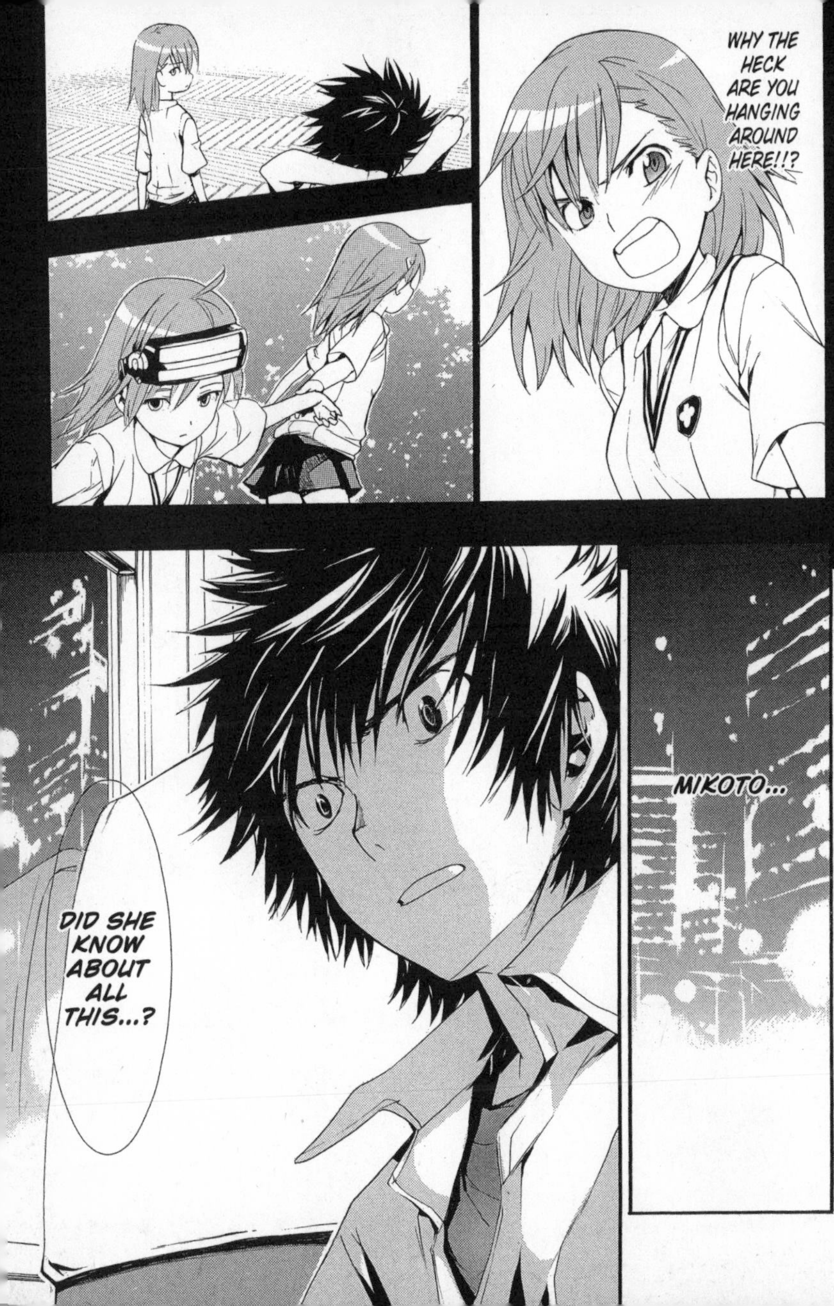
WHY THE HECK ARE YOU HANGING AROUND HERE!!?
MIKOTO...
DID SHE KNOW ABOUT ALL THIS...?

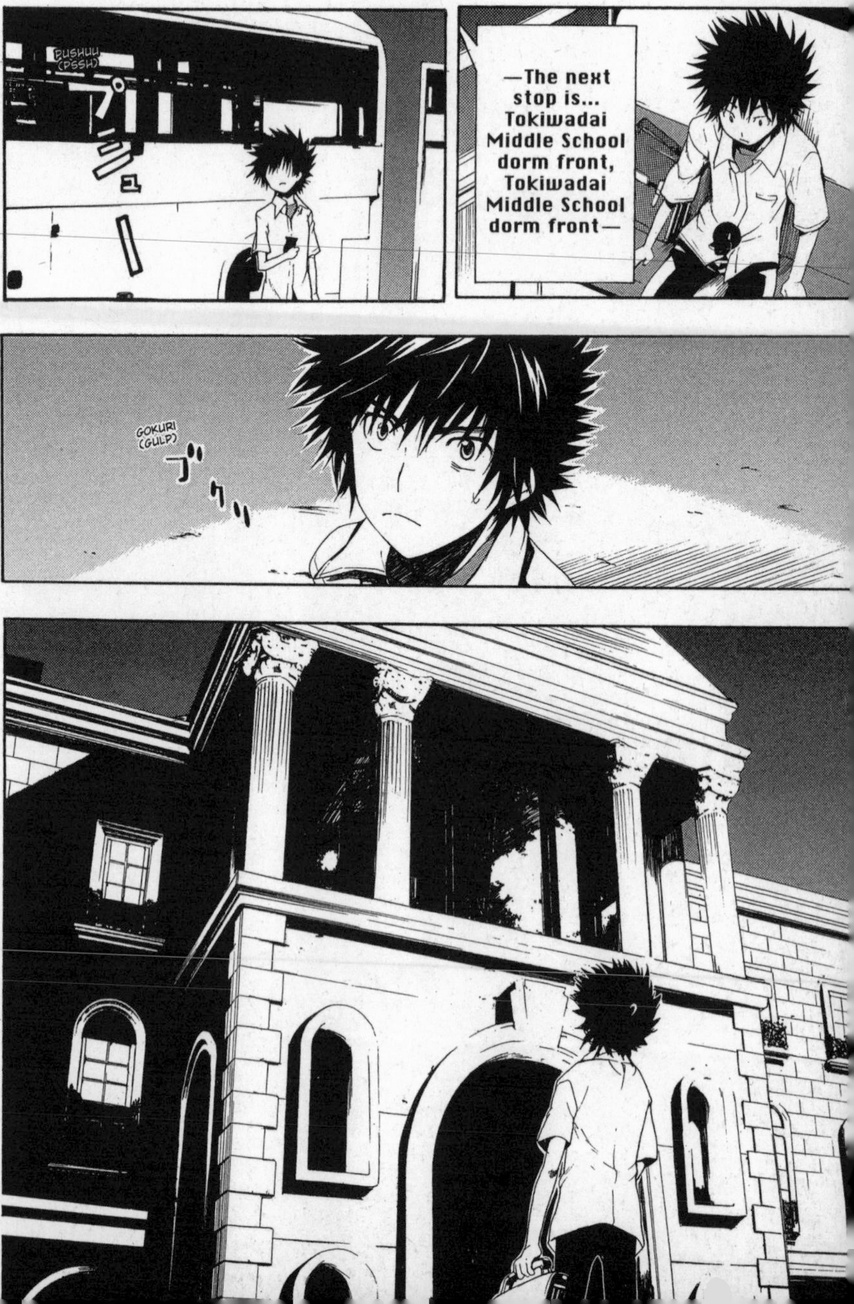
—The next stop is... Tokiwadai Middle School dorm front, Tokiwadai Middle School dorm front—
PUSHUU (PSSH)
プシュー
GOKURI (GULP)
ゴクッ

A Certain
Magical
Index

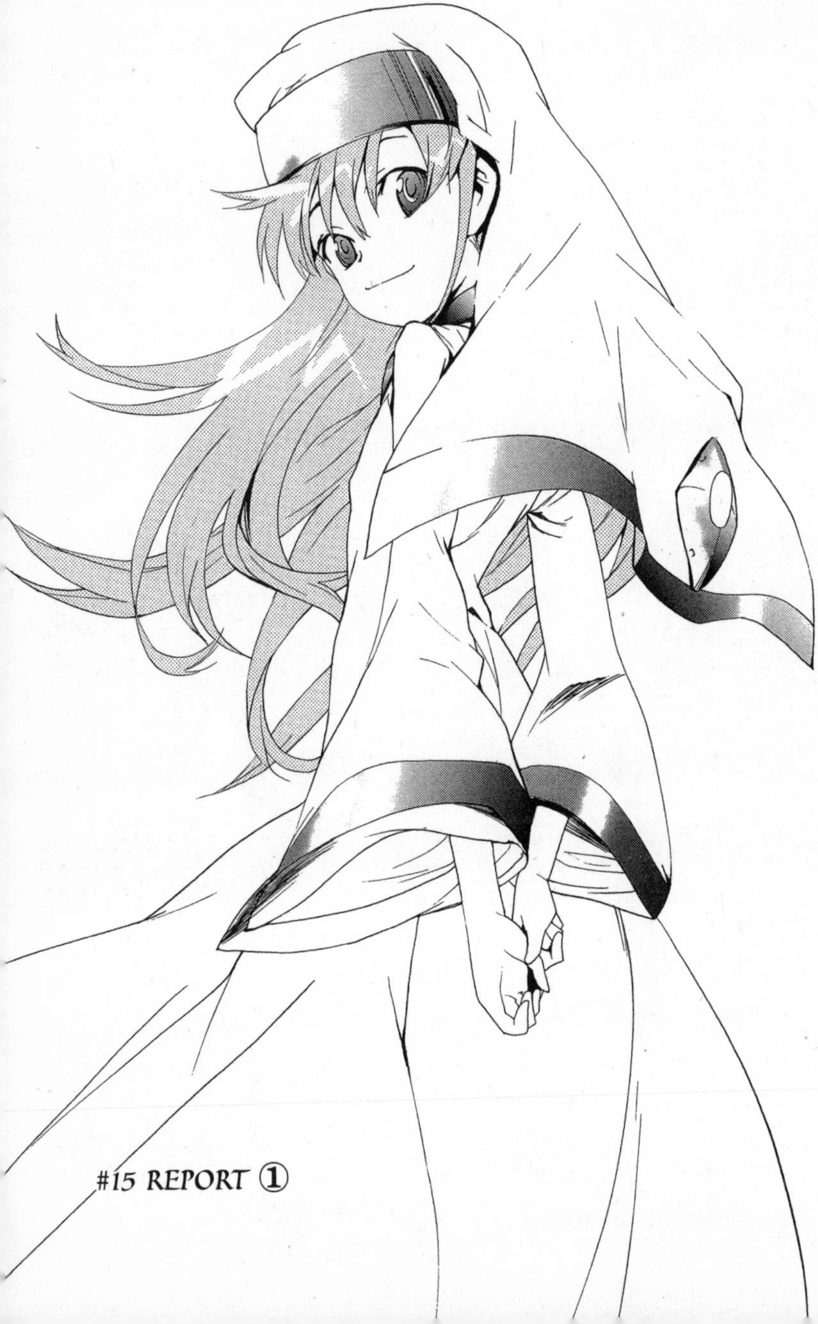

#15 REPORT ①

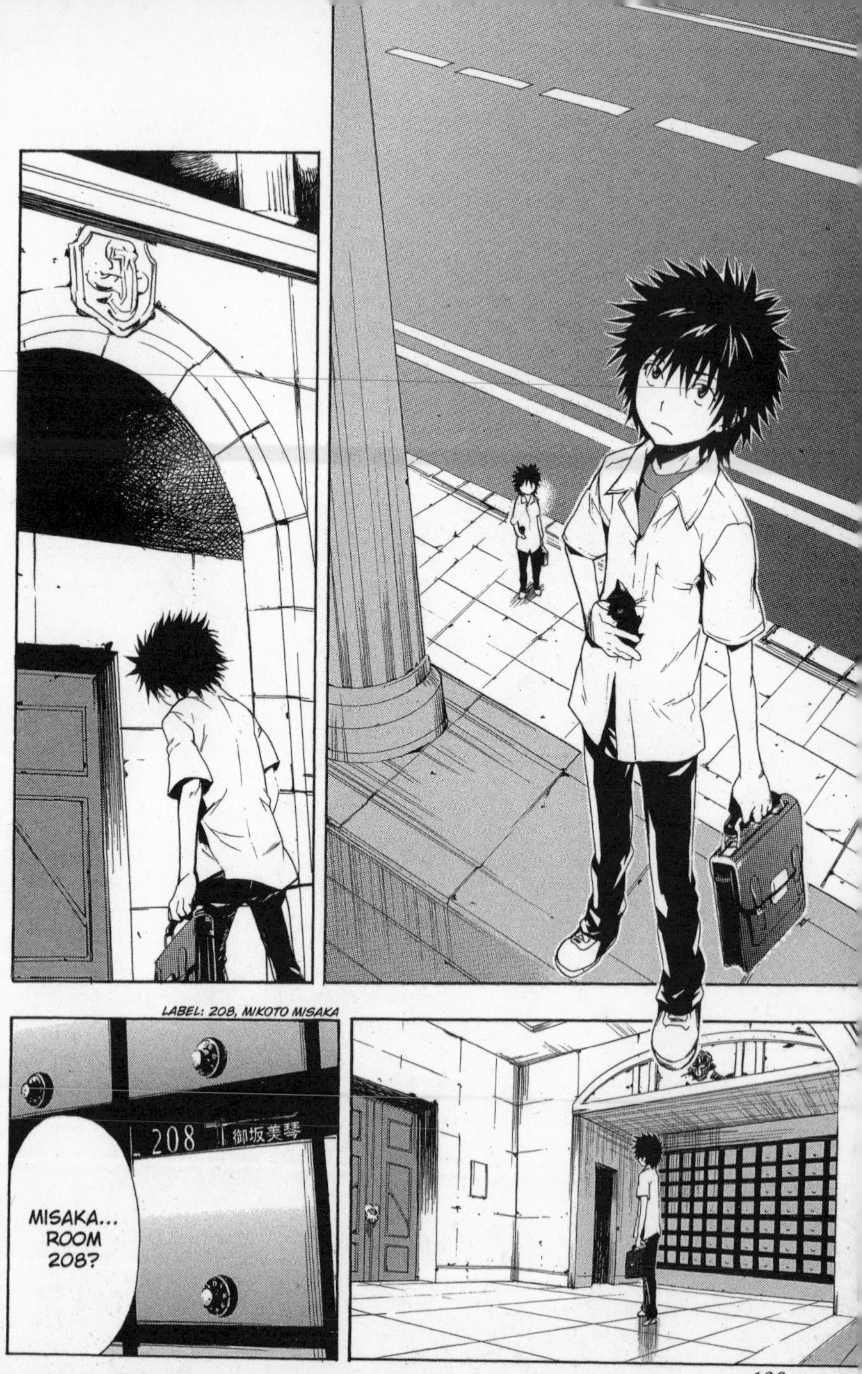
LABEL: 208, MIKOTO MISAKA
208 御坂美琴
MISAKA... ROOM 208?

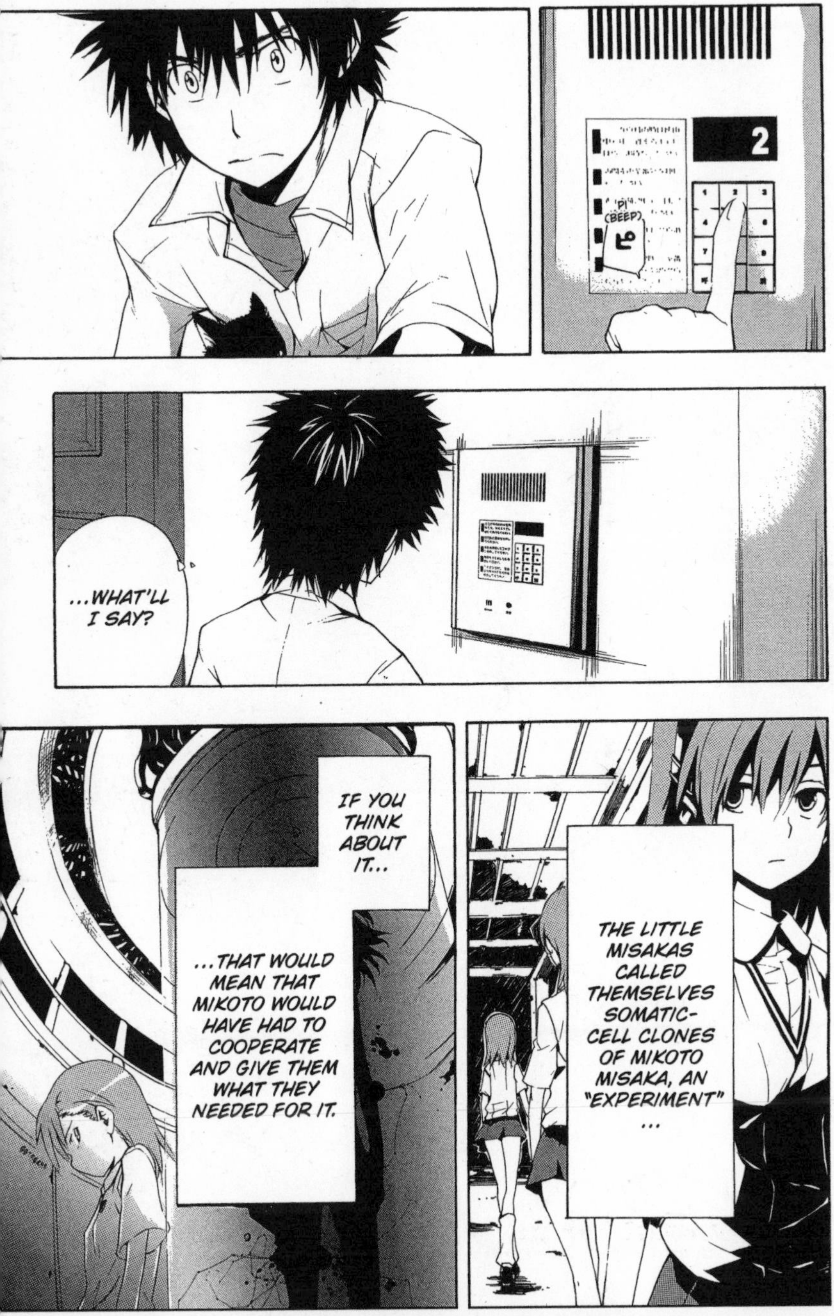
2
PI (BEEP)
ピ
...WHAT'LL I SAY?
THE LITTLE MISAKAS CALLED THEMSELVES SOMATIC-CELL CLONES OF MIKOTO MISAKA, AN "EXPERIMENT" ...
IF YOU THINK ABOUT IT...
...THAT WOULD MEAN THAT MIKOTO WOULD HAVE HAD TO COOPERATE AND GIVE THEM WHAT THEY NEEDED FOR IT.

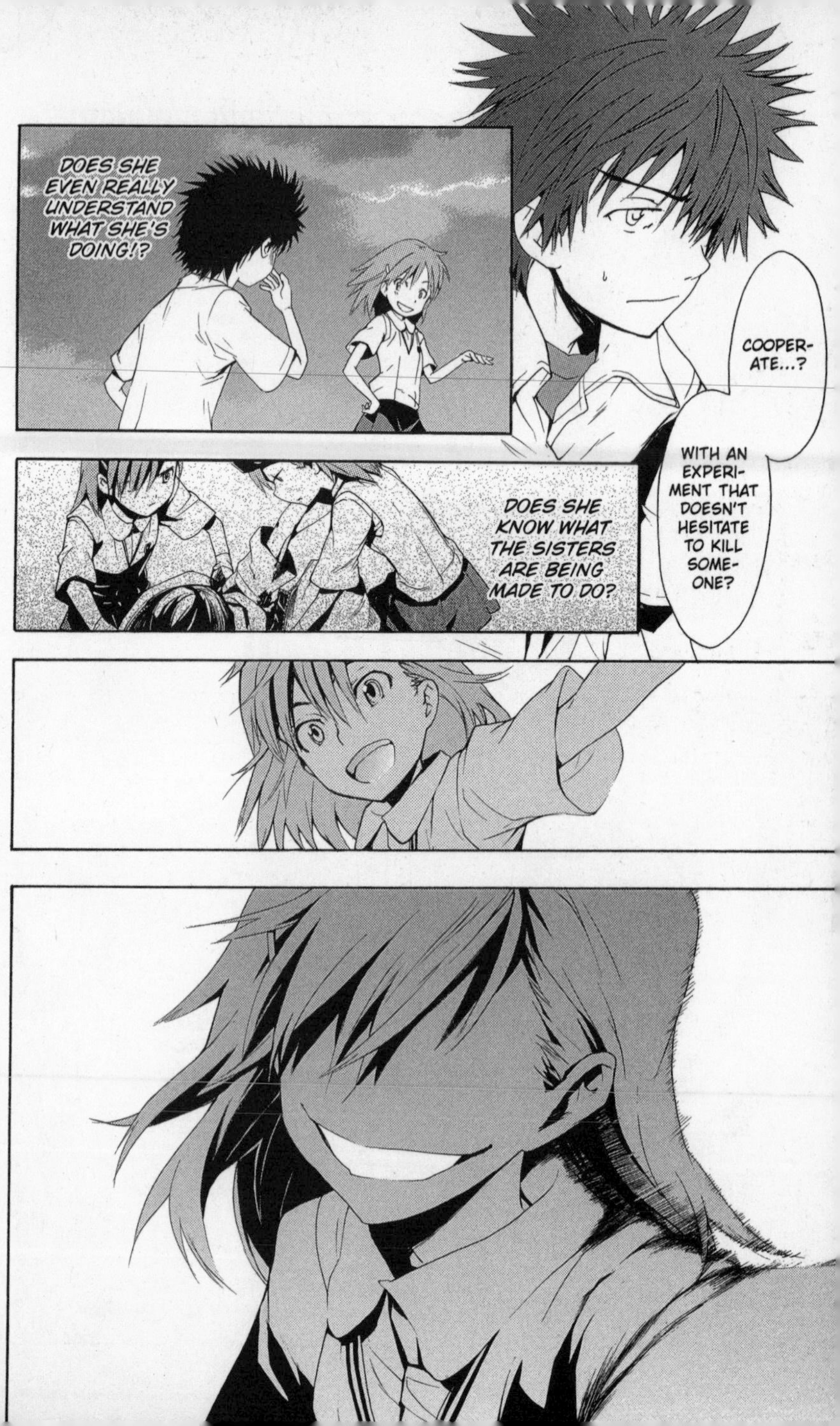
COOPER-ATE...?
WITH AN EXPERI-MENT THAT DOESN'T HESITATE TO KILL SOME-ONE?
DOES SHE EVEN REALLY UNDERSTAND WHAT SHE'S DOING!?
DOES SHE KNOW WHAT THE SISTERS ARE BEING MADE TO DO?

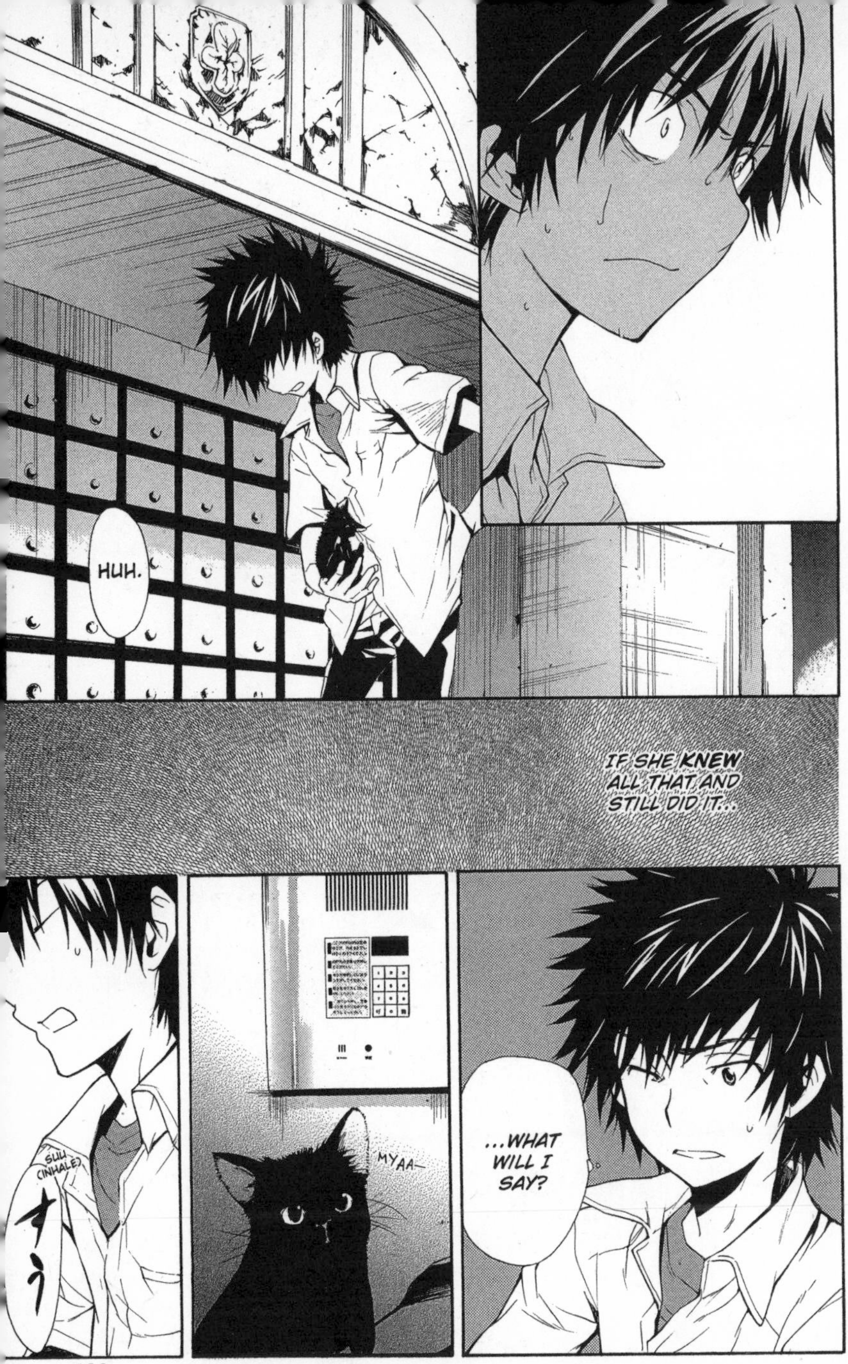
HUH.
IF SHE KNEW ALL THAT AND STILL DID IT...
...WHAT WILL I SAY?
MYAA—
SUU (INHALE)
すう

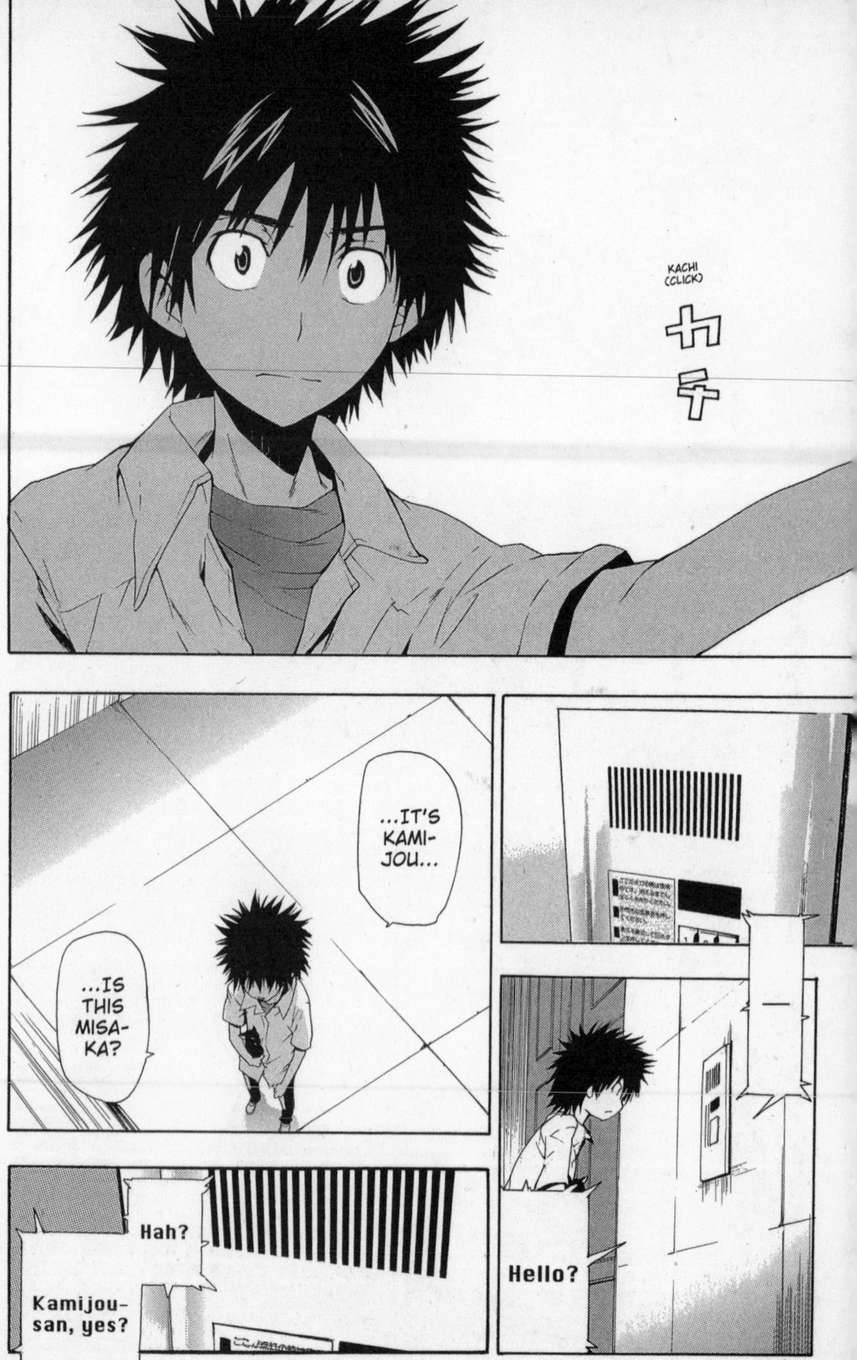
KACHI (CLICK)
カチ
—
Hello?
...IT'S KAMIJOU...
...IS THIS MISAKA?
Hah?
Kamijou-san, yes?

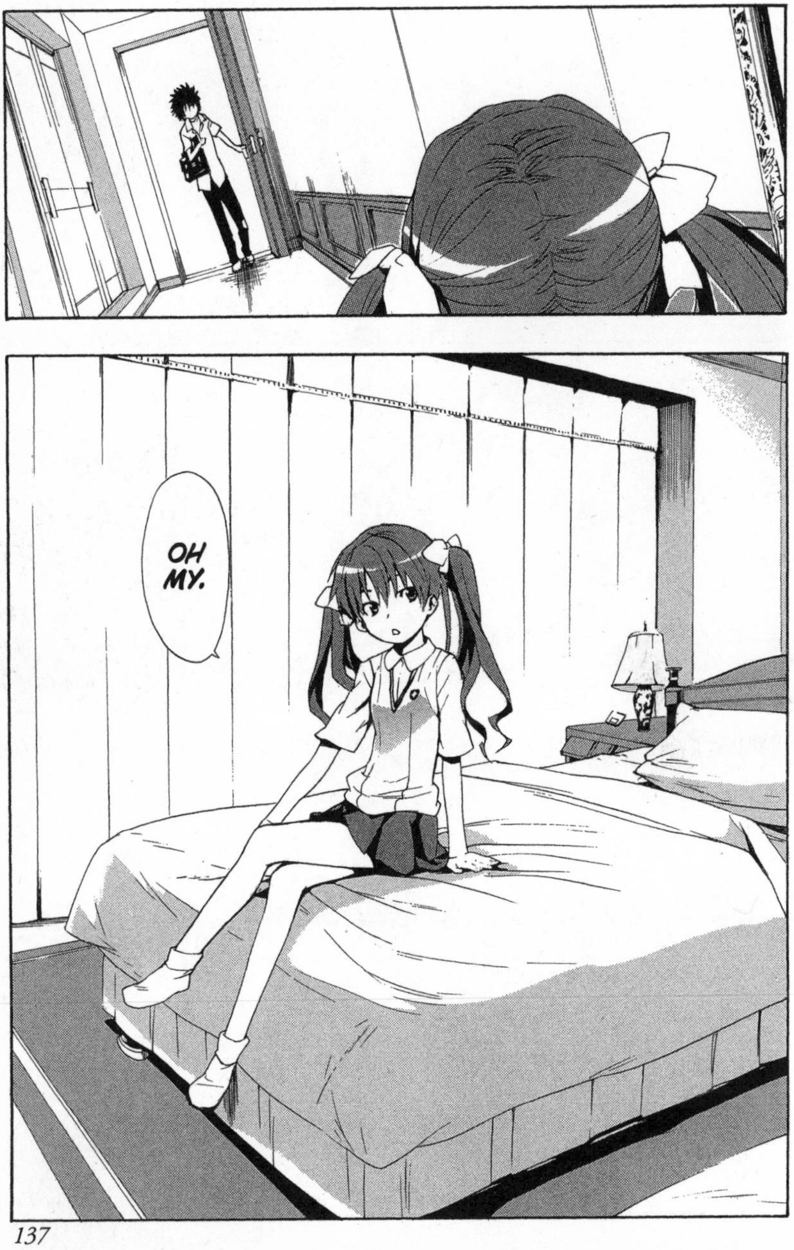
OH MY.

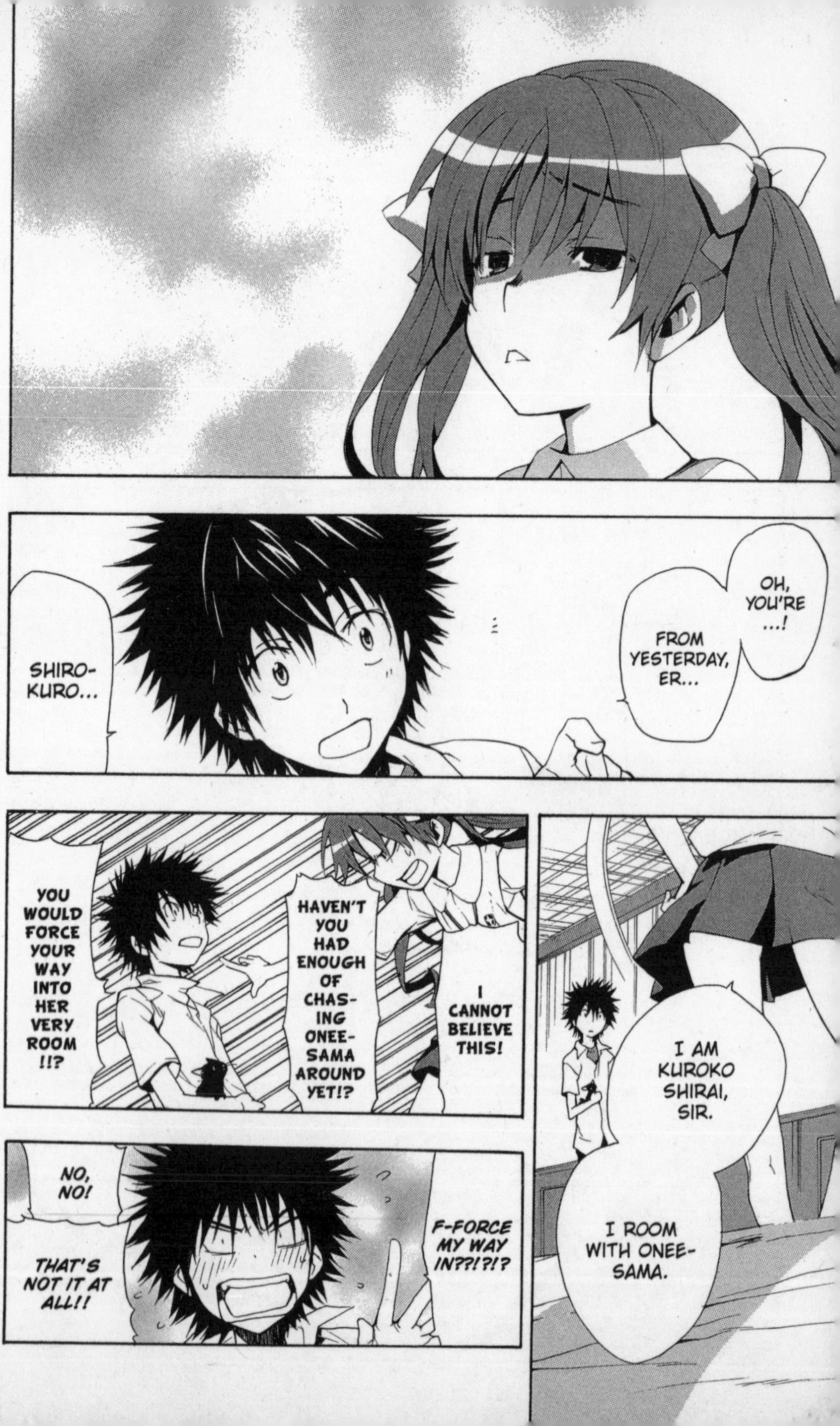
OH, YOU'RE ...!
FROM YESTERDAY, ER...
SHIRO-KURO...
I AM KUROKO SHIRAI, SIR.
I ROOM WITH ONEE-SAMA.
I CANNOT BELIEVE THIS!
HAVEN'T YOU HAD ENOUGH OF CHAS-ING ONEE-SAMA AROUND YET!?
YOU WOULD FORCE YOUR WAY INTO HER VERY ROOM !!?
F-FORCE MY WAY IN??!?!?
NO, NO!
THAT'S NOT IT AT ALL!!

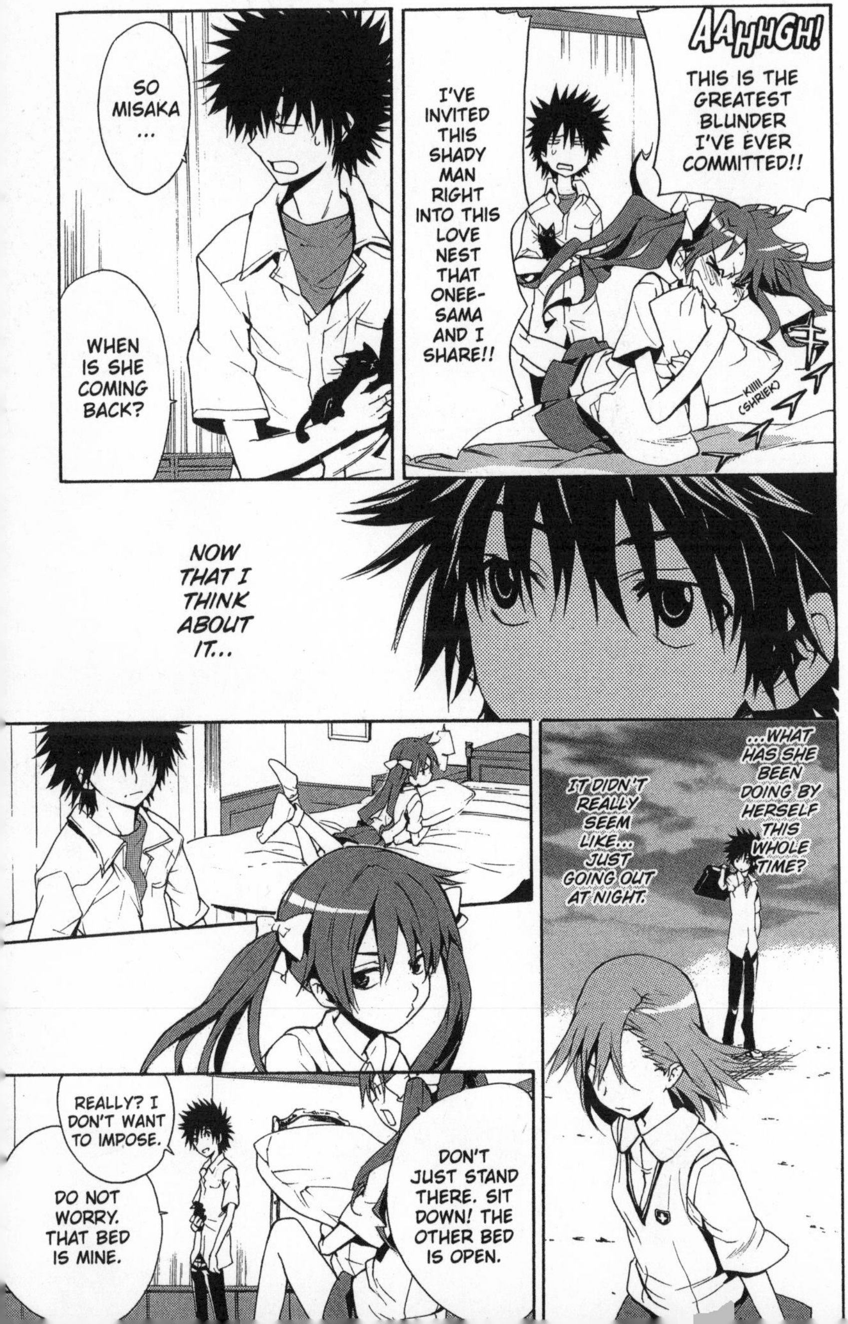
AAHHGH!
THIS IS THE GREATEST BLUNDER I'VE EVER COMMITTED!!
I'VE INVITED THIS SHADY MAN RIGHT INTO THIS LOVE NEST THAT ONEE-SAMA AND I SHARE!!
KIIIII (SHRIEK)
SO MISAKA ...
WHEN IS SHE COMING BACK?
NOW THAT I THINK ABOUT IT...
...WHAT HAS SHE BEEN DOING BY HERSELF THIS WHOLE TIME?
IT DIDN'T REALLY SEEM LIKE... JUST GOING OUT AT NIGHT.
DON'T JUST STAND THERE. SIT DOWN! THE OTHER BED IS OPEN.
REALLY? I DON'T WANT TO IMPOSE.
DO NOT WORRY. THAT BED IS MINE.

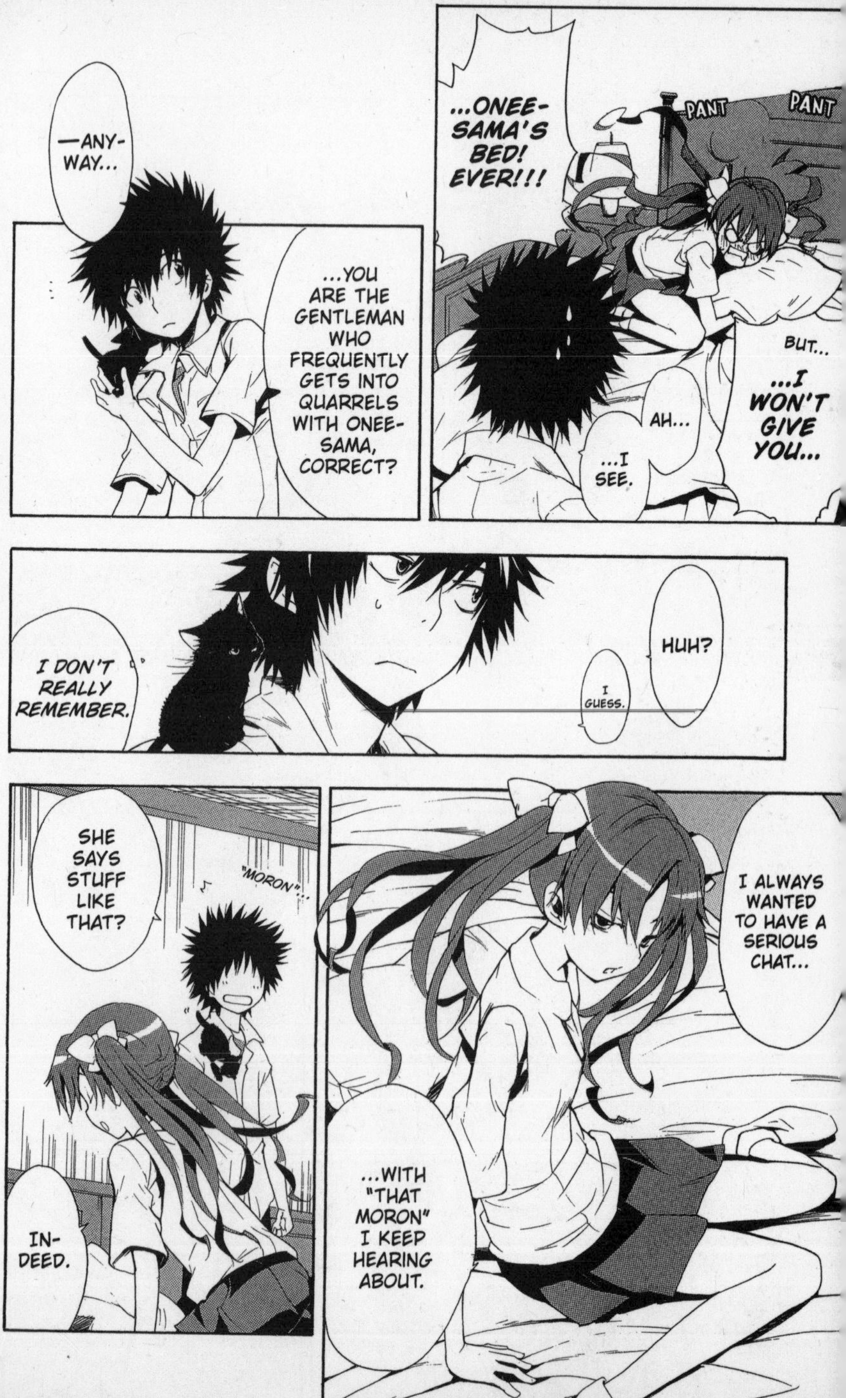

PANT PANT
...ONEE-SAMA'S BED! EVER!!!
BUT...
...I WON'T GIVE YOU...
AH...
...I SEE.
—ANY-WAY...
...YOU ARE THE GENTLEMAN WHO FREQUENTLY GETS INTO QUARRELS WITH ONEE-SAMA, CORRECT?
HUH?
I GUESS.
I DON'T REALLY REMEMBER.
I ALWAYS WANTED TO HAVE A SERIOUS CHAT...
...WITH "THAT MORON" I KEEP HEARING ABOUT.
"MORON"...
SHE SAYS STUFF LIKE THAT?
IN-DEED.

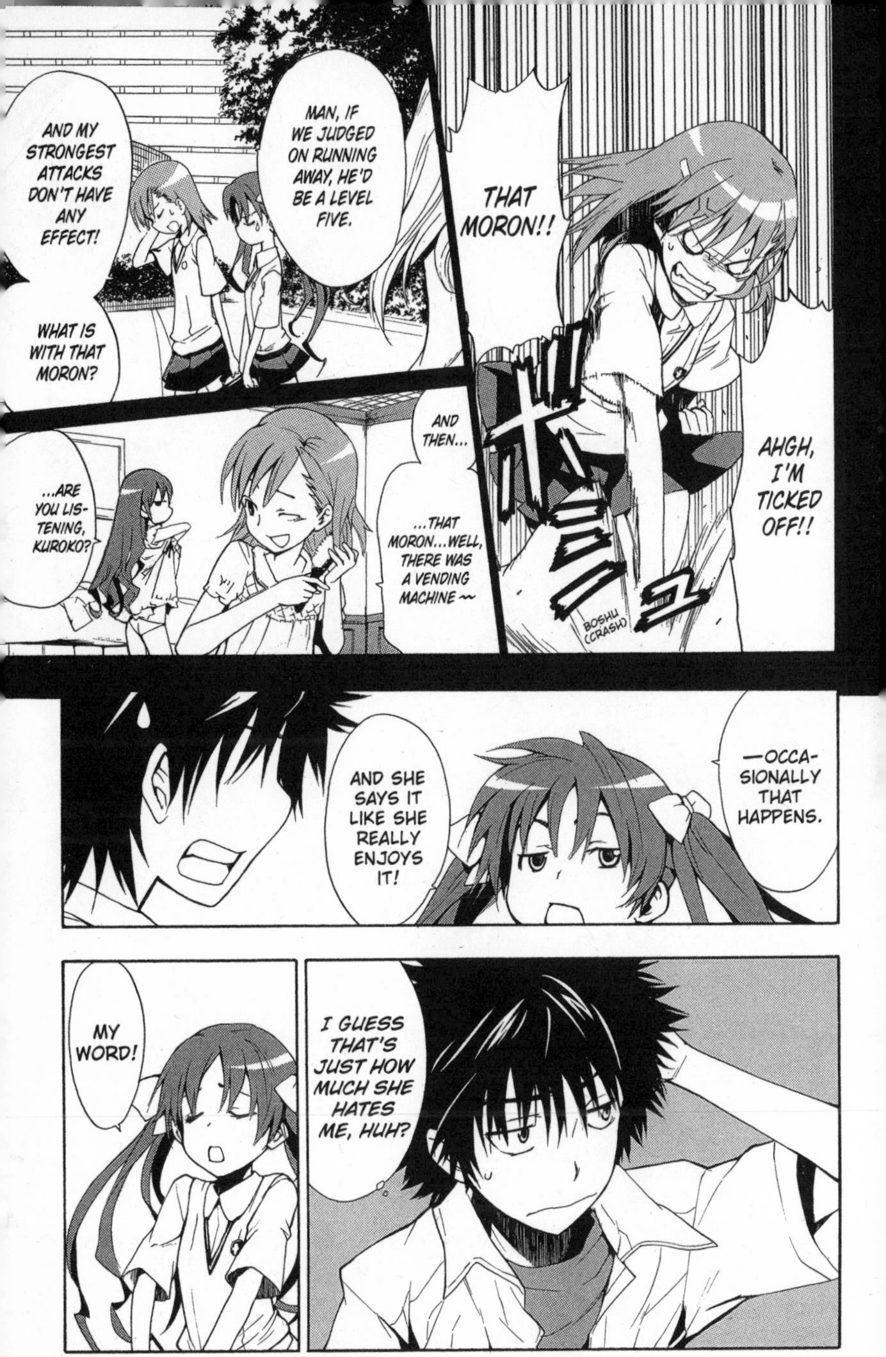
THAT MORON!!
AHGH, I'M TICKED OFF!!
BOSHU (CRASH)
MAN, IF WE JUDGED ON RUNNING AWAY, HE'D BE A LEVEL FIVE.
AND MY STRONGEST ATTACKS DON'T HAVE ANY EFFECT!
WHAT IS WITH THAT MORON?
AND THEN...
...THAT MORON...WELL, THERE WAS A VENDING MACHINE~
...ARE YOU LIS-TENING, KUROKO?
—OCCA-SIONALLY THAT HAPPENS.
AND SHE SAYS IT LIKE SHE REALLY ENJOYS IT!
I GUESS THAT'S JUST HOW MUCH SHE HATES ME, HUH?
MY WORD!

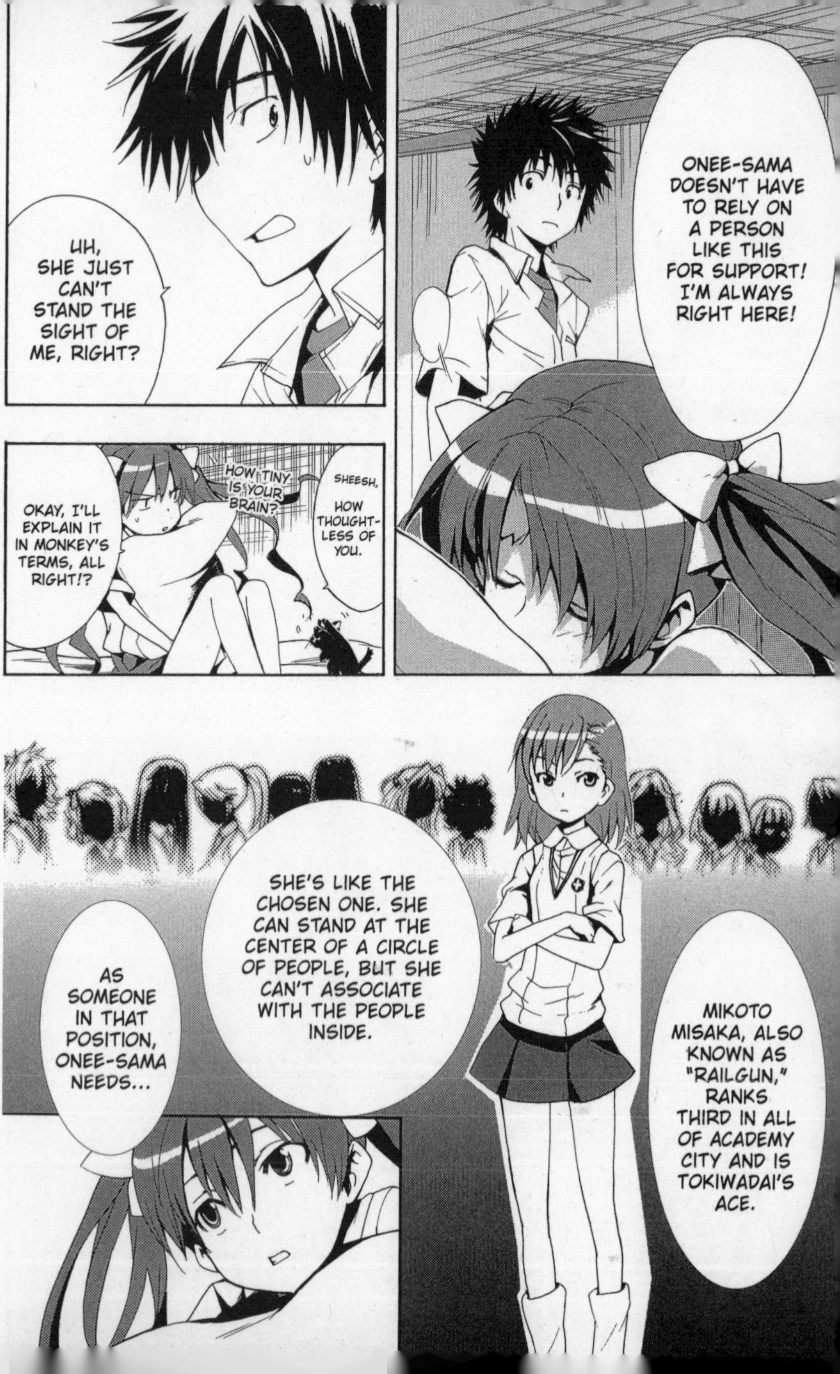
ONEE-SAMA DOESN'T HAVE TO RELY ON A PERSON LIKE THIS FOR SUPPORT! I'M ALWAYS RIGHT HERE!
UH, SHE JUST CAN'T STAND THE SIGHT OF ME, RIGHT?
SHEESH, HOW THOUGHT-LESS OF YOU.
HOW TINY IS YOUR BRAIN?
OKAY, I'LL EXPLAIN IT IN MONKEY'S TERMS, ALL RIGHT!?
MIKOTO MISAKA, ALSO KNOWN AS "RAILGUN," RANKS THIRD IN ALL OF ACADEMY CITY AND IS TOKIWADAI'S ACE.
SHE'S LIKE THE CHOSEN ONE. SHE CAN STAND AT THE CENTER OF A CIRCLE OF PEOPLE, BUT SHE CAN'T ASSOCIATE WITH THE PEOPLE INSIDE.
AS SOMEONE IN THAT POSITION, ONEE-SAMA NEEDS...

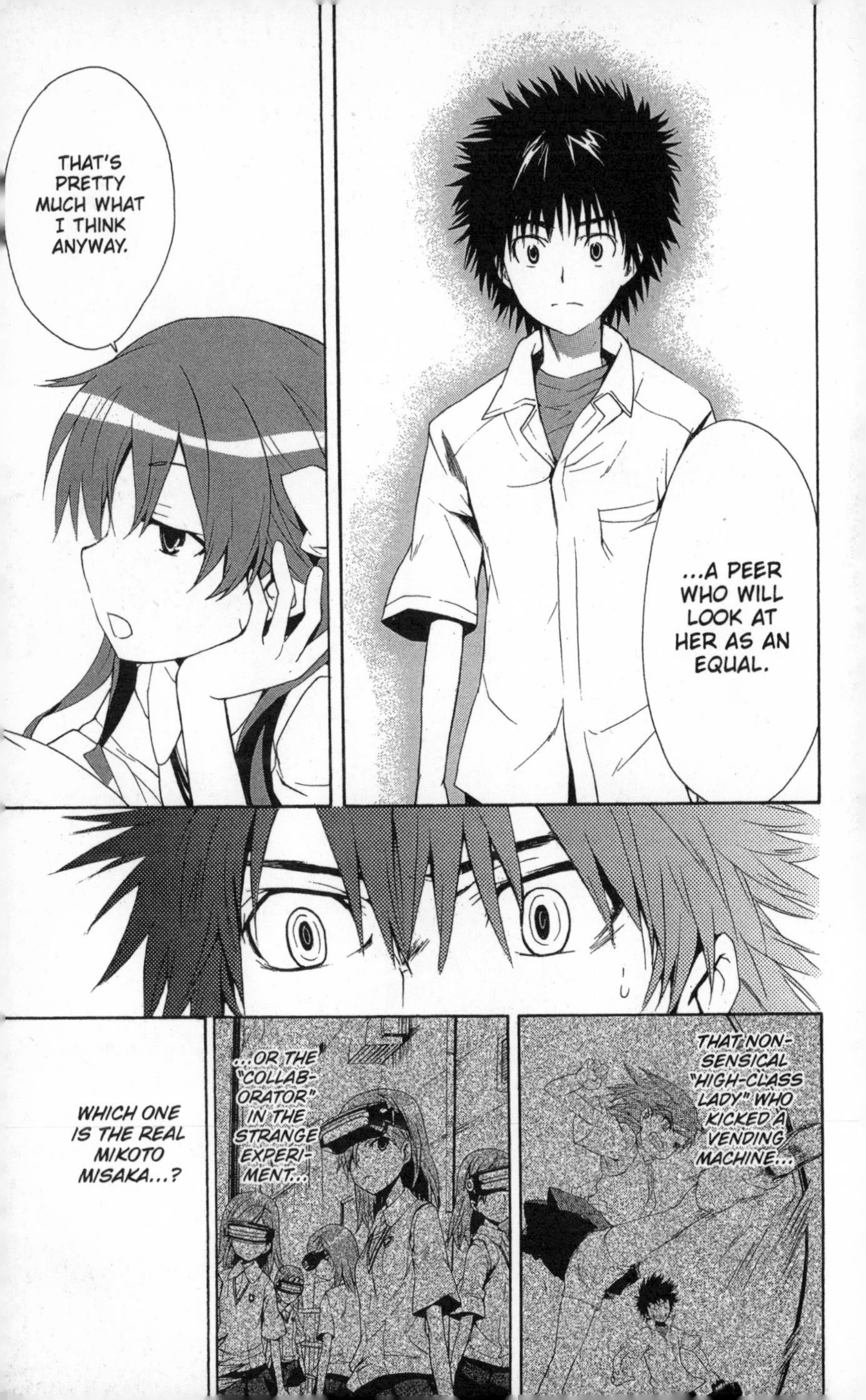
...A PEER WHO WILL LOOK AT HER AS AN EQUAL.
THAT'S PRETTY MUCH WHAT I THINK ANYWAY.
THAT NON-SENSICAL "HIGH-CLASS LADY" WHO KICKED A VENDING MACHINE...
...OR THE "COLLABORATOR" IN THE STRANGE EXPERIMENT...
WHICH ONE IS THE REAL MIKOTO MISAKA...?

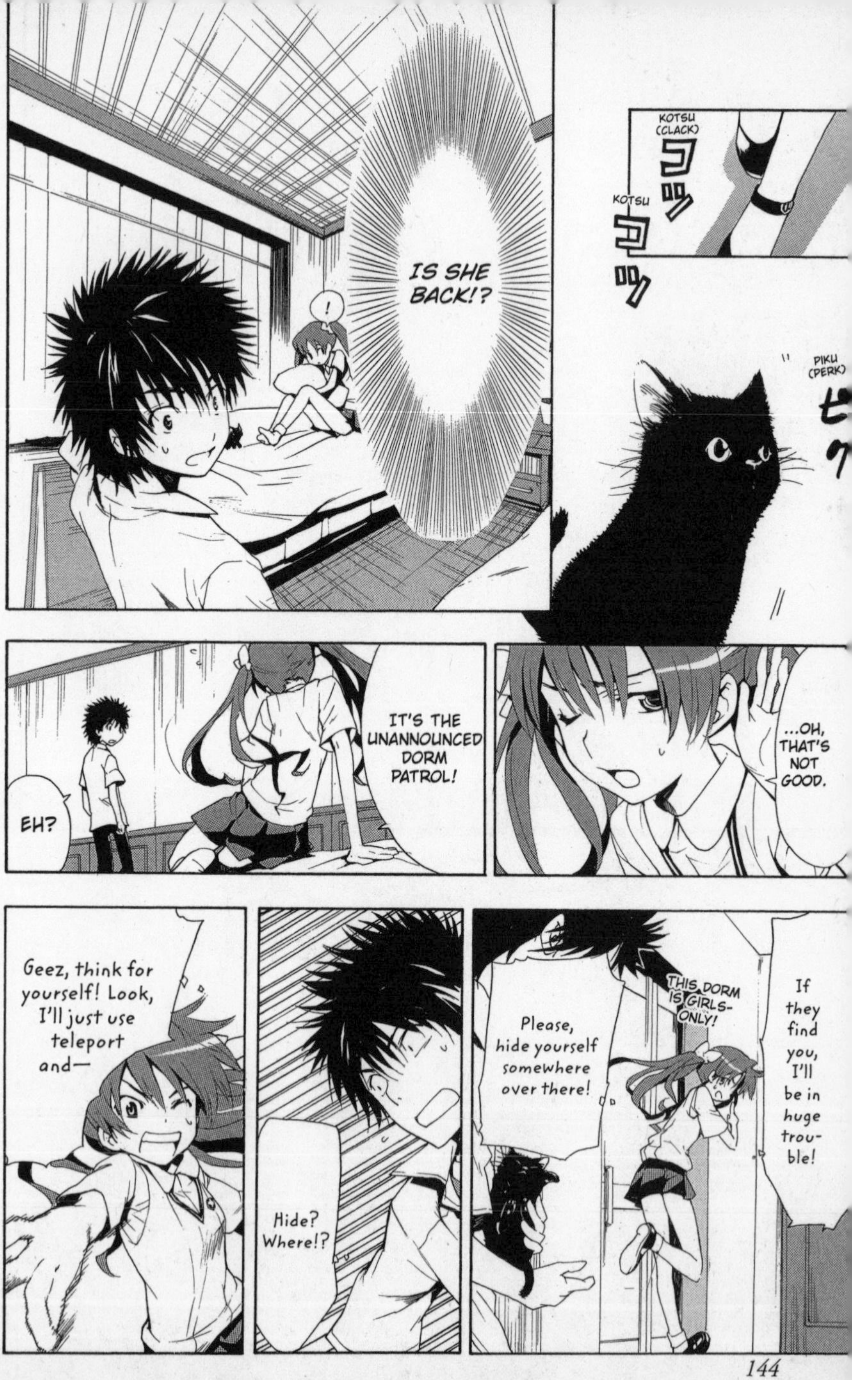
KOTSU (CLACK)
KOTSU
PIKU (PERK)
!
IS SHE BACK!?
...OH, THAT'S NOT GOOD.
IT'S THE UNANNOUNCED DORM PATROL!
EH?
If they find you, I'll be in huge trouble!
THIS DORM IS GIRLS-ONLY!
Please, hide yourself somewhere over there!
Hide? Where!?
Geez, think for yourself! Look, I'll just use teleport and—

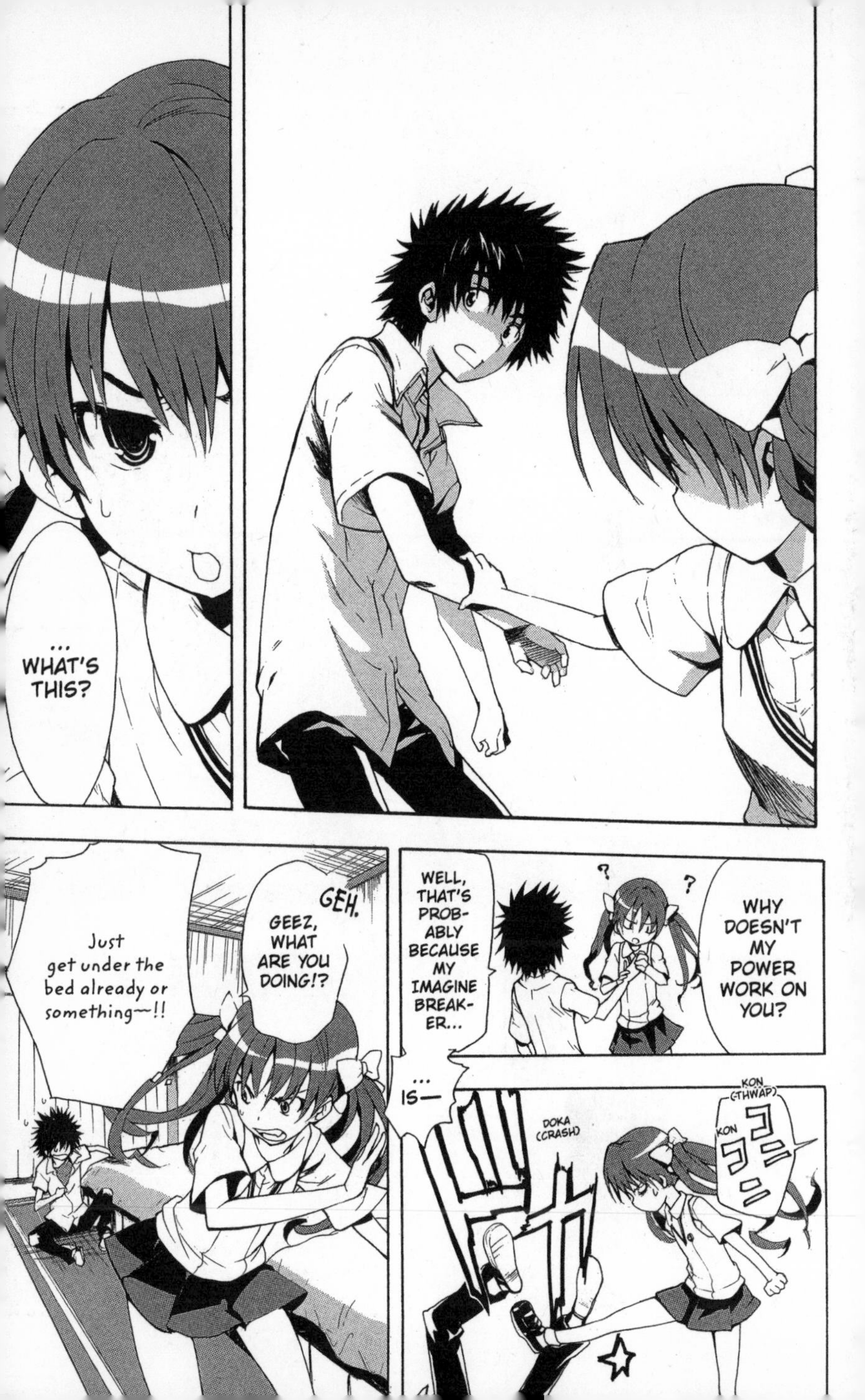
... WHAT'S THIS?
WHY DOESN'T MY POWER WORK ON YOU?
WELL, THAT'S PROB-ABLY BECAUSE MY IMAGINE BREAK-ER...
... IS—
KON (THWAP)
KON
DOKA (CRASH)
GEEZ, WHAT ARE YOU DOING!?
GEH.
Just get under the bed already or something~!!

WILL DO!

OKAY!

...IT'S DINNER-TIME. ASSEMBLE IN THE DINING HALL.

SHIRAI...

GACHA (CLACK)

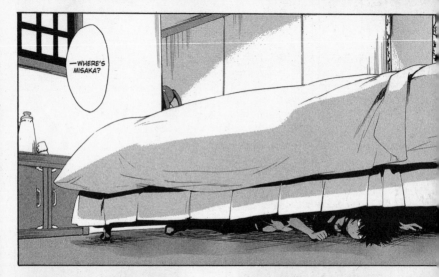

—WHERE'S MISAKA?

OW, OW, DON'T SCRATCH ME!

OW!

BARI (SCRITCH)

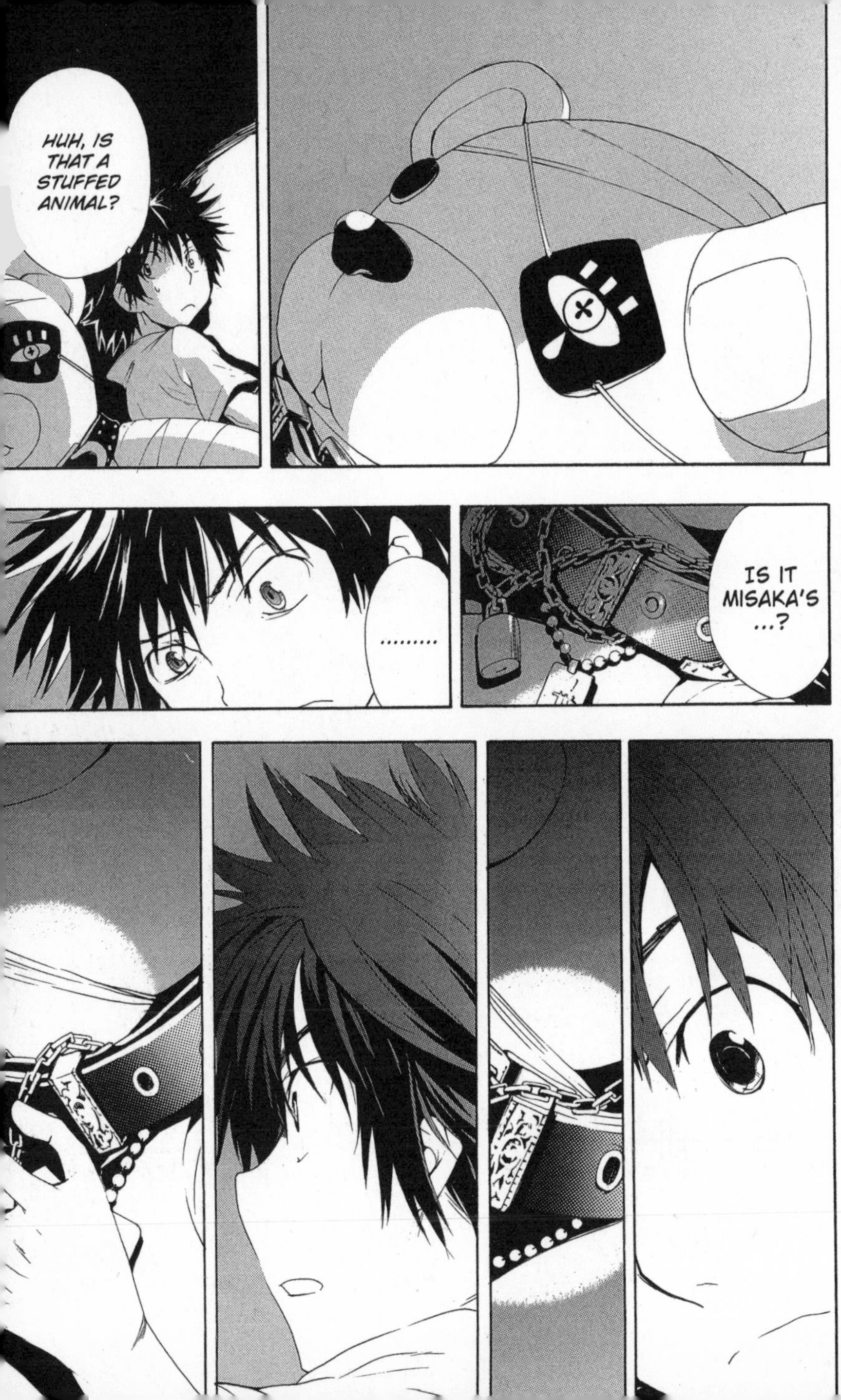
HUH, IS THAT A STUFFED ANIMAL?
IS IT MISAKA'S ...?
....

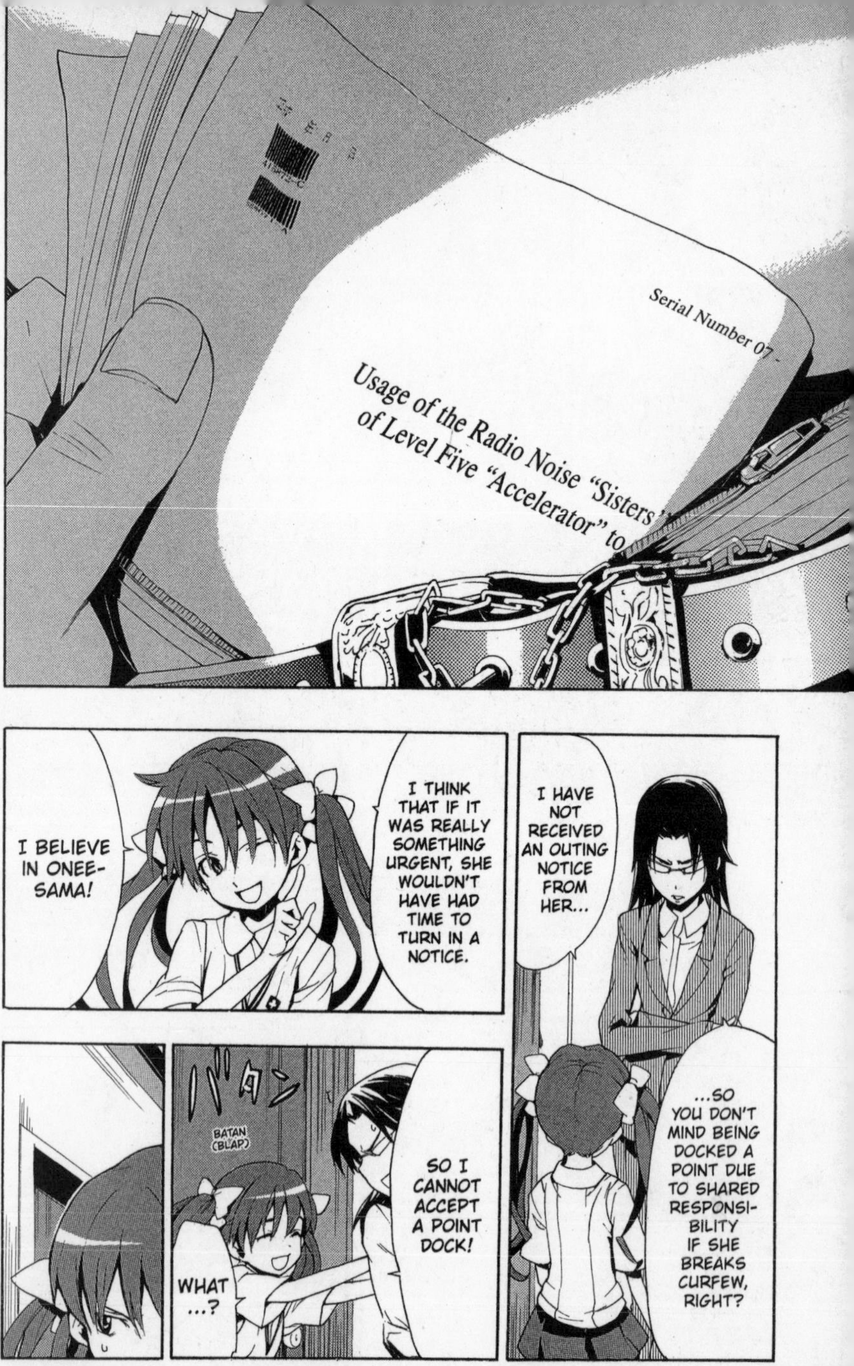
Serial Number 07
Usage of the Radio Noise "Sisters"
of Level Five "Accelerator" to
I HAVE NOT RECEIVED AN OUTING NOTICE FROM HER...
I THINK THAT IF IT WAS REALLY SOMETHING URGENT, SHE WOULDN'T HAVE HAD TIME TO TURN IN A NOTICE.
I BELIEVE IN ONEE-SAMA!
...SO YOU DON'T MIND BEING DOCKED A POINT DUE TO SHARED RESPONSI-BILITY IF SHE BREAKS CURFEW, RIGHT?
バタン
BATAN (BLAP)
SO I CANNOT ACCEPT A POINT DOCK!
WHAT ...?

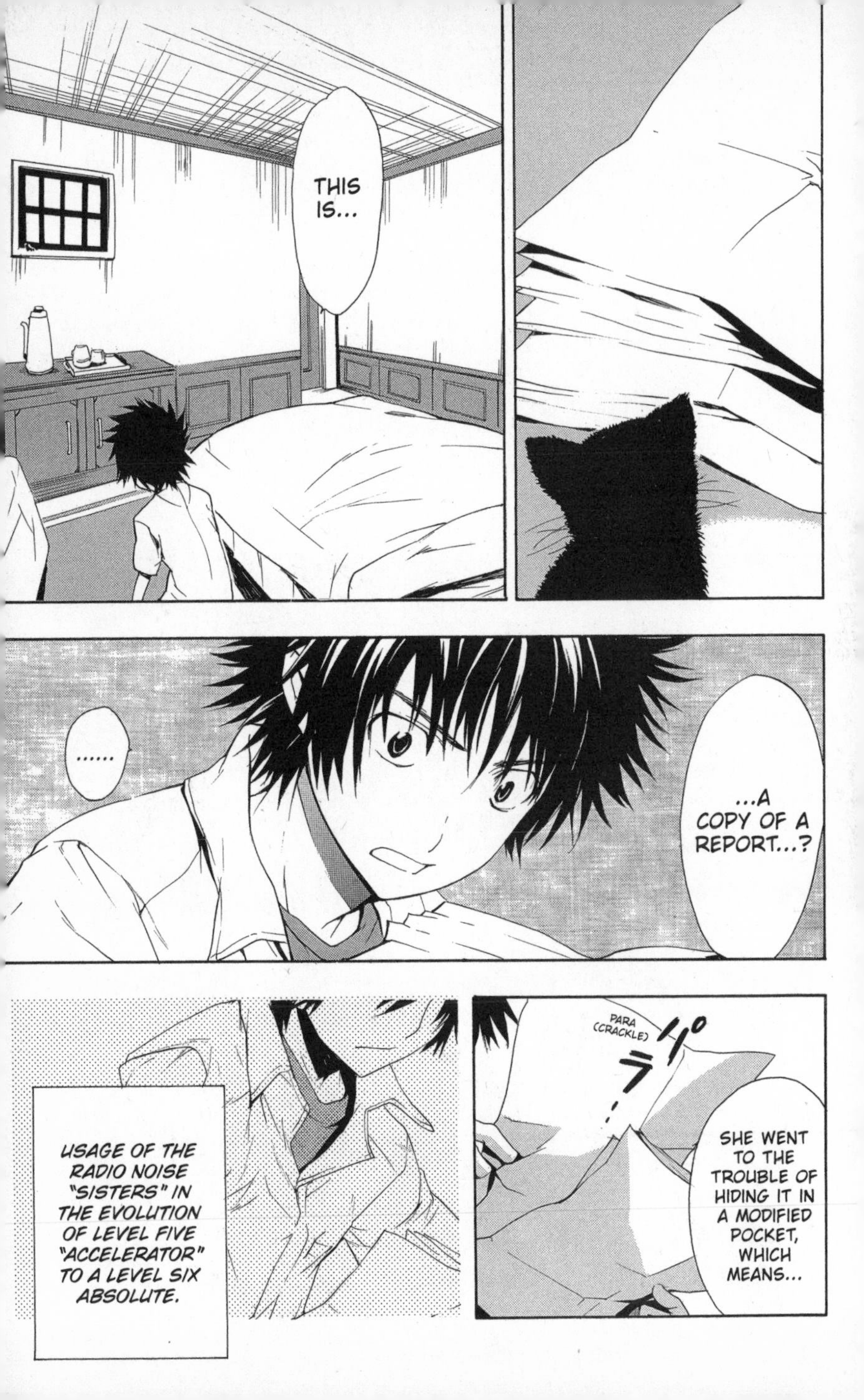
THIS IS...
...A COPY OF A REPORT...?
......
PARA (CRACKLE)
SHE WENT TO THE TROUBLE OF HIDING IT IN A MODIFIED POCKET, WHICH MEANS...
USAGE OF THE RADIO NOISE "SISTERS" IN THE EVOLUTION OF LEVEL FIVE "ACCELERATOR" TO A LEVEL SIX ABSOLUTE.

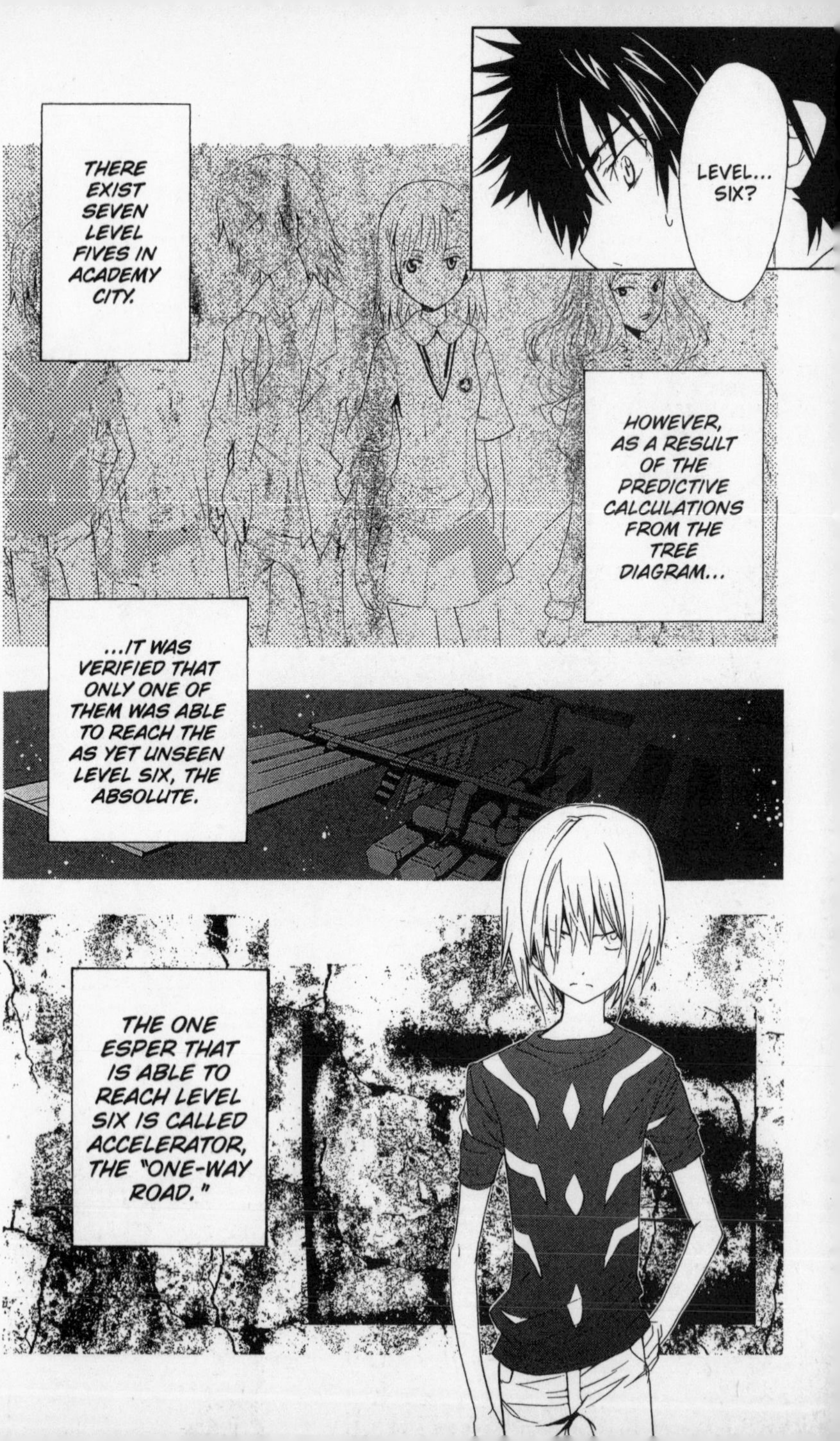
LEVEL... SIX?
THERE EXIST SEVEN LEVEL FIVES IN ACADEMY CITY.
HOWEVER, AS A RESULT OF THE PREDICTIVE CALCULATIONS FROM THE TREE DIAGRAM...
...IT WAS VERIFIED THAT ONLY ONE OF THEM WAS ABLE TO REACH THE AS YET UNSEEN LEVEL SIX, THE ABSOLUTE.
THE ONE ESPER THAT IS ABLE TO REACH LEVEL SIX IS CALLED ACCELERATOR, THE "ONE-WAY ROAD."

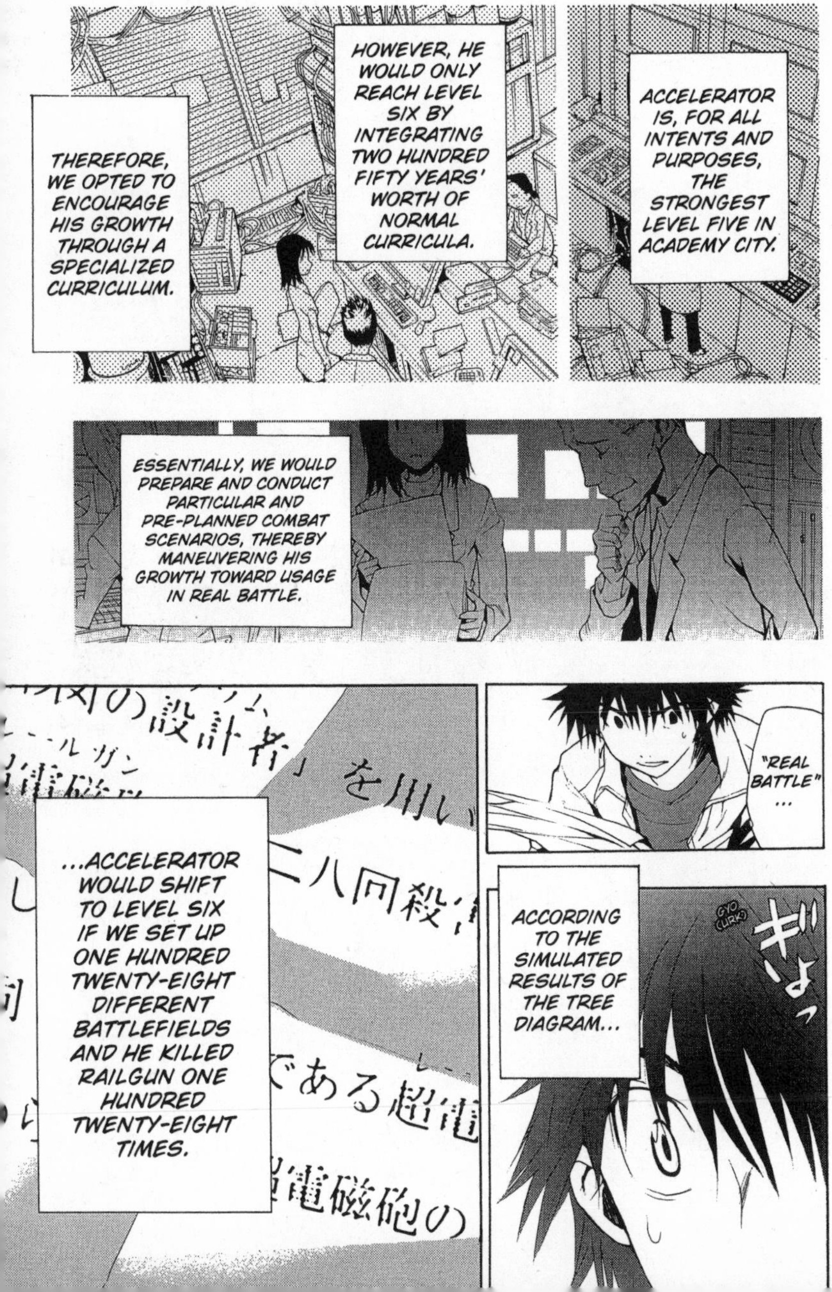
ACCELERATOR IS, FOR ALL INTENTS AND PURPOSES, THE STRONGEST LEVEL FIVE IN ACADEMY CITY.
HOWEVER, HE WOULD ONLY REACH LEVEL SIX BY INTEGRATING TWO HUNDRED FIFTY YEARS' WORTH OF NORMAL CURRICULA.
THEREFORE, WE OPTED TO ENCOURAGE HIS GROWTH THROUGH A SPECIALIZED CURRICULUM.
ESSENTIALLY, WE WOULD PREPARE AND CONDUCT PARTICULAR AND PRE-PLANNED COMBAT SCENARIOS, THEREBY MANEUVERING HIS GROWTH TOWARD USAGE IN REAL BATTLE.
"REAL BATTLE"...
ACCORDING TO THE SIMULATED RESULTS OF THE TREE DIAGRAM...
GYO (URK)
...ACCELERATOR WOULD SHIFT TO LEVEL SIX IF WE SET UP ONE HUNDRED TWENTY-EIGHT DIFFERENT BATTLEFIELDS AND HE KILLED RAILGUN ONE HUNDRED TWENTY-EIGHT TIMES.

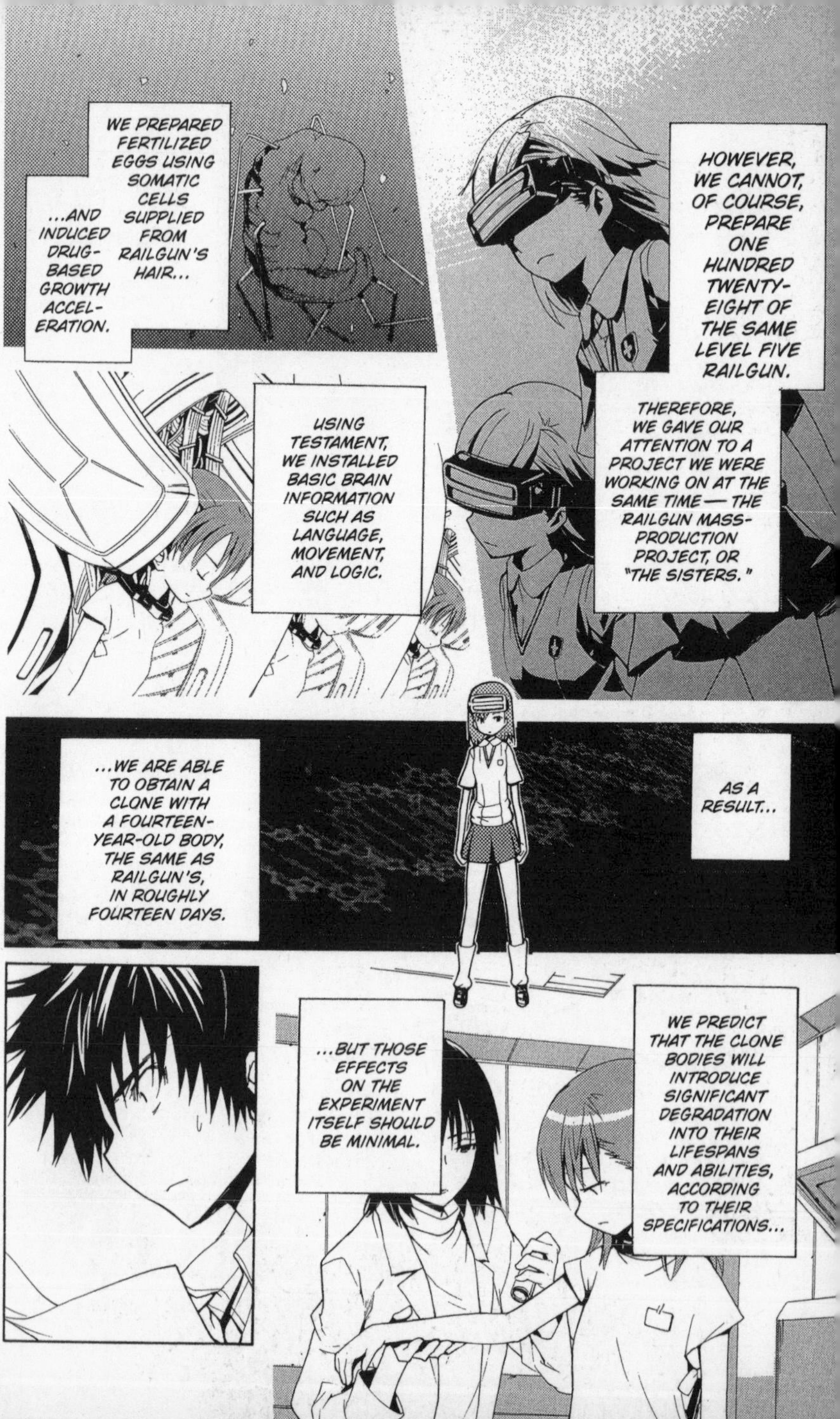
HOWEVER, WE CANNOT, OF COURSE, PREPARE ONE HUNDRED TWENTY-EIGHT OF THE SAME LEVEL FIVE RAILGUN.
THEREFORE, WE GAVE OUR ATTENTION TO A PROJECT WE WERE WORKING ON AT THE SAME TIME — THE RAILGUN MASS-PRODUCTION PROJECT, OR "THE SISTERS."
WE PREPARED FERTILIZED EGGS USING SOMATIC CELLS SUPPLIED FROM RAILGUN'S HAIR...
...AND INDUCED DRUG-BASED GROWTH ACCEL-ERATION.
USING TESTAMENT, WE INSTALLED BASIC BRAIN INFORMATION SUCH AS LANGUAGE, MOVEMENT, AND LOGIC.
AS A RESULT...
...WE ARE ABLE TO OBTAIN A CLONE WITH A FOURTEEN-YEAR-OLD BODY, THE SAME AS RAILGUN'S, IN ROUGHLY FOURTEEN DAYS.
WE PREDICT THAT THE CLONE BODIES WILL INTRODUCE SIGNIFICANT DEGRADATION INTO THEIR LIFESPANS AND ABILITIES, ACCORDING TO THEIR SPECIFICATIONS...
...BUT THOSE EFFECTS ON THE EXPERIMENT ITSELF SHOULD BE MINIMAL.

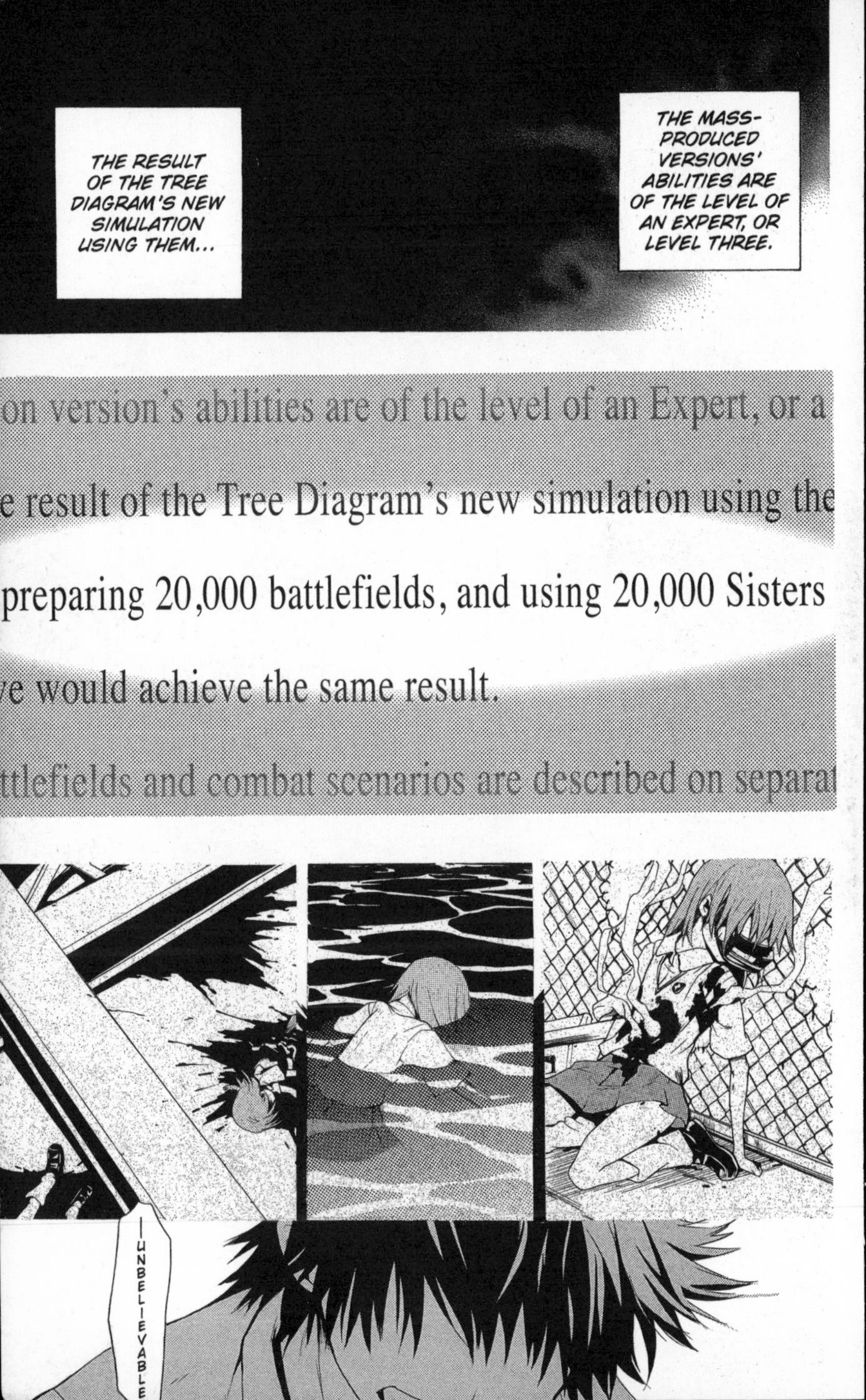
THE MASS-PRODUCED VERSIONS' ABILITIES ARE OF THE LEVEL OF AN EXPERT, OR LEVEL THREE.
THE RESULT OF THE TREE DIAGRAM'S NEW SIMULATION USING THEM...
on version's abilities are of the level of an Expert, or a
e result of the Tree Diagram's new simulation using the
preparing 20,000 battlefields, and using 20,000 Sisters
ve would achieve the same result.
ttlefields and combat scenarios are described on separa
—UNBELIEVABLE

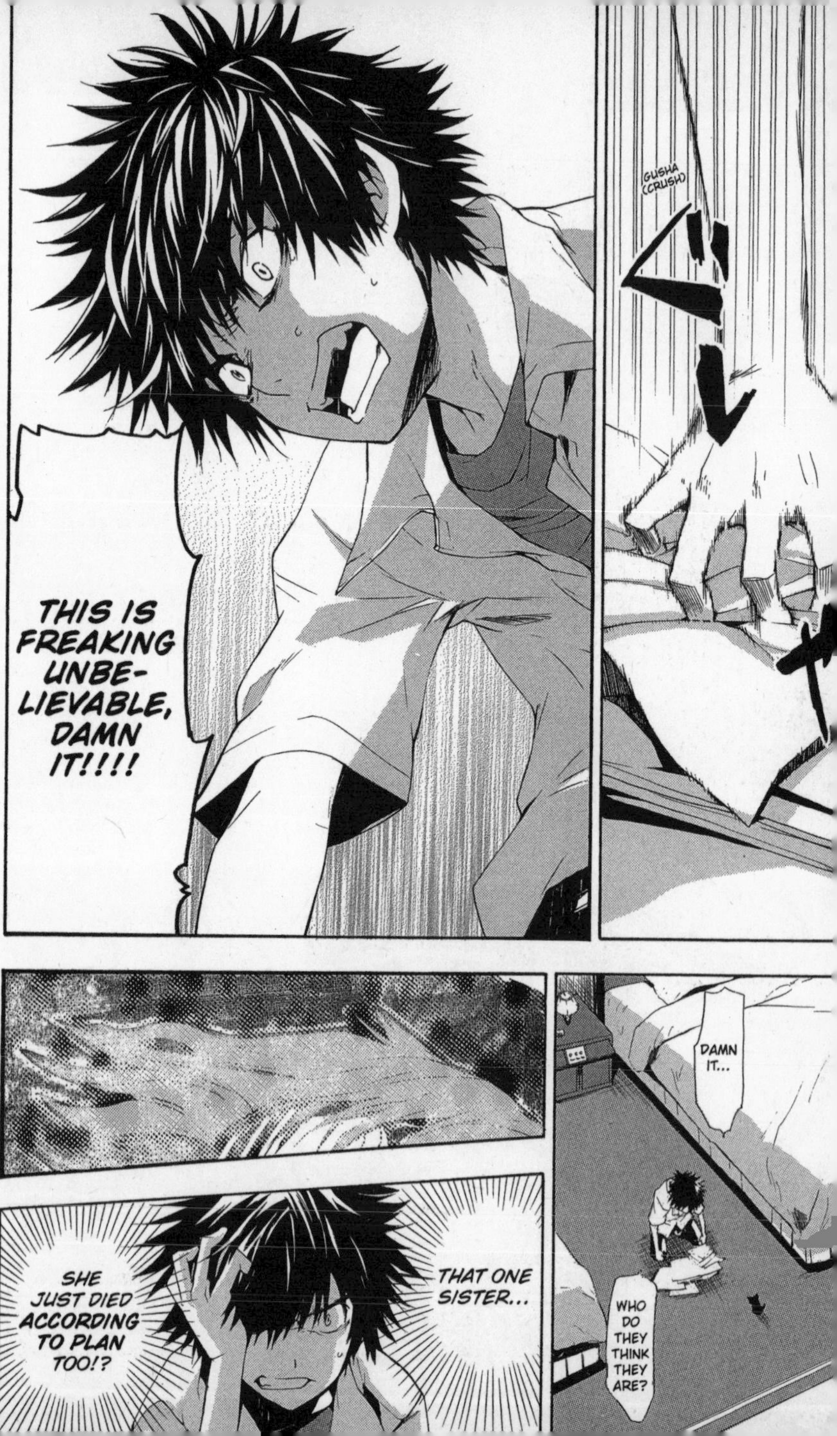
GUSHA (CRUSH)
THIS IS FREAKING UNBE-LIEVABLE, DAMN IT!!!!
DAMN IT...
WHO DO THEY THINK THEY ARE?
THAT ONE SISTER...
SHE JUST DIED ACCORDING TO PLAN TOO!?

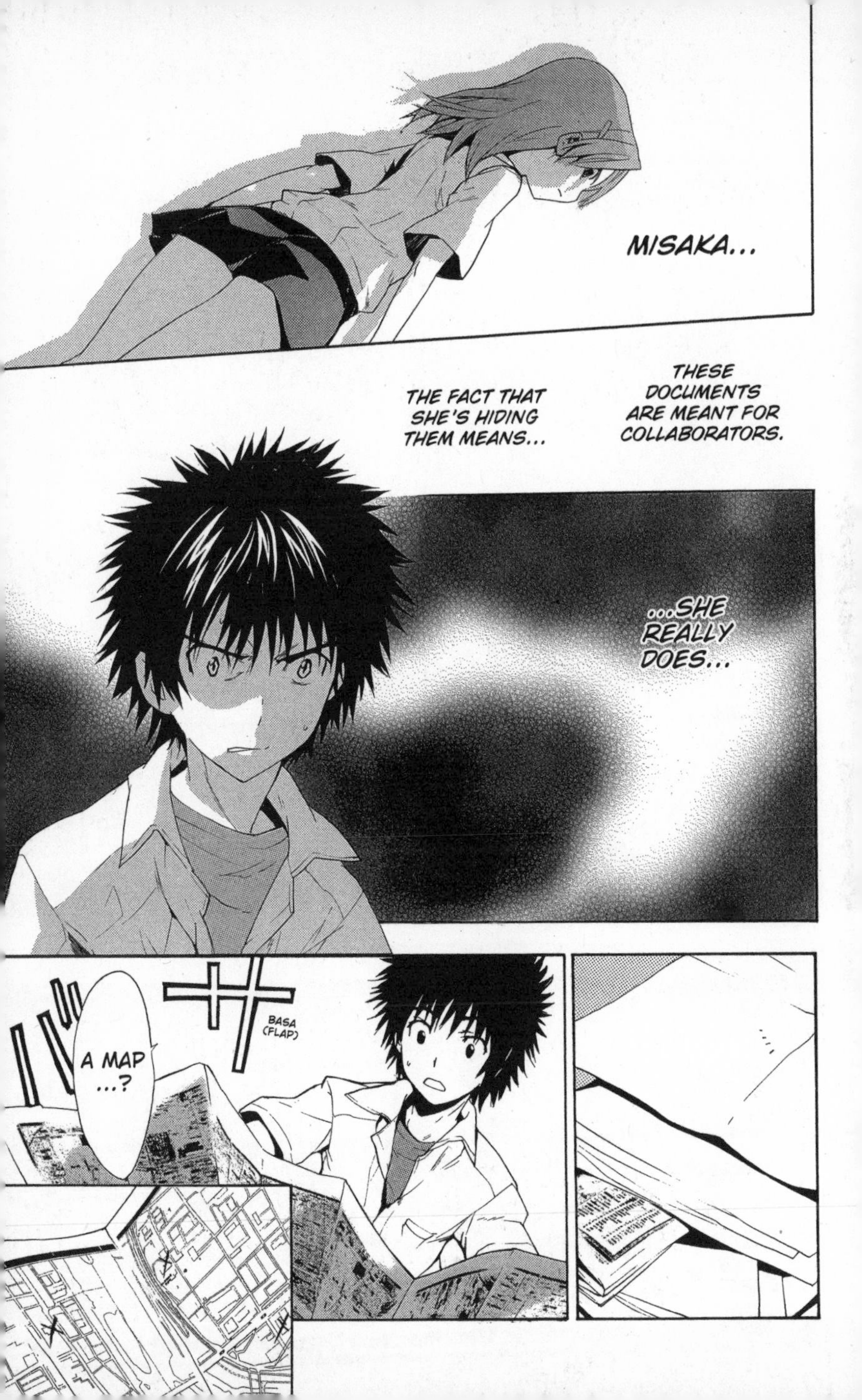
MISAKA...
THESE DOCUMENTS ARE MEANT FOR COLLABORATORS.
THE FACT THAT SHE'S HIDING THEM MEANS...
...SHE REALLY DOES...
BASA (FLAP)
A MAP ...?

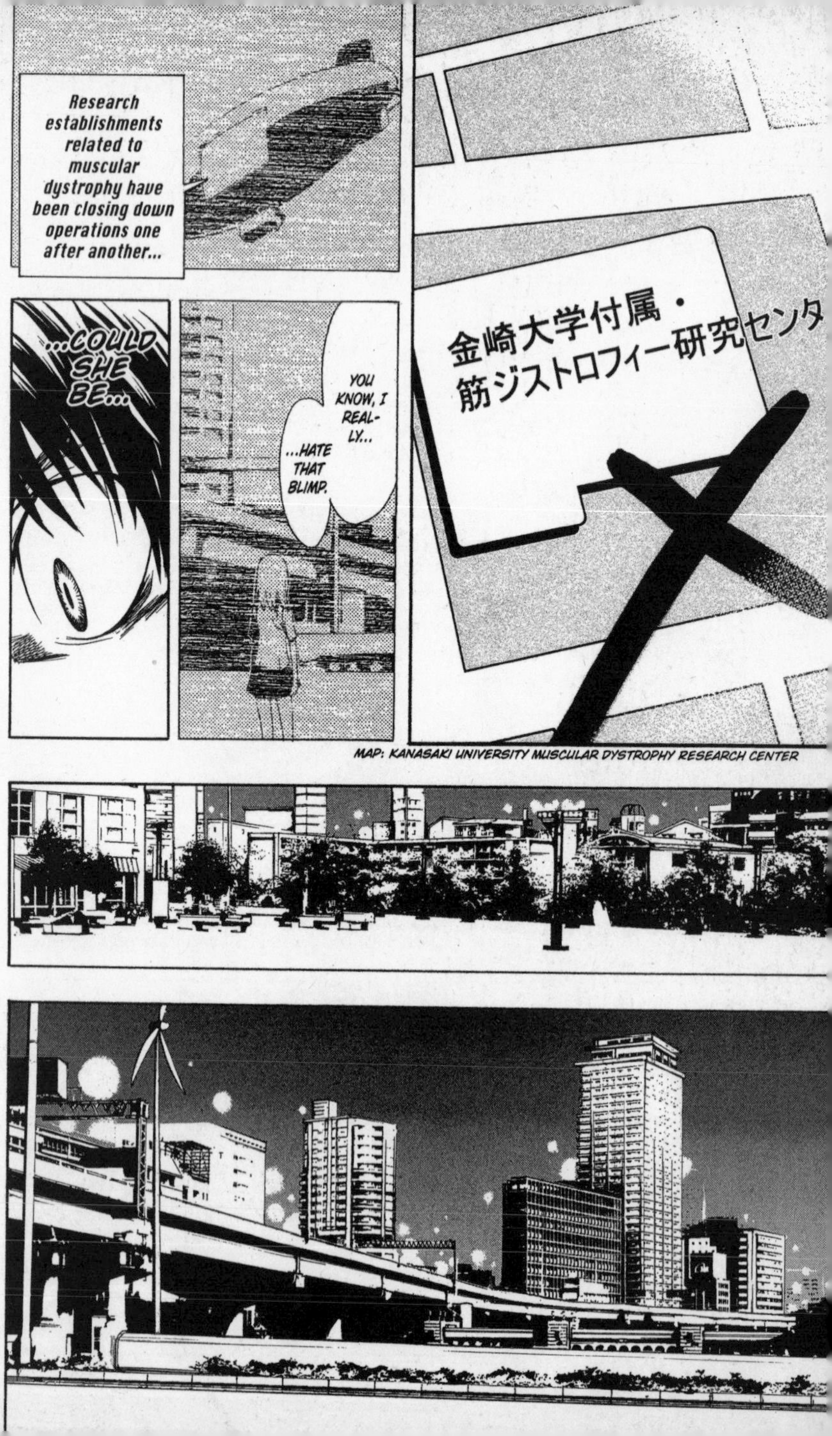
金崎大学付属・
筋ジストロフィー研究センタ
Research establishments related to muscular dystrophy have been closing down operations one after another...
YOU KNOW, I REALLY...
...HATE THAT BLIMP.
...COULD SHE BE...
MAP: KANASAKI UNIVERSITY MUSCULAR DYSTROPHY RESEARCH CENTER

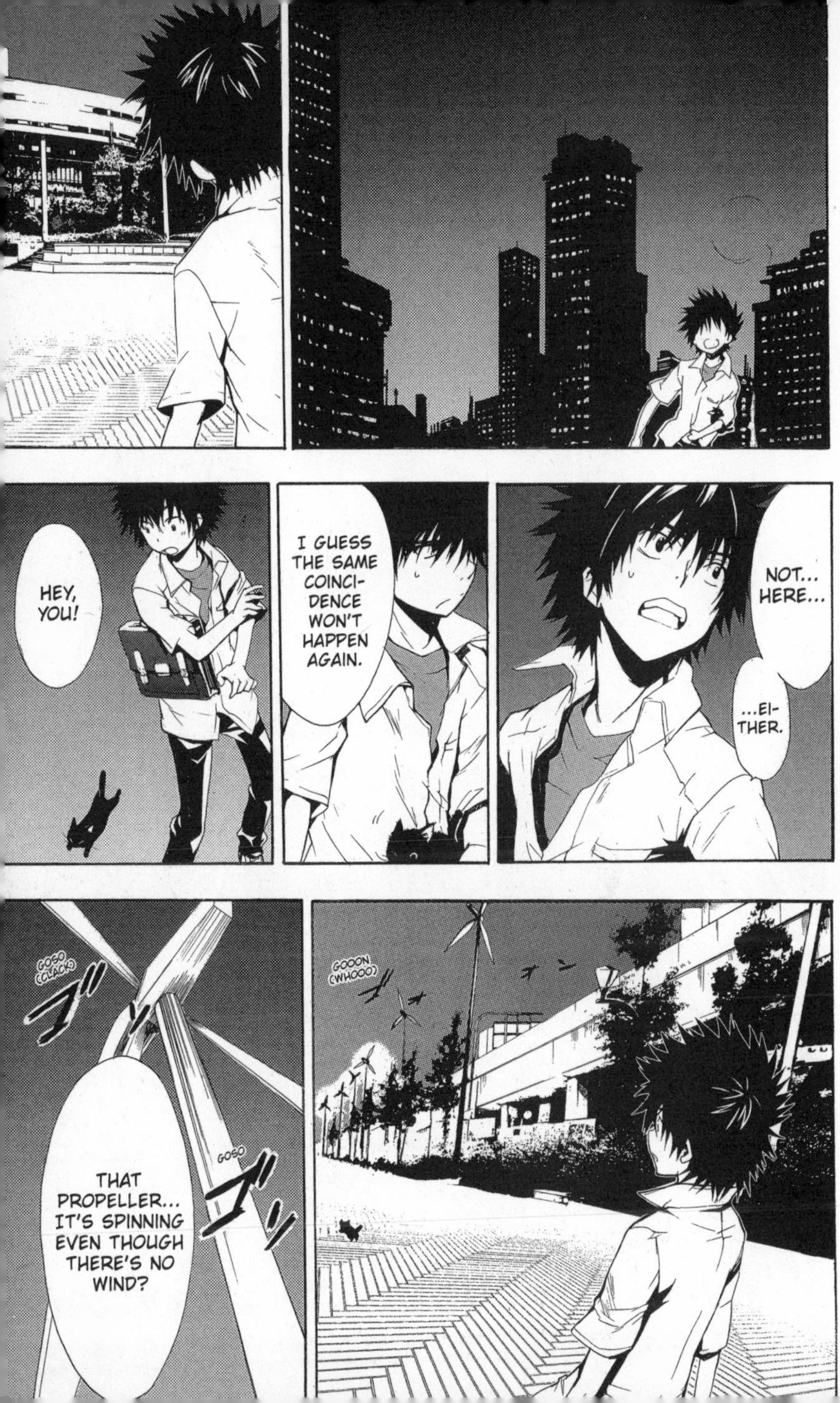
NOT... HERE...
...EI-THER.
I GUESS THE SAME COINCI-DENCE WON'T HAPPEN AGAIN.
HEY, YOU!
GOOON (WHOOO)
GOSO (CLACK)
GOSO
THAT PROPELLER... IT'S SPINNING EVEN THOUGH THERE'S NO WIND?

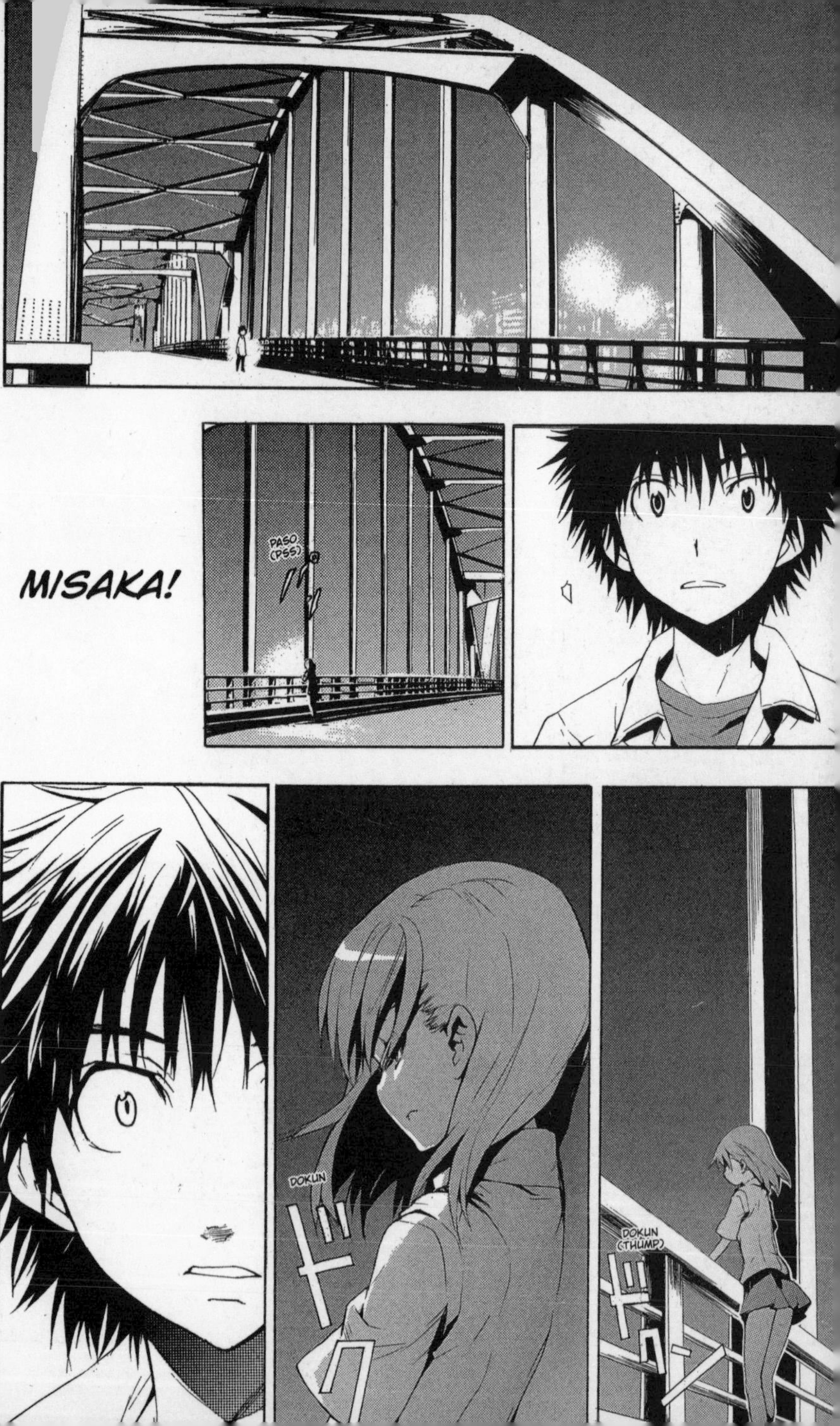
PASO (PSS)
MISAKA!
DOKUN (THUMP)
DOKUN

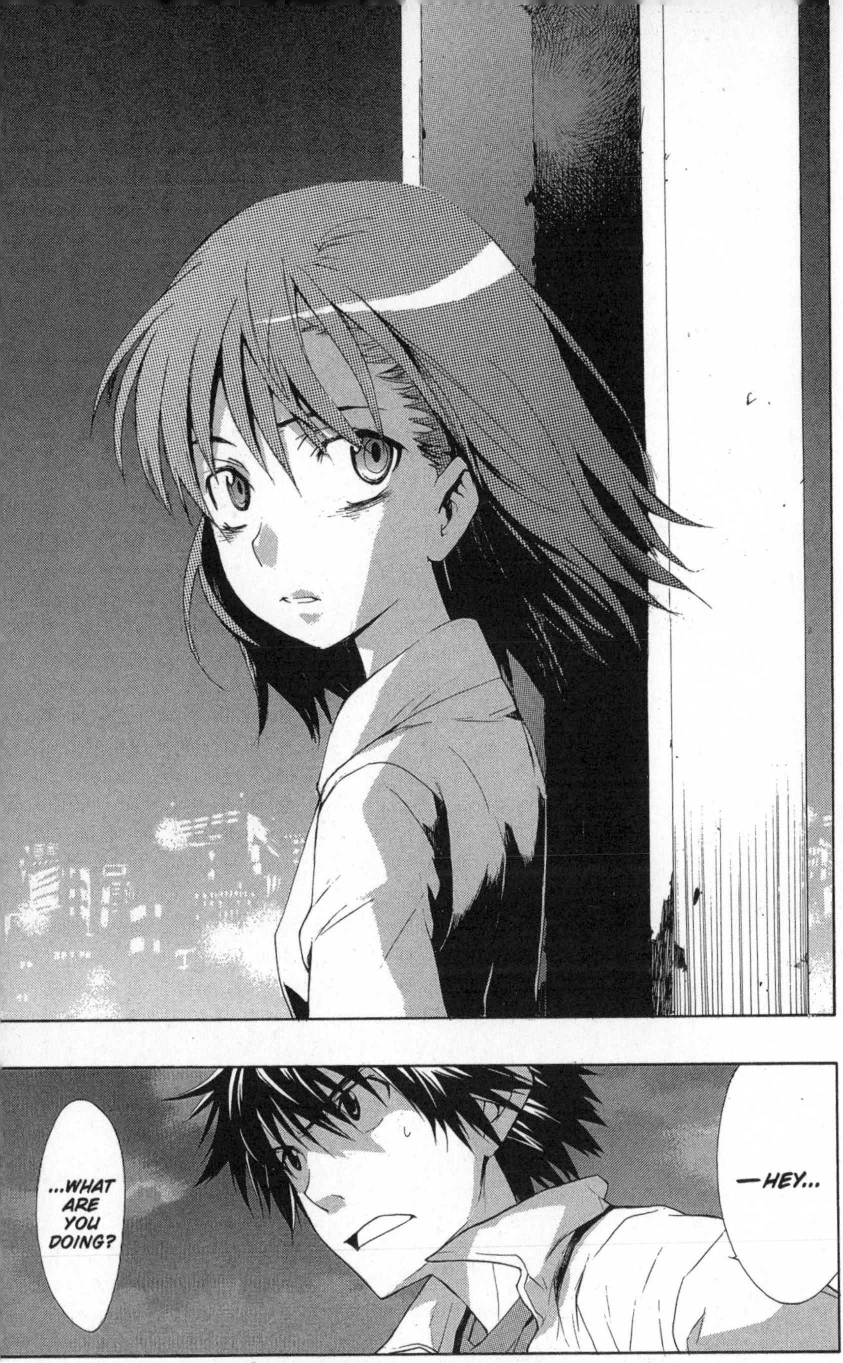
—HEY...
...WHAT ARE YOU DOING?

A Certain Magical Index

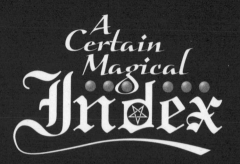

AFTERWORD: SUMMARY OF PREVIOUS EVENTS!?

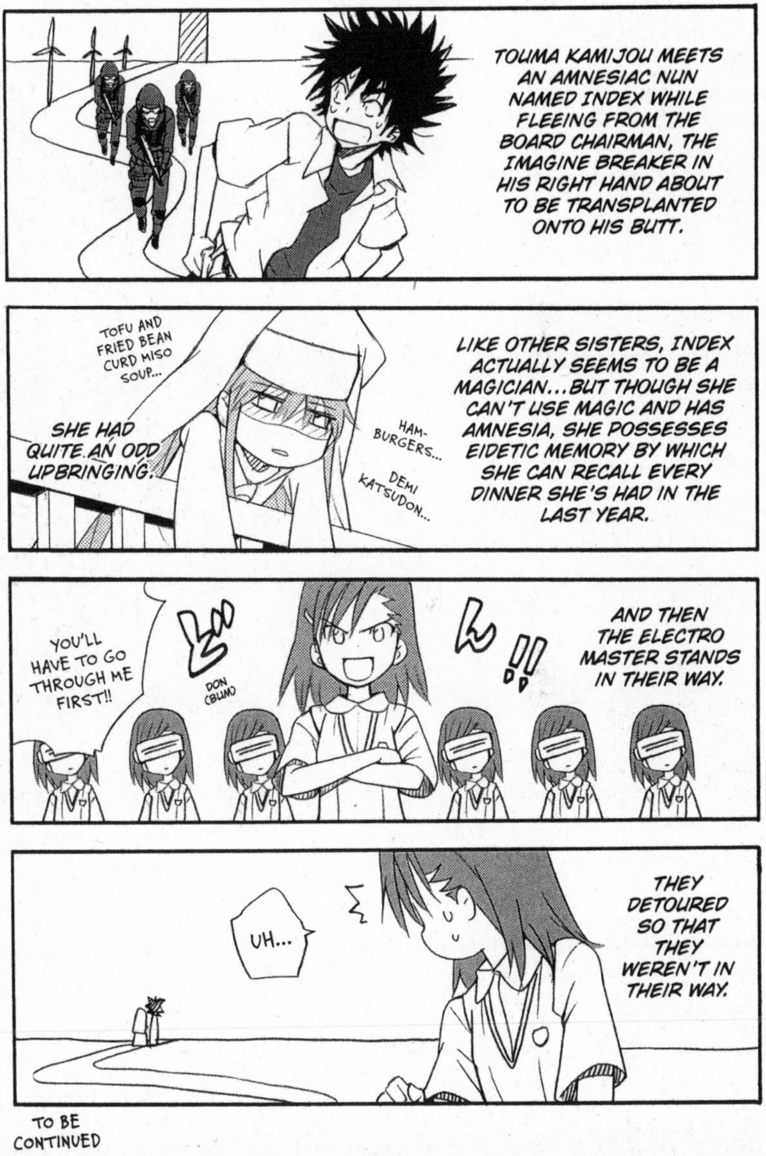
TOUMA KAMIJOU MEETS AN AMNESIAC NUN NAMED INDEX WHILE FLEEING FROM THE BOARD CHAIRMAN, THE IMAGINE BREAKER IN HIS RIGHT HAND ABOUT TO BE TRANSPLANTED ONTO HIS BUTT.
LIKE OTHER SISTERS, INDEX ACTUALLY SEEMS TO BE A MAGICIAN...BUT THOUGH SHE CAN'T USE MAGIC AND HAS AMNESIA, SHE POSSESSES EIDETIC MEMORY BY WHICH SHE CAN RECALL EVERY DINNER SHE'S HAD IN THE LAST YEAR.
HAM-BURGERS...
DEMI KATSUDON...
TOFU AND FRIED BEAN CURD MISO SOUP...
SHE HAD QUITE AN ODD UPBRINGING.
AND THEN THE ELECTRO MASTER STANDS IN THEIR WAY.
DON (BUM)
YOU'LL HAVE TO GO THROUGH ME FIRST!!
THEY DETOURED SO THAT THEY WEREN'T IN THEIR WAY.
UH...

TO BE CONTINUED

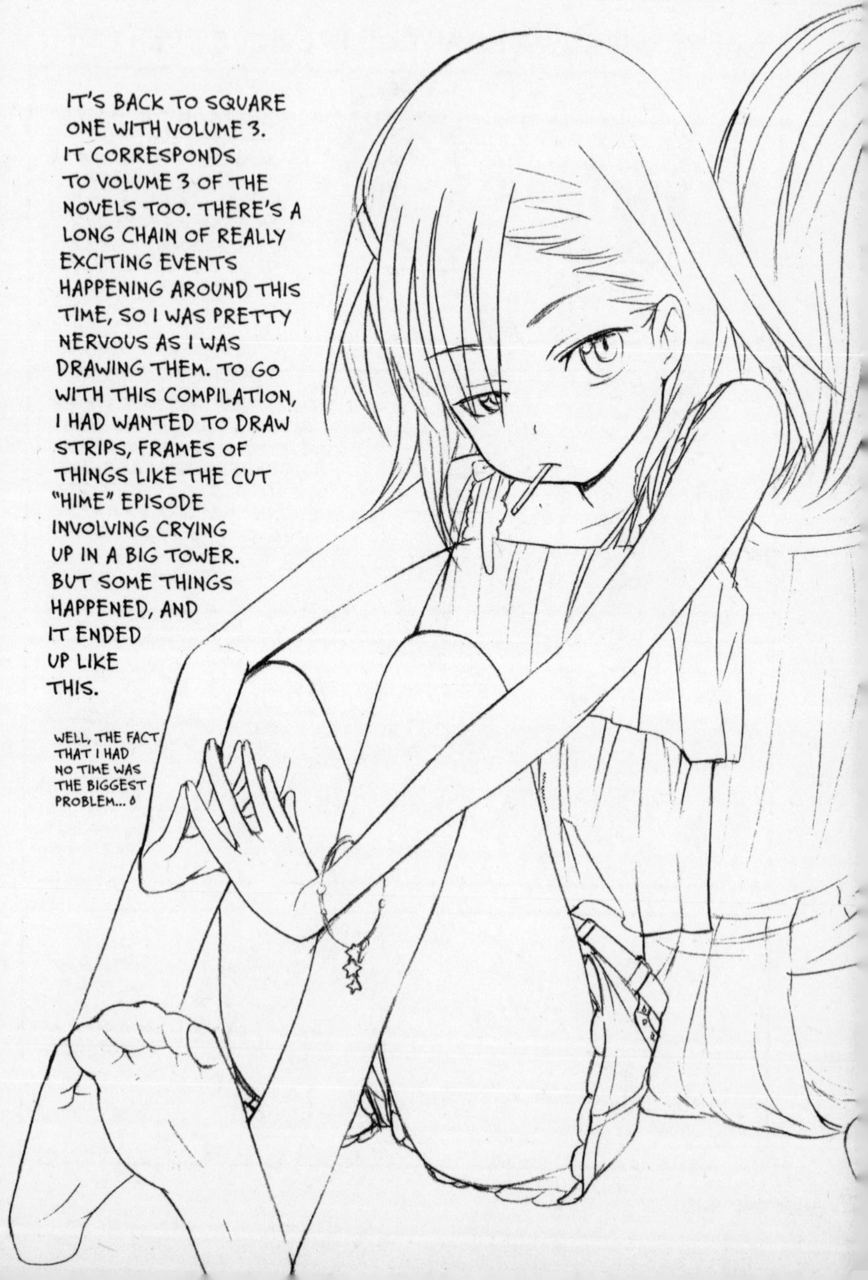
IT'S BACK TO SQUARE ONE WITH VOLUME 3. IT CORRESPONDS TO VOLUME 3 OF THE NOVELS TOO. THERE'S A LONG CHAIN OF REALLY EXCITING EVENTS HAPPENING AROUND THIS TIME, SO I WAS PRETTY NERVOUS AS I WAS DRAWING THEM. TO GO WITH THIS COMPILATION, I HAD WANTED TO DRAW STRIPS, FRAMES OF THINGS LIKE THE CUT "HIME" EPISODE INVOLVING CRYING UP IN A BIG TOWER. BUT SOME THINGS HAPPENED, AND IT ENDED UP LIKE THIS.
WELL, THE FACT THAT I HAD NO TIME WAS THE BIGGEST PROBLEM...

ANYWAY,
THERE ARE PROBABLY MANY OF YOU WHO READ FOR THIS PART OF THE STORY!

KAMACHI-SENSEI,
HAIMURA-SENSEI,
FUYUKAWA-SENSEI...

THANK YOU FOR PROVIDING YOUR FABULOUS COMMENTS AGAIN.

THE SISTERS ARC WILL END IN THE NEXT VOLUME. PLEASE GIVE IT A LOOK!

2008. 10.

近木野中哉
CHUYA KOGINO

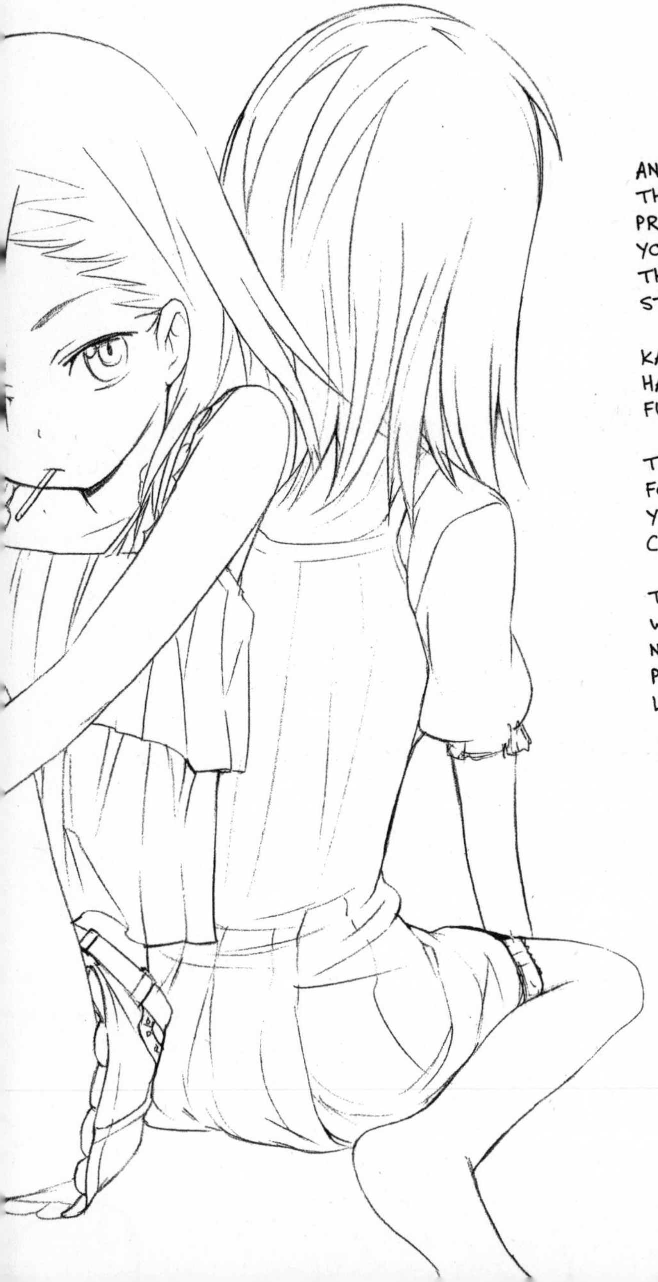

ARCHIVE-SAN

A CERTAIN MAGICAL INDEX ☆ EXTRA EDITION

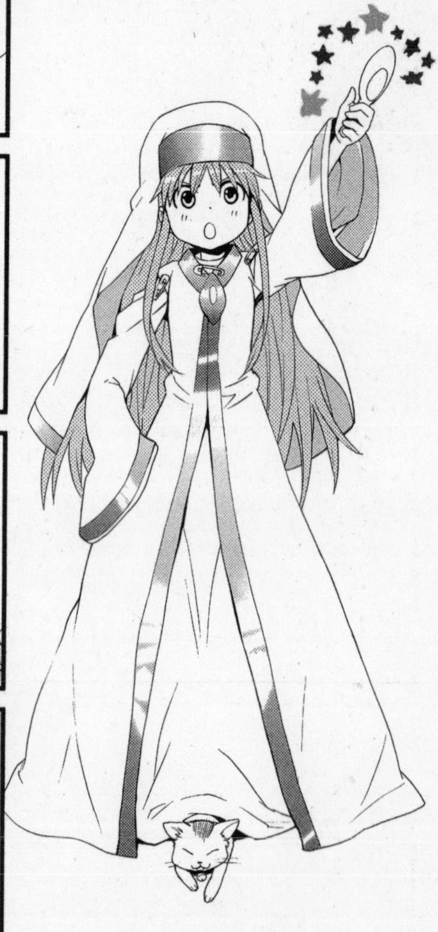

HOMEMADE

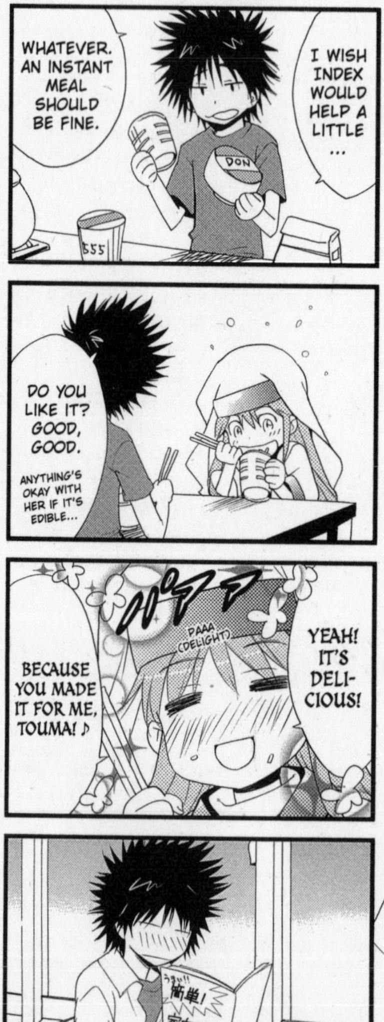
I WISH INDEX WOULD HELP A LITTLE ...
WHATEVER. AN INSTANT MEAL SHOULD BE FINE.
DON
555
DO YOU LIKE IT? GOOD, GOOD.
ANYTHING'S OKAY WITH HER IF IT'S EDIBLE...
YEAH! IT'S DELICIOUS!
パァァ
PAAA (DELIGHT)
BECAUSE YOU MADE IT FOR ME, TOUMA! ♪
うまい!!
簡単!
家庭料理

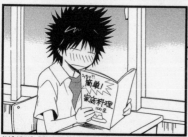

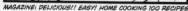

MAGAZINE: DELICIOUS!! EASY! HOME COOKING 100 RECIPES

MICROWAVE

INDEX IS BAD AT USING THE MICRO-WAVE.
PURU (TREMBLE)
CANCEL
STA
PURU
EXPLODE? THAT'S IF YOU HEAT IT UP TOO MUCH.
UUUM.
¥380
BOCHU (STAB)
HI-YAH!
PI (BEEP)
JUST DO THIS... SEE? EASY.
PI
O-OKAY.
TOUMA! ARE YOU OKAY!?
...YOU DID THAT ON PURPOSE! YOU DEFINITELY DID THAT ON PURPOSE......

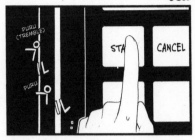

REVENGE

ONEE-SAMAAA!
DOOON (GLOMP)
GABA (GRAB)
HOW'S THAT!? NOW I WON'T FALL FOR THAT EVERY DAY!!
BUSHUU (PSHHH)
...ONEE-SAMA, YOU'VE FINALLY STARTED TO ACCEPT THE BURNING FEELINGS I HAVE FOR YOU!!!!
WHAT?
JIRO (STARE)
UH-HUH...
NUAHH!?
JIRO
GIUUU (SQUEEZE)

EVOLUTION

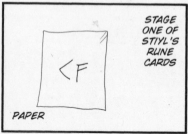

STAGE ONE OF STIYL'S RUNE CARDS
PAPER
STAGE TWO
LAMINATED PAPER
PROPERTIES
• WATERPROOF
• SHOCK-RESISTANT
STAGE THREE
BLADES
SHA (WOOSH)
SHA
YOU CAN ATTACK DIRECTLY WITH IT!
YOU SHOULDN'T TRY THIS HARD, STIYL.
HEH HEH HEH.
CHOIIIIIN (SKREEEEE)

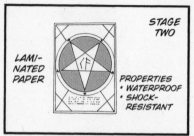

CAT EARS

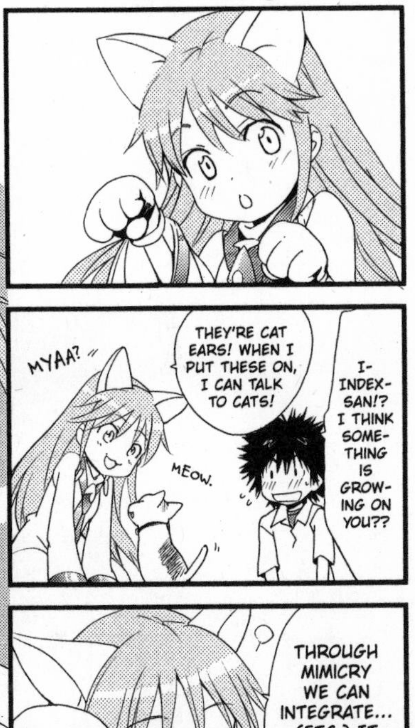
I-INDEX-SAN!? I THINK SOMETHING IS GROWING ON YOU??
THEY'RE CAT EARS! WHEN I PUT THESE ON, I CAN TALK TO CATS!
MYAA?
MEOW.
THROUGH MIMICRY WE CAN INTEGRATE... (ETC.) IT IS ONE OF THE MOST RESPECTED MAGICS, YOU KNOW?
...WAIT, YOU USE MAGIC?
BASHIII (TEAR)
SHE JUST WANTED TO TRY IT OUT ...!!?

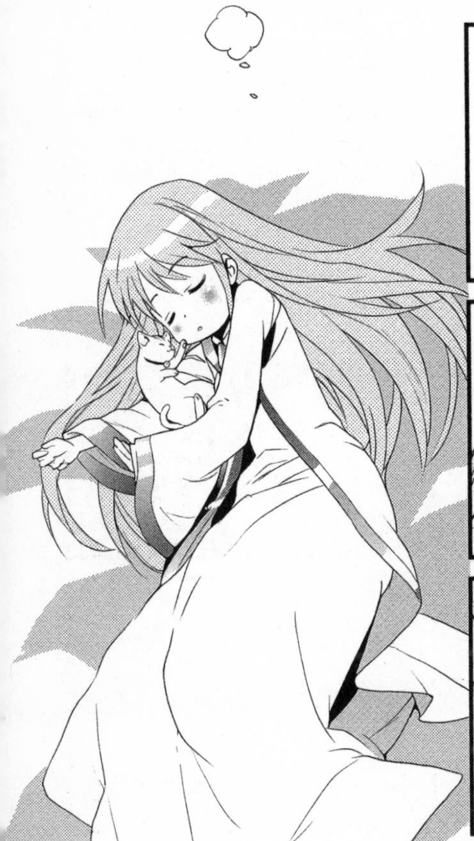

THIS ENDED UP BEING THE THIRD VOLUME OF THE A CERTAIN MAGICAL INDEX MANGA TOO. CONGRATULATIONS.

I AM EXTREMELY GRATEFUL TO KOGINO-SAN FOR BEING ABLE TO SCRUPULOUSLY DEPICT THE SCIENTIFIC SIDE OF THE STORY IN ADDITION TO THE MAGICAL SIDE.
THIS TIME, THE STORY REVOLVES AROUND SCIENCE. I WONDER IF THERE WERE READERS WHO GOT CONFUSED OR FLUSTERED BECAUSE OF IT.

THE STORY OF THE IMPOTENT (LEVEL ZERO) AND THE SUPERPOWER (LEVEL FIVE) IS GOING TO CONTINUE, SO PLEASE ENJOY THE SCIENTIFIC SIDE OF THINGS AS WELL.

KAZUMA KAMACHI

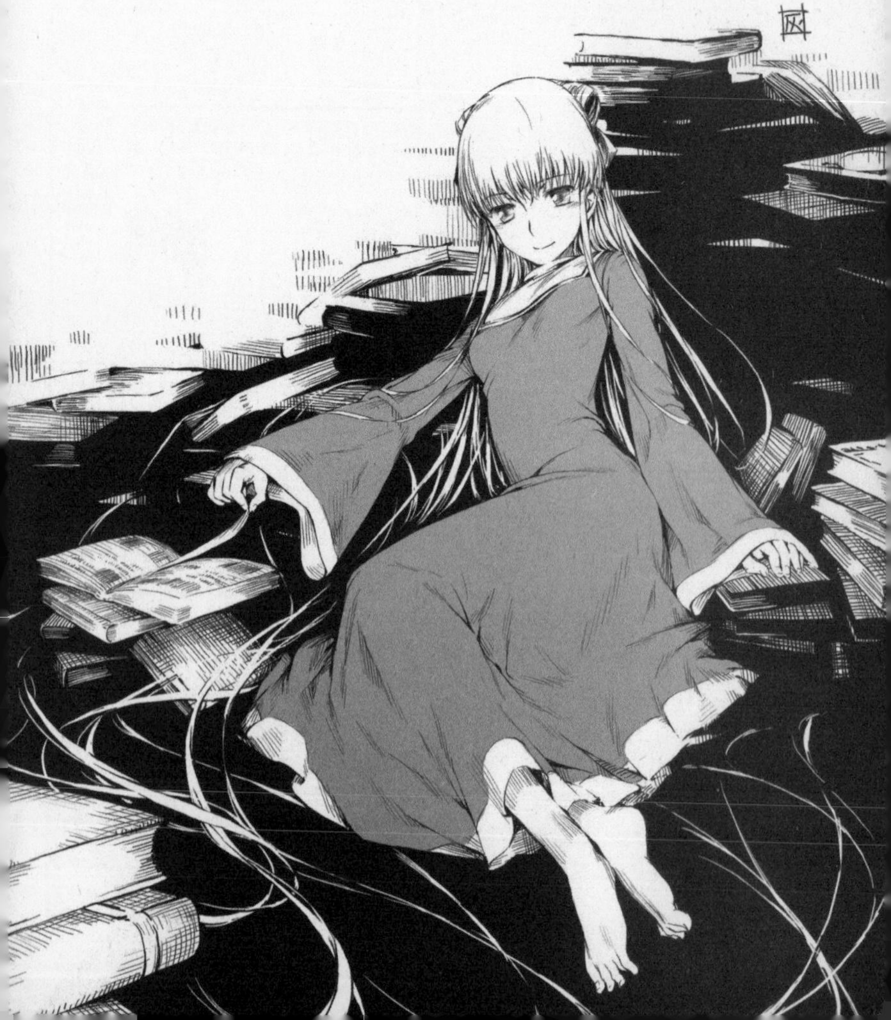

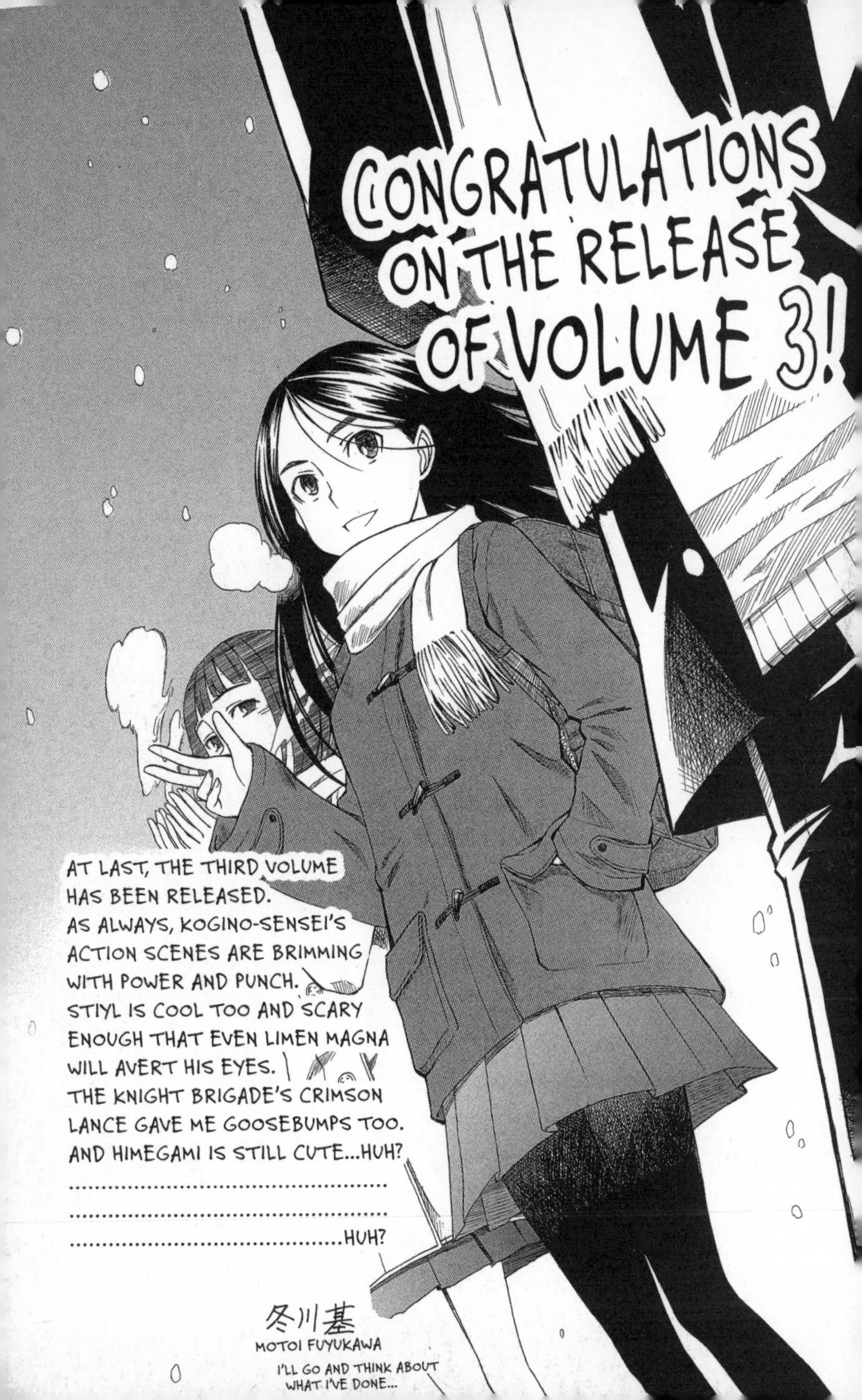
CONGRATULATIONS ON THE RELEASE OF VOLUME 3!
AT LAST, THE THIRD VOLUME HAS BEEN RELEASED.
AS ALWAYS, KOGINO-SENSEI'S ACTION SCENES ARE BRIMMING WITH POWER AND PUNCH.
STIYL IS COOL TOO AND SCARY ENOUGH THAT EVEN LIMEN MAGNA WILL AVERT HIS EYES.
THE KNIGHT BRIGADE'S CRIMSON LANCE GAVE ME GOOSEBUMPS TOO.
AND HIMEGAMI IS STILL CUTE...HUH?
....
....
....HUH?
冬川基
MOTOI FUYUKAWA
I'LL GO AND THINK ABOUT WHAT I'VE DONE...

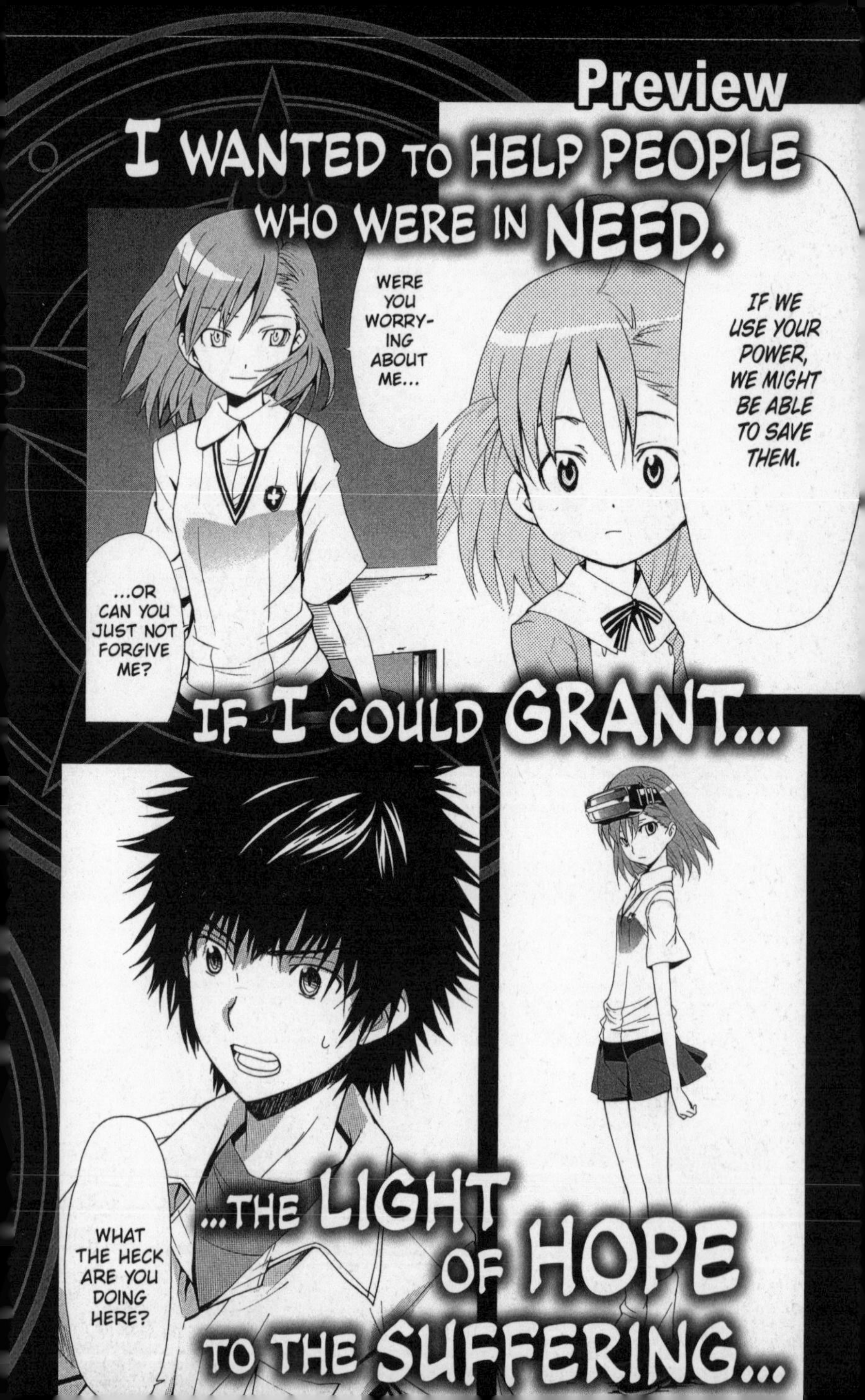
Preview
I WANTED TO HELP PEOPLE WHO WERE IN NEED.
IF WE USE YOUR POWER, WE MIGHT BE ABLE TO SAVE THEM.
WERE YOU WORRYING ABOUT ME...
...OR CAN YOU JUST NOT FORGIVE ME?
IF I COULD GRANT...
WHAT THE HECK ARE YOU DOING HERE?
...THE LIGHT OF HOPE TO THE SUFFERING...

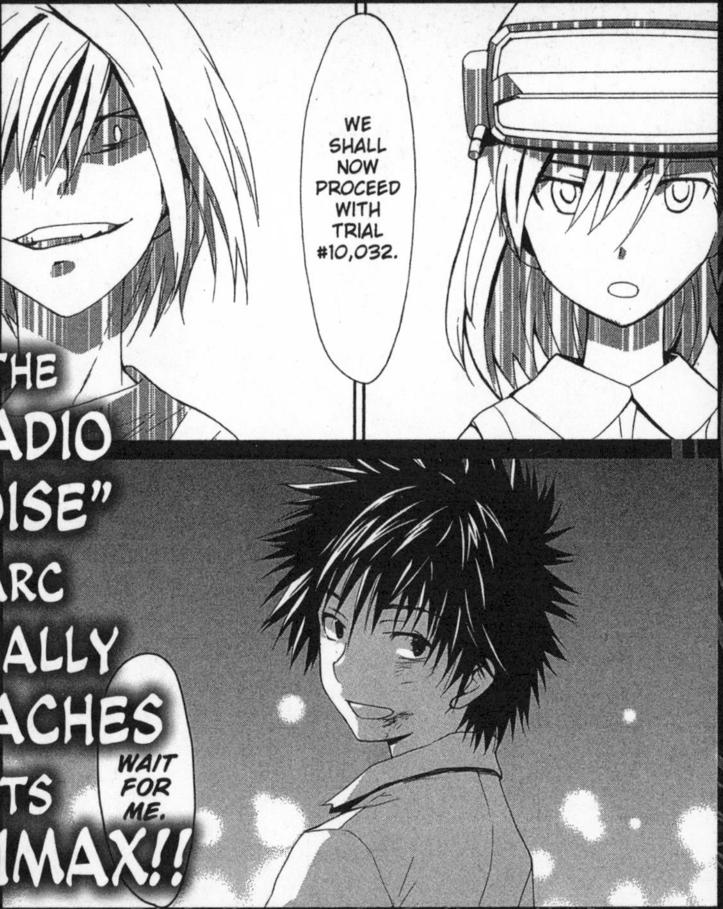
WE SHALL NOW PROCEED WITH TRIAL #10,032.
WAIT FOR ME.

THE "RADIO NOISE" ARC FINALLY REACHES ITS CLIMAX!!

A GREAT MASSACRE UNDER THE GUISE OF AN EXPERIMENT, INVOLVING THE MISAKA SISTERS AND ACCELERATOR, TO BECOME A LEVEL SIX. THIS ACCURSED RESEARCH MUST END—WHAT IS THE CONCLUSION TOUMA REACHES...!?

A Certain Magical Index

Volume 4

Look forward to it!!

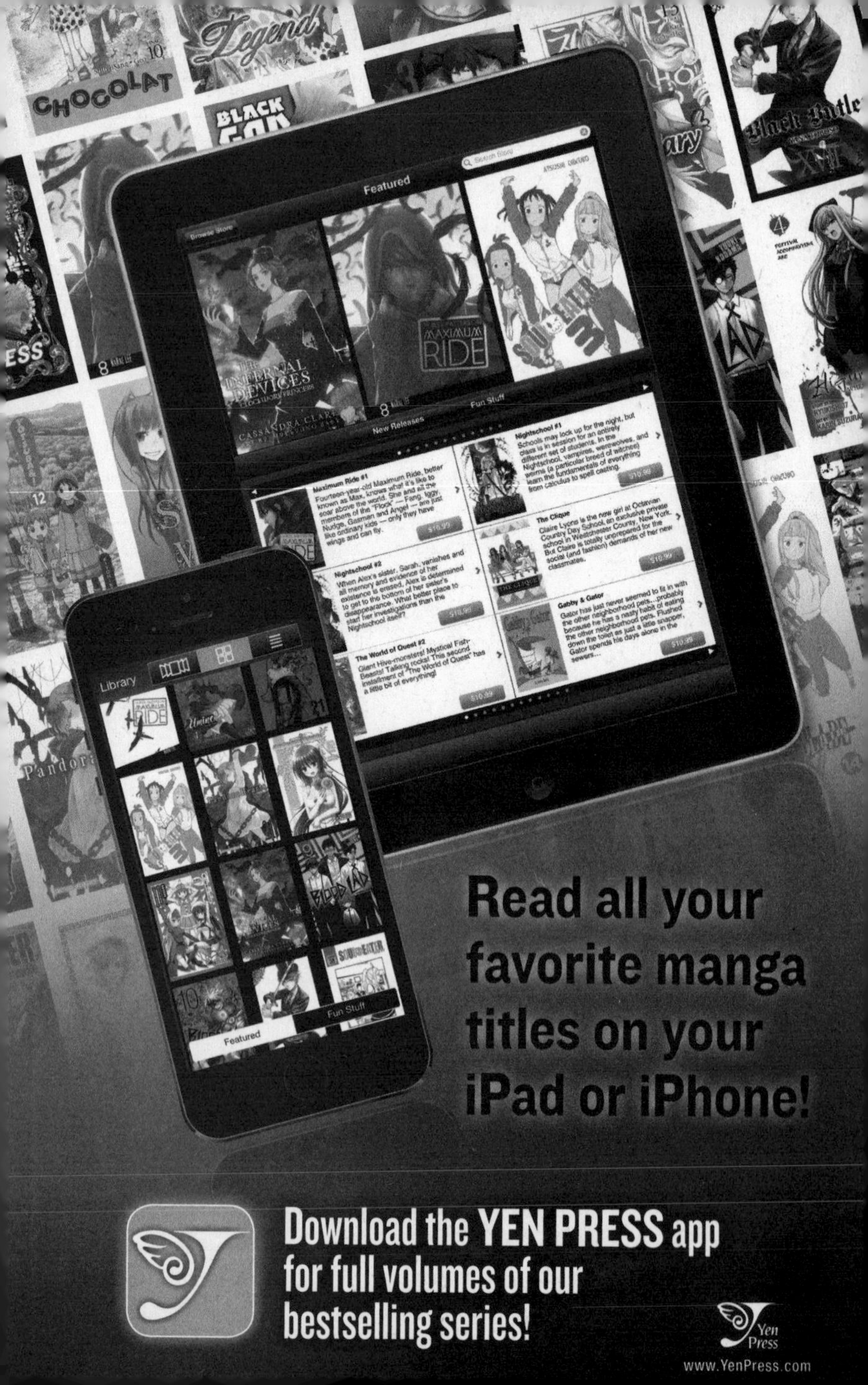
Read all your favorite manga titles on your iPad or iPhone!
Download the YEN PRESS app for full volumes of our bestselling series!
Yen Press
www.YenPress.com

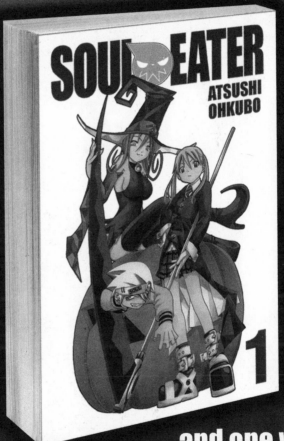

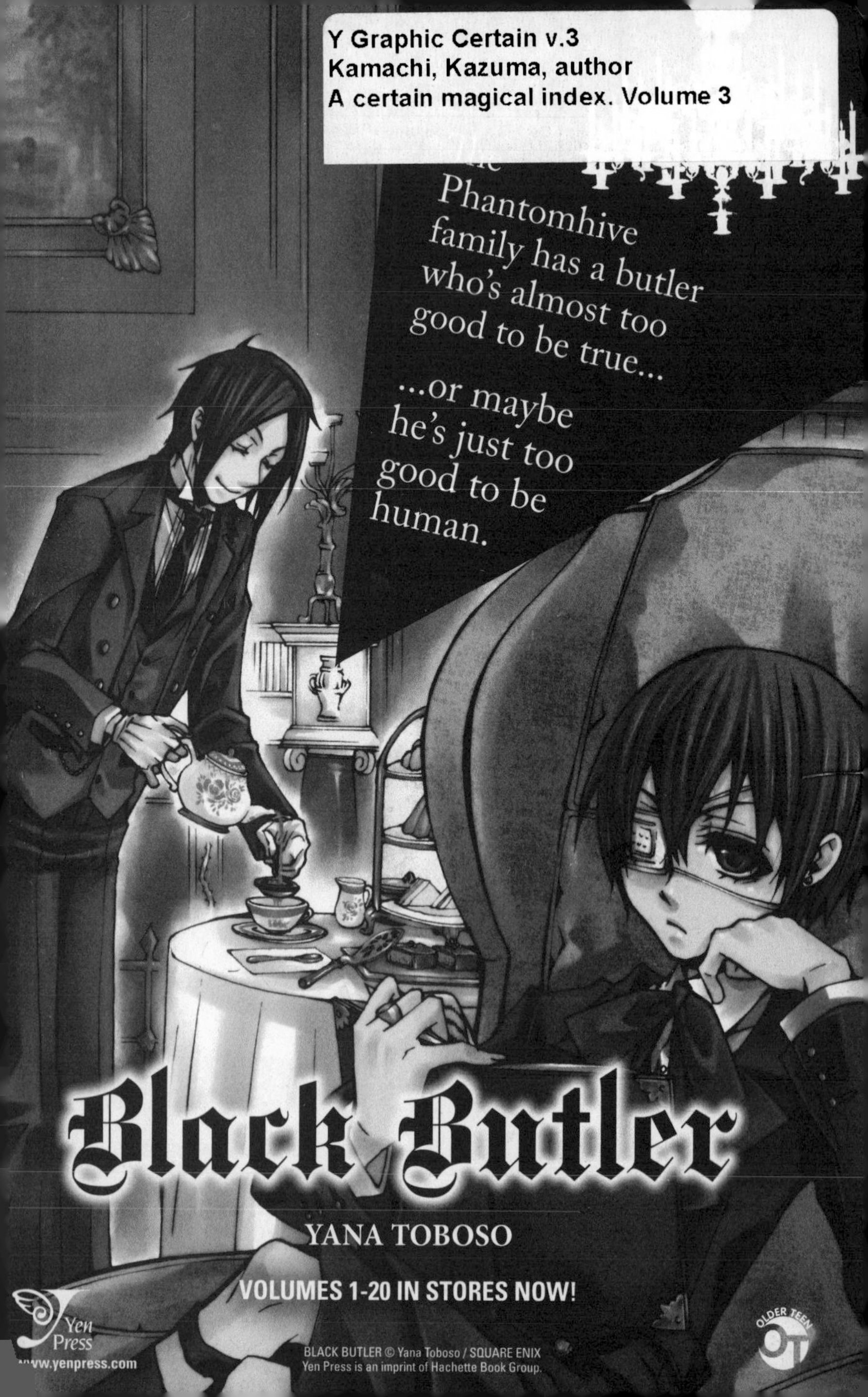
Phantomhive family has a butler who's almost too good to be true...
...or maybe he's just too good to be human.
Black Butler
YANA TOBOSO
VOLUMES 1-20 IN STORES NOW!
Yen Press
www.yenpress.com
BLACK BUTLER © Yana Toboso / SQUARE ENIX
Yen Press is an imprint of Hachette Book Group.
OLDER TEEN
OT

WELCOME TO IKEBUKURO, WHERE TOKYO'S WILDEST CHARACTERS GATHER!!

AS THEIR PATHS CROSS, THIS ECCENTRIC CAST WEAVES A TWISTED, CRACKED LOVE STORY...

AVAILABLE NOW!!

ceya

A CERTAIN MAGICAL INDEX ❸

KAZUMA KAMACHI
KIYOTAKA HAIMURA
CHUYA KOGINO

Translation: Andrew Prowse

Lettering: Brndn Blakeslee & Lys Blakeslee

This book is a work of fiction. Names, characters, places, and incidents are the product of the author's imagination or are used fictitiously. Any resemblance to actual events, locales, or persons, living or dead, is coincidental.

TOARU MAJYUTSU NO INDEX Vol. 3
© 2008 Kazuma Kamachi
© 2008 Chuya Kogino / SQUARE ENIX. CO. LTD.
Licensed by KADOKAWA CORPORATION ASCII MEDIA WORKS
First published in Japan in 2008 by SQUARE ENIX CO., LTD.
English translation rights arranged with SQUARE ENIX CO., LTD.
and Hachette Book Group through Tuttle-Mori Agency, Inc.

Translation © 2015 by SQUARE ENIX CO., LTD.

Yen Press
Hachette Book Group
1290 Avenue of the Americas
New York, NY 10104

www.HachetteBookGroup.com
www.YenPress.com

Yen Press is an imprint of Hachette Book Group, Inc. The Yen Press name and logo are trademarks of Hachette Book Group, Inc.

The publisher is not responsible for websites (or their content) that are not owned by the publisher.

First Yen Press Edition: October 2015

ISBN: 978-0-316-34592-7

10 9 8 7 6 5 4 3 2

BVG

Printed in the United States of America